THE
FRACTURED
20TH CENTURY

THE FRACTURED 20TH CENTURY

by

Jerry S. Grafstein

Library and Archives Canada Cataloguing in Publication

Title: The fractured 20th century / by Jerry S. Grafstein.

Other titles: Fractured twentieth century

Names: Grafstein, Jerry S., 1935- author.

Identifiers: Canadiana (print) 20220249644
              Canadiana (ebook) 20220250219

ISBN 9781771616805 (softcover) ISBN 9781771616829 (EPUB)
ISBN 9781771616812 (PDF) ISBN 9781771616836 (Kindle)

Subjects: LCSH: World politics—20th century. | LCSH: History, Modern—20th century. |
           LCSH: Civilization, Modern—20th century.

Classification: LCC D443 .G73 2022 |
                 DDC 909.82—dc23

Published by Mosaic Press, Oakville, Ontario, Canada, 2022.

MOSAIC PRESS, Publishers
www.Mosaic-Press.com

Printed and bound in Canada

MOSAIC PRESS
1252 Speers Road, Units 1 & 2, Oakville, Ontario, L6L 5N9
(905) 825-2130 • info@mosaic-press.com • www.mosaic-press.com

OTHER BOOKS BY
THE HON. JERRY S. GRAFSTEIN, Q.C.

1. *'Beyond Imagination'* - published by McClelland & Stewart Inc. (1995)

2. *'The Making of the Parliamentary Poet Laureate: Based on a Senator Grafstein's Private Member's Bill'* – published by the Porcupine's Quill (2003)

3. *'The Passage Through Parliament to Establish Holocaust Memorial Day in Canada'*, co-authored with Richard Marceau – published by Jerahmiel Grafstein (2004)

4. *'Suicide Bombings: Parliament Speaks'* – Parliamentary history of Bill 215, an Act to amend the Criminal Code (Suicide Bombings) - published by Jerahmiel Grafstein (2012)

5. *'Parade: A Tribute to Remarkable Contemporaries'* – published by Mosaic Press (2017)

6. *'A Leader Must Be a Leader: Encounters With Eleven Prime Ministers'* – published by Mosaic Press (2019)

TABLE OF CONTENTS

DEDICATION

This book was informed by three major family influences on my life.

First, my father Soloman Simon Grafstein. Second, my maternal grandfather, Israel Isaac Bleeman. Third, my eldest son Laurence Stephen Grafstein.

My father died tragically in 1951 at age 54, hit by a car helping a lame man while crossing a narrow street on the way home from our small synagogue in my birth place London, Ontario, on a cold March 'Purim' evening.

My maternal grandfather was blinded in two accidents in his late twenties near his home in Kensington Market in Toronto around 1915 and then 1917 where he lived and worked with his wife and two daughters, the elder of whom was my mother.

Both my father and grandfather were Polish immigrants. My grandfather arrived in Canada as a young man in his '20s in 1905. He worked to earn enough, first in Antwerp and then in Toronto, to send for my grandmother, Mirel Ethel, my mother Helen Rose[1] and my aunt Betty who arrived in 1907[2], all on their own, from their 'shetel' Drilsch (Ylze in Polish) in southern

---

[1] My mother, Helen Rose Grafstein née Bleeman was born in Drilsch (Ylze), Poland in 1900. My mother's Hebrew name was 'Chaya Ruchel'. She was named by my grandfather after the mother of a famous Ger Hasidic Rebbe of which he was a follower and also after a deceased aunt. Her paternal grandfather was a lumberman and her paternal grandmother was the town's apothecary. My maternal grandmother was born with the surname Topol in Yusapov, a nearby town. My mother, born in 1900, arrived in Canada in 1907 and lived to 102 passing peacefully in Toronto still in charge of all her mental faculties. Her life spanned the 20th century which this book attempts to reflect on events and personalities through the author's eyes, family, study and experience. We each carry within us our ancestors' DNA for us to explore our roots to seek to comprehend the mystery of our life.

[2] It seems when my grandmother, mother and aunt arrived in Canada in 1907, it was the year when America experienced its largest Jewish immigration from Eastern Europe in history.

Poland travelling across Europe by carriage and train, then by crowded ship across the Atlantic, then across Canada from Halifax by train to Toronto where my grandfather eagerly awaited their arrival at Union Station[3]. They eventually settled at 35 Kensington Avenue in Kensington Market in Toronto where he and my grandmother Mirel Etel (nee Topol) started an egg and chicken business in their small backyard. After my grandfather, in two successive accidents became blind, my grandmother helped run their small business while my grandfather devoted most of each day studying the Bible, the two Talmuds and works of the great Hasidic masters[4].

My father, an orphan before twelve, a divorcee, a World War I and Polish War of Independence veteran and a small businessman, came from his tiny village, Waśniów (a tiny population of under 200 over 120 of whom were Jewish), in southern Poland to visit his three of his elder brothers in Toronto in 1927 and his only sister, Anna Silverman, living in New York City. Intending to return to Poland via Argentina where he had relatives and then Asia, my uncle, Morris[5], introduced his youngest

---

3   My orthodox grandmother who wore a dark shiny wig to frame her pale white face and dark bemused brown eyes, was four feet eleven and spoke Yiddish, Hebrew and Polish and yet made it across Europe and Canada alone with my seven year old mother and my five year old aunt in tow.

4   My hardworking grandmother kept up her charitable work. She organized a small group of Orthodox women to donate bridal trousseaux for poor orphan girls in the neighbourhood. Later in the '50s, when I came to Toronto, I would be accosted by several of them who had named their first born daughter after her.

5   My uncle Morris (Moishe), as a youth, emigrated to Canada, settled in Toronto around 1907 and became an organizer in a baker's union. Then he started a dance school. Later he set up a dry goods business at the corner of College and Spadina. He married Goldie of Jewish German-English-Polish descent (on her maternal side, she was related to the Oppenheims, an illustrious German family) and had 8 daughters and 1 son. Seven older daughters were each trained on a different musical instruments and became a band entertaining at weddings and bar mitzvahs while my uncle led the dancing. He was a tall handsome always elegantly dressed bon vivant. Once someone met my uncle Morris, one could never forget him. Five of his sons-in-law served in the armed forces in World War II. His eldest grandson, Robert Kaplan, became a Member of Parliament in 1968 and served in the Pierre Trudeau cabinet as Solicitor General when he reopened the dormant war criminals' files. Bob's given Hebrew name was Jerahmiel. We were both named after my paternal grandfather and his maternal great grandfather.

brother, my father, to my mother in Toronto in 1927. As noted, they fell in love and my father decided to settle in Canada rather than return to Poland. They married and moved to London, Ontario in 1930 where another elder brother Max[6] owned a retail textile business and a small Yiddish and English publishing company[7]. My sister Pauline Beverly

---

6   My uncle Maxwell Wolfe (Melech) Grafstein studied as a youth at the Lomza Yeshiva, the first modern orthodox college in Poland. Then he left early and went on to an extraordinary career as a radical then an impoverished Yiddish actor and producer in Warsaw, then in Europe and later in New York City when my uncle Morris persuaded him to come to Canada and join him in his retail textile business. First Melech settled in Toronto and then London, Ontario, where he worked as a merchant in the 1920's, 1930's and 1940's. My uncle, 'Melech', was also a prolific essayist, stage producer, political activist and publisher who published the collected works of Shalom Aleichem and I.L. Peretz, two of the greatest Yiddish writers in the 20th century in London, Ontario in the late '40s. Melech was also owner and publisher of the *Jewish Observer*, a glossy cultural magazine on Jewish subjects, writers and poets. Melech was a major supporter of the Hebrew Journal, the Yiddish daily published in Toronto. He was closely connected to the thriving Yiddish theatre in New York City and it's itinerate Yiddish actors who staged Yiddish plays across both Canada and the U.S.A. in the '20s, '30s and '40s. 'Melech' was an adherent and early leader of the Histradrut in Canada, an international Jewish labour socialist organization based in then Palestine. He was an accomplished public speaker in Yiddish and English. On a visit with my father to Toronto, we attended the offices of the Hebrew Journal, the Toronto based Yiddish daily, located at 542 Dundas Street West, the building owned by my uncle Melech who supported this daily Yiddish newspaper providing very low rent. We spent time at the newspaper's busy office with Gershon Pomerantz, the editor and himself a published Yiddish writer and poet. Gershon was the father of a classmate of mine at University of Toronto Law School, Joe Pomerant. Melech moved to Miami in the early '50s to retire and quickly was chosen as editor of the leading Jewish periodical magazine called 'Panorama' and was active in efforts to help impoverished Yiddish actors who retired in Miami and became part of the thriving Yiddish cultural life there. Melech married a second cousin, Rose (Mandel) and they raised a large family. Three of his sons, Sam, Manny and Joe served in the armed forces in World War II. Their eldest daughter Pearl was named after my paternal grandmother as was the eldest daughter in each uncle's families. His eldest grandson Norman born in London, Ontario settled in Israel when he retired. Sam settled in western United States and wrote several books of advice to dice and card gamblers.

7   Another uncle Jeremiah (Yermiah) arrived in 1917 from Waśniów, Poland with his wife Leiba and a large family of four boys and two daughters. One was later born in

(named after my paternal grandmother Penina Bayla) was born in Victoria Hospital in London, Ontario in 1933 where I was born later in 1935 in the same hospital.

Both my grandfather and my father were practising Orthodox Jews, followers of the Gerrer Rebbes, an Orthodox Jewish sect that originated in Ger, Poland almost a suburb of Warsaw whose Rebbes visited Israel in the 1920's and in 1940 until the Ger Rebbe, their leader, who returned to Poland, miraculously got out of Europe in 1940 and settled in Jerusalem where the Ger had previously established a Yeshiva named after the 'Sfas Emes', the Rebbe's grandfather, where they are headquartered today in Jerusalem. Unlike most orthodox sects, the Gerrer Rebbes were active Zionists and cofounders of the Agudath Israel, an international umbrella orthodox Jewish organization which is headquartered in Israel. Ger Hasidism had begun to settle in Palestine before World War I[8].

Toronto. Two of his sons served in the armed forces in World War II. The other two were too old or failed their medical. Jeremiah settled in Kensington Market and lived on Baldwin Street where he had a small chicken business and was a 'schochet'. A strict studious orthodox man all his life, he attended nearby synagogues daily. Three of his sons' children, all born in Canada, emigrated to Israel to study during the 1980's where they settled and flourished as business executives, teachers, doctors and professors. Two of Jeremiah's sons, Morris and Samuel, World War II air force veterans, followed, after they retired from their fur business in Toronto, to join their offspring in Israel. Another son Percy, a close cousin who lived in London, Ontario, worked as a furrier. Percy gave me my first job at nine years old helping stretch fur skins before they were cut and stitched into women's fur coats. Two of Percy's daughters, Charlotte and Pearlie, married two Canadian academics and then settled in Israel to raise their children. Percy's youngest daughter Bernice, married a Canadian doctor who became a leading specialist in his field in the United States, who died prematurely. Jeremiah's oldest son, Robert, also named Jerahmiel in Hebrew, settled in Peterborough, Ontario to start a dry goods business where he raised a thriving family. His second son, Murray, an outstanding athlete and businessman was the best man at my wedding in Toronto in 1958. A remarkable family saga.

8   My father, my maternal grandfather and his nephew and my maternal granduncle were all followers of the Ger. My grandfather's younger brother Chaim Elia Bleeman a devout orthodox Jew, had settled in Toronto where he raised a family of three, Murray, Deena and Manny and lived at 22 Lippincott Avenue not far from Kensington Market. Like my grandfather, he was a tall heavy boned man who made a living as a

Born in 1897 in Poland, my father, Solomon (Simcha) orphaned at twelve years old and Orthodox Jew, volunteered for the Polish Army in 1914 and fought in World War I until 1916. In 1918, he rejoined his Pilsudski Brigade and fought in the Battle of Warsaw in 1920 that led to Polish independence in 1921. He was wounded twice in battle and was decorated for bravery on the battlefield by Marshall Pilsudski himself. Then in 1921 after discharge from the army, he returned to his home-town of Waśniów in southern Poland to join his eldest brother Nathan ('Nusin')[9] in their small family businesses[10]. My father became active in the community affairs of his small town serving as Chairman of the

---

house painter, but he had an artistic bent. He decorated synagogues with astrological signs. His work can still be seen in tiny synagogues scattered around Toronto. He also designed the calligraphy and supervised the carvings on the tombstones of my grandmother, his brother my grandfather and my father. My blind grandfather composed as beautiful acrostic poem for my grandmother and then when my father died for my father each line starting with a letter of the deceased's name. My grand-uncle composed an acrostic poem and designed the art work and the calligraphy on the tombstone when my grandfather, his eldest brother predeceased him. Both my maternal grandparents are buried in Toronto at the Eitz Chaim Cemetery on Rose-lawn Avenue in Toronto. Chaim's oldest son Murray at 17 ran away from home in 1939 to enlist at the beginning of World War II in Hamilton. He died in the Dieppe Raid. My grand-aunt never fully recovered from the loss of her first born. She kept a large coloured picture of Murray in uniform in her small living room where she sat rocking in a chair for a few minutes daily.

9   Both my father's parents passed before he was thirteen. Brought up by his eldest brother, Nusin, head of the Grafstein family in his birthplace, Waśniów. Nusin had a large family of four daughters and seven sons. The Germans arrived in Waśniów in 1940 and the entire family including the cousinhood was transported to a nearby town and separated. Nusin and his wife, two elder married children, their families and the cousins were transported to Treblinka. Three brothers were sent to slave labour camps in Bezin and just before liberation in 1944, two escaped only to be killed by Polish Partisans who stripped them of their meager valuables. Samson Grafstein, a first cousin, the youngest son of Nusin, and Mendel Haiven, a third cousin, were sent to Auschwitz. Samson survived because of Mendel, a baker was given work in the camp bakery.

10 My father Solomon (Simcha), orphaned at 12, was brought up by his eldest brother, Nathan ('Nusin'), in his birthplace, a small town in southern Poland, Waśniów. His father Jerahmiel, an orthodox Jew, my namesake, was the leading merchant of his

County Library located next to the only church across the grassy small square from the shops owned and operated by the Grafstein clan. His friend was the Catholic priest in his hometown who, like my father,

---

small town. Jerahmiel died prematurely about 1909. His wife Penina (nee Mandel) who came from a family that originated in Alsace-Lorraine died about the same time. Her name was taken by the eldest daughter in each of the Grafstein brothers and sister families. My paternal grandparents came from different orthodox sects. My paternal grandfather was a 'Hasid' and my paternal grandmother came from a 'Misnagdic' orthodox Jewish family – two warring orthodox sects. By all accounts, it was a stormy marriage. Nathan, the eldest sibling, inherited the family businesses (lumber, distilling, transport, hardware, textiles and pub), his three younger brothers having left and emigrated to Canada from 1907 to 1917. Nathan, his immediate family and extended cousinhood, 67 in all, perished in Poland in the Holocaust except two. Only two cousins survived. One, Mendel Haiven, emigrated to Canada right after World War II due to my father's efforts. The other, Samson Grafstein, came with his family in 1966 to Canada from Poland then behind the Iron Curtain due to my efforts. No other Grafstein in Poland, France, Germany or Belgium survived World War II to the best of my knowledge. I was named Jerahmiel after my paternal grandfather and Samson, my second name, after my paternal great-grandfather. My grandfather Jerahmiel, my uncle Melech wrote, was a fierce hasidic Orthodox Jew and merchant leader of his hometown of Waśniów and who was elected in the 1880's and 1890's to represent his district in the Kielce Provincial Assembly. Earlier Grafsteins had settled in Radom before the 1850's and two were published authors. The Grafstein family name originated in Austria in Carinthia where they were in the wine growing business and produced white wine and apple brandy in the 17th century. This brandy is still produced and sold in Austria called 'Grafensteiner'.

The Graffensteins, Grafensteins, Grafsteins (German), Grafzstains (Polish), an uncommon name can be traced to Austria, in the Province of Corinthia according to my late father's fragmentary notes. Three Grafstein brothers, who were in the wine business there, decided to leave Austria in late 1780's to seek more hospitable homes. Isaachar Dov, my branch of Grafstein family, made his way to welcoming Poland while one went to Germany and the other to Belgium near the French border where I discovered a tombstone with the name Grafstein in 1995. Isaachar Dov settled in the town of Izbica in Poland (59 km southeast of Lublin, the regional capital), a Jewish village composed of orthodox Hasidic Jews that had created an independent Jewish community (Kehilla). Izbica was first settled by Jews in 1713. These religious orthodox Hasidim (Chassidim) were followers of the Przysucha Rebbe (also spelled Pyshishkhah), Yakov Yitzhak who called himself 'Yehuda' – 'the Old Jew' (also called 'Yehudi – HaKodosh' – The Holy Jew). Isaachar Dov's grandson Samson, my paternal great

spoke many languages and was well educated. By this time, his only sister
Anne Silverman (nee Grafstein), the eldest in the family, had long settled
in New York City (where several of her family served in the American

---

grandfather, left and then made his home in Radom, about 1840 then travelled south
to settle in the small village of Waśniów where my grandfather Jerahmiel was born
and where in 1897, my father was born. Samson was an astute businessman but also
a devout orthodox Jew and became a follower of the Przysucha Rabbi (1766-1814).
After Yaakov Yitzhak died in 1814, his group of dissident Hasidic Jews were led by
R. Simcha Bunim (1765-1827). My great-grandfather Samson would regularly travel
to and attend the court of the Przysucha especially on Passover. Samson befriended
R. Simcha Bunim's son Jerahmiel after whom my paternal grandfather was named,
his eldest son and my namesake. My father was named by his father Simcha after
Simcha Bunim and because as the youngest son in the family he was born on Jewish
festival of 'Simchas Torah' – celebration of the Torah. I named my eldest son's second
name Simcha after my father. I was named after my paternal grandfather Jerahmiel,
from the Aramaic, meaning the 'mercy of God' who was a Prince of Judah and son of
King Jehoiakim who died in 597 BC in the siege of Jerusalem before his successor also
King Jehoiakim and 3000 of his followers were exiled to Babylonia after the destruction of the First Temple of Jerusalem.

After Simcha Bunin, this Hasidic line was continued by R. Menchem Mendel of
Kotzk (1784-1859). Then came the Alexander Rebbe and finally the first Ger whose
leader visited the Holy Land starting in 1919, then 1920, and then through to the '30s
and finally escaped Europe in 1940 to the 'Holy Land'and became the leader of the
Agudas Israel, a leading orthodox group of various orthodox sects that supported
the establishment of the State of Israel. Today, their successors continue to lead the
Agudas Israel in the State of Israel from their Yeshiva 'Sfas Emes' Headquarters in
the heart of Jerusalem which I visited and met the Ger Rebbe Pinchas Menachem
(Pnei Menachem) AHL in the 1990's. I was told then that the Ger say Yahrzeit each
year for my maternal grandfather to commemorate his death. My maternal grandfather was a student of the 'Sfas Emes' and colleague of the 'Imrei Emes', the son of
the 'Sfas Emes'.

The founder of this line of rabbinic masters was the 'Przysucha' (also 'Pryshiska')
who challenged the Hasidic establishment. This led to an internal war. The Przysucha were considered contrarians. They refused to conduct themselves in way
that seemed synthetic, false, or reeked of self-deception, be it to honour religious
leaders or a particular religious practice. They equated pretension and self-deceit
with worshipping idols. A person needed to struggle daily with his ego to drive out
false motivations whether the desire for honour or the urge towards conformity
which placed a barrier between the individual and his creator. Both my father, my

armed services) and one daughter played in the New York Philharmonic as a violinist while brothers Morris, Max and Jeremiah had settled in Toronto and each had raised large families.

In 1927, my father, the youngest sibling, still a bachelor, left Poland for a tour first across Europe, then to Canada to visit his three other brothers in Canada and his only sister, Anna, in New York City. He had planned to visit relatives in Argentina then visit parts of Asia and return back to Poland. When my father met my mother in 1927 in Toronto, introduced by my uncle Morris, he fell in love, courted her for three years and then married her in 1930 in Toronto and decided to settle in London, Ontario where my sister Pauline Beverly (Penina Bayla) and I were born. My father, educated, erudite, orthodox Jew, a gifted linguist, inveterate letter writer, sometime Yiddish short story writer and diligent reader with a remarkable memory, was fluent in over 11 languages, lost his small retail dry goods (textiles) business in London early in the 'Great Depression'. Thereafter, my father struggled to make a modest living in various jobs (baker, caterer, teacher, custodian, interpreter, translator and

---

paternal and maternal grandfather, were followers of Ger as is my cousin Abraham Bleeman, a first cousin of my mother, a Holocaust survivor who is a lay leader of the Ger in Toronto. Read 'The Quest for Authenticity - The Thought of R. Simcha Bunim' by Michael Rosen (Urim Publications, New York, 2008). *Souls on Fire: Portraits And Legends Of Hasidic Masters* by Elie Wiesel translated from the French (Jason Aronson Inc. Printing, 1993).

My paternal great grandfather Samson was a strict orthodox man who became a successful leading merchant in the small town of Waśniów. He came from Radom around 1850. He was also a talented scribe. In the 1850's, he undertook to write a Sefer Torah on fine Russian parchment. My father brought this family Sefer Torah to London, Ontario when he settled there in 1930 and donated it to his small orthodox synagogue, B'Nai Moses Ben Judah on Horton Street. Years later, the Sefer Torah fell into disuse as some letters had fallen away. When I discovered this, I acquired it, brought the Torah to Toronto and hired a scribe recommended by Rabbi Zalman Grossbaum, a key Lubavitch leader and friend. The scribe spent over two years to meticulously repair the old scroll using similar lettering to the original. When it had been completely repaired, I loaned it to Beth Tzedec Congregation, my synagogue on Bathurst Street in Toronto, where it is now in regular use, probably the oldest Torah scroll in the synagogue's possession, if not Canada.

founder and publisher of the London Jewish Calendar) for my mother, my sister and me until his premature death, killed by a teenager in a fast car while crossing a narrow street, Horton Street, helping a lame man from his small orthodox synagogue, in 1951.

After my father's sudden tragic death, my mother Helen Rose worked as a saleswoman at a tiny millinery shop on Dundas Street[11] in downtown London, Ontario to earn a modest living. She had left primary school early to help support her family. My mother was working in a high fashion store on Bloor Street West when my father started to court her in the late 1920's. My mother always loved high fashion. My mother believed a woman wasn't well dressed unless she wore a hat and gloves. Later after my father's death she acquired the small shop in downtown London where she had worked, renamed it The Helena Rose Hat Shoppe, where she designed and sold ladies hats and gloves until I forced her to retire and move to Toronto at age 75. She lived on her own until 88 and then went to live at Baycrest where she loved to socialize and renewed old Toronto friendships and where she sang in the choir and followed the news, especially political news, daily, and died peacefully at 102 with all her faculties intact.

Both my father and maternal grandfather were lifelong daily students of the Bible and the two capacious Talmuds (the Jerusalem and the Babylonian versions)[12] that provided intricate Rabbinic glosses on the Old Testament, on biblical interpretations and history. Each studied one page of the Talmud each day of their adult lives except the Sabbath (and when my father served in the Polish army). This book is dedicated to them, their lives, their intellectual curiosity and their insatiable thirst for learning that they sought, each in their own delicate way, to transmit to me.

---

11 My mother, Helen Rose, called her tiny shop the Helena Rose Hat Shoppe where she became known for her stylish designs and tastes.

12 The two Talmuds are different. The older is the Jerusalem Talmud, more fragmentary and difficult to decipher, written in Aramaic, the language of ancient Palestine, was preferred by my grandfather and father. My father studied from the same Jerusalem Talmud that his father Jerahmiel studied before him. Their numerous handwritten notes are still visible in this volume.

To these two influences, I add my eldest son Laurence Stephen, a graduate of Jewish Day School at Beth Tzedec Synagogue and Upper Canada College in Toronto, whose academic interests led him to Harvard and on to Oxford, then the Sorbonne and later back to the University of Toronto Law School and whose journalistic and scholarly interests broadened my perspective on the turning points in the 20th century. Rummaging through my son's thesis at Harvard and the sources of his thesis at Oxford on the causes of World War II gave me different new insights into those turbulent times.

Most important, my grandfather, my father and my eldest son, Laurence Stephen[13,14], each in their own way, sought endlessly to find meaning behind manmade events and humankind. All three occupied strong beliefs in the Almighty, the search for moral conduct and the unfolding mysteries, the vagaries of life and the human condition.

Amongst my blessings, I count the ability to travel extensively, across Canada from sea to sea to sea, Europe[15], east and west, and throughout

13   My second son, Michael Kevin, a big burly man with a heart bigger than his outsized body lives in Toronto where his outgoing personality endears him to everyone he encounters. He is a voracious reader and an avid knowledgeable movie buff.

14   Laurence Stephen born in 1960 married Rebecca (née Weatherhead) from Winnipeg, who met at University of Toronto Law School, then settled after graduation from Law School in New York City in 1990 as an investment banker and she a lawyer where they raised my three grandsons Daniel, Edward and Isaac who like their father all graduated from Harvard College in Cambridge, Massachusetts.

15   In the late 1980's, I first visited Poland and the birth places of my father and mother in southern Poland in my father's village – Waśniów in the Province of Kielce and nearby Ylze (Drilsch), my mother's tiny birthplace. In Waśniów, all that several older Poles could remember was that the Grafstein family and cousinhood that made up of about a third the village population of 192, left suddenly in 1940 when the Germans arrived. One elderly woman recalled as a youngster, 'Rachmeel', as she called him, my grandfather driving a heavy freight wagon, led by large white draught horses that he bred. In Ylze (Drilsch) my maternal great grandmother's apothecary was still extant. My maternal great grandfather, Nusin, was a woodsman chopping trees and then cutting and selling lumber for a living. All my father's family perished in the Holocaust save two, Mendel Haiven, a second cousin who arrived right after World War II and Samson Grafstein, a first cousin in 1966. Both settled in Toronto and raised families here. One distant cousin, Bodo Grafstein, I discovered perished in Berlin

China, parts of Asia, all states of the United States and much of South America and parts of the Middle East, especially Israel and Jordan, while deepening my knowledge of these places and people, failed to quench my endless curiosity in politics, culture and history that never ceases to stand still and continues to attract my attention.

during World War II and the other cousin, Renée Grafstein, a skilled seamstress in a haute couture house in Paris also perished in World War II. How Samson survived the war in the camps was told in my book '*Beyond Imagination*' (McClelland and Stewart Inc., 1995)

EXPLANATION

"As he went on talking about himself, not realizing
that this was not interesting to others as it was to him."
– *'The Cossacks'*, Leo Tolstoy.

This book contains my reflections and observations on each decade of the 20th century.

My father was born in 1897 in Poland and died in London, Ontario in 1950. My mother was born in Poland in 1900 and died peacefully at 102 in Toronto. The purpose of writing this book is to make sense of their 20th century and mine, for myself and perhaps others. History is like an unfinished novel where the writer knows in advance how it turns out or is sometimes surprised. The writer chooses the facts and the characters to amplify his version of history.

Born in 1935 in the midst of the Great Depression in the small town of London, Ontario in modest circumstance, I was surrounded by my father's books in Yiddish, Hebrew, Aramaic, English, French, Spanish, German, Polish, Russian, Latin, Greek and other languages my father spoke and wrote. His library included exotic dictionaries like French to German, Polish to Russian, Latin to Greek, and so on. I understood not a word, but these books were a source of endless fascination and curiosity. My father was an inveterate letter writer. Writing for him was a ritual. He would place a large blotter in a leather case on the dining room table, carefully put on his rimless reading glasses, examine his blue Parker Pen for ink, fill his pen, set thin letter paper on the blotter and slowly begin to write with care, pausing with every sentence before writing another in clear European style script. Illiterate immigrants neighbours would come by and ask him to write letters to Europe in their language mostly Russian and Polish which he did with great care.

THE FRACTURED 20TH CENTURY

My father, an avid stamp and coin collector, I would witness as he carefully made additions to each collection and explained the background of each new find which I rarely understood. As a slow learner, having been held behind to repeat kindergarten to my mother's chagrin, at my mother's insistence, my father was cajoled to home teach me to read and write starting with reading the London Free Press in 1939 when I was over four years old early each morning. After reciting the morning prayers, my father taught me to learn to read, aloud, first the headlines and captions under the pictures. Then my father would give me quick simple history lessons behind those headlines and the captions on pictures that were emblazon across the front page of the newspaper. Slowly, my father aroused my curiosity and I became Eurocentric, as it was the onset of World War II and these early morning lessons continued as the War progressed during the early forties[16].

The war in Asia broke out after the sneak Japanese attack on Pearl Harbour in 1941 and so the exotic Far East became another source of curiosity and learning. These daily early morning lessons went on until the late forties after my Bar Mitzvah until my father was tragically killed in 1951. To understand literature, my father bought me 'Classic Comic Books' like *The Count of Monte Cristo*, *A Tale of Two Cities* and *Les Misérables* to trigger an interest in classic literature. It did!

My father also taught me to read the sports pages so my early heroes were not only political leaders but hockey[17], baseball and boxing stars. By osmosis, I became equally fascinated with sports, especially boxing,

---

16   My three best friends in public school and afternoon Chedar (Hebrew and Bible classes) in London, Ontario were my distant cousin Murray (Monue) Brickman, Irwin (Milky) Goldstein and Bennie Feldman – who became doctors and an accountant. During World War II, we used to play 'The Big Four' - Churchill, Roosevelt, Stalin and Chiang Kai-shek. I chose Winston Churchill! Murray Brickman was my first business partner who lived next door to me. When we were five, we got some ripe lemons from his father, a fruit peddler and some wooden crates and got into business selling lemonade for 1 cent a glass. Ice included was 2 cents. We did well.

17   I became a fan of the Toronto Maple Leafs when my Uncle Barney Wolfe took me to my first hockey game at Maple Leafs Gardens when I was ten. This interest in hockey flagged but my wife, older son and grandsons remain avid hockey fans to this day. Every Saturday night Carole watches her beloved Leafs alone on TV and then replay

and history in the making during the turbulent '40s. I started voluminous scrapbooks of my sports heroes. My father, a keen grassroots Liberal volunteer, took me as a youngster to polling stations where he served as a scrutineer and where I got my first taste of politics.

My mother, who possessed a lovely soprano voice, sang in a choir, took me to movies, especially technicolour musicals, hence my lifelong interest in music[18]. My sister Pauline, my only sibling, two years older, was smarter and quicker than I, and a top student unlike me who in her middle age, launched a brilliant business career[19].

Mother would converse with my father in Yiddish, Hebrew or Polish and used Polish when she didn't want me to understand their conversation.

My father whose wartime experiences as a Polish soldier in World War I and the following Polish War of Independence where he was wounded twice in battle, once during World War I and once during the Polish War of Independence, he never recounted. When I pointed to his two scars from bullet wounds, he would smile and change the subject. He would repeat that old saw that those that did not remember and learn from history were doomed to repeat the worst of it. This search for history and

---

the game with a son or grandson over the phone – a raucous experience as I hide away in my library for peace and quiet.

18 My father, a superb cook in the European style, taught me early the joy of preparing a fine repast. An avid gardener, he also taught me to put down dilled cucumbers, pickled green tomatoes and beets, alas, a lost art. Although he did not drink, he made homemade red wine from grapes he grew and sweet wine from red cherries he bought. I retain one of his bottles of red wine still tightly screwed and as yet unopened in the back of my wine cellar. My father bought second-hand art books and taught me about the European masters and modern French art that I later came to appreciate more when I became the Chair of Hermitage Foundation of Canada affiliated with Hermitage Museum in St. Petersburg, Russia – the largest collection of both old European masters and modern French paintings in Europe and possibly the world that I was privileged to visit and tour many times. Every room is intriguing and a delight to the eyes and mind.

19 Pauline, my exceptionally talented sister, worked as an executive secretary in Toronto, became a superb creative cook as well because of my father's influence. In her 30's, she developed an original food product called 'Honeycup Mustard' that soon was sold throughout Canada, the Americas and Europe due to her culinary and marketing expertise.

its meaning held my rapt attention for decades and haunts me to this day. I never quite understood what my father meant until I was mature enough to witness egregious history repeating itself endlessly before my eyes. My father was a grassroots Liberal and a believer in progressive reform so the idea of progress which he early tried to explain was and remains an endless elusive search. My father took me to polling stations during elections when he served as a scrutineer for the Liberals. *"Daddy, why are we Liberals?"* I asked him. *"Because my son Liberals help people that cannot help themselves."*

For this book, at first I thought I would focus on the '90s. When the chapter on the 1990's decade was completed, I looked back at the 1900's at the beginning of the 20th century and finally decided to complete the book with reflections on all the decades in between. This meandering book uncovers the deep fractures of the 20th century observed through my eyes and from my studies as history continued to roll by. All history travels via a winding staircase as humanity endlessly seeks the prospect of something better – peace, progress and prosperity.

What has the history of the 20th century taught me? The human condition remains the same, unchanged, unrepentant, searching, aching for improvement even while it takes dives in regression. Progress remains episodic and, at best, diffuse. Each of us imagine history through the lens of our own family history, culture, education and work experience. We try to connect the dots, altered by the moving parts of our own experiences.

This book describes the chaotic fractured 20th century, the political and cultural landscape, the seismic changes and quick sketches of its leading and lesser known characters that struck my interest. The needless endless deaths from civil and international wars, droughts and pestilence is noted.

Some of the turning points of the 20th century emerge and some, I thought, were turning points at the time. The uses of history remain as opaque as ever. Written histories change with times. Giant strides in science and technology has not altered the fierceness of humanity. Outbreaks of regional and international epidemics are continuous. Droughts reoccur. Natural disasters never leave us. Innovation continues to compound at an ever accelerating rate. Science races to uncover the unknown. With each conquest of new frontiers accompanied by these dizzying advances, violence has become more graphic and in the moment, as history repeats itself, endlessly, while science races to keep ahead of barbarity[20]. The uses and abuses of history continue as war, civil and foreign, remain a norm[21]. Progression and regression march forward, lockstepped together and then backward, in lurches and leaps. Still progress, dim as it seems at times, inches inexorably forward.

The meaning of recorded history, and the residue of its fragmented shards, largely ignored, haunts and taunts us. Who or what can restrain humanity from its delusions and excesses or remain on guard against its continuing barbarity, as progress inevitably advances, remains an unanswered question.

---

20 The relationship between science and the invention of instruments of mega destruction of life continued to be a puzzle of human nature in the 20th century.

21 It is estimated that there were at least 240 wars including civil wars and insurrections in the 20th century. The 21st century's miserable record continues as the number of people displaced by war already exceeds 40 million and never seems to recede. Syria was the vicious civil war that induced largest immigration (totalling over 15 million) since World War II and continued based on the misguided inaction or collaboration of other nations. Russia's war with Ukraine continues as a miserable blotch on the civilized world.

ACKNOWLEDGEMENTS

This book would not have been possible without the encouragement of Howard Aster and Matt Goody at Mosaic Press, my wife and fierce critic Carole and my assistant Naaznin Pastakia whose patience on my endless revisions passes understanding. *Caveat lector* – reader beware. This book was edited for only grammatical errors, so I take full responsibility for its contents and beg the reader's indulgence. Google was helpful when checking dates, esoteric information and certain statistics. All errors, omissions or repetitions are mine and mine alone.

THE LAST GREAT DECADE

THE 1990'S AND THE 'NEW WORLD ORDER'

*"Nobody knows about the generation that follows them and
certainly has no right to judge."* – Ernest Hemingway

*"To ascend faster on the stairs of life, keep the thinking shorter!
Think fast and act fast!"* – Mehmet Murat Ildan

*"We are tied down to a language which makes up in obscurity what it lacks
in style."* – 'Rosencrantz and Guildenstern Are Dead'*, Tom Stoppard

Suddenly, the world we knew changed on November 9, 1989. The Berlin
Wall came tumbling down[22,23]. The 'Cold War' ended with a whimper.

---

22 In 1987, I was invited by the Federal German Government to join a small group of
Parliamentarians from Europe to observe the West German Federal Elections. This
highly contested election pitted Helmut Kohl, leader of the Conservatives Chris-
tian-Democratic Union (CDU), and its main coalition partner from Bavaria, the Chris-
tian Social Union (CSU) led by Franz Josef Straus against Johannes Rau, leader of the
Social Democrats (SPD). For one week, we travelled in a swift cavalcade with Helmut
Kohl and in the second week, we travelled with Johannes Rau. It was an amazing experience as I observed at close hand how deeply the democratic ethic was imbedded in the
West German psyche from the major cities like Berlin (then divided into western and
Soviet controlled zones), Munich, Cologne, Bonn and Hamburg to the small towns and
villages dotted across the rich carefully cultivated agricultural areas of West Germany.

   The democratic 'idée fixée', I learned, was practiced at every level of political
activity. Each German political party had its own well-framed 'shiftung' ('think
tank'), financed mostly by the Federal Government to debate, research and develop
thoughtful party policies and democratic practices. Each 'stiftung' was named after
a party icon. I participated and spoke at the 'Friedrich Naumann Stiftung' of the
'Freie Demokratische Partei' (the Free Democratic Party, F.D.P.) akin to the Liberal
Party of Canada but more to the right. Both the FDP and Liberal Party of Canada
were members of Liberal International. Each party 'stiftung' had extensive outreach
programs to help developing democracies learn practical democratic processes and
principles. The party leader served as Chair of his party's 'shiftung'.

23 At a meeting of the annual 'Atlantik-Brücke' (the Atlantic Bridge) fostered by the
Marshall Plan after WWII in Munich that I attended in late October 1989, a few

3

Hope swirled around the world. Peace, concrete peace, lasting peace, was the high expectation. Talk of a 'new world order' based on democracy, peace and prosperity became part of the freshly transplanted lexicon. The heaving, heavy yoke of Communism had been lifted. The old division between 'east' and 'west' dissolved. Or so it seemed.

In June of 1989, the flames of democracy, quickly ignited across China fueled by student protests, had been even more quickly doused in Tiananmen Square in Beijing as the world watched[24]. But Europe, Europe, east and west, would be different.

My naïve belief that this 'new world order' heralded an end to anti-Semitism, would finally allow me to condemn my voluminous files on this topic to the shredder.[25]

---

weeks before the Berlin Wall came down – only one of the experts from Canada and Germany (comprised of politicians, business leaders, academics, security specialists, writers and journalists) - John Halstead, an academic, former Canadian diplomat and friend - predicted the early reunion of East and West Germany after the quick demise of East Germany while all others questioned or scoffed at this far-fetched notion.

24   Throughout the '80s and early '90s, I had travelled extensively across China. In 1985, my wife arranged for us and our two young sons to follow the ancient 'Silk road' from northwest China into the Chinese heartland. I was amazed at the electrification of the countryside and how quickly rural China was advancing with brick plants everywhere and how mud huts in the communes were changing to brick houses. I became Vice-Chair of the Twinning of Toronto and Chongqing in Szechuan Province and was in Chongqing when the Tiananmen student rebellion broke out. Governor of Beijing, Wong, attacked students with tanks. My friend Mayor Yang of Chongqing sent buses to the University campuses surrounding the outskirts of this crowded city, brought thousands of students to the centre of the city daily by bus, fed, and rebused them in the evening until the student rebellion ebbed and stopped. Not a single student was hurt or killed in Chongqing.

25   When the Berlin Wall came down in 1989, I actually believed that moment finally marked the end of the most murderous century in history. Let me recap by some numbers:

1. In the 11th century, one out of the five Jews were murdered.

2. In the last Millennium, before the 20th century, two out of every five Jews were murdered.

3. Then when we reached the 20th century ('The Killing Century') the mathematics accelerated. Over two hundred million human beings were slaughtered and, the Jews were always at the head of the list. One out of every three Jews was murdered.

Words of a 'unipolar' world led by 'Pax Americana' and its democratic allies dominated the public narrative. The lessons of the 'Cold War' were ripped up and destined, so we believed, to the dustbins of history. It was the springtime of hope for the future.

Under towering Helmut Kohl, a peaceful Germany, West and East, swiftly reunited with American accord under George H. Bush, as a united Germany quickly became the most successful economic anchor of Europe and European Community[26].

There was a faint pause of peace. While outbursts of violence continued, these felt more like the residue of a bygone era. The mega-bloodshed of the 20th century had seemed endless. Crushed between the 20th century bookends starting with pauses of peace between empires at the beginning of the century in 1900 to the end of the first decade in 1910, and then another peaceful pause between the 'great' powers ending in the last decade, from the start of 1990 to 2000, the ceaseless century-long slaughter suddenly appeared to dissipate. The deep freeze of the 'cold war' was defrosted. It was as if the air was escaping, deflating like a mighty early 20th century Zeppelin helium balloon warship fluttering down to earth, never to rise again.

Even the cycle of Mid-East wars slowed as contesting Shiite and Sunni dominated Arab states in the Iran-Iraq war came to an uneasy end that killed over a million Muslims and injured more than half a million. We witnessed Ayatollah Khomeini, the supreme radical religious leader

---

Mathematics teaches Jews to be alert. Mathematics keeps us awake. Still Jews, despite these murderous mathematics through the ages, maintained their fidelity to monotheism – in the belief in one God and their belief in democracy and progress! *"What did God do during the Holocaust to Jews?"* one survivor demanded of his Rabbi. *"What did man do?"* the Rabbi replied.

26 Little noticed on November 13, 1990 was a hard hitting speech in the British Parliament by Sir Geoffrey Howe, the British Foreign Minister in the Thatcher government that signalled the coming schism in the U.K. about U.K. membership in the European Union. Howe's speech announcing his resignation from Thatcher's cabinet ultimately brought down her government. The issue was Thatcher's skepticism about the EU and the loss of British sovereignty. Howe and others in her cabinet disagreed. In retrospect, this marked the start of the tremors in British politics that led to the schism on Brexit three decades later.

of Revolutionary Iran (who had returned to Iran after years of political asylum in France) obscenely, serenely, grotesquely, inspecting lines of his 'child' soldiers on TV matched by the equally obscene Saddam Hussein in the Iran-Iraq war over a small disputed stretch of seacoast between these two antagonistic Muslim nations. Even this seemed surreal and a throwback to an era that would be quickly arrested and reversed in the fresh liberating air of the 'new world order'[27].

The Oslo Accords – the peace agreement between Israel and the PLO concluded at the White House, in front of TV cameras, augured a peace resolution to the Israel-Palestine conflict in 1993 as did the Oslo II Accord signed with Egypt in 1995. I happened to be in Jerusalem shortly after Oslo II was being implemented and had a long informative meeting with Prime Minister Yitzhak Rabin and his Chief of Staff Eitan Haber, who were both plainly exhausted after seeking to correct a mistake in the map on the boundaries near Taba in the Sinai. Taba is a small Egyptian town near Eilat, Israel, on the Red Sea which I later visited. Rabin, puffing one cigarette after another, was cautiously optimistic but repeated an early admonition he gave me back in 1973 when he predicted there would be no peace for Israel until a settlement was reached with Syria.

The 1990's – and what seemed like, at last, a quiet decade to finish the 20th century - was an exhilarating moment in my time. After a century of contesting ideas, finally liberal democracy had triumphed over the last of the miserable 'isms' - communism[28]. The good guys had won!

History was on steroids.

---

27 Too competing autocratic Muslim venal leaders encapsulated the false narrative of the 'rule of law' to legitimize and capture the fealty of 'true believers' – one Shia and the other Sunni. Both transformed the Middle East and then the world. Ayatollah Ruhollah Khomeini (1902-1989) and the other Osama Bin Laden. Both were profound Quranic scholars and both were mired in the paradox of the revenge ideology and utopian hope for true believers following in the deep autocratic distorted footprints of Stalin, Hitler and Mussolini.

28 Little noticed was another event in March 1989 that was to change the course of history in the 21st century forever. An unknown software expert, Tim Berners-Lee, submitted a plan to collate research data for an open computer network called 'Information Management System'. The proposal received a grant from CERN the European organization for advanced Research. This was the birth of the World Wide Web.

In 1990, the Charter of Paris was signed by the heads of 35 Europe states (except for Andorra and Albania) together with U.S.A. and Canada. A brand new international political organism, the Organization for Security and Cooperation in Europe (OSCE) dedicated to democratic principles and practices, human rights and economic cooperation sprang to life. The OSCE covered territory was from 'Vladivostok to Vancouver', nations from Russia, south and west, including all of Europe, Canada the United States.

In 1991, the Soviet Union formally disbanded, cratering the second largest communist state in history[29]. Gorbachev and Reagan, each in his own way had triggered the Soviet Union's collapse. 'Perestroika' became Gorbachev's slogan that opened the doors to democracy. The reach of democracy flashed across Eastern Europe, its satellites and the steppes of Russia like a comet[30]. Francis Fukuyama, an American historian,

---

How scientific enquiry in the 20th century transformed our perceptions of the world and beyond can be found in *'When Einstein Walked with Gödel: Excursions to the Edge of Thought'* by Jim Holt (Farrar, Straus and Giroux, 2018).

29 China was and remains the most populous communist state in history. I travelled extensively across China, mostly alone, from the '80s to the early '90s.

30 Between August 24th and September 1991, following the Baltic States (Estonia, Latvia and Lithuania), Ukraine, Belarus, Moldavia, Azerbaijan, Kazakhstan, Kyrgyzstan, Uzbekistan, Tajikistan, Georgia and Armenia declared independence from the Soviet Union. Most of these countries I had visited. The sudden bloodless collapse of the Soviet Empire was the most unparalleled counter-revolution in modern history, over, without war, domestic or foreign. I travelled to most of these new states. In Kazakhstan, I became friends with their foreign minister and then Speaker of their national assembly, now President, Kassym-Zhomart Tokayev. He dined with me in my home in Toronto when he visited Canada for an OSCE-PA meeting in the '90s. Tokayev's career trajectory was fascinating. Trained in Moscow and a devout Communist, he moved across the political spectrum and became an open-minded pragmatist and a believer in democratic tolerant practices.

During a visit to Astana, the modern capital of Kazakhstan, I asked Tokayev if there were any Jews in his capital. He arranged for a visit to a recently built beautiful white painted synagogue not far from the centre of the new metropolis. I was surprised in this Muslim country there were no guards at this synagogue and the ornate gates were open. There I met Rabbi Israel Cohen, the chief Rabbi of Kazakhstan who was a follower of the Lubavitch Rebbe and who was born in Brooklyn, in Crown Heights, where the Rebbe's home and headquarters was situated.

proclaimed it was 'the end of history' and we believed it. East and West Germany had quickly reunited boosting Germany's explosive economic growth. Ukraine became an independent country for the first time in its tortured history. Soviet vassal states across Eastern Europe, the Caucuses and the Baltics crumbled and quickly regained their independence as democratic elections spread like a wild fire destroying autocratic structures and replacing them with democratic assemblies[31].

We experienced a mind blowing vortex of change.

During the late 1980's and all through the 1990's, I was elected a senior officer, first as Treasurer, then as Vice-President and head of the Liberal Political Group under the purview of the Organization for Security and Economic Co-operation in Europe - Parliamentary Assembly (OSCE PA) – headquartered in Copenhagen[32]. As a senior officer representing

---

Cohen travelled regularly across Kazakhstan, the third largest in the world, sometimes by train, and had never encountered animosity. Incredible.

31 Nothing was quite as romantic or newsworthy as the 'Velvet Revolution' between the Czechs (led by a former imprisoned dissident, philosopher, playwright and writer Václav Havel who became the first Czech President of the renewed Czech Republic) and the Slovaks as they divided into two separate states that was consummated amicably on January 1, 1993. The Czech lands were composed mostly of Bohemia and Moravia, a medieval remainder that lie at the heart of the Holy Roman Empire. Amazingly, Slovakia, a Nazi collaborator state, had gained wartime independence under Hitler and had been reunited with the Czechs after WWII under Josef Tito, a Serbian wartime Communist Partisan leader. These rearranged states retained their ethnic based origins and national impulses while emerging as fledgling democracies.

32 The Secretary-General of the OSCE-PA, Spencer Oliver, and its International Secretariat was and remains located in Copenhagen. Spencer Oliver, an American was one of the most knowledgeable experts on European politics I have ever encountered. We became fast friends. Other American pals included Congressmen Steny Hoyer (now Democratic Majority Leader in the U.S. House of Representatives), Alcee Hastings, Chris Smith and Ben Cardin (now Senator). The OSCE was divided into two – the government arm was located in Vienna and the parliamentary arm in Copenhagen where I travelled regularly after I was elected a senior officer for over a decade, first as Treasurer, then Senior Vice-President. I was also elected and re-elected Chair and Leader of the Liberal Group at the OSCE-PA for over a decade that gave me an influential role in both the make-up of the organization and its debates and policies.

During this same period I was annually elected by all Canadian parties for 15 years Co-Chair of the Canada-U.S. Interparliamentary Group that liaise regularly

Canada, I was invited to join, help organize and co-lead international election monitoring teams first in Ukraine, then Georgia, then Russia, then Romania and later Montenegro gaining a close-up and personal view of the deep popular desire for democracy practices and democratic elections in Eastern Europe. OSCE expanded rapidly as these new nascent democracies rushed to become full fledge active members dedicated to the OSCE principles and practices of democratic institutions and the 'rule of law'.

Like a star burst, the rays of democracy spread rapidly into the dark corners of Eastern Europe. It was a breathtaking time. One could barely keep up with the news surging across Eastern Europe and the Caucuses, the Balkans and the Caucuses, the Baltics as century-old animosities appeared to dissolve overnight. Democratic sunshine brightened that dismal war-torn landscape. New boisterous fourth estates blossomed across Eastern Europe and the Baltics in print, radio, TV and on the web. A babble of different voices could be seen and heard in a democratic melee of viewpoints.

In May 1998, India, the world's most populous democracy, ignited a series of three underground 'nuke' tests following an earlier test in 1974. Prime Minister Atal Bihari Vajpayee immediately declared India a 'nuclear power' while the United States and Canada criticized India's actions. The United Kingdom, France and Russia refrained. None of the above issued sanctions. Even these few nuclear explosions seemed far off and didn't change the global narrative of a new peace world order.

'Frozen conflicts' remained (e.g. northern Ireland, Korea, Cyprus, Taiwan, Sakhalin Islands, etc.). I was asked to join a trio of OSCE-PA parliamentarians - by Spencer Oliver, a most knowledgeable American and the founding Secretary-General of OSCE PA who became a lifelong friend

---

with a parallel group from Congress to deal with trade irritants like lumber, salmon, potatoes, cattle, etc. We met regularly mostly in the U.S. Friendship were developed with Senators Leahy, Frank Murkowski, Grassley, Crapo, Klobuchar, and Biden and Congressmen Amo Houghton, Cliff Stearns and Cohen Peterson just to name a few. We began to meeting U.S. Governors as well attend their annual meetings held in every region of American when we learned that almost all political issues, like Canada, were local in origin.

and advisor – to attempt by direct mediation to resolve the smoldering issue between Moldava and 'the 'breakaway' region of the Transnistria (formerly known as 'Bessarabia'). We had high hopes the strong winds of democracy would be felt even there[33].

With 'Glasnost' coined by Gorbachev as the 'thaw' erupted in Russia and access to the KGB archives finally uncovered the lucid truth behind the death by execution in 1940 of Isaac Babel considered one of the greatest short story writers in the 20th century after his 'show' trial in the '30s. 1990 saw the publication of Isaac Babel's *Complete Works* edited by his daughter Natalie Babel, a literary feast followed by a superb English

---

33　I was selected by OSCE PA to join two other Parliamentarians, a Finnish social demo-crat and a German conservative to mediate a settlement on the 'frozen' conflict between the warring parties of Moldavia and the separatist' enclave of Transnistria ('Bessarabia') which was supported by the Russians. There had been violent clashes between the parties since the demise of the Soviet Union. We agreed to organize 'face to face' meetings with the two major protagonists, both brawny war-scarred leaders. We chose the Aland Islands lying in North Sea waters (where 90% of the islands were of Swedish origin and 90% were Swedish speakers) between Sweden and Finland, long a disputed region, which dispute had been settled by the Finns accepting Swedish language with minority rights while maintaining Finnish hegemony and a high degree of local autonomy, utilizing the mutual recognition of both languages equally. This dispute had been settled by the League of Nations in 1920. This was an essentially bilingual federalist solution – hence OSCE PA interest in having a Cana-dian participant with federalist political experience in the smoldering conflict.

We arranged for a formal encounter at a sparsely furnished Nordic wood clad community centre meeting room on the main scenic island, once a settlement for wealthy seamen who made a healthy living as whalers. The initial morning meeting did not go well. We decided to have lunch in a sun-drenched room at a local restau-rant. My wife Carole was with me. We decided that Carole who spoke no foreign languages should sit between the two angry war-scarred leaders, one with one arm lost in battle and the other with scars on his face and only three fingers on one hand. Both were angry men who had never talked to one another. Both spoke Russian. Carole, as if she was having lunch at Acadian Court in Toronto, turned to one then the other, and without an interpreter, started making small talk asking about their families until they started to chat to each other about their children. It was bizarre. But it worked. The two leaders began to speak to each other without anger or rancour, sharing family experiences. The afternoon meeting made progress as disputed issues were discussed more rationally. To date, this 'frozen dispute' has yet to fully thaw, but the killing stopped.

translation with more literary gems to follow like a bubbling brook of once repressed existence running clean, fresh and free.

Finally in 1991, Ivan Bunin's collected works were published in Russia for the first time. Included was Bunin's eye witness accounts of the Russian Revolution particularly in Moscow and Odessa[34] considered a cultural beacon of artists, musicians and writers, entitled *'Cursed Days'*. Bunin is considered the heir to the superb Russian writers like Pushkin, Turgenev, Chekhov and of course, Tolstoy. Nominated for a Nobel Prize in Literature in 1925 when he fled to the west, he was finally awarded this award in 1933, the first Russian writer and first author in exile to gain the coveted recognition. Bunin opposed Bolshevism and the Soviet Empire from the advent of the Revolution in 1917. Considered the first and best known Soviet dissident Bunin continued his activism, unabated, until his death in Paris in 1953.

Poets and writers from Russia especially women, now freed of government restraints, flowed with a wave of innovative works. Izabella Akhatovna 'Bella' Akhmadulina, one of Russia's greatest female writers of the 20th century, opened complex themes from a female perspective. 'New Wave' playwrights like Lyudmila Petrushevskaya uncovered

---

34   Odessa was considered the cultural centre of Russia, though located in Ukraine. Carole's maternal grandmother was born in Odessa, hence my interest in its colourful history and its endless stream of outstanding poets, musicians, artists and writers from Pushkin to Babel, the philosopher Martin Buber, the painter Ilya Repin, the musician David Oistrakh, just to name a few. Leon Trotsky born a Ukrainian, recounts in his autobiography how his family moved for him to attend school in Odessa in 1888 and how his education in Odessa changed his life and world outlook. Isaac Babel, one of the greatest essayists of the modern era, wrote eye-opening accounts of life in Odessa and later as a member of the Red Cossacks as they fought across eastern Europe especially Poland. Vladimir Jabotinsky, the founder of Revisionist Party in Israel and the Jewish Self Defense League in Europe (that later morphed into the Haganah – the Israeli Defense Force), was born in Odessa, an outstanding speaker/writer, wrote colourful reminisces of his youth and early education in Odessa. Internationally acclaimed musicians and artists were born and started their careers in Odessa. Chaim Bialik, a Yiddish poet was one of the pioneers of modern Hebrew poetry and came to be recognized as Israel's national poet through he never lived there. Musicians included Emil Gilels and S. Richter. Interestingly, George and Ira Gershwin's parents and Bob Dylan's grandparents came from Odessa.

revelations of repressed disintegration and moral turpitude adding new chapters and insights to this decade's literary explosion. Others like Yevgenia Ginzburg opened new windows to frame life in Soviet Russia from a feminist perspective. Literature was bubbling and flowing in a rising tide of new and exciting books. One could barely keep up.

Two astonishing Russian authors and close friends, the poet Joseph (Josip) Brodsky and the author Sergei Dovlatov, both from Leningrad (now St. Petersburg), succeeded to emigrate to the United States – Brodsky in 1972 and Dovlatov in 1977. Both had been expelled from the Soviet Writers Union. Brodsky became a Nobel Prize winner for literature after his poems were published in the United States and critically acclaimed. Dorlatov, unable to be published in Russia, was finally published in the United States. Both authors are revered and read by millions of Russians.

None were more prolific in the 1990's than 'Bella' Akhmadulina, a celebrated poet, screenwriter and novelist. She married writer Yevgeny Yevtushenko, a favourite of mine, the dissident poet whose poem, 'The City of Yes and the City of No' made him, already a legend within Russia, well known beyond, in the west. In the 1990's, Akhmadulina published a flood of poems, novels and short stories and is considered one of the top five Russian women writers-poets of the 20th century, a treasure trove of innovative startling insights and exciting writing, so different in style and nuance from the western mainstream[35].

Music from America was transformed to catch the changing tenor of these swift changing times. In 1991, the rock band REM led by Michael Stipe (singer), Mike Mills (bassist) and Peter Buck (guitarist) wrote,

---

35 In 1990 on a visit to Moscow for the opening of the MacDonald's with a group of Toronto friends of George Cohan, the founder of MacDonald's in Russia, I acquired several paintings of the so-called 'Secret Art of the Soviet Union'. These were fine paintings of various styles that eschewed the Soviet government's directed style of 'social realism'. Travelling across Eastern Europe over the years thereafter, my collection of these wonderful paintings grew as I acquired most of them from the artists or their families or friends and expanded to over 350 canvases and is still growing. The Russian techniques were superb. Impressionist, post-impressionist, surreal, cubist, modern, post-modern styles influenced by European and American artists flourished underground during the Communist era throughout Eastern Europe. Art like history is cumulative and adaptive.

performed and produced *'Out of Time'*, a breakout alternate rock album with songs titled: *'Losing My Religion'*, *'Radio Song'* and *'Shiny Happy People'*, that sold over 80 million albums world-wide. Their songs caught the public mood and mirrored this newly arrived sense of universal freedom[36]. American music, and especially music from England, could be heard across Europe, East and West. The world seemed in a hungry search to digest the next 'new' idea in every direction - politics, literature, film culture and business, and especially music.

The 'Third World', a common generalized word entered the global dialectic replacing the 'Underdeveloped World' as the latter term diminished, fluttered around the globe and was shoved aside as these regions were given secondary consideration. Civil war burst out in San Salvador in the Americas and Sri Lanka in Asia. South and Central America began to topple autocratic leaders. These appeared as minor positive disruptions that did not disturb the broader global pacifist mood. Some were the residue of communist infiltrations, others corrupt autocrats, bursting forth from clogged rusted ideological sewage pipes that begin to spring leaks.

Still, some lessons from history were quickly forgotten. The exuberant rapid expansion of NATO eclipsed the objections and warnings from a weakened Russia, and went unheeded. The Russian obsessive paranoia about 'encirclement' still simmers below the surface. Previous restrictive

---

36 Of course Canadian born Buffy Sainte-Marie added her songs and voice as did Joan Baez who earlier caught the public's attention after the disruption of popular music during the Vietnam War and its aftermath that gave rise to new forms of musical, at times jarring, at times melodic expression. Other Canadian born singers and songwriters like Neil Young, Ian Tyson and Sylvia Tyson, all members of the Canadian Songwriters Hall of Fame added their voices and music to create a distinct Canadian texture and sound. For a time, in the '80s, I was a lawyer for Sylvia Tyson whose voice and music animates me still. Peter Newman, one of Canada's foremost political authors and columnists was also for a time a client that gave me insight into writers' travails. Peter was an avid fan of Stan Kenton and wrote while he listened to Kenton and his band. Peter Newman's gifted wife for a time, Christine, a friend, was his editor and in her own right was a distinguished journalist and author. Mea Culpa. In her book, *'Grits: An Intimate Portrait of The Liberal Party'* (Macmillan of Canada, 1983), I was the subject of one chapter.

agreements reached between the west and the Soviets that assumed containment of NATO were forgotten[37].

The myth of the 'Non-Aligned Movement' (NAM)[38] that represented nearly two-thirds of UN members and 55% of the world population, as projected in the West, that in truth had always been in synch as 'fellow travelers' with the Soviet Union, imploded. The Soviets had been experts on creating international and cultural organizations to foster Communist/Soviet interest under so-called 'neutral' cover. There were few so-called 'neutral' countries. Examples include Cuba, Yugoslavia, India, Indonesia, Mongolia and Iran. They self-designated themselves as 'non-aligned' and the 'Third World', another misnomer.

---

37 In 1975, the West had reached a massive comprehensive settlement with Soviet Union as proof of 'co-existence' between the two contesting ideologies. The West and its allies (35 nations in all) including Canada and the U.S.A., signed the Final Act of the Helsinki Accords to respect Soviet borders and those of its Soviet Eastern European and Baltic satellites in exchange for reductions in 'nuke' arsenals and especially Basket III – mutual respect for 'human rights'. This gave fuel to the Russian 'dissident movement'. Later during 'glasnost' and 'perestroika' (openness and transparency) to make socialism work more effectively in part by liberalizing the Soviet economy, Reagan and Gorbachev reached affirmation on a similar treaty agreement, to respect the borders of the Soviet empire including Eastern Europe and the Baltics in exchange for mutual reductions in U.S. and Soviet 'nuke' arsenals. These undertakings by the West were forgotten as NATO rapidly expanded across Eastern Europe after 1991, a source of Russian discontent to this day. The Helsinki Accords led to the creation of the OSCE after the Conference on Security and Cooperation in Europe (CSCE) commenced regular meetings. In 1990, the CSCE morphed into two organizations under the rubric the Organization for Security and Economic Cooperation (OSCE) and both play an active role in its planning and committee work. The OSCE is one of the few European based multilateral organizations where United States and Canada are full voting members, both its governmental arm (OSCE), headquartered in Vienna and its parliamentary arm (OSCE-PA) in Copenhagen.

38 The so-called Non-Aligned Movement (NAM) (that followed the Bandung Conference in 1955) was dreamed up by Josip Tito, the lifelong communist leader who became disenchanted with Russian Soviet hegemony. So in 1961, he gathered other leftist leaders, Nehru (India), Nasser (Egypt), Nkrumah (Ghana) and Sukarno (Indonesia) to combine to resist Communist and American hegemonic leadership. NAM leaders were all 'soft' on Communism and the Soviet Union. Later Fidel Castro (Cuba), by this time, a devout communist became the elected head of NAM.

While the tide of freedom was rising across Europe, the deep undertow of ancient animosities in the Balkans was felt, straining and heaving below the surface. The 'new world order' was not yet perfected in this turbulent region simmering to revise history and recapture antique long lost 'homelands'. The Balkans arrested once again the narrative of freedom washing across western and eastern Europe. The source of this dark backwater was Yugoslavia, an outlier Communist state patched together into a multi-ethnic federation by Josip Tito, a successful Communist guerilla leader in World War II who with the advocacy of Englishmen like Winston Churchill's son Randolph he had befriended during the war, came to be admired by the western allies as a 'good' communist. Tito squirmed away from the smothering Soviet grip to enjoy economic growth across polyglot Yugoslavia. Tito, in designer sunglasses, reveled in an ostentatious luxurious life style, clad in white tailored uniforms, was photographed enjoying his beautiful homes, powerful cars and sleek motor-boats accompanied by his stunning dark-eyed, dark haired, formidable wife, a World War II guerrilla comrade, always at his side. Tito who became a leader and charter member of the so-called 'non-aligned' states, and as an independent communist state, had become a pin-prick in the rear of the Soviet behemoth. For a time, the darling of Communist worldwide, Fidel Castro became the head of the non-aligned nations as a glorified world leader.

After Tito's death in 1980, the Yugoslavia Federation of six ethnic states, Croatia[39], Slovenia, Serbia, Montenegro, Kosovo, Bosnia and Herze-govina began to unravel. First Croatia, then Serbia and Slovenia returned

---

39 Croatia's key ally in its breakout from the Yugoslavian federation was the erstwhile German Foreign Minister Hans-Dietrich Genscher. Croatia had been a Nazi ally during WWII and sent troops to assist Nazi war aims. This breakout triggered the disintegration of the multi-ethnic Yugoslav federation and the ensuing ethnic cleansing and the resulting deplorable conflict in the Balkans. Genscher was an 'architect of German reunification where his diplomatic skills excelled. He and I became acquainted at meetings of his party, the Free Democratic Party (FDR) in West Germany and at OSCE in Vienna where he served as Chairman for a period. However his role in projecting Croatia to independence opened the door to the horrific slaughter and 'ethnic cleansing' that followed in the Balkans throughout the 1990's.

to their World War II predilection for 'ethnic cleansing'. No state was more active than Serbia in these deplorable actions against the integrated Muslim minorities in the regions of Bosnia and Herzegovina and Kosovo. Sarajevo, the capital of Bosnia and Herzegovina, had been a multicultural city made up of Muslims, Jews and various Christian sects.

It was said of the Jews of Sarajevo, expelled from Spain in 1492 during the Inquisition that had settled there, that each Sarajevo Jewish family descended from those Spanish Jews kept a family tradition. They passed down the antique keys of their homes in Spain as a reminder of that turbulent past. Jews are inseparable from their memories. All these religious groups, Christian, Muslim and Jewish, got along and were physically indistinguishable from one another.

Under the charming leadership of Tony Blair, Bill Clinton[40], then mired in the notorious 'Lewinsky Affair' was nudged, perhaps to 'wag the dog', to bomb Serbia forcing a brokered peace settlement by 2000 called the Dayton Accords. Slobodan Milošević, the ultra-nationalist Serb President, was later imprisoned and convicted as a war criminal at the International Court of Justice at The Hague where he died, unwept, unrepentant, behind bars.

In the muck and mire of the Balkans (especially the outrage at the UN inspired 'safe zone' in Srebrenica where thousands of Bosnian Muslims were slaughtered when a Dutch-led UN peace-keeping force allowed Bosnian Serbs to massacre innocent Muslim men, women and children)[41], one Canadian, General Roméo Dallaire, head of a UN Peace

---

40 Up close and in person both Blair and Clinton were charming, witty and careful listeners and compelling speakers.

41 The UN Report of 1995 on the Srebrenica massacre detailed the failure of Kofi Annan, the UN Secretary-General and the senior UN officials who encouraged Srebrenica as a 'safe haven' and then stood by and remained neutral during this massacre and, still failed to take full responsibility for this outrage. This outrage was genocide within the UN accepted definition of genocide. Annan's failures include dismissing warnings of the genocide in Rwanda and the transformation of the UN Human Rights Commission into an absurd organism run by a cabal of representatives from nations with horrendous records of human rights violations which they studiously ignore while the world's worst human rights offenders go free of UN criticism. One nation, Israel, has garnered more resolutions of criticism for alleged breaches of 'human rights'

Keeping Force, emerged as a hero. Romeo later joined me in the Senate of Canada where I came to know and understand this resolute, passionate, brave soldier who gained world renown for his outspoken voice against 'ethnic cleansing', while giving voice to the plight of refugees, crumpled human rights and 'child' soldiers. Once the Balkans stabilized, the 'new world order' narrative was restored.

In this last decade of the 20th century, the world population continued to grow, reaching over six billion[42]. The UN membership tripled from 51 states at its founding in 1945 to 189 states by the year 2000. Immigration flows accelerated with more open borders, hastening, as most thought, the long awaited good cycle from vice to virtue that would intensify 'progress'. 'Civil wars' largely displaced wars between nation states. Asymmetrical wars, so called 'microwars', fomented by radical minority entities came crashing to the fore eroding the established conception of 'war between states', upending conventional international law built on the Augustinian thesis of 'just war' between states[43]. But these were considered 'disturbances' and didn't break the overarching narrative and hope of 'peace in our times'.

Smoldering American domestic 'civil wars', came to the public attention via nightly TV, especially from the decay of the inner American cities like Los Angeles divided by depressed black, Hispanic and white precincts where gang wars, violence, and looting periodically broke out to capture an instant of wider viewing. In New York City, led by strong civic leadership under Mayor Rudy Giuliani, a rebirth of urban civility and security was launched with dramatic crime reductions[44]. Urban scrawl

---

than all the nations combined in the world from this 'faux' commission on human rights abuses and the UN itself.

42 At the start of the 20th century in 1900 the world population was just over 1.6 billion.

43 Read 'Civil Wars: From L.A. to Bosnia' by Hans Magnus Enzensberger, New York Press (1990) who cogently essayed these phenomena.

44 After 9/11, my wife and I, backed by a small group of volunteers, led a large contingent of thousands of Canadians from coast to coast to New York City, where we met and enjoyed the company of Mayor Giuliani and who later visited our home in Toronto. See chapter of 'The Miracle on 52nd Street: Canada Loves New York Weekend' in my last book 'Parade: Tributes To Remarkable Contemporaries' (pg. 237, Mosaic Press, 2017). For a fuller history of this memorable event, read 'Chicken Soup for the Canadian Soul'

was erased and 'shattered windows' were fixed. Open street drug dealing dissipated while police patrolled the dangerous inner city precincts serving as a constant visible presence. The forgotten and rotting inner cities began to regenerate. Harlem was a stunning example. The 'benign neglect' of the inner cities by all political classes, had been pointed out by Daniel Moynihan in the '60s, slowly, too slowly, began to evaporate. *"Benign neglect"*, Moynihan coined it and so it was. Poverty, if not being erased, was beginning to ameliorate, and still only by fits and starts.

---

by Raymond Aaron, Janet Matthews, Jack Canfield and Mark Victor Hansen (Health Communications, Inc., 2002). It was said by several observers at the time, that this was the largest invasion of Canadians to the United States since the War of 1812 – estimated at over 26,000 Canadians who travelled from across Canada, all at their own expense, to visit New York City that remarkable weekend.

THE 'FREE TRADE' EXPLOSION IN THE 1990'S

The 1990's acted as a punctuation mark to the end of political protectionism and national divisions as wave after wave of 'free trade' agreements and easier border transit were ushered in, reaching every corner of the globe. The sweet siren call for 'free trade' crossed domestic political lines. A broad consensus for 'free trade' began to solidify.

The Europe Free Trade Agreement expanded the European zone as one prosperous 'free trade' region. In 1991, the Maastricht Treaty established the Euro as the common currency for the most of European Free Trade zone easing trade, travel, tourism and commerce across European borders while accelerating economic growth.

The ASEAN Free Trade Area (AFTA) Agreement was signed on 28 January 1992 in Singapore. When the AFTA agreement was originally signed, ASEAN had six members, namely, Brunei, Indonesia, Malaysia, Philippines, Singapore and Thailand. Vietnam joined in 1995, Laos and Myanmar in 1997 and Cambodia in 1999. AFTA now comprised the ten countries of ASEAN.

In 1993, the European Community changed to new attire under the mantle of the European Economic Union (EEU) demonstrating that forgotten thesis that 'free trade' has always preceded democratic expansion. In 1995, even reluctant Austria, France and Sweden joined the EEC expanding its cross border trade flows further and faster.

In 1994, in North America, NFTA between U.S.A., Canada and Mexico created the largest 'free trade' agreement in the world negotiated by the Liberals under Jean Chretien. The opposition to 'U.S.A.-Canada free trade' evaporated earlier in 1988 under Brian Mulroney after the clear-cut Conservative election victory. Finally there was a political consensus of the benefits of 'free trade' that took almost a century after Laurier was defeated in the 1911 federal election campaign on the issue of a mutual reduction of tariffs between Canada and the U.S.A., based on the premise of 'Reciprocity'[45].

In 1994, in South America, the Mercosur Free Trade Agreements first between Brazil and Argentina, then between Brazil, Chile, Paraguay, Uruguay and Venezuela and other adjacent associated states created yet another a large 'free trade' bloc.

Nothing was more important to global 'free trade' than in 1995, when the World Trade Organization (WTO) replaced the outmoded General Agreement on Tariffs and Trade (GATT). One hundred and twenty-three countries joined, including Canada and the U.S.A. India became a founding member of WTO and 'free trade' exploded in Asia[46]. China, the most populated country in the world, and Indonesia, the largest Muslim country in the world, were soon to follow.

Even in the backwater Middle East, states along the southern Mediterranean littoral - North Africa - established 'MENA' - 'free trade' relations between some Arab countries like the Ottoman Empire of old. More importantly, regional 'free trade' zones (QIZ) in Jordan and Egypt

---

45 'Free Trade' with the U.S.A. had been explored by Mackenzie King several times but, always cautious, he retreated, at the least hint of opposition, especially from Quebec. King, ever the careful student of the Canadian mindset, recalled Sir Wilfrid Laurier's lost election based on 'Reciprocity' – reciprocal trade with the U.S. in 1911. St. Laurent had moved forward with the St. Lawrence Seaway to facilitate better trade efficiencies, despite opposition especially from Quebec, but broader attempts at free trade were deferred. Diefenbaker's Minister of Trade, George Hees led trade missions abroad. Mike Pearson succeeded with the introduction of the 'Autopact' in 1965 as a key free trade component in Canada-U.S.A. free trade relations that then followed with the FTA under Brian Mulroney in 1988 and then NFTA under Jean Chretien in 1994.

46 China joined the WTO in 2001 and world trade - global trade - reaching every corner of the earth – was never the same. There is no turning back. China and India became home to the fastest growing middle classes in the world. China soon nudged the U.S.A. seeking to overtake American and to become the largest and fastest-growing domestic market in the world. The transformation of India into a modern economy was also accelerated. Both nations became 'free trade' opportunities joined by other Asian 'tigers' like Indonesia, Korea, Taiwan, Malaysia, Thailand, Philippines, Singapore, Vietnam and of course, Japan. Malaysia is the largest Muslim country in the world.

were created by the U.S. Congress led by George W. Bush aimed to foster economic partnerships between Jordan, Israel and Egypt businessmen by stimulating jobs and growth allowing products assembled there to be exported to U.S.A. tariff free. Jobs were swiftly created as activist businessmen from Jordan, Israel and Egypt worked together as business partners in their common economic interest. The economic growth of Gaza festers as its leaders remain more convulsed by violent ideology than economic progress[47].

Earlier in 1985, U.S.A. had entered its first Free Trade Agreement with Israel. Canada followed in 1996 with its first Free Trade Agreement with Israel. Other Free Trade Agreements followed. These agreements were one major source of Israel's explosive economic growth where its per capita income rivalled some parts of Europe in the next decade. West Bank per capita income continued to grow higher than any other Muslim state in the Middle East except the oil rich emirates and Saudi Arabia and began to approach income levels in Europe. This startling fact was rarely covered by the media.

Ironically, Canada did not have 'free trade' between the provinces of Canada despite the 1867 BNA that expressly stated there was to be free trade between provinces for goods and products produced in other provinces[48].

---

47 Youth unemployment in the Middle East, over 60%, remains the highest in the world. This is a major rationale that triggers violence in that troubled region that also has the highest youth population in the world.

48 The great irony of the Conservative and Liberal Parties respective beliefs in free trade with other nations is that Canada does not have free trade, free of provincial tariffs and other trade barriers, within Canada. See The Report of The Senate Committee in Banking, Trade and Commerce that I led as Chairman of the Senate Banking Committee in 2007-2008 on direct or indirect provincial barriers to trade within Canada notwithstanding the clear language of the 1867 British North America Act Section 93 that remains as part of Canada's constitution unamended to this day. Recent efforts in 2018 by the Justin Trudeau government to name Minister Dominic LeBlanc to focus in removing inter-province trade barriers held promise. Regretfully Dominic fell ill, retired from Cabinet and now, restored to health, returned to this post in the Cabinet. The Supreme Court of Canada failed to recognize the clear words of the Canadian Constitution recognizing free trade between provinces.

It was as if the wind of liberty blowing across the globe affirmed the nexus between 'free trade', economics, growth, democratic progress and yes, demonstrated that the inherent strength of liberalism that could change 'hearts and minds'. The great German economic leader Ludwig Erhardt who led Germany's economic 'miracle' after World War II argued, *"It was 'mogenpolitik' ('stomach politics')"* that was a profound preparation for democracy. *"Eating is believing."* – Full stomachs, Erhardt felt, gave the best foretaste of democracy. The history lesson was never clearer. 'Free trade' and full bellies had always preceded and accelerated peaceful democratic change.[49] It was as if the antique Hanseatic League of 'free cities' open to trade along the Baltic Sea was reborn again – this time in the form of a united free trade zone open border Europe[50].

What was less obvious was the struggle, within each liberated Eastern European state, to rip each economy from the decaying stifling grasp of Communism and state ownership and introduce 'market economy' reforms. Those states that delayed reforms with internal squabbles economically languished while others like Poland, that digested market based reforms, propelled by breathtaking economic growth, surged ahead. The proof was in the pudding.

The most gratifying event to welcome the '90s took place in South Africa where long imprisoned Nelson Mandela on February 11, 1990 was released from prison after 26 years for opposing apartheid and then established a Peace and Reconciliation Commission to bring whites and blacks together while illuminating South Africa's egregious policies of segregation.

The infamous 'beer' case. In 2018 on April 19, the Supreme Court of Canada overruled that section 21 of 1982 Constitution that states 'goods must be admitted free as they move from province to province' - that is clear and unambiguous language in the Constitution.

49 See Speech Index #53 *'Ruminations on Turkey, Toronto, the Ottoman Empire and Hanseatic League, Russia and the Internet'* later in this book for fuller exegesis the impact on democratic processes and the 'rule of law'.

50 The Hanseatic League composed of 'Free Cities' and towns along the North Sea (1356-1862 CE) demonstrated that commerce and commercial law via free trade were precursors to democratic practices, civil laws and principles.

1900 TO 1910 - LOOKING BACK - THE FIRST DECADE - THE BIRTH OF THE 'MODERN'

Looking back, the first decade at the beginning of the 20th century was equally liberalizing as the last. 1900 was a demarcation line between the old 'bourgeois' society and the new 'civil' society. A glimmer of tolerance for human rights, especially womens' rights, began to gain popular traction.

The essence of the expanding civilizing hegemony was personified by the greatest empire in the world – the British Empire or so the Imperialists believed. Remember our public school history book replete with maps showing the pink swatches of lands of the Empire on every continent including British colonies in South America reaching the Falkland Islands off the tip of South America. The British Empire covered more than a fifth of the globe, a quarter of human race – 450 million people of every race and religion living on every continent and islands of all the oceans and in every time zone. It was said, *"The sun never sets in the British Empire"*[51]. Larger than the Greek or Roman or Ottoman or Spanish Empires, the only problems for Imperial Britain were periodic revolts and violent eruptions in its Asian and African colonies. British bureaucracies, British-style education and limited assemblies planted the seeds of democracy in these colonies, many of which became Dominions under British leadership as later the Empire morphed into the Commonwealth[52]. The 19th century where millions upon millions had

---

51 There was a dichotomy of narratives. England lived in 'splendid isolation' went one strong trope, whilst British imperialism touched every part of the globe. Perhaps both narratives while contradictory were appropriate at the time. 'Consistency' may be 'the ogre of little minds'.

52 British Imperialists believed their brand of imperialism drove 'progress' as historians like Macaulay, Carlyle, Gibbons and then Reade who wrote *'The Martyrdom of Man'* programmed British youth like Churchill to believe that British Imperialism was inseparable from 'progress' and civilization. David Hume, the Scottish born

been displaced by impoverished conditions, famine and plagues, was left behind. Few foresaw the mega terrors looming ahead in the 20th century. Civilization – western civilization - was on the march![53,54,55]

Imperial Germany, Russia, the Austro-Hungarian Empire, France, and tiny kingdoms of Belgium and Holland continued to vie for colo-

---

philosopher, took a more realistic view of the Imperial idea as it was based, he wrote, on violence and greed. Churchill, a staunch Imperialist, after encountering President Roosevelt and his generals strong anti-colonists biases in his famed meeting with Roosevelt and his aides in 1942 aboard ship off Newfoundland wrote Roosevelt in retort, *"I make bold to suggest that spread and is spreading democracy more wildly than any system of government since the beginning of time."* This debate continues to this day. Did the Imperial British administration in far off lands lay the foundation stones of democracy?

53   Nowhere was economic growth more viable and visible than in statistics on wheat crops. In 1900, Russia produced 738 million bushels, the U.S.A. 581 million bushels and Canada 71 million bushels. By 1910, Russian wheat production had reached 1,027 million bushels, U.S.A. 763 million bushels and Canada 231 million bushels. Canada had exceeded both Russia and U.S.A. in percentage growth during the decade – over three times. Canada's economic growth fueled by immigration, manufacturing, lumber, agriculture and cheap energy achieved record heights. The 20th century began to belong to Canada as Sir Wilfrid Laurier predicted in 1911.

54   Canadian wheat became Canada's most successful agricultural product due to Doctor William Saunders and his son Dr. Charles Edward Saunders (1867-1937) born in my hometown of London, Ontario. Together they bred and launched Marquis Wheat in 1904. Marquis Wheat was a higher yielding, earlier maturing, robust, higher in gluten, by crossing Red Fife, then popular in Canada with Hard Red Calcutta from northern India brought by Percy Saunders, Dr. William Saunder's eldest son, from India. This new wheat, excellent for baking, that ripened earlier, became throughout the 20th century a mainstay in Canada and one of its leading export products.

55   Sir Frederick Grant Banting (1891-1941) was a Canadian born doctor, medical scientist and painter born in London, Ontario, my hometown. He started his medical practice in London and became a lecturer at the University of Western Ontario. In 1923 he discovered insulin and that year shared the Nobel Prize for this discovery.

While Banting was the best known, Canadians won Nobel Prizes starting in 1908 in chemistry, medicine, literature, physics, economics and two for peace (Pearson and Pugwash) – 19 in all throughout the 20th century. Canadian advances in science, agriculture, art (e.g., Group of Seven, Riopelle), public health, manufacturing, mining, energy resources, lumber, aluminium, steel, brewing, liquor and merchandizing began to make international waves. In 1914 Connaught Laboratory was founded in

nies overseas, in the Far East and Africa, as they nudged and prodded each other across Europe and competed in Africa and Asia for resources to sustain their Europe-based Empires. Spain and Italy, once proud empires, languished under tottering monarchies.

At the beginning of the 20th century, each major Empire held a different set of internal organizing ideas. Britain's ideals was based on a framework of individual liberties stemming from the 12th century Magna Carta where the ruler agreed to adhere to Parliament and the 'rule of law'. While France was imbued with the Republican virtues of the French Revolution – liberty, fraternity and equality – France failed to inject these virtues into their colonies. The Austro-Hungarian Empire was glued together by the Hapsburgs with topical respect for minority rights deemed necessary to hold this diverse Empire together[56]. The Imperial Empire of Russia maintained its religious-autocratic sentiments of divinity under the Czar with a crush on western 'progress' – first instigated by Peter the Great. The Russian Empire had in three centuries grown to the largest contiguous land mass in the world ever obsessed with 'encroachment' of its borders. Imperial Germany did not appear to cleave to an internal philosophic structure, except love for militaristic prowess exemplified by the lineage

---

Toronto and made vaccines for typhoid, diphtheria, insulin and other vaccines, a leader of vaccine making in the world.

Sir Adam Beck (1857-1925) born in a village in Upper Canada, then moved to London, Ontario where he built a successful small business with his brother and then became a leading provincial politician. A pioneering advocate for hydroelectricity, he spearheaded the founding of the Ontario Hydro Electricity Commission and building the giant turbines to harness Niagara Falls on the Canadian side. Beck's Turbines were installed on Niagara Falls in 1922, the U.S. started earlier in 1895. Beck's majestic modernistic statute adorns University Avenue just below Queen Street in downtown Toronto. I first became acquainted with Beck's history when my high school London Central Collegiate was a fierce sporting opponent of Sir Adam Beck Collegiate in the east end of the city.

The first hydroelectric plant was built in by Nikola Tesla and George Westinghouse in the U.S. in 1895, not Edison. These started the electrification of North America. Earlier smaller models were at work in 1882.

56 Sometimes history erases pages. Such was the case of an early Hapsburg, Phillip II of Spain who reigned England for a short period as King (1554-1558).

of Frederick the Great, but was obsessed with its military losses and what it deemed 'lack of respect' and so became addicted to power, especially military power and modern forms of firepower, terrestrial and maritime, both surface and submarine[57].

Britain was a key player in the 'balance of power' politics playing one European power against the other[58]. Germany's strategy was to take all comers at the same time in its race for military supremacy. Yet the first decade of the 20ᵗʰ century was a quiet period of graceful, calculated diplomatic exchanges between the central powers of Europe as they raced for hegemony over their far off colonies and riches and resources to replenish their homelands[59].

---

57   In 1916 and 1917, German submarines attacked and sunk U.S. ships after U.S. warnings were ignored. These attacks triggered President Wilson to declare war on Germany and the late American entry into World War I. Wilson, like Franklin Roosevelt in the late '30s and before the Pearl Harbour attack on December 7, 1941, wanted to pivot from his earlier refusal to enter the European wars until public opinion caught up with their leadership aims for greater foreign involvement. Both wrapped their decision in patriotic words, e.g. Wilson '14 Freedoms Speech' to justify America's entry into war. Roosevelt was endless in his patriotic musings from his fireside chats on a radio to his powerful speeches on freedom and liberty. In 1941, in his State of Union address 11 months before Pearl Harbour, Roosevelt accelerated his preparation of public opinion in his speech entitled the 'Four Freedoms', fundamental freedoms that people 'everywhere in the world should enjoy' – too slow for some historians that raised question of his leadership and his preference to follow public opinion as opposed to leading.

58   Suddenly in that first decade of the 20th century, the British Empire yanked itself from its 'splendid isolation' that kept it untangled from European alliances, to 'balance' European threats to its security. In 1902, Britain entered into an agreement with Japan to check Russian expansion. In 1904, the British Empire with France entered into a security alliance to check Germany's rise as a naval and military threat. And then in 1907, the Triple Entente fused Britain, France and Russia together to hold Germany in check and curb its militaristic ambitions as Germany continued to isolate itself. 'Brexit' is a British continuum and variation of 'splendid isolation' untangling itself from Europe.

59   Required reading for any student of politics of the 20th century includes Walter Litppman's 'U.S. Foreign Policy' (Little, Brown and Company, 1943), Martin Wight's 'Power Politics' (Royal Institute of International Affairs, London, 1946), George F. Kennan's 'Realities of American Foreign Policy' (Princeton University Press, 1954),

The horrific and beastly rule by Belgium King Leopold the Second in his African colony in The Congo that he founded and owned as a private fiefdom, was ripped from his control by the other embarrassed European colonial powers in 1908 when the first grisly 'genocide' of the 20th century came roaring to western attention from the Congo[60]. The gaping blood wounds of savage rule of the Republic of the Congo was swiftly

---

Abba Eban's 'The New Diplomacy: International Affairs in the Modern Age' (Random House, 1983). But the magisterial work of Henry Kissinger 'Diplomacy' (Simon Schuster, 1994) remains a classic work that outshines them all. And as Abba Eban once wrote, "*Kissinger was 'the only Secretary of State under whom two Presidents served'.*" Of course, for Canadian students, 'Radical Mandarin: The Memoirs of Escott Reid' (University of Toronto Press, 1989) along with L.B. Pearson collected speeches, essays and memoirs especially 'Mike: The Memoirs of the Right Honourable Lester B. Pearson' (University of Toronto Press, 1972) provide an essential insight into the breakout of Canadian diplomacy called Pearsonian Diplomacy in global affairs.

Abba Eban also cogently opined on 'balance of power' diplomacy. He wrote, "*... the alternative to a 'balance of power' is an imbalance of power which was usually resulted in wars and has never consolidated peace.*" The most influential teacher and writer on international diplomacy in the 20th century, certainly the latter period, was Hans J. Morgenthau (1904-1980). Morgenthau, a German Jewish immigrant and scholar who escaped the clutches of Nazi Germany just before World War II. His book 'Politics Among Nations: The Struggle for Power and Peace' (1978 New York, Alfred A. Knoff) established him a major founder of the School of 'Democratic Political Realism' in international affairs. Morgenthau influenced all the above, and Reinhold Niebuhr, Raymond Aron, George F. Kennan and Arthur J. Schlesinger to name but a few.

A professor and writer, he taught and lectured at numerous universities in America and abroad especially at the University of Chicago and Harvard University. His book was required reading at over 100 universities and outsold all other works in this field combined. Morgenthau advocated the 'balance of power' as key to peace and stability while recognizing that the 'human condition;' is flawed and unchangeable over all of the course of history. An opponent of the Vietnam War, his analyses on 'a just war' have led him to be compared to Aristotle and St. Augustine. Even more relevant is his later book 'The Roots of Narcissism' co-authored with Ethel Person of Columbia University (The Partisan Review, 1978) that explores leadership and the aphrodisiac of political power. Morgenthau and his voluminous books, articles and reviews are a must read for any student of foreign affairs.

60 Clearly no history of the late 19th or early 20th century is more chilling than the horrifying tale of the shrewd and avaricious King of Belgium, Leopold II, lusting to expand his miniscule divided kingdom into African colonization. Leopold II,

cauterized by the 'Great Powers' via a quick amendment to the Treaty of Berlin, 'transferring' ownership of this benighted African colony from Leopold II to the sovereignty of Belgium[61].

Little noticed and largely unheeded in the West was the rapid rise of the Japanese Empire that emerged as the first Asian world power at the turn of the century. In 1905, Japan challenged Russia in the Japanese-Russian war and became the first Asian power to defeat Russia in land battles and then annihilated her Russian Navy in the Battle of Tsushima. Russia lost two-thirds of their naval forces. Theodore Roosevelt brokered a peace treaty between the two in 1905 called the Treaty of Portsmouth in New Hampshire. For this, Theodore Roosevelt was awarded the Nobel Peace Prize in 1906. Still the East was on the rise. After the turn of the century, the European powders including Japan intervened in the anti-trade anti-west rebellion in China to protect its trade and economic interests, including the opium trade, interest and helped put down the Boxer Rebellion which led a decade later to end the Manchu Dynasty that had ruled China for two thousand years and in turn laid the seeds of Communist takeover half a century later[62].

---

by stealth and corruption, privately acquired large tracts of land along the Congo River basin into uncharted west and central Africa. In the process, aided and abetted by the notorious African explorer William Stanley (not his true name) (who later became a leading Labour Member of Parliament and a hero to many notables such as Bertrand Russell for his pacifist views), Leopold II hoodwinked the United States President Arthur along with the other Central European Powers, especially figures such as Bismarck, to gain pseudo international recognition and thereby subjugate over 800 native tribes and a landmass 1/13 of the African continent, 26 times larger than Belgium, for his African fiefdom. By allowing chunks of this region of Africa to be colonized by France, Portugal, Germany and others, Phillip II successfully played the British Empire to agree, always anxious to encourage divisions amongst its European competitors in the exercise of its 'balance of power' strategy.

Read 'King Leopold's Ghost: A Story of Greed, Terror and Heroism in Colonial Africa' by Adam Hochschild, First Mariner Books 1990 for a spell-binding account of this period.

61   Belgium, Portugal and Holland, minor powers, had larger overseas colonies with larger populations than Germany adding to landlocked German 'angst', envy fuelling its imperial ambitions.

62   No nations experienced more transformative history in the 20th century than China, Japan and Russia. From their medieval origins at the turn of the century,

Meanwhile in Europe, the Empires – the so-called 'Great Powers' – maneuvered against each other by parading public demonstrations of military strength and firepower. Publicity attracted by so-called 'War Games' demonstrated muscular militarism across the face of Europe as Empires were vying for balance of power stances. The Austro-Hungary Empire under aging Emperor Franz Joseph, sensing the dissipating grip of the Ottoman Empire, moved to annex Bosnia and Herzegovina with the rationale that the Austro-Hungarian Empire sought only to protect the embattled Muslim minorities, to the dismay of their Christian neighbours Serbia and Montenegro and their senior ally - Imperial Russia. This 'Balkan Crisis' in 1908 was quickly papered over by the 'Great Powers'

China and Japan both rose to world economic power. The complex origins of the rise of both came alive as in the west, American and European powers demanded trading concessions from both. Japan rose to an aggressive military power first giving Russia a military major loss and thus emboldened invaded China and Korea. Embargoes, quarantine and most times sanctions were the west's efforts to contain Japan. The causes of the World War II with Japan resulted in these futile efforts especially by the United States vying for hegemony in the Pacific. However what was most remarkable was how the war loving Japanese, being the first nation to be atomic bombed to end World War II, was transformed into a model democracy and economic power that insisted that war be outlawed in its post-war constitution.

General MacArthur's equally remarkable stewardship of Japan after World War II transformed Japan into a thriving democracy that included freedom of press, union organizations and recognition of women's rights. China, weakened by civil war, morphed under reformist Communism into a functioning modern state and into the second leading economic power of the world after the United States by the end of the 20th century, a miracle of economic self-determination with the fastest rising middle class in the world followed by India. Taiwan and South Korea both have made giant economic strides via the practice of democracy to increase the rapid growth of their respective middle classes. In retrospect, Russia, under autocratic Stalin suffused by Leninist ideology based on Marxism, became the most expansive explosive world power occupying most of Europe and infiltrating their ideology into Western Europe, Africa, South Asia, South, Central and North America, a story yet to be told. Economic growth in Russia was artificial and failed to increase the prosperity of the middle classes. My next book, *'Leadership and Failure of Leadership – Roosevelt, Churchill, de Gaulle, Stalin and Mao Zedong'* – recounts how Roosevelt and advisers like Marshall 'lost' China and Mao emerged as the most impactful leader of the 20th century and beyond, is in the works, due for publication in 2021.

as they amended the Berlin Treaty in 1909 to assent to the Austro-Hungarian annexation of Bosnia and Herzegovina, attempting to muffle the fires of nationalism slowly burning below European surface.

This collective action by the 'Great Powers' laid the seeds of the outbreak of World War I when Archduke Ferdinand, the heir to the aging Austro-Hungarian throne was assassinated in Sarajevo, five years later in 1914 by a Serbian nationalist. The templates of 'balance of power' began to shift below the surface.

The feverish race for naval supremacy on the high seas had begun in earnest especially between Britain and Germany. A deadly race between Britain and Germany building larger, ever more lethal gigantic dreadnoughts, began with stiff nationalist resolve.

The Trans-Siberian Railway was completed linking the far-flung massive Russian landmass even closer together under Russian Imperial rule.

In 1899, Winston Churchill, a devout supporter of the British Empire, heard the clanging bells of the Boer War[63] and sped to South Africa where

---

63 Canada participated with patriotic fervour as did other members of the British Empire like Australia and New Zealand giving Canadian military their first military foray overseas in the 20th century in the Boer War in South Africa. Earlier between 1860 and 1865 in the American Civil War, 23,000 and 56,000 Canadians from Upper and Lower Canada (a.k.a. British North America before Confederation in 1867) volunteered, mostly for the Union side.

Many Canadians were decorated for bravery in these two wars. The influence of the American Civil War can be seen in Canada in the checks and balances and unifying powers of the central governance in the 1867 British North America Act. Sir John MacDonald, the father of Confederation, saw the establishment of Canadian Senate as a check and balance against 'democratic excess' as he witnessed the American Civil War. Both these chapters in Canadian history has been almost forgotten. In the Boer War, four Canadians received the Victoria Cross, 19 received the Distinguished Service Order, 17 received the Distinguished Conduct Medal and Canada's senior nursing sister, Gwynne Pope was awarded the Royal Red Cross. Canadians were the key factor that won many pitched battles against Boers including the Battle of Paardeberg, the first major victory of the war. The Boer War instigated a number of monuments to commemorate Canada's role after that first major war where Canadians fought overseas with bravery and determination. Sir Wilfrid Laurier led Canada

as a rabid war correspondent, he was captured and escaped, emerging as a hero to catapult his career in 1900 into Parliament. His early books of the Boer, Cuban and African wars were exciting historical accounts. Only later, much later, in retrospect, Churchill came to realize the Boer War was the first eruption of the blood-soaked, war-obsessed, 20th century. *"The age of peace had ended"*, as Churchill reflected on his Boer War experience many years later. *"There was no lack of war. There was enough for all... and enough to spare."* The world had entered the century of Churchill[64].

Churchill started earning his living first as a journalist and a writer publishing *'London to Ladysmith via Pretoria'* and *'Ian Hamilton's March'* in 1900. His account of the war in the Cuba insurrection is still riveting[65]. His major income thereafter flowed from his prolific pen. In 1906, he published a two volume book of his late father, Lord Randolph Churchill who became Churchill's lifelong beacon to emulate. His mother, an American born beauty, Jennie Jerome, had married Randolph Churchill. When he died in 1900, she was not left enough to maintain her lavish lifestyle. So in 1908, she published her own memoirs *'The Reminiscences*

---

to support the British Empire's war in South Africa causing a split in his Cabinet when Henri Bourassa left and planted fresh seeds of Quebec's separatist impulse that grew as the 20th century unfolded and came alive in World War I and World War II as Quebecers on the whole, refused to join the British Empire's conflicts. Many Quebec based regiments gained recognition for their military prowess, and veterans played key roles in the political and business affairs of Quebec. It was like a symphony with conflicting themes played in minor and major keys.

64   My friend, now deceased, Charles Krauthammer, America's most astute political observer in the latter part of the 20th century, in an article on Dec. 1999 labelled Churchill *'The Person of The Century'* and described his indispensability.

65   During his Cuban sojourn as a war correspondent to cover the Cuban uprising against Spain in 1895 Churchill picked up his lifelong habit of smoking Cuban cigars mostly of the Romeo y Julieta brand, a taste I came to share. In recent historical accounts of Churchill, it is said that he started his cigar habit in New York City during an earlier visit with Bourke Cochrane, an American politician and mentor who befriended Churchill during a book tour there. Churchill and Clémenceau are the only two leaders to have cigar sizes named after them, both oversized to match their personalities. Churchill's regular champagne bottler had a Pol Roger 1979 vintage champagne Churchill preferred named after him, expensive but excellent.

of Lady Randolph Churchill' that was a success on both continents, but did not earn enough to cover her high living expenses or enough to sufficiently supplement his son's lavish living style.

In 1904, Halford Mackinder published a ground breaking article that provided fodder for Imperial expansion and '*bella casus*' for war in Europe – '*The Geographical Pivot of History*' that posited the European 'Heartland Theory' of world domination. Later in 1917, Mackinder expanded his strategic theses ('*Democratic Ideals and Reality*'):

> "*Who rules East Europe commands the Heartland;
> who rules the Heartland commands the World-Island;
> who rules the World-Island commands the world.*"[66]

In 1900, Paris held the World Exposition which marked the explosive beginning of the 'modern' in Europe and elsewhere. Diesel engines, talking films, recording devices and escalators were exhibited. The 'Age of Electronics' was launched. The Eiffel Tower was lit with electric bulbs for the first time to add glitter to the romantic capital of the world. Overnight, Paris became the eternal 'City of Lights'.

Paris dominated women's world fashion. 'Haute couture' became a buzzword of high fashion before the turn of the century coined by an expat Englishman Charles Worth. By high styled designs and tailoring, deploying live models in the first of its kind fashion shows, the House of Worth became the largest fashion house and pacesetter for Europe. By 1900, Worth employed a staff of over 1,200 tailors, sewers, and craftsmen and women.

Madeline Cheruit, an ambitious young seamstress in Paris, rose to become the first woman to organize and head a leading fashion house in

---

66 Robert D. Kaplan in his book, '*The Return of Marco Polo's World: War, Strategy, and American Interests in the Twenty-first Century*' (Random House, 2018) opined that Mackinder's strategic analyses and ideas are 'no longer premature' as both Russia and China seek to expand their hegemony. His book explains both Putin's reading of history and a renewal of Russian expansionist plans, few in the west understand or have the patience to renovate realistic policies towards Putin's Russia, especially as China, India and Malaysia continue to rise as economic world powers.

1900 with her own couture designer, Paul Poiret, creating the business model for other great fashion houses to follow later, led by Chanel, Schiaparelli, Dior and others.

Perfume fabricated by an array of floral infused synthetic aromas for the first time, by the House of Guerlain. In 1900, Guerlain introduced new scents like *'Jicky'*, then *'Mouchoir de Monsieur'* in 1904 and *'Après L'Ondée'* in 1906, to become within the decade, the world leader in women's scents and continued its leadership throughout the 20th century and beyond[67].

While Paris dominated women's high fashions, London became the leader in men's 'bespoke' clothing. Located on Savile Row, Henry Poole employed 300 tailors and cutters and produced 1,700 tailored men's three-piece suits annually[68]. Customers included the Royal Heads of Belgium, Italy, the Tsar of Russia Nicholas II and the Emperor of Mexico. Edward the III, a dandy himself, gave Poole the Royal Warrant. Turnbull and Asser, who designed and sold bespoke distinctive men's shirts and ties, moved to Jermyn Street (pronounced 'German') in London and other men's specialty shops swiftly followed making it the man's shopping street of world renown. Savile Row, Jermyn Street and old Bond Street for men's fashions in London rivalled Place Vendome and Rue St. Honoré in Paris for women's fashions as they do today.

---

67 In the early 1900's a looming battle for leadership of women's face cream was ignited between two women, Helena Rubenstein, a Russian immigrant living in Australia and then America and Elizabeth Arden, a Canadian of English descent. Rubenstein using lamb fat, in plentiful supply, started selling her creams first in Australia, and quickly spread via her shops in America and Europe. Arden followed suite opening shops to sell her beauty products to compete with Rubenstein. These brand names led by these two extraordinary entrepreneurs continued throughout the 20th century.

68 In the early 1990's, my late pal, David Graham, a Canadian expat living in London introduced me to Savile Row where three tailors, one for the jacket, vest and trousers, fitted me for my one and only Savile suit. It still fits, almost. A few years later, he insisted I attend with him at Charvet, an old French fine men's shift and tie maker off Place Vendome in Paris founded in 1838 and one of the oldest extant shirtmakers in the world. Charvet was acquired after World War II by a Jewish Rumanian immigrant who I met while shopping there where we discussed how, as an immigrant tailor, he desired to provide and sell the best men's wear, especially shirts and ties, in France.

The First International Congress of Philosophy was convened in Paris in 1900 as the thinkers raced to keep abreast of the changing world. There, Bertrand Russell, Henri Bergson[69] and Henri Poincaré and other notable minds joined in the clash of philosophic ideas that ruminated through the 20th century between rationality and emotion causality.

This delightful period was the tail end of the equally mesmerizing period called 'Belle Époque'.

In 1908, the world was captivated by the exoneration for treason of Alfred Dreyfus, a Jewish officer in the French army, first in the French courts and then in the French Assembly. Emile Zola, a French journalist and novelist, led the fight to repeal the military court's decision after he instigated a global outcry with his article 'J'Accuse' bravely published in a French newspaper *L'Aurore* owned by Georges Clemenceau, who later became the Prime Minister of France) that was reprinted around the globe.

France and the western world became divided between 'Dreyfusards' mostly on the 'left' and anti-Dreyfusards mostly on the 'right'.

Anti-Semitism, so deeply embedded yet barely disguised, within the psyche of the French military and the French political, commercial and educational establishment, was demonstrated by this egregious case, that became a visible dark chasm dividing the French elites and the French public[70, 71]. France was still a far cry from the egalitarian Napoleonic

---

69 Henri Bergson's school of philosophy that emphasized individual emotions over abstract reason reverberated throughout the 20th century and was a precursor of 'identity' politics in the 21st century.

70 *"Anti-Semitism is a special form of madness, one of the features of which has always been at every step of history, choosing the right words to make its madness look reasonable."* – Bernard-Henri Lévy, *'The Genius of Judaism'*, Random House (2017)

71 The Dreyfus Case exposed a deep divide between liberals called 'Dreyfusards' and reactionary conservatives across Europe and America that resonated throughout the 20th century. By the end of the 20th century, the extreme left took leadership in 'anti-Semitic' sentiment and stole rhetoric and 'pseudo fascism' away from the extreme right. Now both extremes of political spectrums share common attitudes that keep the coals of anti-Semitism hot and burning beneath the surface. The rapid rise of Islamism has fuelled civic violence. Anti-semitism remains a patent for failed politicians, religious extremists, ideologues and even disgruntled groups to distract from their own political flaws and failures. Blame 'the other'. Alas.

decrees that opened French citizenship to Jews in 1794 – the first in Europe. The court martial for treason was concocted against Dreyfus by other French officers to protect the officer who had sold military secrets to Germany, to cover his and their own tracks. Dreyfus wrongly accused of treason was found guilty in a French Military Court, stripped of his military insignia with sword broken on parade and then sent to Devil's Island where he languished for almost a decade until his case was reopened in 1908 over public outcries felt around the world. The first decade of the 20th century produced an apparent respite from the endemic and offered justice through the 'rule of law'. Pogroms in Russia triggered worldwide condemnation. The ease of international communications through print media as typified by the Dreyfus case in that first decade opened the doors to global interconnectivity. The 'Fourth Estate' was firmly established as a watch dog against injustice, at home and abroad. A refreshing wave of liberalism and calls for justice echoed across the globe.

In 1903, the first massacre of Jews in the 20th century took place in Kishinev, the smallish capital of Bessarabia in the Russian Imperial Empire[72]. This massacre of 49 Jews, large number of rapes, hundreds of wounded and 1,500 homes and small businesses destroyed was called a Pogrom ('to advance') as this word entered the 20th century lexicon. Worldwide attention came as funds were raised to help these impoverished Jews. The spurious *'Protocols of the Elders of Zion'* were concocted by the Czarist Police written, disseminated by the Czarist government and read at this time to rationalize Russian barbaric attacks on innocent Jews. This incident intensified worldwide anti-Semetic attacks that ripped through the remainder of the 20th century like crashing waves with ever greater increasing intensity and devastating effect. The Protocols of the Elders of Zion have shown renewed life as they are published and republished in Arabic throughout the Muslim Middle East today.

In that first stunning decade in the 20th century, from 1900 to 1910, the world also witnessed the birth of the 'modern' in North America as well.

Autos starting with steam and then the combustion engine were the first mass produced mobile products especially the sturdy Ford Model

---

72 *'Pogrom: Kishinev and The Tilt of History'* by Steven J. Zipperstein (WW Norton, 2018)

T[73] and the Ford Models A as they began to scurry along the dusty roads of North and South America. Freed from railways, this was the first gulp of individual mobile freedom became a reality in the 20th century. Oil created wealthy barons, like the Rockefellers, as cartels were formed to satisfy the craze for oil reserves worldwide. Steel cartels followed in the U.S. led by Andrew Carnegy.

Swift ships by sail and then fueled by coal and finally oil, brought America and Europe closer together. The Atlantic had been cabled. The first wireless transmission of the Morse Code was sent from Newfoundland to Ireland. Electricity expanded in the cities and farmlands. Sanitation works in cities accelerated. Running water became widely available. The first electric typewriter was introduced. The Wright Brothers launched their first flimsy canvas-winged aircraft as a harbinger of the coming decades of airplane and space travel. Vaccines for the scourge of tuberculosis was discovered. The American Congress passed the first Pure Food and Drug Act in 1906 and the Meat Inspection Act. Public health was ushered into national political debates[74].

In 1909, Louis Bleriot flew the first plane from France to England bringing the European continent closer to the U.K. The first silent movies appeared in nickelodeons. In 1906, the first full-length silent movie

---

73 In 1952, I acquired my first 'used' car, a 1922 Ford Model T from a local farmer for $25, a four-door, canvas topped convertible that was still in good working condition, the first auto owned by my family. I proudly drove it around the streets of my hometown of London, Ontario for two years, then the T-bar froze in winter. It was quickly replaced in the spring with another T-bar traded for the canvas top from another farmer just outside of London and I drove it for another year till I traded up for my second car, the first 1926 Ford 6-cylinder auto. Both were fuel efficient and easy to fix. This led to a string of second-hand car trades including a 1935 12-cylinder eight-seat Cadillac limo while at Western till I ended up in a 1946 Chrysler Fluidmatic then a 1947 Buick Road Master when I came to attend Law School in Toronto in 1955, all before I acquired my first new car in 1958, a wonkey wing-tailed Plymouth sedan.

74 The 'progressive' era had been launched under the exuberant power of the leadership of Theodore Roosevelt, a Republican, after he became President and took over McKinley's lead on 'progressive' issues when McKinley was assassinated in 1901. Until recently, McKinley was not given adequate credit for his ambitious 'progressive' agenda labelled as the first 'modern' President (see footnote 79 below).

'*The Kelly Gang*' from Australia made its entrance into popular culture. Telephones, a Canadian invention, inaugurated the new electronic 'person to person' communication era. In 1906, a little known Canadian, Reginald Fessenden, broadcast the first radio signals from Quebec. The neon light was invented in 1901. The Victor Talking Machine with the trade-marked dog listening intently to the cauliflower speaker, the first popular recording device was introduced in 1906. Recorded music in the home quickly became a necessity. Vacuum cleaners began to alleviate household drudgery. Peace and stability swept across the western world.

In 1900, Max Planck introduced the Quantum Hypothesis. Quantum Physics had arrived. Enter the modern era of physics. In 1904, Pierre and Marie Curie, she a Polish immigrant to France, discovered the elements of radium and polonium whose properties gave birth to the Atomic Age. Physics was changed forever.

In 1900, the Americans declared an 'open door' policy to the mysterious 'Middle Kingdom' - China - and the world was propelled into the global mercantile era. Chinese furniture, Chinese bone china, pearl and jade, embossed screens[75], Chinese silk brocades and artifacts became the rage. It was the springboard of change in styles and taste.

The Russo-Japanese war, started in 1904, ended swiftly in 1905. President 'Teddy' Roosevelt[76] won the Nobel Prize in 1906 for brokering 'peace in our time' between the warring Russian and Japanese Empires. The Japanese however never forgot what they felt was America's disrespect for their political and economic aspirations and culture. Nor did China forget how the European powers under 'kumquat' diplomacy demanded access to the China market and expanded the opium trade with China and the West. The Asian sensitivities to insensitive western influence triggered later seismic changes throughout the east in the 20th century.

---

75 Carole and I, two years after we married spent almost our entire savings on an antique 200 year old Chinese screen and lived with an empty living room in our capacious duplex apartment apart from our small kitchen and two bedrooms and a folding card table and chairs for over a year until we could afford to start to furnish the rest of our spacious quarters.

76 Roosevelt's first job was Police Commission of Police of New York City. Nothing prepared him better for the American Presidency.

In 1906, the San Francisco earthquake punctuated the decade where over 300,000 people died. City structures thereafter became earthquake proof. Building codes that focused on safety became a norm across both Canada and America.

In 1900, Winston Churchill (1874-1965) was first elected to the British Parliament at age 25[77] and started his career as the greatest parliamentarian in western history for almost all of the century. In 1904, under the tutelage Lloyd George (the Welsh Liberal dynamo), Churchill turned from Tory Conservatism the party of high trade tariffs and protectionism to become a Manchester Liberal on the issue of 'Free Trade'[78]. George and Churchill, then a budding protégé, together became the leading advocates of 'free trade' over the Imperial Preference of tariffs to promote 'free trade' across the Empire and beyond. Their leadership of 'free trade' resonated in Canada. Liberals under Sir Wilfrid Laurier led the battle for 'reciprocity' – freer trade with the U.S.A.

In 1901, President McKinley, considered the first 'modern' President[79], was assassinated and his Vice-President, the vigourous, ebullient Theodore Roosevelt, became President[80]. The age of 'progress' and 'progressives' was

---

77 Churchill ran for Parliament in five different constituencies 17 times winning 12 out of 17 elections.

78 Manchester was the birth place of the English 'free trade' movement led by Richard Cobden and John Bright, both MPs in the mid-19th century. Read my essay '*Churchill is a Liberal*' in my book '*Parade: Tributes To Remarkable Contemporaries*' (pg. 71, Mosaic Press, 2017) for a precisé of the astounding aspects of his astounding career and '*Churchill as a Zionist*' (pg. 54). Charles Krauthammer in his marvelous book of essays '*Things That Matter: Three Decades of Passions, Pastimes and Politics*' (Crown Forum, 2013) called Winston Churchill '*The indispensable man of the 20th century*' – which he was.

79 The book '*The Triumph of William McKinley: Why the Election of 1896 Still Matters*' by Karl Rove (Simon and Schuster, 2016) gives support for the thesis that McKinley's understated achievements laid the foundations for Theodore Roosevelt's 'progressive' reputation. McKinley's Pacific expansionist policies (Hawaii, etc.) have largely been forgotten. History has begun to shed more attention on McKinley's undeniable accomplishments as America's first 'modern' President. McKinley sought to rein in economic disarray in the U.S.A. as he moved on social justice fronts.

80 Theodore Roosevelt became the first President to aggressively pivot away from the isolationist Monroe Doctrine - keeping European interests out of the Americas. Roosevelt, using his 'bully' pulpit, became a vigourous advocate to broaden

upon us. A leading 'progressive', Robert LaFollette, became the Governor of the State of Wisconsin in 1900 and later a Senator in 1906.

Theodore Roosevelt, author of 47 books[81], numerous pamphlets, essays and articles (on wide ranging subjects from conservation to the history of the Americas to economic policies), became the great 'reform' American President. Together these two reformist politicians and mostly sparring partners, each pushed his own 'progressive' agenda

---

American's interests in global affairs as inseparable from America's 'national interests'. In 1904, Roosevelt advocated a 'Corollary' to the Monroe Doctrine arguing America's right to intervene in other states to protect them from European hegemony and make them 'safe for democracy'. Roosevelt expanded America's interests to include the Pacific, especially the Philippines. Roosevelt's policies exhibited a dichotomy between 'progressive' social issues and expansionist foreign policy that whet America's appetite for foreign hegemonies by most successive Presidents. This 'globalism' of American 'interests' led to the U.S.A. rationale for interventions, military and otherwise, in other states throughout the 20th century and beyond, in over 149 countries at last count.

This expansive posture gave deeper texture to the American doctrine of 'Manifest Destiny' – trumpeting American 'Exceptionalism'. Of course, the United States especially after World War II chronically meddled in the flood of democratic elections in Europe, East and West, including Russia, Ukraine, the Baltics, the Caucasus, the Middle East, Mexico, Central America, Asia and Africa – a subject worthy of historical consideration and perspective. This American meddling intensified after 1989 when the Berlin Wall came down and those newly liberated Communist states scrambled for democratic elections. American meddling focused on countries with large popular Communist parties and personalities and parties inimical to American perceived interests.

Of course not to be forgotten is the American, British, French, Canadian-led failed military excursions into Russia to support the 'white' Russian led military attempts to overturn the Soviet Revolution after 1918.

81 Roosevelt's first book, 'Naval War of 1812' (Modern Library) was published in 1882. In the book, he described the naval war on the Great Lakes and the east coast between U.S.A. and Britain implying U.S.A. won the war of 1812. America did not! And never invaded Canada again. In 1814, in Treaty of Ghent, Canada gained recognized borders from the United States. This didn't preclude Americans from perpetually interfering in Canadian affairs, economically, politically and militarily (e.g. Norad) throughout the 20th century. Americans could not resist a penchant for meddling in any nations' affairs throughout the 20th century, especially in North, Central and South America.

of minimum wages, lower working hours, 'native' rights, progressive taxation, public health, worker compensation for injuries and preservation of public lands into an expanding string of National Parks. It was the 'Age of the Progressives' and it was a thundering age of reform in all directions across all segments of American civic society.

President Teddy Roosevelt told a gathering of students in 1910, *"It is not the critic who counts; not the man who points out how the strong man stumbles, or where the doer of deeds could have done them better. The credit belongs to the man who is actually in the arena, whose face is marred by dust and sweat and blood; who strives valiantly; who errs, who comes short again and again, because there is no effort without error and shortcoming; but who does actually strive to do the deeds; who knows great enthusiasms, the great devotions; who spends himself in a worthy cause; who at the best knows in the end the triumph of high achievement, and who at the worst, if he fails, at least fails while daring greatly, so that his place shall never be with those cold and timid souls who neither know victory nor defeat."*[82]

"Keep your eyes on the stars, and your feet on the ground." - Theodore Roosevelt.

A shorter version of the high purpose of human endeavours and politics follows.

"Far better is it to dare mighty things, to win glorious triumphs, even though checkered by failure... than to rank with those poor spirits who neither enjoy nor suffer much, because they live in a gray twilight that knows not victory nor defeat." - Theodore Roosevelt

Theodore Roosevelt understood the power of 'Bully Pulpit' of the U.S. Presidency and deployed it to its fullest[83]. *"Speak softly and carry a big*

---

82 *The Man in The Arena* - Excerpt from the speech '*Citizenship In A Republic*' delivered at the Sorbonne, in Paris, France on 23 April, 1910. This passage was quoted by the American Presidents later in the 20th century by both John F. Kennedy and Richard Nixon.

83 Roosevelt understood the power of the press to make his case to the public for reform. He assiduously cultivated the leading journalists of the day, especially those known as 'Muckrakers', Ida Tarbell, Lincoln Steffens and others. The early 'Muckraker' group was called 'McClures' after its founder Samuel McClure, a skilled editor and journalist who founded his own magazine by that name to which the others contributed.

stick", he extorted at home and abroad[84]. Roosevelt believed in American seapower and America's ability to seek hegemony in the west Pacific.

The 'progressive' movement did not mature in a vacuum. The rise of unbridled capitalism in America led by the financial genius JP Morgan who then single-handedly rescued the U.S. markets from a collapse in 1907 triggered the 'progressive' agenda. The unbridled capitalism and crude labour practices by the barons of oil (Rockefeller), steel (Carnegie) and mining (Guggenheim) and railroads (Harrman) gave the 'progressives' easy targets.

The Communist Party of Canada was founded in 1921 in Guelph led by Elizabeth Rowley. It was illegal at the time. At its height in the '40s, the Party never exceeded 2,500 members.

The Socialist Party of Canada, affiliated with the World Socialist Movement was founded in Winnipeg in 1931 led by Phyllis Corriveau, a British Columbia politician.

The Socialist Party of America, founded in 1901, ran its first nominee for President in 1904. The Party received 6% of the vote, Eugene V. Debs as Presidential candidate in 1912 and 1916 received just under one million votes[85]. In all Debs ran five times for the American Presidency. Later, under President Wilson, considered 'progressive'[86], Debs was imprisoned

---

84 Teddie Roosevelt was a devoted student of Alfred Thayer Mahan and his book '*The Influence of Sea Power Upon History: 1660–1783*' (New York 1890). Roosevelt believed in American sea power to expand 'American exceptionalism' across the Pacific.

85 The first Socialist to be elected to Congress in 1911 was Victor L. Berger, a German born Jew from Wisconsin. He was followed by Meyer London, a Jewish immigrant from London, England, another Socialist from Manhattan (from 1915-1919 and then 1921-1923). Samuel Dickstein replaced London in Congress in 1922. The history of the Socialist Party was revived by the Democratic Socialists of America (DSA) founded in 1982 by Michael Harrington with about 600 members.

86 Wilson as President misled the U.S.A. and its allies when he publically advocated 'self-determination' for all during and after WWI. Meanwhile, he secretly arrayed military forces against revolutionary socialist and communist parties in South and Central America, Mexico, Russia and elsewhere. Woodrow Wilson had selective vision about 'self-determination', supporting only those whose ideology with which he was in agreement. Wilson was a scholar of the American Constitution and wrote a massive book. Yet his acceptance of its principles was limited to United States and

for two years for his political views, became ill, received early release, never recovered fully, and passed away in 1924[87].

The American Communist Party (called the Communist Party of the United States of America) was founded in 1919 in New York City under the leadership of C.E. Ruthenberg (1882-1927), a Lutheran German immigrant who was first a socialist. He was buried in the Kremlin. In the '40s, the Party had over 80,000 members.

The first Labour Party was founded in Australia in 1901 and shortly thereafter won a string of governments there. James Keir Hardie, a Scottish socialist founded the British Labour Party in 1900. He formed the first Labour government in 1924 in the U.K.

And in 1904, the Socialist International Congress convened in Europe called for the establishment of Labour Day to promote an eight-hour working day.

The first socialist party in Canada was founded in 1904 in British Columbia with a labour base and a Marxist orientation[88]. Plaques on Vancouver's waterfront attest to the birth of organized labour in Canada.

---

even then he held a Southerner's view of its application to all American citizens equally.

87 Eugene V. Debs, a socialist, was arrested and convicted under the U.S. Sedition Act when he publicly declared that WWI was instigated by capitalism while *"our hearts are with the Bolsheviks"*. He was sentenced to 10 years in prison and later released early due to ill health. Socialism began to morph into Communism. Communism in America grew in the '20s via the American Communist Party and underground cells of American citizens, agents of the Comintern to keep them following the Bolshevic party line while Soviet recruited a myriad of spies committed to stealing advanced American technology especially of a military nature to advance Soviet military goals of hegemony proliferated across America.

88 Though other provinces founded provincial socialist/labour organizations, no socialist/labour federal party was created until 1920 under the name Federal Labour Party of Canada. The Communist Party of Canada began in 1921 from a meeting of 21 men in a barn in Guelph, Ontario which led to the creation of the Communist Party. In 1924, the Party had abandoned some of its early Marxist policies and replaced the Communist Party of Canada based on the Marx's Communist Manifesto of 1848. In the later forties, Tim Buck, a history teacher at my high school in London, Ontario, London Central Collegiate Institute, was then head of the Communist Party of Canada. Some socialist labourites and Marxists, were elected to city councils,

Theodore Roosevelt had written his first of many books starting as a 23 year old student at Harvard in 1882, on the War of 1812 entitled *'The Naval War of 1812'*. Roosevelt concluded that, while the U.S. Navy won some skirmishes on the Great Lakes in the War of 1812 against the Canadian colonies of Upper and Lower Canada, and a major naval victory at the Battle of New Orleans, these had little effect while the land battles decisively were won by Canadians, Aboriginals (both Canadian and American tribes led by the great Tecumseh[89]) and British forces which together halted and prevented the American conquest of the Canadian colonies. The decisive result of the War of 1812 is still not accepted by some American historians. They are loath to recall the burning of the White House on August 24, 1814 which took place in retaliation for burning Fort York in Toronto. The American anthem was written to celebrate the fact that the American flag still flew over Washington after this military debacle. That was almost the end of America's appetite to

---

provincial legislatures and in Parliament. The impact of Marxism and Communist ideology in Canadian politics remains to be written.

It was in 1932 in Calgary, Alberta, that the Co-operative Commonwealth Federation was established under the leadership of J.S. Woodsworth who had earlier obtained a seat in Parliament. In 1933 in Regina, Saskatchewan, the Party adopted a socialist platform called the Regina Manifesto – nationalizing key industries, universal pensions, healthcare, shelter allowances, unemployment insurance and workers' compensation. The Party immediately became affiliated to the Socialist International. In 1944, the CCF under Tommie Douglas became the first socialist government in Canada in Saskatchewan. In 1939, Woodsworth was the only Member of Parliament to oppose the declaration of war against Nazi Germany and fascist Italy leading to World War II in 1939. In 1958, David Lewis, the first Canadian Rhodes Scholar and President of the Oxford Union, the famed debate forum, and long-time CCF party secretary and organizer, became the first Jew to head a federal party, the CCF. In 1961, the CCF was renamed the New Democratic Party, labour-socialist in ideology and orientation. I came to know Lewis and his son Stephen as both articulate and thoughtful potential leaders.

89 Tecumseh, a Shawnee leader of the First Nations confederacy, where he gained other first nation allies, gathered a large number of warrior bands in America, came north to Canada to fight against the Americans in the War of 1812 as the Americans had breached their pledge to preserve aboriginal hunting grounds and sold aboriginal lands to settlers. He was made a Brigadier General in the British army.

conquer Canada. America withdrew from Canadian territory after that war – 'mission accomplished'. Canadians won that war. Still most Americans either shuffled the result under the rug or remain in denial. Check the paintings of this war on Capitol Hill in Washington D.C.

The lust for American sea power supremacy reaching across the Pacific was launched by Theodore Roosevelt as a result of his research into the War of 1812. As President, he sent a massive flotilla of warships, painted in bright white, across the Pacific to expand American presence into the far reaches of Asia[90].

In 1901, the first Nobel Prizes were launched and made an impressive international impact. Peace, Science, and Literature were topics propelled by the recognition given by these Prizes. Civilization was doing the quick step. The first Rhodes Scholarships were awarded and became coveted awards for budding scholars with athletic prowess to study at Oxford for the rest of the century and beyond[91]. International education became an indicia of a 'liberal' education.

Tecumseh died in the Battle of the Thames along the Thames River basin around 60 miles from my home town of London, Ontario, in a battle that stopped the American invasion in its tracks. Tecumseh was deserted by some of his aboriginal cohorts. The Americans retreated, never to return. Tecumseh's burial grounds were never discovered. Three of his remarkable speeches were published and widely circulated after his death. Tecumseh should be considered one of the founding fathers of Canada. A public primary school in south London, Ontario that I attended, for a time, is named after Tecumseh triggered my early interest in him where his large, handsome, memorable portrait adorned the school assembly hall.

90   When Thayer Mahan, a leading U.S. Naval Academy officer and teacher published 'The Influence of Sea Power Upon History, 1660 to 1763' in 1890, he was influenced by Theodore Roosevelt's first book 'Naval War of 1812' published in 1882. Roosevelt, as President, put Mahan's theses into action. Hence the voracious appetite for American influence across the Pacific, especially in the Philippines. Franklin Roosevelt too was deeply influenced by Mahan, his book and his theories, especially in the Pacific. Roosevelt revered Mahan's book and led to his interest in American naval strategic sea power and it was this expertise that allowed Franklin Roosevelt to let his guard down on Japanese naval expansion and advances in the Pacific.

91   My eldest son Laurence was elected the first Canadian born President of the Oxford Union in 1984-85. The first Canadian was David Lewis. Lewis was born in Poland. David Lewis became a Rhodes Scholar in 1934-35 when he was elected President

In 1902, '*The Tale of Peter Rabbit*' appeared selling millions of copies and sequels unleashing a stream of books and films about animals who act like humans but are much nicer.

The death of Queen Victoria deconstructed staid conformity and unleashed wild diversity in art, music, literature and invention. It was the robust start of the 'modern'. It was the start of the Edwardian period chocked full of reduced morals and wild amusements. Sex came out of the closet.

Oliver Wendell Holmes, America's greatest judicial reformist, was appointed to join the Supreme Court of United States in 1903, later to be joined by Louis Brandeis and together called the 'Great Dissenters' who launched a judicial movement upending the absolute 'right of property' to make way for even more 'progressive' reforms in the '30s, later mimicked by Canada and others[92]. Brandeis cobbled together the 'right' of privacy, not in the Constitution, from articles and court decisions. This 'right' had serious implications for the 'right' to abortion later decided in Roe versus Wade the famous Supreme Court of United States precedent in 1973.

And in 1908, Theodore Roosevelt launched the FBI, the first American federal police force, to contain crime that seeped over state borders. Criminal law remains primarily a state power in U.S.A. unlike Canada where the Criminal law was and is under the federal jurisdiction.

The first New York Subway was completed in 1914, almost 15 miles long within four years on time and on budget.

"Si c'était à refaire, je commencerais par la culture" – **"If I were starting over, I would begin with culture"** - Jean Monnet[93].

---

of the Oxford Union. My son Lawrence, a Rhodes Scholar in 1983-85, when he was elected President of the Oxford Union. Boris Johnson (later Mayor of London and the leading MP advocating Brexit and recent Prime Minister) was his Treasurer at the Union.

92 Pierre Trudeau rejected the 'right of property' in the 1982 Canadian Constitution despite fierce opposition based on the same rationale.

93 Jean Monnet, an avuncular French wine merchant by trade, can be rightfully called a 'godfather' of the European Common Market after World War II. His singular role as a private citizen and advocate with a gift for special relationships in America,

Culture and power have always been interwoven down through the annals of history including 20th century. Art and culture were manifestations of

---

France and Germany, tirelessly instigated moves towards reunification of Europe politically and economically before the time of the Marshall Plan which in turn, due to American largesse, accelerated European growth and the start of political and economic European community has been forgotten in the recent steps to dismantle the Common Market and the European Union and borderless Europe, by Brexit, the U.K.'s referendum to withdraw. Jean Monnet's autobiography 'Memoirs' (Doubleday Books, 1978) remains the best history of the origins of Common Market – the precursor to the European Union. Leadership by private citizens has been forgotten in homogeneity of the public classes and the focus of media on political leaders. Brexit, of course, was triggered by the sudden immigrant flood of refugees from the Middle East especially Syria into the heart of Europe and it was this reaction and the irritation of mindless regulations of Common Market instituted by bureaucrats in Brussels with little political accountability that led in large measure, to the Brexit vote in the U.K. to leave the EU. One forgotten footnote to Monnet's remarkable career. In 1940, he and an English M.P. called Arthur Salter produced a memo that sketched out a detailed political and economic union between France and England including one Parliament and one government, a custom's union that persuaded Churchill to get his government's concurrence which he did to persuade the French to join in a common effort against Germany. The French Cabinet refused and instead under Petain signed a disastrous agreement with Nazi Germany with all its negative consequences to allow Germans to occupy most of France led by Marshal Petain called Vichy after the small Vichy that became the compliant French government seat. French President Francois Mitterrand, a socialist favourite, served in Petain Vichy's invidious government and even earned a medal for his efforts which was not publically disclosed until after his Presidency.

What's not well known about Monnet was the active role he played with de Gaulle during World War II in London and then in Washington during World War II. Monnet, a delightful compelling conversationalist influenced President Roosevelt's key advisors to support Britain's efforts to obtain naval, military and financial support to aid Churchill's beleaguered government which was virtually fighting alone against the Nazi military, naval and aerial juggernaut (except for the Commonwealth - Canada, Australia, New Zealand, South Africa et al) in 1939, 1940 and 1941. Monnet befriended Felix Frankfurter, a serving Supreme Court of United States, an Anglophile, who enjoyed numerous privileges and protégés in the Roosevelt administration, who worked together to support Churchill's urgent requests for military and financial aid. Read 'The Brandeis/Frankfurter Connection' by Bruce Allen Murphy (Oxford University Press, 1982)

power from the dawn of history in ancient Egypt, Greece, Rome, Japan, Mexico and South America, throughout Russia, medieval Europe onto modern Europe.

With the advent of the 20th century, art and culture exploded in all directions – music, architecture, painting, sculpture, poetry and novels. Each genre, influenced by the others, took on a dizzy array of new forms.

Every major novelist of the 20th century, at least after 1920, studied and sought to imitate the voluminous pages of the 'tour de force' written by Marcel Proust published in 1917 in France – *'In Search of Lost Time'* – translated into dozens of languages. This masterpiece, over 700 pages in length uncovered the intimate relationships of French society of that era. It remains a primer for any budding writer or novelist. Proust, a 'Dreyfusard' and struggling writer self-published his masterpiece.

Autocratics, followed in the footsteps of Royal precedents. Stalin, Mussolini, Mao and especially Hitler, each took a direct interest in all aspects of art and culture. Stalin's 'social realism' in art and print followed the Soviet party line becoming government directives. All else was 'degenerative' art.

Hitler and the Nazis agreed with Stalin's theses. Hitler 'ethically cleansed' Jewish actors, writers, musicians, art and artists. Books and art paintings were publically burned to popular applause. This another 20th century manifestation of 'cancel culture' aside from the Catholic Church's list of prohibited books considered 'blasphemy'. The Communists in Russia and under Mao in China also led in censorship. Mussolini's earliest advisors were art and literary experts promoting new art forms while castigating the 'old'. Mao Zedong used art and literature to project his party line to shape and inculcate the Chinese masses while he eviscerated Confucius thought from Communist China that had kept the 'Middle Kingdom' intellectually culturally and politically united.

With the rise of the Nazis to power via the Third Reich in the '30s, art censorship took on a lethal form as it did earlier in the Soviet Russia and later in China when Communists took over.

The history of the relationship of art and power and the forms that culture took that accompanied the 20th century continues to be explored especially its impact on civil society.

One clinical comprehensive fascinating perspective was meticulously explored by Lynn H. Nicholas, an art historian in 'The Rape of Europa: The Fate of Europe's Treasures in the Third Reich and the Second World War' (Vintage Press, 1995)[94]. She describes repeated infernal paradoxes. Art treasures were demonized and ostracized then confiscated, first by 'legal' means then looted as plunder, as Nazis occupied European state after state.

Greed and avarice amongst the Nazi leadership elites, especially Hitler himself and Goering, who both favoured art dealers, was without parallel.

Jewish own art collections were especially targeted. The 20th century is replete with such paradoxes.

This complex book is a difficult, detailed masterful account how nations about to be occupied or occupied protected or hid their nations art treasures.

As World War II wore on allied liberators, American, English, Canadian, France and Polish were favourably lobbied by their nationals interested in art to protect these artifacts of civilization against the destruction of war. Russia did as well hiding their art treasures across Russia with care and devotion. In the result, so-called 'Monument Men' were added to military forces to urge their military cohorts to avoid destroying inhibited by war those national treasures.

More complicated were the detection and discovery of 'treasure troves' secretly hidden by the Nazi leadership. Some were found, many not. Some were returned after the war to surviving original owners or their heirs, most were not.

The narrative takes surprising twists and turns. The Soviets led by Stalin were clear headed and focus especially about German art. Of all the allies, no doubt Russia suffered the most from the Nazi 'scorched earth' policies. Stalin demanded reparations including German art treasures. Special army brigades under the Soviet Trophy Commission were dispatched to uncover hidden treasure troves in a race with the American and English 'Monument' men. Over 200,000 paintings and

---

94 Another fascinating book of this genre is 'The Faustian Bargain: The Art World in Nazi Germany' by Jonathan Petropoulos (Oxford University Press, 1999)

other artifacts were laded unto guarded trains. On arrival in Moscow, they were met by Stalin who directed this plunder to be divided especially to the Pushkin and Tetriak museums in Moscow and the Hermitage in Leningrad (now St. Petersburg).

The Americans were divided about the German art treasures they discovered and stored. After World War II, the public debate continued. A large shipment of German art was sent to the National Gallery in Washington and exhibited to massive crowds. After a raucous public debate, most of the art was returned to Germany.

The restoration of stolen art to rightful owners and heirs continues in the courts - over six decades later. This page in history is still being written.

Back to the dawn of the 20th century, my favourite essayist, George Orwell, was born in 1903 in Motihari, Bengal in 20th century British India. Orwell became and remains the prime conveyor for 'truth' in the endless political discourse to isolate and segregate propaganda that infected benighted 20th century, deployed by both by autocrats and democrats alike, and continues unabated to this day.

At the turn of the century, George Bonnard and Edward Vuillant, leaders of the Nabis (Hebrew word for prophet) used new colour combinations to startle art lovers. 'Avant garde' impressionist and abstract art burst onto the scene. Paris became the mecca for art experimentation ushering in a new era of art appreciation.

'Post impressionism' coined in 1906, swiftly followed by Fauvism, Cubism[95], Dadaism, exploded on the cultural scene and art was never the same. The birth of abstract art introduced modern art to new vistas

---

95 Picasso and others whose interest in Cubism was influenced by native artifacts flooding the European market from African colonies. Picasso, a Spaniard by birth, painted in many traditional styles until his disruptive work of fractured faces and figures became the leading edge of modern art. No one could match the consistency of Joan Miro's style of disruptive modern art throughout his long 20th century career. Miro started his career in Barcelona, and like that city and its architecture and its separatist politics cleaved a different path in the art world. One of the most beautiful art museums in the world is dedicated to Miro works on a hilltop overlooking Barcelona. Its modernist dining room offers a superb cuisine.

of visual expression and popular consumption. In 1907, Gustav Klimt painted haunting pictures of women like the '*Woman in Gold*' fusing traditional faces with modern gauzy backgrounds and undulating forms that went on to haunt the 20th century. Wassily Kandinsky, a Russian born painter and art theorist, launched his 'impressionist' painting career in 1903 using shimmering bright colours that floated off his canvas almost independently of the objects themselves.

The doyen of art and literature in Paris in the early 1900's was the wealthy expat American Gertrude Stein, who was a mentor and promoter of modern art and literature in Paris. Her salon was a meeting place for young writers and artists and she influenced both. Her own experiments in writing were not successful while her 'bon mots' like '*a rose is a rose is a rose*' remain iconoclastic. She attempted to deconstruct the written word as cubism did in art. Her written works, at times studded with startling aphorisms, were lumpy, disruptive and failed to glide easily to retain the reader's attention. Still her taste and influence on writers like Hemingway and painters like Picasso were indelible[96,97].

------

96 Pablo Picasso painted a portrait of the formidable looking Gertrude Stein seated in her famed salon in Paris, a contemporary copy reputedly done by one of his students which I acquired. Stein's remarkable career extended to Nazi occupation where she was left in Paris unhindered during World War II. Stein's influence on art and modern writing and writers, on Ernest Hemingway, F. Scott, Fitzgerald and a Canadian writer, Morley Callaghan, an early chum of Hemingway from their time together as reporters for the Toronto Star, is unquestioned. Morley Callaghan, a rabid supporter of the Liberal Party especially Mr. Pearson and later Pierre Trudeau, became an interesting companion who lusted for gossip of the goings-on in Ottawa whenever we would periodically meet for a chat or coffee. I was first introduced to Morley by his son Mike who was for a time, a classmate at law school. It was Morley who knocked out Hemingway when Hemingway challenged him in post-World War I in Paris which Hemingway denied. Read '*That Summer in Paris*' by Morley Callaghan (Exile Editions, 2014). I believed Morley. Read '*A Moveable Feast*' by Ernest Hemingway, Charles Scribner's Sons (1964). Morley was one of Canada's greatest novelists in the 20th century.

97 Max Jacob (1876-1944), born in Brittany met Picasso in Paris when Picasso was a struggling artist and Jacob, though dressed as a dandy, was also a struggling artist, writer and poet. They became best friends and Jacob even served as a model for Picasso including in the iconic Picasso painting called '*Three Musicians*'. Both were

No one invented more creative new modern art forms (paintings, sculptures and ceramics) than the Spaniard Pablo Picasso who together with the French Degas, Matisse and Cezanne were the radical agents of the 'modern'. Earlier Camille Pissarro, the Danish-French painter of Jewish origins, served as a mentor to them all. Space and light bathed in soft colour, new harmonies for the hungry eye. Of course, the celebrated encounters of Paul Gaugin and the Dutch painter, Van Gogh, again transformed the eye and appreciation for their colourful powerful new images and forms. Gaugin's works from the South Seas Islands stand alone as do Van Gogh's sundrenched French landscapes and bright starlit woozy night scenes. By 1912, Duchamp's painting 'Nudes Descending a Staircase No. 2' after years of experimentation finally was completed and this took the art world by storm. Movies and art, in motion, combined.

Painters and sculptors and photographers streamed into Paris to create a combustible concoction of modern art. A diaspora of Jewish artists from isolated eastern Slavic 'shetels' and small eastern towns were attracted to Paris, the most exciting capital of art experimentation in the world. Zadkine, Pascin, Kisling, Kemény, Chagall, Lipchitz, Soutine and Brâncuși flowed in Paris. Brassai, the photographer captured many in photos that jolted the eye and influenced the art world and photography forever. Look at Brassai's early photo of Picasso. Picasso's dark eyes searing like burning coals exude the passion and brilliance captured in his works.

Sigmund Freud's book on 'Interpretation of Dreams' was released in 1900 which sold only 600 copies in 8 years. Still, Freud ushered in the 'Age of Pyschoanalyses' that oscillated across the rest of the world throughout the 20th century and beyond till today. 'Freudian slip' entered the modern jargon. The 'id' and 'ego' took on lives of their own.

---

pioneers in the cubist movement, in painting and Jacob in writing and poetry. Jacob, born a Jew, converted to Catholicism and found it did not save him from being shipped to Drancy, a collection site near Paris in World War II. Jacob died in 1944 awaiting transfer to Auschwitz. Picasso, who survived in Paris during World War II, perhaps in remorse for not assisting Jacob provided drawings for Jacob's poetry books published after World War II. Both were leaders in disruptive art forms Picasso in painting and Jacob in literature and poetry.

The feverish exploration of the 'psyche' and 'self' began. Emil Durkheim focused his philosophic palate on 'individualism'. Writers and thinkers began to compete to explore the anatomy of 'personality' and 'sexuality'. The 'cult' of the personality took thinkers and scientists captive. The new frontier was open to behavioral science as the mind and emotions were plumbed, deconstructed and explored in the endless search for sounder health. 'Depression' and 'neuroses' became essential parts of the modern medical lexicon as the gyrations of the inner psyche and mental health became equal partners with physical health in health care.

Italy too witnessed the rise of the modern by its disruptive 'Futurist' school of painting. Influenced by French modernism, the Italian 'Futurist'[98] school flourished. Its best works can still be seen collected in a jewel of an art gallery, the Museo Moderna d'Arte located in the lush Borghese Gardens in the heart of Rome built by Benito Mussolini in the '30s. Mussolini in turn had been influenced early in his climb from socialist to fascist by his Jewish mistress, Margherita Sarfatti[99], his biographer and elegant cultural advisor who savoured an immaculate taste for art, architecture and literature,. Like Hitler, both Stalin and Mussolini used art 'modern realism' as propaganda tools to promote their extremist ideas. Each dictator understood the powerful relationship between art forms and populism as vital political teaching tools. Art and power became inseparable. Each dictator shaped their propaganda art to illustrate their version of modern utopia.

---

98   Futurism is from 'Futurismo' in Italian founded in 1909 in Milan by the poet Filippo Tommaso Marinetti who wrote the 'Second Political Manifesto of Futurism' in 1910. The founding of the Venice Biennale, that continues to this day, preceded the Futurist movement. Mussolini adopted modernist Futurist art and architectural designs to his Fascist movement.

99   Ruth Sarfatti, Margherita Sarfatti's granddaughter, is a fine ceramic artist living in Jaffa who Carole and I met in Israel during my first visit in 1973 when I acquired a modernist steel statue of Moses done by her husband Moishe Schternschuss, a teacher of the Canadian sculptor Sorel Etrog. Later when I mentioned to Sorel I had met his teacher, Schternschuss, born in southern Poland like my father, who in 1903, emigrated to Palestine, settling finally in Jaffa in 1926, who, no doubt, had influenced his work, Etrog abruptly changed the subject. Ah, artists!

Mussolini clad his street ruffians in black shirts, rather than just armbands, later to be emulated by Hitler's appetite for uniforms to unite his followers. Visible conformity was the essence of gaining auto- cratic followership. Wearing a uniform merges the individual into the collective.

The Italian 'Futurists' sought to coalesce their new art with tech- nology. The Futurist school extended to architecture, crafts and litera- ture. Painters and sculptors like Umberto Boccioni, Carlo Carà, Giacomo Balla, Luigi Russolo, Gino Severino created art in a profusion of colour and dazzling forms, while the architect Antonio Sant'Elia designed clean high rise buildings of concrete and steel girders with elegant elevators on exterior walls. Meanwhile the poet P.T. Marinetti fused the Tuscan cultural past with the Italy economy, mired in crafts and agriculture to propel Italy into the future. And it was Marinetti who fused Futurism with Mussolini and Fascism at its earliest stages.

With the advent of the first Italian car made by Giovani Agnelli who cofounded Fiat in 1899 in Turin, Italy became obsessed with sleek autos, trains, bikes and above all, speed. Ford racing cars designed and managed by Carroll Shelby (1923-2012) beat the Agnelli racing cars at the Le Mans in Europe towards the end of the century. The Mustang Shelby GT350 was introduced in 1965 was the first American 'muscle' car that set world trends[100]. Propelled by modern design and crafts, movement was the 'leitmotif' in the Italian cultural awakening as beautifully crafted objects were hurled into spatial repetitions. 'Transit' in art and objects became a touchstone of this fascinating school of modernism.

'A Modern Utopia', a novel published by prescient H.G. Wells in 1905, predicted a world government, promising a global 'brave new world'.

Havelock Ellis published the first of his six volumes studies on sexu- ality pushing sex out of the bedroom into public scrutiny and ignited the first revolution of sexual liberation.

William James, associated with the philosophic school of prag- matism, published in 'A Review of General Psychology' in 1902 and then

---

100 For a while I owned at 1974 a two door Oldsmobile 4 cylinder 442, a family version
     of the 'muscle' car.

'*The Variation of Religious Experience*' that still resonates with the current toxic mix of religion and politics.

Meanwhile back in U.S.A., Booker T. Washington published '*Up From Slavery*' in 1900 and W.E.B. DuBois published his works bringing 'racism' to the scratchy surface of American conscience. W.E.B. DuBois was perhaps the most influential civil rights activist that preceded Martin Luther King in the 20th century. Receiving his post-graduate degrees at Harvard University and University of Berlin before the turn of the century, DuBois became a skilled journalist, educator, polemist, writer and organizer for the black civil rights movement in U.S.A and beyond. In 1903, he published '*The Souls of Black Folk*', the most influential book on par with the earlier '*Uncle Tom's Cabin*' that gained broader support in white America for civil rights while igniting black activism. DuBois went on to become a leading co-founder of the National Association for the Advancement of Coloured People (NAACP). Originating with the 'Niagara Movement' that he co-founded, he advocated equal rights and continued to write, persuade, cajole and be involved in the organization and every aspect of the black rights movement till just before his death in the '60s when the Civil Rights Bill was passed under Lyndon Johnson in 1964 after Kennedy's tragic assassination in 1962.

There is an interesting, little known Canadian connection to the U.S. civil rights movement. DuBois and other early activists who he called the 'Talented Ten' met in 1905 in Fort Erie, Ontario, at a lake front hotel - the Erie Beach Hotel - where blacks were not colour barred. The 'Niagara Declaration', written and approved at Fort Erie, set the base-line for American activism in search of equal rights. DuBois persuaded a few white supporters to join with him as he galvanized his small activist base.

DuBois enlisted the help of key Jewish American 'progressives' like Lillian Wald and especially Joel Spingarn, who became first Chairman of The National Association for the Advancement of Coloured People (NAACP). Both were activists in the 'progressive' movement in that first decade leading to the creation of the Progressive Party in 1912. Before Spingarn died years later, an annual award was established in his honour by the NAACP. The Spingarn Prize is awarded annually to the person who contributed most to the advancement the cause of civil rights. Martin Luther King, when finally awarded the prize in 1957, relished this award above most he received[101]. When Spingarn died, Supreme Court Justice Thurgood Marshall, the first black member of the Supreme Court of the United States, and black activist Roy Wilkins gave Spingarn's eulogy in 1963.

DuBois's activism was not limited to civil rights in America. DuBois was an early pacifist. He lobbied for equal treatment of black soldiers in World War I and beyond in Europe. He co-organized Pan-African Congresses to bring attention to the plight of blacks in Colonial Africa and elsewhere. Then he organized the first legal department of NAACP with the help of Joel Spingarn's younger brother Elias whose detailed work led directly to the formulation of the Civil Rights Act in 1963. Martin Luther King acknowledged the key role that these American Jews and others played in the American civil rights movements, a chapter in American history now sadly neglected[102].

New music came brashly marching into the 20th century. Mahler and Schoenberg changed classical music with their discordant modern atonal symphonies, not to everyone's taste.

---

101 King expected to win the coveted award in 1956 the year before but it was granted instead to Jack Roosevelt Robinson the first black baseball player in the National League. Robinson, a World War II veteran and college graduate played for the Montreal Royals in the International League a farm team for the Brooklyn Dodgers. When Robinson came to play the Toronto Maple Leafs, he could not obtain upscale hotel accommodations in Toronto because he was black. Instead he stayed at Warwick Hotel co-owned and managed by my late father-in-law, Harry Sniderman, a sandlot baseball star in the '20s and '30s in Toronto who welcomed Joe Louis when he came to Toronto with his all black fast team 'The Joe Louis Punchers'. Louis Armstrong also stayed at Warwick when he came to Toronto to play with his band.

102 American Jews, young and old, made up a majority of the white northern Americans that joined Martin Luther King in his first march to Selma, Alabama, is now largely forgotten, especially by surviving and successor black civil rights activists. In 1964 a trio of youth, one black, two Jews, James Chaney, Andrew Goodman and Michael Schwerner were murdered by the Klan whose bodies were buried and then recovered in Mississippi.

The 'Tango' originating amongst Italian immigrants in Buenos Aires, Argentina[103], travelled to the brothels of Europe and quickly became a dance craze in Europe, Asia and America. The Americans first detected the syncopated beats of the Blues and Jazz that travelled from the plantations of the deep south through New Orleans that then blossomed in the north to change popular tastes with their catching rhythms forever. The swift rise of the middle class changed the popular musical culture, and dented a wider public consciousness with strange and different sounds.

Of course, there were violent disruptions in that first decade. But those were in far off mysterious lands. These played in the minor key while the major key was 'the modern'. The strikes against 'sweat shops' and mining practices in American barely scratched the public consciences of Americans and Canadians. The first outburst of the first Russian Revolution in 1905 ended with the Czar establishing the first Duma – the first popular assembly in Russia. Stalin, then a young organizer, assassin, agitator and bank robber under Lenin's leadership, was jailed for the first time in 1905 in Tbilisi, Georgia, the country of his birth where he started his agitation, revolutionary activities, banditry and terrorist acts[104,105].

---

103 In 2015, as part of my 'bucket list', I travelled to Argentina with Carole and Michael when I took tango lessons in an antique café in Buenos Aires on the River Plate whose walls were lined with old fading sepia dance photos. The tango was reputed to originate in Argentina when lonely male Italian immigrant workers began dancing with each other for amusement in the 1880's until it shifted to brothels at the turn of the century when women joined the erotic dance.

104 I acquired a fine painting of a church tower on a high promontory where Stalin was reputedly first imprisoned in 1905, overlooking the river rushing through in the heart of scenic Tbilisi, the capital of Georgia, where I visited a number of times especially to help monitor the first Georgian democratic election in 1991. In nearby Gori, Stalin's birthplace, his massive statue until recently held a place of pride in the centre of this thriving city. A museum dedicated to Stalin in Gori was jammed with visitors.

105 I travelled across Europe, east and west. It was my habit to visit a local synagogue. History and current events can be quickly and easily uncovered there, I found. On a visit to Tbilisi, Georgia, I was guided to an antique synagogue in continuous use for over 2,000 years. My visit coincided with the 'Festival of Palms' ('Sukkot'). My young Georgian guide and I entered through a gate cut in the high wooden wall surrounding the picturesque stone block and brick structure with a high round

The Boxer Rebellion in China, reacting to the 'opening' to China to foreigners, broke out and was quickly quelled, while the seeds of Communist ideology planted in China in the early '20s, gained early Chinese adherents like Mao Zedong and Zhou Enlai, the endless 'troubles' in Ireland, unrest in the Balkans, the Romanian Peasant uprising, periodic pogroms in Imperial Russia, slave trade in Africa and slaughter of millions especially in the Congo, the tribal wars in Africa led by Zulu warriors, the short-lived Boer War in South Africa barely creased the public conscience in the West as the Victorian era had come to a sudden end with the death of Queen Victoria in 1901.

Canadians served with honour, skill and distinction for the first time overseas gaining a well-deserved reputation for their bravery and professional military prowess in the Imperial Forces in the Boer War in South Africa exhibiting both courage and toughness as resourceful soldiers. Laurier's decision to support the British in the Boer War split the Canadian government as Henri Bourassa[106] dissented and resigned, planting the seeds of separation in the 'Belle Province'.

---

window forming a stained glass Star of David. In the inner cobblestone paved courtyard and surrounding the building lounged a dozen or so Jews smoking heavily. Emerging through the wooden door entrance in a high wooden fence surrounding the beautiful old synagogue, my young female guide was aghast. A tall dark skinned handsome man with a heavy black Georgian style moustache strode towards the wooden gate to leave the synagogue precinct as we were entering. *"He is the leading poet of Georgia and a Member of Parliament"*, she stuttered. She forgot to tell me his name. We quickly exchanged greetings as I made my way up the broad stone staircase to enter the sanctuary. There I encountered the Rabbi, a Lubavitch Hasid who was handing out 'etrog' and 'lulavs' – lemons and palm leaves – used to celebrate the ancient Hebrew festival of Sukkot. In a small study room off the entrance, I noticed a large coloured poster of the Lubavitch Rebbe. His image, I found, was in small synagogues throughout the Balkans and Eastern Europe. I was shocked a decade later when I was exploring the new excavations under the Wailing Wall in Jerusalem to be accosted by the same handsome dark haired man, now clean shaven, who had left Tbilisi with his family to settle in Israel. Life is full of happy coincidences!

106 Henri Bourassa, a leading Quebec politician and publisher, went on to oppose World War I and conscription. His repeated agitation for independence of Canada from Britain, especially for an independent Canadian navy, helped gear Canada's slow moving peaceful transition from a colony to a self-governing Dominion

The mighty Imperial Empires of Britain, Germany, Austro-Hungary, Russia, France and Japan continued to expand their reach now joined by the U.S.A. as the newest emerging world power. Meanwhile the tottering Ottoman Empire growing weaker whetted the European imperial powers appetite for expansion in the mid-east and beyond to Asia, later called the 'grand game'. Regional outbursts of violence were contained, almost remote and far removed from the rapid progress of the new western way of life swiftly transforming the globe and barely noticed in the west.

The Hague Convention was adopted in 1907. While not the first time in the modern era, it was the first time 'war' was universally condemned – and rules of humane conduct in war became more widely accepted. These evolving rules of humane conduct in war entered conventional international law. This new concept of the 'rule of law' to contain barbarianism in war originated with the Lieber Code that Lincoln had adopted in 1964 in American Civil War four decades earlier to impose for the first time, humane treatment of prisoners of war and prisoner exchanges. This was followed by the First Geneva Convention with rules for the humane treatment of war prisoners and injured. International law began to institutionalize the Hague Conventions' 'rules of war' and then along with the later Geneva Accords together marked the beginning of the 'human rights' movement that cascaded throughout the 20th century with growing political support and wider consensus.

---

in the Commonwealth. Henri Bourassa was the grandfather of Robert Bourassa who was the Premier of Quebec during the 'October Crisis' based on F.L.Q.'s (the extremist separatist group) kidnapping of a British diplomat and the murder of a Liberal minister. Pierre Trudeau introduced the War Measures Act in 1974 to crystallize public opinion and take strong action. Opinion remains divided as to whether this extreme action was helpful or hurtful to the 'separatist' cause which Trudeau abhorred. While I initially disagreed with Trudeau, at the time, his actions, I now believe in retrospect, were correct, considered and needed drastic measures to lance the 'boil' of creeping separatist sentiment. Still, when amendments of the War Measures Act came before the Senate Committee for consideration, changes suggested by Serge Joyal and I that were later adopted by the Senate and by the Commons. The major amendment we suggested was a 'sunset' clause so the emergency legislation would be regularly revisited and kept up to date.

And the 20th century welcomed the birth of my mother, Helen Rose, who was born in a small 'shtetel' Ylze ('Drilsch' in Yiddish) in southern Poland in 1900. In 1907, as a 7-year old, she immigrated to Canada, accompanying her diminutive (less than five feet tall) mother (who spoke only Yiddish, Hebrew and Polish), Mirel[107], and younger 4-year old sister Betty who together crossed Europe, the Atlantic and then

---

107 My maternal grandmother, Mirel Etel Bleeman nee Topol – born in Yusapov, Poland
    – had deep Hasidic roots. She was born in Yusapov, a nearby village and came from a
    distinguished line of Hasidic Rabbis. Her maternal great grandfather was the Solis-
    czer Rebbe who in turn was a direct descendent of the 16th century Hasidic master
    called the 'Sheloh Hakodosh' (Isaiah Horowitz) after his majestic works – *Shnei
    Luchot Habrit*' ('*The Two Tablets of the Covenant*') who in 1621 emigrated to the Holy
    Land after serving as Chief Rabbi of Prague and before in Posnan and Frankfurt.
    The Sheloh's roots go back before the Second Temple in Israel.
        Isaiah Horowitz, born in the Czech lands can trace his family name and roots
    to a small town in Bohemia called Horovice. His ancestors came there in the 14th
    century after his family fled from Girona in Catalonia after the 1391 massacre of
    Jews. There the family name was Beneviste whose family tree lived in Gerina whose
    leading Rebbe at the time was Nachmanides (Ramban), a Talmudic scholar and
    writer. In turn the Beneviste roots can be traced to Aragon in Spain and Narbonne in
    11th century France and then back to the Holy Land.
        After his wife died, the 'Sheloh' decided to leave his established sons, also
    Rabbis (one who followed him as Chief Rabbi of Frankfurt), to study the Kabbala, a
    school of 12th century Jewish mysticism, in Safed (Sfat), a small town in the northern
    part of the Holy Land. He first settled in Jerusalem and set up a 'yeshiva'. Elected
    the first ashkenazic Chief Rabbi of Jerusalem around 1623, he was imprisoned by
    the Ottomans, held for ransom, then released after ransom was collected by Jews
    around the Mediterranean basin and paid. On his way to Safed (Sfat), he died near
    Tiberius where he is buried there in a small cemetery next to Moses Maimonides,
    the 12th century philosopher and a leading exponent of biblical interpretations of
    Jewish religious practices. Maimonides sought to rationalize faith with science
    ('*Leo Strauss on Maimonides: The Complete Writings*' by Leo Strauss, University of
    Chicago Press, 2013). Less than ten great Rebbis are buried there including Maimon-
    ides father. Menachem Mendel of Vitebsk who emigrated from Russia in the 1780's
    with a small group of devout Hasidic Jews to settle in the Holy Land is buried in a
    small cemetery in Tiberius near the cemetery where my ancestor Isaiah Horowitz –
    the 'Sheloh'. Maimonides collected centuries of rabbinic interpretations of the Bible
    and the two Talmuds into a book called '*Mischneh Torah*'. Maiminides is also buried

Canada travelled by rail from Halifax to join my devout grandfather who had left Poland earlier in 1904 to seek freedom to practice his religion in the new world. My grandfather, Israel Isaac Bleeman was a perpetual Talmudic student and a follower of the 'Gerrer' Rebbes[108] who led a dominant Orthodox group in Europe and later in Israel.

---

in the same small cemetery in Tiberius as is his father. For his prolific works, he was called from 'Moses to Moses' to signify the biblical law as declared by Moses was made more clear by the collection of Talmudic interpretations assembled by Maimonides. Maimonides' leading work called *'The Guide To The Perplexed'* is still rigorously studied in Yeshivas around the world as are the 'Sheloh' works. The Sheloh's siddur (prayer book) is also still in use especially by the Lubavitch. The first Lubavitch Rebbe kept the Sheloh's siddur on his desk as he wrote his magnus opus *'The Tanya'* (*'The Way'*) the key work studied by the Lubavitch to this day. *'The Tanya'* was first published over 200 years ago.

108 My maternal grandfather, Israel Isaac Bleeman, as a youth in Poland had studied with Hasidic masters - the Sfas Emes AHL, the 'Mouth of Truth', AHL (1847-1905), and was a colleague of his son and successor 'The Imrei Emes' AHL, the 'Lip of Truth', AHL (1866-1948), named after their masterpieces of biblical interpretation, who both taught that every word spoken and written was powerful and possibly destructive so great care should be taken with the use or misuse of any words, in speech and especially in writing. Blinded by a tragic accident in 1919 in Toronto, my grandfather continued daily his Talmudic studies with friends until he knew their works and the Torah and Talmud by heart. My grandfather was a 'Ger' Hasid, follower of the 'Ger' line that expanded from a small fellowship of hasidic Orthodox Jews in a suburb of Warsaw called Ger to become a broad based group across Europe, Canada and both North and South America. The fifth and the sixth Ger of the line emigrated to Israel well before WWII. Today the Ger is considered the most influential orthodox group in Israel with branches around the world. Perhaps not by fateful coincidence, my late father and his father and grandfather (after whom I am named) were adherents of the Ger in Poland. My father, Solomon, after six years of service first in the Polish army during and then after World War I in the Polish War of Independence (1919-1921), an orthodox Jew, arrived to visit his older brothers in Toronto in 1927. My astute uncle, Morris (Moishe) anxious for my father to stay in Canada introduced him to my mother. The fact that my father and his paternal predecessors were also 'Ger' adherents persuaded my maternal grandfather to approve my father's courtship with my mother. They fell in love, married in 1930 in Toronto and then settled in London, Ontario where I was born in the midst of the great depression in 1935 at Victoria Hospital. To my mother's deep disappointment, I was born just past midnight on January 2nd, too late to collect the baby buggy and

Though blind from his mid-twenties from a heavy beer-wagon accident in Toronto, he authored a book called 'For the Love of the World' based on his notes from his Talmudic studies. The 'Ger' Hasidism believed in daily rigorous prayer and daily study to foster self-improvement and to make a 'better world'.[109] My grandfather had travelled first from southern Poland to work for a time in Antwerp to gain sufficient income to take him to Toronto where he settled in Kensington Market in 1905. Then he sent for his young courageous wife and two young daughters where they were reunited at Union Station in Toronto in 1907 and shortly thereafter bought their new home in the heart of Kensington Market, a narrow attached brick house next to a lane at 35 Kensington

---

other goodies 'awarded' to the first baby born in my home town in 1935 that my mother had planned to receive. Thereafter my mother would never fail to remind me when I was lazy that I lacked "push" and needed "push" to get ahead in the world.

109 My cousin Abraham Bleeman – a Holocaust survivor (also a devout follower of the 'Ger') who emigrated to Toronto in 1945 sponsored by my grandfather, collected my blind grandfather's early notes and published them in a slender book in Aramaic, following Talmudic tradition, titled 'For The Love of The World' 20 years after my grandfather's death based on my grandfather's notes from his studies with the 'Sfas Emes' AHL and the 'Imrie Emes' AHL before and after he emigrated to Canada in 1905 and thereafter till he was blinded and lost his sight in 1917. Most Rabbinic authors are usually named after their great works. 'Sfas Emes' means the 'Mouth of Truth' while 'Imrie Emes' means the 'Lip of Truth'. These works anticipated with detailed rules the current obsession with 'politically correct' language or speech meant to hurt or defame another. The 'Sfas Emes' taught 'words can kill'. Idle gossip can damage a person's reputation and should be abjured. More egregiously, an order from afar to kill people is more potent than a murderous knife in the hand. 'Words can kill', they taught.

More than two decades ago or so, I visited Rabbi Adin Steinsaltz in his office in Jerusalem, one of the world's outstanding scholars on the Old Testament and both the two Talmuds, to read my grandfather's book and see if I could get it translated into English in Jerusalem. Steinsaltz was in the process of publishing his multi-volume version of the Old Testament in English, a joy to read. Rabbi Steinsaltz advised me later that my grandfather's book would be almost impossible to translate because it would be voluminous and would still depend on the reader comprehending the layers of glosses on the Old Testament, Talmudic texts, and 'Mishneh Torah' collected by Maimonides and an intricate knowledge of these and other works my grandfather referred to in his slender volume of notes.

Avenue that still stands. This intrepid tale of immigration to the new world was repeated thousands upon thousands of times. These stories of hope and persistence are keys that combined to make Canada the great country it has become.

In 1901, a study published in Toronto attributed the high infant mortality rate with bacteria from sewage and water. The city fathers were jolted to take action. Toronto accelerated the separation of water and sewage and persuaded most Torontonians homeowners to connect their waste and water to freshly constructed city trunk lines. Public health officials lobbied reluctant civic leaders to commence construction of Toronto's first filtration plant on Toronto Island followed by another plant in the east end at Bay, screening waste from water drawn for Lake Ontario, Toronto's primary water source. Public Health became a civic priority. In 1907, the invention of the first flush toilet quickly became a household staple. Concern for public health emerged as an early benchmark of the 20th century in Canada.

The T. Eaton Company became Canada's largest retailer and first department store which expanded from Toronto to Winnipeg in 1905 led by Toronto Eaton's third son, John Craig Eaton who gained a Knighthood for his pioneering efforts. John Eaton opened buying offices around the globe, especially in England and France, to bring the world of style and fashion and tailoring to Canada. Eaton's became a pace setter with the Eaton's catalogue allowing small towns and farmers, anticipating Amazon success (via the internet), to buy items by mail order. There's nothing new under the sun, only better, if not cheaper.

In 1899, Joe Atkinson, a sharp aggressive newspaperman, with the help of Sir Wilfrid Laurier and other Liberal financial backers acquired an ailing evening Toronto newspaper. Then in 1900, Atkinson renamed it the Toronto Daily Star. The Star went on to become the largest daily circulation newspaper in Canada and a robust supporter of liberalism and the Liberal Party, its preferred vehicle of reform. In the '20s and '30s, the Toronto Star was a leader in the fight against rising anti-Semitism in Toronto fomented by the growing number of Swastika Clubs starting in the Beaches. The Star with the Winnipeg Free Press became two of the most the powerful voices of the 'progressive' movement in Canada.

In 1904, the Canadian Red Cross was formed to join the established Red Cross Committees across Europe and then around the world.

Before the turn of the century, two mighty successful Canadian missionary movements, originating in Toronto, targeted western China. 'Civilizing' China by teaching the gospels was the illuminating call to Christian consciences. The Protestant stream led by the key financial support of Lady Eaton[110] (mostly from the wealthy churchgoers at Timothy Eaton Church on St. Clair West, Toronto) and others and the Catholic stream led by the Scarborough Fathers were both based in Toronto. These two schools of dedicated missionaries intensified their teaching of the 'social gospel' as engines of 'conversion progress' and western civilization in China. They set up schools teaching Chinese to illiterate Chinese youth, hospitals, and China's first dental school in south-west China in the most populous province - Sichuan[111].

It was the sons of these Canadian Protestant missionaries that Mackenzie King and O.D. Skelton, his principal assistant, an academic King enlisted from Queen's University, attracted as a young well-schooled staff nucleus that became the Canada's Department of External Affairs located in the East Block next to King's and the Cabinet offices in the late twenties in Ottawa, when King decided to create a foreign policy, distinct and independent from Imperial Britain during the '20s. And it is why the 'social gospel' germinated at the core of Canada's foreign policy, from the very beginning, as it does to this day[112].

---

110   The spiraling cost of maintaining the growing demands of the Protestant missionary movement in western China underwritten by various Protestant churches in Canada resulted in the formation of the United Church of Canada in 1925, a tale forgotten in Canada's long history with China.

111   The founder of Time Magazine, Henry Luce, born of American missionary parents, studied at a school in Chefoo in western China established, run and funded by Canadian missionaries. The Royal Ontario Museum in Toronto acquired a large collection of old Chinese artifacts from Archbishop White, a leading missionary leader who smuggled them out of China and donated them to the ROM. Chinese lions, thus unlawfully obtained, can be viewed outside the ROM on University Avenue in mid Toronto near Bloor Street West.

112   During a visit to Chongqing (formerly Chungking, where the Nationalist Movement of Chiang Kai-shek moved in World War II and built tunnels to safeguard his

In 1897, the First Zionist Congress had been convened in Basle, Switzerland under the visionary leadership of Theodore Herzl with 200 participants from all parts of the diaspora (17 countries in all) to finalize the Zionist platform with the paramount Zionist goal to seek *'for Jewish people a publically recognized legally secured homeland in Palestine.'*[113] Of the

---

government from Japanese attack) in Sichuan Province, to establish 'city to city' twinning relations with Toronto, I encountered the head of the Communist Party in Sichuan Province, the most populated in China. He took me by surprise when he told me he had been taught to read and write Chinese as an illiterate youth in a missionary school established by Christian missionaries who came from Toronto. I also befriended YaYu Shan, the leading sculptor of China, who became head of Chongqing Institute of Fine Arts as a reward for winning the China-wide contest to sculpt the outsized white marble statue of Mao in his mausoleum in Tiananmen Square in Beijing. Shan gave me his favourite maquette, a two foot plaster statuette of Zhou Enlai, his mentor, who chose Shan to sculpt the large statue of Mao, which I cherish. Based on that small maquette, an outsized statue of Zhou Enlai was sculpted by Shan as a national monument to that extraordinary leader in China who was his patron.

At a later visit to Chongqing to a painters old age home, I acquired from Son Guangxu, an elderly painter, who was the leading wood cut artist of China, a black and white limited numbered print, #19 done in 1924, of Lu Xun, a leading liberal writer of China and admired by Mao. A copy of this print was Mao owned himself. I acquired a 20 volume collection of Lu Xun's works in English where the original wood cut I acquired was the frontpiece of each volume authorized and dedicated by Mao himself, which took years to read, and remains unfinished.

113   Theodore Herzl was a Hungarian-born assimilated Austrian Jewish journalist, author and playwright. He covered the Dreyfus trial in Paris as a journalist. He encountered visceral anti-Semitism when Karl Lueger, a populist candidate for Mayor of Vienna won office on an anti-Semitic platform. *"Hep, Hep, Hep"* was the street rant. *"Hierosolyma est perdita"* - *"Jerusalem is lost"*. In 1895, Leuger won the office of Mayor of Vienna. He was denied the office as the aging Franz Joseph II, the Austro-Hungarian Emperor was convinced that the election of a blatant anti-Semite in Vienna, where a strong minority of mostly assimilated Jews lived and worked, was contrary to the Empire's equal treatment of minorities that glued the polyglot Austro-Hungarian Empire together. After two years from his election and pressure on the Emperor in 1897, caused him to succumb to this 'populist' Mayor who took office. Pope Leo XIII intervened to support Lueger. The Ring Road ('Ringstrasse') around Vienna is still named after Karl Leuger. His party was a union of the German National and Christian Social factions and became the seeds of the Nazi Party. Hitler was born in Austria and influenced by Lueger. A crowd photograph of this period includes a youthful Hitler in Vienna.

200 delegates form 17 countries were women who were not allowed to vote until the next World Zionist Congress in 1898. Herzl wrote in his diary that year, *"At Basle, I founded the Jewish State."* This was followed by a stream of annual and biennale Zionist Congresses in Basle and elsewhere[114].

The idea of annual World Congresses was adapted by Herzl from the noted America's experience of delegated Congresses that was a democratic key to yanking America's independence from Britain. Herzl, a visionary, organized national congresses across the diaspora made up of delegates from every region and every political fraction and every Jewish organization. In turn, these national congresses would vote to send delegates to the annual World Zionist Congress.

Democratic selection of delegates to democratic rules of procedure and policies were baked into Herzl's Zionist idea of 'Israel' and the return of exile for Jews to the 'Holy Land' from the onset.

The Dreyfus Affair uncovered the deep core of anti-Semitism splitting the French Republic. Émile Zola published 'J'accuse', a polemic against the bias in French military and political establishment. Zola was convicted of slandering the French military and left France before being jailed. Read *'The Disappearance of Émile Zola'* (Faber and Faber, 2017) who fled to England until he was allowed to return to his France. Anti-Semitism was alive and well in France.

114   It was Herzl who decided that the recognition of a Jewish 'homeland' under international law required the construction of democratic, secular based institutions like the Zionist Congress and the Jewish National Fund. The Jewish political experience was steeped in democratic institutions and practices to prepare for statehood and legal recognition. Like the elements of classical music of which Herzl was a devout fan, he embedded his Zionist vision with an opening exposition incorporating a central theme, repetition, and then a climax. He made the first case in the 20th century for institutional democracy building as a precursor to a democratic state by creating annual Congresses with a recurring central theme – return to the Promised Land with Jerusalem as its 'eternal' capital. Some Jewish Orthodox sects bitterly opposed Herzl and Zionism which they believed was a break from the biblical prophecy that there could be no Jewish state in the Holy Land until the coming of the 'Messiah'. Others like Ger Rebbes and some of their followers made 'aliyah' (going up) to the Palestine before WWII. The 'Imrei Emes', the fourth Ger Rebbe of the Ger dynasty in Poland and a co-student and colleague of my grandfather, co-founded Agudas Israel to foster Jewish education in Poland. Agudas Israel went on to become the most powerful Orthodox Jewish organization and one of the most influential orthodox political forces in Israel, as it is today.

Herzl's stunning clarity of vision was premised on his theses that Jews could only receive equality of treatment with 'sovereignty' and recognition under international law in a state of their own. Assimilation, even rights to citizenship or religious fervour was not the answer to anti-Semitism. 'Equality' could only be achieved by the relentless practice of democratic principles gained from the work done by delegates at each annual congress, adapted from the American experience. From selection of delegates, to voting procedures, to creating democratic institutions could the return to the 'Promised Land' be possible and viable. Herzl's organization genius rallied World Zionism (Zionism means Temple Mount in Jerusalem) in a few short years that mesmerized and unified the divided Diaspora of Jews from every religious sect and every shade of political ideology - left to right. All this, he accomplished without the benefit of 'mass media' or major funds. Herzl's ideas and words spread like wildfire through the ubiquitous Yiddish press across Europe and the Americas. Every opinion would be considered in these congregations where raucous debates took place before decisions were taken and implemented. 'E Pluribus Unum.[115, 116]

Herzl understood the power of unifying symbols. The first Congress approved a national anthem – Hatikvah (The Hope). The Second Zionist Congress elected delegates climbed to over 600 as the diverse groups

---

115   The best example of democracy building in the 20th century is Israel. The organizing idea was called 'auto-emancipation' coined by Ahad Ha'am, a Zionist writer and polemist who preceded Herzl. Israel's democracy was built from the bottom, up from ordinary people to the leadership, a history that should be carefully studied by other budding democracies.

116   Israel today practices robust, sometimes painful minute democratic processes – 'a light into the nations' as the Bible taught and the only relentless democracy in the Middle East where every voter demand to be heard, and sometimes is! It enjoys a robust press, strong unions, excellent accessible education, health care, women's rights, gay rights, minority rights and independent judiciary that cover the political spectrum from healthcare, to defense policy, to economic and foreign policy, all in open sometimes raucous always serious debates in the Knesset, Israel's parliament, located in the heart of Jerusalem.

Martin Luther King Jr., in 1968 after the Six Day War: "*I see Israel, and don't mind saying it, as one of the great outposts of democracy in the world, and a marvelous example of what can be done. How desert land almost can be transformed into an oasis of brotherhood and democracy. Peace for Israel means security and that security must be a reality...*" King also equated an attack on Zionism as 'anti-Semitism'.

and countries sent representatives. In 1900, for the first time, the Zionist Congress was held in London, England while Jews were fleeing Russian pogroms and anti-Semitic persecution especially from Romania was felt by every Jew. Zionism's main thrust for public support shifted from continental Europe to England.

1900 witnessed the birth of the Jewish National Fund (JNF), an international charitable fund dedicated to buying unoccupied land and forestation and cultivation of the arid lands in desolate Palestine. JNF became the first green movement in the 20th century. Every Jewish family I knew kept a blue and white can (a *'pushkah'*) or two to deposit coins for this cause.

Thereafter at the Fifth (1901), Sixth (1903), the Seventh (1905) Zionist Congresses that ended with a eulogy to Herzl who had passed away – Zionist Jews re-shifted the emphasis from Uganda proposed by England rather than Palestine as the 'homeland' for the Jews. Henceforth the idea of 'return to the Holy Land' never wavered amongst Jews scattered in a diaspora around the globe. *"If I forget thee, O Jerusalem, let my right hand forget her cunning."* - Jews have pledged and repeated at their annual Passover Seder celebrations throughout the centuries since the first diaspora before the birth of Christ and they simply refused to forget.[117, 118, 119]

---

117 The Zionist movement's extensive international recognition for a Jewish homeland in all of Palestine started formally with the Balfour Declaration in 1917. Then after WW I the San Remo Treaty approved by the League of Nations in 1922 granted all of Palestine west of the Jordan River as a 'homeland' for the Jews. . At the same time, Britain reneged in its promise to grant all of Palestine as a 'homeland for the Jewish people'. Palestine, east of Jordan, was awarded to the Arabs as the Kingdom of Transjordan under the Hashemite King Abdullah for his participation in the WWI on the side of the British against Germany. Abdullah and his brother Faisal 'of 'Lawrence of Arabia' fame had led the revolt against the Ottoman Turks who sided with Germany. Faisal was awarded the Kingship of Syria. This was opposed by the French. Abdullah, gave up his Kingdom in Syria and gained the Kingship in Iraq (together with Transjordan, Syria and Iraq, the Arabs were granted sovereignty over more than 90% of Palestine including the rich oil resources). The San Remo Treaty granted all of Palestine to the Jews, was ratified by all the western powers including Canada. When the League of Nations was replaced by the United Nations after World War II, all treaties and obligations by the League was acceded by the UN and remains part of UN legal obligations, unamended, to this day, including the San Remo Treaty of 1920. Under conventional international law, both east and west Jerusalem never occupied by

In 1907, Henri Bergson, a French philosopher, published '*Creative Evolution*', drawing parallels with Darwin theories of plant, bird and animal evolution.

the Palestinians but by the Jordanians, the West Bank now occupied by the PLO is 'disputed territory'! Under conventional international law, any country is not inhibited from recognizing Jerusalem as Israel's capital as the United States did in 2018, nor the Golan Heights captured after Syria attacked Israel.

118   The Zionists vigorously supported the Allies in World War I which in turn led to the Balfour Declaration in 1917 by the British government under the Liberal Lloyd George. George considered himself a Zionist as did numerous other leading politicians from both the Conservatives and Liberals like Winston Churchill. C.P. Scott, the editor of the liberal '*Manchester Guardian*' led his paper to become the leading advocate for Zionism. Lloyd George had written to his brother in January 1917, "*I am looking forward to achieving something generations of the chivalry of Europe failed to accomplish*" (a Jewish homeland for the Jews in Palestine). In 1919, Balfour, after meeting U.S.A. Supreme Court Judge Louis Brandeis, an American Zionist leader, wrote to Brandeis, "*Of course, these are the reasons that make you and me such ardent Zionists.*" Palestine, before World War I, was a province under the sovereignty of the Ottoman Empire. The Ottoman Empire supported Germany in WWI. Palestine became a British mandate under the League of Nations after WWI. Zionists throughout the world and Palestine supported the Allies. Chaim Weizmann, a young immigrant from Russia, settled in England and became a scientist at Manchester University, where he made a significant contribution to the British war effort in World War I. In 1946, at the World Zionist Organization, a conflict arose about procedure. Weizmann correctly assessed there was a question of his leadership. Rather than be compromised, he resigned to be replaced by a committee led by David Ben-Gurion, his major antagonist on the policy direction of the Zionist movement. The Zionist movement was politically divided by socialists led by Ben-Gurion and the Revisionists led by Ze'ev Jabotinsky which political divide continues to this day. Both Weizmann and Ben-Gurion conspired with the British after Jabotinsky who was expelled from Palestine by the British administration in 1930 for alleged violent acts, never proven, to keep him out of Palestine to weaken the growing political power of the Revisionist Party he founded and led. Jabotinsky died in 1940 in New York City. His bones were later reburied in Israel in 1964 on Mount Herzl Cemetery. Nate Silver, a Polish immigrant and law client of mine in Toronto, who later settled in Israel was an avid Revisionist supporter of Begin gave me long lectures on this aspect of Israel's history that was muted if not submerged in Ben-Gurion's historical versions of Israel's founding steps.

119   Chaim Weizmann, no longer President of WZO remained Zionism's leading advocate, later convinced Harry Truman in 1947 to support the UN vote and

In 1909, Martin Buber broke through as a leading Jewish philosopher when he published his *Ecstatic Confessions: The Heart of Mysticism* challenging rationality with mysticism, the various forms of which are contained in all theologies. In that first decade, Buber published a stream of books about Jewish teachers and mystics and others including *The Tales of Rabbi Nachman* (of Bratislava) (*Rabbi* means teacher), *The Legend of the Baal Shem Tov*, and *The Sayings and Parables of Chung Tzu*. In the process, he opened new vistas of thought for Jews and Christians and Muslims alike while he explored the mystical interior of individuals as the contest between the inner turmoil and outer serenity of the individual and the endless, daily, internal struggle between vice and virtue. Also in this process, the Jewish rationalization between science and biblical revelation began by Maimonides centuries earlier was modernized and advanced. The 20th century conflict between collective conformity and individual free will erupted with articulate advocates on both sides of this intellectual divide[120].

---

recognize Israel. He went on to become Israel's first President selected by his sometimes adversary and rival David Ben-Gurion, the first Prime Minister of Israel. The President of Israel's powers are limited to advice much like the Crown in Canada. Ben-Gurion was a polymath who spoke and wrote over 12 languages from Arabic, European and Slavic languages, Greek and Latin. His modest two-storey home in Tel Aviv, on a street named after him, contains four libraries of over 20,000 volumes, maintained now as a museum.

120 Vladimir 'Zeev' Jabotinsky, born in Odessa in 1880, an early Zionist writer, orator and polemicist, who is considered the founder of the Zionist stream of Revisionism, never ceded the idea of one united Israel including west and east of the Jordan River as the 'Jewish homeland' was promised for all of Palestine, on both sides of the Jordan, in the 1917 Balfour Declaration then was unilaterally limited to all the territories west of the Jordan River as agreed by the San Remo Treaty of 1922 by the victorious allies or ratified by the League of Nations and all its members including Canada. Considered by some a liberal democrat, Jabontinsky preached: *"Every man is a leader, every man, a king."* contributing to democratic activism that is part and parcel of life in Israel. 'Jabo' as he was called served for a time was a British army officer who had organized 'Betar', a youth movement dedicated to Jewish self defense in Europe between the wars. He was the key founder of the Jewish self-defence movement first in Poland, then in Palestine leading to the Jewish Legion in World War I a precursor to the Israeli Defense Force – the Haganah.

The second International Peace Conference held at Hague deeply influenced the Zionist movement. At the 1905 Zionist Congress welcomed a Russian born English chemist teaching at Manchester University, Chaim Weizmann, who thereafter rose to become the leading advocate for the Jewish homeland in Palestine. During WWI, Weizmann used his inventive chemical scientific skills, especially in explosives, on behalf of the Allied Cause. Weizmann, a biochemist developed acetone that was critical to mass manufacturing of explosive devices[121]. From a tiny acorn, a mighty oak tree grows[122].

Under his leadership, Jews lobbied to form a Jewish Regiment within the British army. Finally the Zion Mule Corps was formed and saw service in the disastrous Battle of Gallipoli and were then allowed to form units in other established British regiments to be called the Jewish Legions. Menachem Begin was his fervent follower and followed Jabotinsky's policies until the first peace accord with P.L.O. engineered by Jimmy Carter in Washington in 1978.

121   In WWI, Britain was desperate for explosive materials for their extensive land and sea heavy weaponry. Weizmann from his laboratory at Manchester University developed a synthetic inexpensive source for acetone used in cordite that had explosive power but would not overheat the gun barrels. Extensive distillation processes were necessary, mostly from maize, then in scarce supply in Britain. Distillers in Canada and U.S.A. were engaged where maize was plentiful. A major distillery owned by Gooderham and Worts located in the Distillery District in Toronto contributed to this war effort providing 1,000 tons of acetone and other distillates a year compared to 253 tons produced in Britain in 1917. Weizmann was at heart a scientist. Every advance leads to another, he believed. His breakthrough work on distillation and separation of micro-organisms led to modern distillations in the manufacture of antibiotics and vitamins. In 1934, when he settled in the Holy Land, he headed a new research institute later named the Weizmann Institute and where his home can be found, kept as a museum.

122   The relentless political squabbles between different Zionist factions and diverse democratic groups from left to right dominated each Congress. Weizmann himself was a victim when he resigned as President of WZO in 1946 and became a respected elder statesman. Later he was made first President of the State of Israel. An excellent primer in the squabbles between different fractions can be found in the biography of 'Lioness: Golda Meir and the Nation of Israel' (Schocken, 2017) who became the first woman Minister of Defense and the Prime Minister of Israel, one of the first females in the world elected to hold the leadership of any democracy.

If Herzl was the visionary who envisaged Israel as a secular modern democracy at every level of life, Weizmann held an equally compelling corollary to the modern democratic state. He advocated from the turn of the century at Zionist Congress after Congress the early establishment of a modern secular university to educate the population in the liberal arts and sciences. And in 1917, 50 years before the establishment of the State of Israel, Weizmann laid the first foundation stone to Hebrew University and supervised 12 others (the twelve stones each to represent a tribe of Israel). In 1922, in the presence of a distinguished local group representing all faiths and an equally distinguished group of international politicians and academics including Winston Churchill, the then Colonial Secretary, Lord Balfour who gave a stunning inaugural address to the 7,000 assembled audience. Then Weizmann opened the doors to the newly constructed Hebrew University on Mount Scopus overlooking Jerusalem. There were three academic divisions – Jewish studies, Math and Science.

The foundation stones of the State of Israel were earlier imbedded in 1900 at the World Zionist Congress. Democratic institutions, an independent judiciary, a free press, independent unions, secular education, scientific research, reclamation of desolate mosquito infested swamps, planting trees, agricultural settlements mostly in desert areas, self-sufficiency and self-defence, the templates of the modern democratic state. Most remarkable was the revival of the ancient language of Hebrew that became the cultural gravity that bound the vast linguistic diversity of Jews from the diaspora together as a united people[123, 124].

---

123 Jews in the west from the turn of the 20th century were divided in their beliefs in Zionism prior to the formation of Israel in 1947. There were four main camps – religious Zionism, labour-socialist Zionism, revisionist Zionism and anti-Zionism. In Canada, there were three transparent organizations - Mizrachhi (religious), Histadrut (labour-socialist) that overlapped the Worker's Farbund) (labour socialist communist) and the Revisionists inspired by Jabotinsky and led by Menachem Begin, the 'Irgun Ze'ev Leumi' – a military underground group in Palestine before the establishment of Israel in 1948.

The Grafstein family loyalties were likewise divided. My father, Solomon (Simcha) was an ardent activist in Mizrachi of Canada (religious Zionism), my uncle Max (Melech) was a key organizer, leader and speaker with Histadrut of Canada

In the 1900's, women's rights took a leap forward when France legalized divorce opening the door wider for women's rights. The suffragette movement was on the march in Europe and America.

(socialist-labour Zionism) while my uncle Morris (Moishe) was an active, if muted, supporter and fundraiser for the Irgun (Revisionist Zionism). Of course, the anti-Zionists Jews were vocal but less visible. They believed that Zionism called in question their loyalty to Canada. Most large Canadian Jewish family contained similar political fissures.

124　No better historic example of the absurd exists than the controversy surrounding the 'Western Wall' or 'Wailing Wall' or 'Kotel' located at the base of Temple Mount in Jerusalem considered the holiest site in Judaism. The Temple Mount is the site of King Solomon's Temple (circa 960 BCE). Destroyed by the Babylonians, it was replaced by the Second Temple (circa 560 BCE) and was laid to waste by the Romans under Titus (circa 70 BCE). The Temple is not mentioned in the Quran. The Al-Aqsa Mosque – the Dome of the Rock considered the third holiest site in Islam as Muhammad, according to legend, rode to heaven on his horse was constructed on the top of the Temple Mount (circa 621 A.D.). The Al Aqsa Mosque is not mentioned in the Quran. The Grand Mufti of Jerusalem in the 1920's started the narrative that it was one of the holiest Muslim sites. Until then, it was just one of the numerous Muslim mosques built over Christian or Jewish places of worship well after Muhammad's death.

Jews, over the centuries, though barred from time to time, have prayed at this ancient wall inserting small hand-written paper notes into the crevices of the large foundation stones from the Second Temple. Jews persisted in the practice through the ages.

In 1920, Jews were allowed periodic access to the Wall via a narrow walkway littered with refuse from close adjacent houses. In 1928, 137 Jews at prayers were killed and 335 injured by attacks inspired by the Grand Mufti of Jerusalem and his circle, early adherents of the Muslim Brotherhood. From time to time, rocks and refuse were flung down on the Jews praying. The issue went to the League of Nations. Petitions were sent to King George V. And in 1931, permission was reluctantly granted by the King of Jordan for restricted access. In 1948, Jews were expelled from the site by the Jordanians, considered the custodians of the Temple Mount until 1967. Jordanians invaded and occupied East Jerusalem in 1948. On June 10, 1967 after a short savage battle with soldiers from neighbouring Muslim states, Israel gained control of all of Jerusalem and created an open space for prayers and meditation from the narrow garbage and refuse crowded walkway – till then a desecrated Jewish holy site.

In 2017, President Trump became the first sitting President to visit and pray at the Western Wall. Previously George N. Bush, Bill Clinton, George W. Bush and

The turn of the 20th century brought an outburst of not only exciting new music and dance, but books. The number of libraries in England increased to 352, double the previous number a decade earlier. The number of books published doubled from 1896 to 1911 from 26 to 54 million in England alone.

Barack Obama each visited as private citizens. John Diefenbaker as former Prime Minister of Canada was the first Canadian Prime Minister to visit Jerusalem after his retirement. During that visit, he said Canada that should recognize Jerusalem as Israel's capital. I was present in Jerusalem in 1973 when John Diefenbaker, then a former Prime Minister, made this declaration. In 2018, Prince William became the first member of the British Royal Family to visit Jerusalem and pray at the Wailing Wall.

Though annexed by Israel in 1967 after Israel was invaded again, when it was considered 'terra incognita' – ' disputed territory' – or 'released territory' under conventional international law, the Western Wall is still considered by most countries as 'occupied territory' though it is not clear what the designation means as the site was never occupied or controlled by Palestinians. The Dome of the Rock was placed under the custodian of the Kings of Jordan. President Trump in 2018 implemented a long stretch unanimous Resolutions of Congress recognizing Jerusalem as Israel's capital and opened its embassy there in May 2018 followed several days later by Guatemala, the second country to do so. Guatemala was the second country to recognize the State of Israel in 1948. Later President Trump recognized the Golan Heights annexation by Israel. For a comprehensive and definitive view of international law on this issue, read *The Legal Foundation and Borders of Israel Under International Law*' by Howard Grief (Mazo Publications, 2008). The Western Sahara Desert in North Africa between Algeria and Morocco is also considered disputed territory under international law.

For a different narrative from a Palestinian perspective, read *The Hundred Years' War on Palestine* by Rashid Khalidi (Metropolitan Books, Henry Holt And Company, New York, 2020). While ignoring the history of conquest by the Romans, Christians and Muslims by Saladin in 1120, the author starts history of the 'Holy Land' in the last 100 years. 'Occupation' becomes inflated beyond recognition in international law. Yet the author presents a full review of the divisions of the Arab states without Palestine and the divisions deep down within Palestine itself. Arabs neglected to build democratic institutions. Arab's maximist demands for One Palestine have been self-defeating and remains the cause of the failure to reach a negotiated settlement from ground up following Israel's example. The author, a participant to many of the failed peace initiatives is fair in his criticism of the deep divisions within the Arab community that continue to this day.

'*Anne of Green Gables*' was first published in 1900 to become a core of Canadian experience, literature and culture. '*Call of Wild*' and '*White Fang*' by Jack London introduced the north to the world. '*The Hounds of Baskerville*' by Arthur Conan Doyle, '*The Wonderful World of Oz*' by L. Frank Baum, '*The Cherry Orchard*' by Anton Chekhov, '*Peter Pan*' by J.M. Barrie, '*Sister Carrie*' by Theodore Dreiser, '*Kim*' by Rudyard Kipling, '*The Phantom of the Opera*' by Gaston Leroux, '*Up from Slavery*' by Booker T. Washington, '*The Souls of Black Folk*' by C.B. DuBois, '*Youth*' included in a volume called '*Youth, A Narrative*' by Joseph Conrad, '*The First Men in the Moon*' by H.G. Wells, '*The Importance of the Voter*' by Emily Parkhurst in 1908. Bestsellers from 1900 to 1910 included '*The Four Feathers*' by A.E.W. Mason, '*The Scarlet Pimpernel*' by Baroness Orczy and '*The Blue Lagoon*' by Henry De Vere Stacpoole - all entered popular culture in that first decade and resonated with increasing impact throughout the rest of the 20ᵗʰ century. Our outlook and actions were shaped by these classic and popular words of literature.

It was the '*Heart of Darkness*' by Joseph Conrad, a Polish born writer who learned English after immigrating to England before the turn of the century, published in 1900, that opened western eyes to the horrific practice of black slavery and barbaric murders, the first mass murders and genocide in the 20ᵗʰ century, especially under the aegis of King Leopold II of Belgium's privately owned colony in Congo that led major powers to compel Leopold II to give the Congo independence in 1908[125].

And in 1900, four remarkable writers, Joseph Conrad, Rudyard Kipling, Ford Maddox Ford and Henry James, all lived within miles of each other in the lovely English countryside of Kent and Sussex honing and deepening their literacy skills with letters and visits to each other. George Bernard Shaw, barely scratching out a living, supported by the founders of Fabianism, the Webbs, gave him cheap room and board, when he wrote '*Major Barbara*', a feminist play in 1905 leading to his breakthrough as playwright and political activist. Emily Pankhurst founded the Women's Social Polit-

---

125 The fruits of Leopold II's illegal riches can be visibly seen today in his family's massive gated estate next to Cap D'Antibe on the Coté d'Azur - the lush southern coastline of France.

ical Union – an all women suffragette organization to advocate and wrote '*My Own Story*' that ignited the fight for women's right to vote in 1903 and solidified the suffragette surge towards women's rights. "*Deeds not words*", she demanded.... still a useful political mantra.

In June 1908 in London, a remarkable march to promote and protect women's rights took place headed to the Royal Albert Hall that numbered over 10,000 women. A group of 1,000 within the crowd marchers hoisted heavy silk banners naming famous women, especially women authors like Elizabeth Barrett Browning, Mary Wollstonecraft and most interesting an author, almost a century old, Jane Austen. Women's marches have taken a different turn.

And in 1904, Sir Wilfrid Laurier declared the 20th century belongs to Canada and so it did.

Little noticed and published in 1902 was a booklet written by an obscure Russian revolutionary fresh from release as a political prisoner who changed his name to Vladimir Lenin called '*What Is To Be Done!*' that sets out the revolutionary path for Russia that transformed the 20th century. It was here Lenin broke ranks with other radicals when he advocated a 'dictatorship of the party' to accomplish the Communist goal of a socialist utopia[126].

In 1909, Winston Churchill, as Minister of the Exchequer under the Liberal Prime Minister Lloyd George, introduced the 'People's Budget'.

---

126 All political ideas germinate from deep roots and are constantly adapted to suit the times. Lenin appropriated the title to his booklet '*What Is To Be Done*' from an earlier novel written by N.G. Chernyshevsky. Chernyshevsky was a renown Russian philosopher and leader of the radical 'intelligentsia' (a Russian word) whose searing novel '*What Is To Be Done*' published in 1863 tells the tale of an ascetic revolutionary dedicated to 'socialist' revolution who sacrifices his life for 'the cause'. This book became a classic in the Soviet era. It is said that Lenin was deeply influenced by his works, as it did for others like Dostoyevsky and even Plekhanov. One summer, Lenin, as a youthful student, read it five times searing its lessons in his brain. Lenin had changed his surname from Ulyanov to protect his family when he became a revolutionary. Stalin, who also had changed his name to mimic Lenin, later read it and was deeply influenced by its ideas as was Lenin. So, coincidently both read this book, Lenin first in 1887 and Stalin in 1898. Lenin's 1902 booklet entitled '*What Is To Be Done*' was devoured by millions of communist true believers.

Ten percent of the population earned 80% of the income and owned 80% of the land and so a modest new tax was introduced on income. The top rate of income tax was increased to 5.8% and on incomes higher than £2,000, the rate was increased to 8.3%. The top 0.01% then took in 11% of all income. The estate taxes and others in this budget helped finance welfare reform. Democracies took up the movement to increase taxation on the upper income earners and corporations and never glanced back. In 1916 in Canada, corporate taxes and then income taxes was passed as a 'temporary measure' in 1917 as the Income Tax War Act covering both personal and corporate income.

AFTER 1910: ENTER THE ERA OF THE MODERN ARMS RACE - THE CRUSHING ARRIVAL OF MEGA DEATHS – THE '20S, '30S AND '40S

> *"It is always possible to bind together a considerable number in love, as long as there other people left over to receive the manifestations of their aggressiveness."*
> – Sigmund Freud

Then, with the advent of the second decade of the 20th century, the avalanche of death and destruction after 1910 began to strike with a psychic vengeance. The modern arms race in Europe accelerated unabated with more and more deadly weapons for land, sea and air, from tanks to poison gas to landmines to tanks to dreadnoughts to submarines to aerial bombers and fighter planes. 'Nihilism' then 'anarchism' introduced the age of terror with violent outbursts against innocents across Europe and Asia. Yet the world barely noticed the birth pangs of the 'Age of Terror' in that first decade. The world did take notice of the startling mathematically based discoveries by a little known young patient official called Albert Einstein that became a turning point in world history[127].

---

127 Starting in 1905, the world did take notice of the remarkable papers published by Albert Einstein while a young clerk in a Swiss patent office, in his 20's that led to his Theory of Relativity that turned science upside down, questioned the Newtonian laws of gravity, redefined time and transformed the way we looked at the world above us and questioned quantum physics entering the 20th century mainstream. Einstein's three papers on Brownian motion, the photoelectric effect and the special theory of relativity were each transformative in their field. Led by Einstein, scientists changed the way we perceive our world and time, energy, light, sound and opened new dimensions of perception. Our world has never been the same as he uncovered the thought that the universe around us is ever expanding. Read *'When Einstein Walked With Gödel: Excursions To The Edge of Thought'* by Jim Holt (Farrar, Straus and Giroux, 2018) and *'The Order Of Time'* by Carlo Rovelli (Penguin Publishing

The rise of the most deadly 'isms' followed - Nationalism, Communism, Fascism, Nazism, and the embryo of Islamism each showed their distorted secular and ideological and twisted religious terrorist faces.

Each of these deadly 'isms' had at its core the insatiable lust for power, conformity of ideas, and appetite for endless territorial expansion.

Each 'ism' starts with a search for an imagined 'utopia', a dreamland, and most end in marginalization, death and destruction of the 'other'[128,129].

The Balkan Wars, the Ottoman genocide of Armenians and end of World War I where 17 million lost their lives on the killing fields of France,

---

Group, 2018) whose books give the untutored easy access to this complex material. Holt's book of essays plumbs the origins of Einstein's theory of relativity and the little known scientists behind quantum physics, quantum mechanics, the nature of infinity, the string theories, the ongoing debates and changing perceptions of our universe, the nature of matter and energy, the invention of the atomic and nuclear bombs, and the origins of the computer that transformed the way we interact and deal with our world in the 20th century and beyond. Rovelli writes with clarity about the centrality of time in our times, or what we think is 'time' – still an active debate. Recent photos from the 'Black Holes' in the universe confirm Einstein's theories of 'time', 'light' and 'energy'.

128   Ideology, the desire to shape utopian ideas that can change the course of history, drives politicians' zeal. This begs the question whether history is disrupted by facts, ideas or emotions. The most astute observer of British Parliamentarians political behaviour is the British historian Sir Lewis Namier who wrote, "... *to treat political ideas as the offspring of pure reason should be to assign them a parentage as mythological as Pallas Athene... what matters most is the underlying emotions, the music of which ideas are the mere libretto, too often of a very inferior quality.*"

129   Two towering leaders, each with his vision of utopia, transformed the 20th century. Vladimir Lenin with his dream and ideology of creating the new man, 'the Soviet man' – the Leninist idea that narrow party control of the state could strip man of his religious and cultural beliefs and replace them with a secular bias imbued with principles of equality. President Woodrow Wilson with his idea of nation building via 'self-determination' that could transform man free of old biases by organizing into a collective of modern states to create a peaceful democratic world via an organization like the 'League of Nations; that the U.S. Congress did not support Woodrow. Wilson in 1919 was the second U.S. President to win the Nobel Prize who won his for founding the League of Nations. Read *'1917: Lenin, Wilson, And The Birth Of The New World Disorder'* by Arthur Herman (Harper Collins, 2017). Both ideas, advocated by these two world leaders, resulted in more deaths than at any prior time in history, yet inclined the world towards a progressive direction. War, and the threat of war, more destructive than ever, remains with us.

the Russian Revolution, the murder of the Romanovs – The Russian Imperial family led to a sane period of peace making structure and treaties. After World War I - the 'war to end of all wars' – peace movements sprang up especially in the North American and across Europe led by women groups, 'progressive' political parties, organized labour, libertarian organizations and civil liberation groups. International law from the time of St. Augustine to Hugo Grotius, considered the founder of modern international law in the 17th century, was valorized by the declaration of a 'just war', based mostly on the rationale of a 'just' defense. This was the major 'casus belli' for 'a just war' for centuries. The Geneva Convention and the Hague Protocols had invested international law with new humane norms and rules of treatment of war prisoners and damage to general civilian populations. 'Just war' and 'just defense' continued to be recognized justification for war under international law.

Suddenly these organizing principles underlying international law were disrupted by the ideas of a Chicago commercial lawyer, Salmon Levinson, who after careful study, concluded that international law should be premised on the principle to 'outlaw' war. He persistently wrote articles, essays and pamphlets dedicated to 'outlaw war', placing 'war' beyond the acceptable boundaries of civil society. No 'war', just or otherwise, was acceptable in the modern world. That was a residue of the 'old world order'. John Dewey, a widely respected American teacher, writer and philosopher, helped bring Levinson's ideas to the attention of the public and politicians. Levinson wrote an article in the New Republic[130], a leading Liberal journal, called 'The Legal Status of War' in 1918 that was widely quoted.

In the spring of 1932, Poland evicted Jewish students from Polish universities. At the same time, Jewish citizens were attacked and beaten on the streets of the Polish capital, Warsaw, and in major cities such as Krakow, Lublin, Vilna and Czestochowa. The English 'Jewish Chronicle' editorial at the time declared 'Polish Jewry is on the road to annihilation. Jews had lived in Poland for over a thousand centuries. These outrages took place before Hitler became Germany's Chancellor in 1933 and well before the Nazi invasion of Poland in 1939 with the express agreement of Soviet Russia under Stalin.

130 As a student at Harvard in the '80s, my son Laurence worked as a summer intern for the iconic New Republic then led by Martin Peretz. Later when the New Republic encountered financial difficulties, Laurence became the Chairman and part owner of the New Republic for a time.

The French Prime Minister, Aristide Briand, took up this cause in France and convinced Frank S. Kellogg, the American Secretary of State who had earlier rejected Levinson's ideas, to reconsider. Together they prepared a Treaty called the Briand Kellogg Pact that did precisely that – 'outlaw war'. This Pact came into effect in the United States on July 24, 1929[131]. Congress approved it unanimously with one vote exception.

By then and shortly thereafter, 62 states including the United Kingdom, Germany, France, China, The Soviet Union and Canada ratified the Treaty. This treaty contained the organizing ideas that 'war crimes', 'crimes against peace', 'crimes against humanity' was rooted in mankind's barbaric past. For their efforts, Kellogg and Briand received the 1929 Nobel Peace Prize.

Although the United States Congress made no changes to the Treaty when it first approved it, later Congress passed a law that interpreted the Treaty as not affecting America's 'right to self defense'[132]. One consequence in the United States was a string of Neutrality Acts passed by Congress from the mid to late '30s that hamstrung Roosevelt to slake American appeasement and help Britain at the outset of World War II (see footnote 144).

No recourse to war is still the law of the land of each ratifying state. When World War II was declared by the Canadian Parliament in September 1939, only one Member of Parliament, J.S. Woodsworth, leader of the CCF (now NDP) voted against it.

---

131   The Briand Kellogg Pact as it was known was formally titled 'General Pact for the Denunciation of War'. There were only two major short articles.

"*Article 1: The High Contracting Parties voluntarily declare in the names of their respective peoples that they condemn recourse to war for the solution of international controversies, and renounce it, as an institution of national policy in their relations with one another.*
Article 2: The High Contracting Parties agree that the settlement or solutions of all disputes or conflicts of whatever nature or whatever origin they may be, which may arise among them, shall never be sought except by pacific means."

132   Japan imbedded in its post-World War II Constitution a prohibition against war as did some others.

The animating principles embedded in the Briand Kellogg Treaty continued to reverberate throughout the balance of the 20th century[133]. How effective they were remains for history to judge. Peace movements continued to proliferate throughout the entire 20th century yet had little impact or a prophylactic effect as millions upon millions were slaughtered in wars between states and within states.

Meanwhile in 1928, as the Paris Accords dedicated to 'outlaw' war was gaining momentum, the Muslim Brotherhood was founded by an Egyptian Islamist thinker and activist, Hassan Al Banna. In its ideology as proposed by Al Banna, declared 'war' as a means of erasing non-believers and to cleanse the world of 'impurity' was both a political and religious objective. Muslims have been at war amongst themselves since Muhammad's death and his acolytes were split into two – Sunni and Shiites. These two divisions in the Muslim faith has been the source of more Muslim deaths from within Muslim followers than without. This lens is necessary to understand the history of the Muslim faith and its impact on the modern era.

In 1954, Yassid Qutb, also an Egyptian Islamist scholar and an adherent to the Muslim Brotherhood, while imprisoned by Nassar wrote and published a short exegesis in Arabic entitled '*Milestones*', later translated in English as '*Signposts on the Road*'). This slender volume became one of the most influential books in the last half of the 20th century and inspired the Al Qaeda and Isis whose leaders Osama Bin Laden and Ayman al Zawahiri who were both faithful adherents of the Muslim Brotherhood. Other groups, the Hezbollah in Lebanon, the Hamas in Gaza and the Houthis in Yemen became activist followers of the Muslim Brotherhood and 'jihadi' fighters following Qutb and Al Banna's ideas.

So while one ideology in the Paris Accords in 1928 sought to 'outlaw' war, war as the means to a political end, another encouraged a contesting ideology for its followers to believe that global conquest by war was necessary to achieve their political and religious aims.

---

133 The key legal basis for prosecuting Nazi leaders at Nuremburg after World War II and Japanese leaders at the Tokyo Trials a year later was the charge that these leaders had committed the crime of 'aggressive war' under the Paris Pact of 1928. This was to avoid the legal defense of retroactive criminal law enforcement.

A brief background to these two Muslim leaders. In 1906, both these two men were born in Egypt in different circumstances, one Qutb from impoverished roots, the other Al Banna from a middle class distinguished family of scholars. Both became ideological leaders of the 'jihad' movement that rumbled through the 20th century with increasing intensity and violence. When Hassan Al Banna founded the Muslim Brotherhood in 1928, his aim from the outset was to establish the Muslim faith under Sharia Law around the globe. Sayyid Qutb's career, with fragile health and limited means, took a different turn. Qutb spent several years in the late '40s in the United States as a university student in Colorado. There he encountered prejudice as a result of his dark skin and while observing the American way of life sharpened his disgust with what he considered the licentiousness and depravity in the western civilization. On his return to Egypt, now a key thinker in the Muslim Brotherhood, he wrote, starting in 1951 until 1965, 30 volumes, starting with the first volume published in 1954. This magnus opus was entitled *'In the Shade of the Qur'an'*[134]. Then in 1964, he published a slender volume in Arabic called *'Milestones'* or later in English translation *'Signposts on the Road'* that had a major global impact on Islamist adherents.

Hassan Al Banna was assassinated, it is believed by Egyptian authorities, in 1949. Sayyid Qutb was executed by Nassar in 1966 for his opposition to Nassar's secularism that he believed had polluted Islamist ideology.

Both advocated throughout their lives the global expansion of Islamism via 'jihad' as a means of Muslim exceptionalism[135,136].

So in the late '20s and '30s, waves of economic and violent unrest continued unabated[137,138]. The League of Nations dedicated to peace and

---

134   Qutb's 30 volume *'In the Shade of+ the Qur'an'* matched the 30 sections of the Quran was published in English in a 30 volume set in 2017 by Kube Publishing Ltd.

135   Two quotes, one from Qutb and one from Al Banna encapsulate their ideas. Qutb: *"Islam cannot accept or agree to a situation which is half Muslim and half 'jahillyya' (separate from God)"*. Al Banna: *"It is the nature of Islam to dominate, not be to be dominated, it imposes its law on all nations the extent of its power..."*

136   For a more extensive concise discussion of these two Muslim leaders, read *'The Internationalists: How A Radical Plan To Outlaw War Remade The World'* by Oona A. Hathaway and Scott J. Sharpiro (Simon and Schuster, 2017), especially chapter 17.

137   With the great market crash in 1929, the world's economics, just beginning to interconnect, began to tumble and reverberate from America around the globe. Winston Churchill by happenstance was a guest of the New York Stock Exchange and

peaceful reconciliation of disputes between nations, continued to falter[139]. The eruption of Communism in China with founding of Communist Party of China in 1921 led to civil war, the Arab uprisings, Arab attacks on Jewish farming communities in Palestine, the Japanese invasion of China (most ghastly was the pillage, rape and massacre of Nanking where it is estimated 200,000 to 300,000 were massacred and 80,000 women were sexually assaulted by Japanese troops), the Italian invasion of Ethiopia that weakened the League of Nations, the Spanish Civil War, the Lenin and Stalin rural collectivization programs in the '20s and '30s that resulted in starva-

---

witnessed the crash overlooking the trade floor. Economic nostrums failed and exacerbated the 'Great Depression'. People lost their homes, their life savings and were driven to desperation. The '30s political machinations cannot be understood without the impact of the Great Depression, that started in United States, moved across the Americas north and south and then into Europe, east and west. Every continent was detrimentally effected. The rise of the miserable 'isms' of Communism, Nazism and Fascism was baked in the economic downtown in the world's economics. Only war and the race for armaments raised the world's economic profile in the late '30s and the '40s and moved especially North America to growth and full employment.

138   In America, the depression also provoked a flood of great novels; William Faulkner's novels including 'The Sound and The Fury', Hart Crane's 'The Bridge', John Dos Passos 'U.S.A.', Katherine Anne Porter 'Flowering Judas', F. Scott Fitzgerald's 'Tender Is The Night', John Steinbeck's 'The Grapes of Wrath', Nathanael West's 'The Day of The Locust', Richard Wright's 'Native Son', Ernest Hemingway's 'For Whom The Bells Toll' and my favourite Henry Roth's 'Call It Sleep'. Each book is a timeless feast. It is a fact of history wherever deep fissures appear in society, after a brief period, literature, music and art begin to fill the cracks.

139   December 11, 1931 was a date often overlooked and little celebrated in Canadian history. The Statute of Westminster was approved by the British Parliament establishing Canada, Australia and South Africa along with New Zealand as independent sovereign states still connected to the Queen and Commonwealth and the residual British Empire. Canada's independence marks the evolution of the Canada Dominion as a sovereign nation still with bonds to Britain yet free to make its own decisions of statehood. A lesson in history, rarely repeated by other nations, which usually failed to reach peaceful transitions to self-governing democracies.

Evolution from the British Empire branded its principles of the rule of law into Canada's national psyche is a lasting constitution to Canada's independence as a sovereign state.

Mackenzie King contributed to the League's weakness and demise when he forbade Canada's representative to support action against Mussolini's invasion of Ethiopia.

tion and death of untold millions, the Holodomor in Ukraine, the regular
Stalinist purges and mass murders ('The Great Terror') assisted by Stalin's
formation of the Gulag network across Siberia[140], failed to neutralize
Communist fellow travelers in Europe and America - everywhere – considered by the so-called 'left' as a necessary evil to the birth pangs of the new
'Soviet man', the 'Long March' retreat to north-western China led by Mao
Zedong, the 1936 militarization of the Rhineland by the Hitler's Germany,
Hitler's Austrian 'anschluss' in 1937, the 1938 dismemberment of Czecho-
slovakia, all greased by the pervasive odious appeasement movement in
Europe and America (called by some the 'locust years')[141], the infamous

---

140 It is conservatively estimated that the Soviets murdered at least 1,500 established
published writers who perished while imprisoned in the Gulags. Earlier Lenin's
decimation of Russian farmers in the '20s was exceeded by Stalin's policies of
rural collective farms in '30s resulted in over 20 million deaths or more. No actual
numbers have been collated of these collectivist efforts. The Communist ideology
was ingested and advocated amongst a wide range of notables in the west. The
century's earliest four most extravagant dupes were H.G. Wells, George Bernard
Shaw and Sidney and Beatrice Webb (founders of the socialist Fabien movement and
members of the Bloomsbury Set). Wells who after an audience with Stalin in 1934,
Sydney Webb reported he had never *"met a man more candid, fair and honest"*. See
'Koba the Dread: Laughter and the Twenty Million' by Martin Amis (University Press,
2002). Franklin Roosevelt was another Stalin dupe. Read *'Leadership and Failure of
Leadership and How Roosevelt Lost Post WWII to Stalin and Soviet Style Communism'*,
Jerry Grafstein (Mosaic Press, due for release in 2022).

141 Little noticed by the world, the Soviet Politburo, directed personally by Stalin beginning in the '20s, started to 'cleanse' the Soviet Union of its 'most hostile anti-Soviet
elements' targeted against the so-called' Enemies of the People', essentially those
who disagreed with Stalin, his cronies and their belief that they were creating a 'paradise' for the masses by the state religion of Bolshevism or more appropriately based
on Marxist-Leninist ideology with Stalin's innovations after Stalin had consolidated
his leaders. Stalin's personally directed arrests exceeded 767,397 and 386,718 execu-
tions that destroyed families and made their orphans trained by the Soviet State. At
the same time 'ethnic cleansing' commenced on a grand scale that included most of
the Polish Communist Party and their families and friends - 350,000 arrested and
247,157 executed. Other nationalities deported included Kurds, Greeks, Finns, Esto-
nians, Iranians, Latvians, Chinese and Armenians. Included were 4% of the Mongo-
lian population and 6,311 priests and this was just the beginning. Stalin practiced
genocide to fullsome extent before Hitler. Read *'Stalin: The Court of the Red Tsar'* by
Simon Sebag Montefiore (Vantage Books, New York, 2005).

non-aggression Soviet pact[142], the outbreak of most deadly World War II, triggered by the Nazi lightning invasion of Poland[143], then Norway, then

142 Stalin's 1940 non-aggression pact with Hitler was not Stalin's first sellout. In 1927, Stalin signed a non-aggression pact with Chiang Kai-shek resulting in the deaths of countless Chinese including many thousands of Chinese communists. This 1927 Stalinist action has been little noticed in history especially by Communist true believers and their fellow travellers.

143 Time is required to place the turning points in proper perspective. No better case is the role of Poland in the 20th century. Poland, the historic middle ground of Europe between the West and East is a case in point. Poland was populated by an ethnic diversity of Slavs, Scandinavians, Germans, Armenians, Jews and Muslims. Poland was the first country in Europe in 1791 to have passed a written constitution setting out rights especially between town and ennobled gentry. Poland before the 20th century was attacked by French, Germans, Russians and Nordic nations to name a few and fought to preserve the middle space of the 'motherland' and was an early adherent to Catholicism in the 10th century rich in art, culture, literature and science. Madame Curie was a Polish born Nobel Prize winner in the 20th century.

By the birth of the 20th century Poland was host to more churches, synagogues and mosques than anywhere in Europe. It had long and glorious military traditions. It was King John III Sobieski and his Polish forces that saved Vienna in Europe from the invading Turk Muslim forces in 1683. Sobieski was educated in Krakow at one of the oldest universities in Europe – Jagiellonian University founded in 1364 - as was Pope John Paul II in the 20th century. Its motto *"Let reason prevail over force."* It was Piłsudski whose Polish military brigade forces beat the larger and better equipped rampaging Soviet army led by Trotsky intent on advancing across Europe at Battle of Warsaw in 1920 considered one the great battles of the 20th century. It was Poland that fought briefly and bloodily against Nazi and Soviet forces on Polish soil in 1939 leading to World War II. During World War II, 'free' Poles forces, army air force, navy and intelligence fought with the Allied Forces in Europe and the Middle East. In 1943 the 22,000 Polish officer corp was decimated at Katyn by the Soviets. The leader of the Polish air squadron in the 'Battle of Britain' destroyed and damaged more Nazi aircraft than any other. Pilot Tad Kosciuszko - 769 'kills', 177 damaged and 252 not accounted for. Polish army units fought with distinction in Italy and at Normandy and in the Polish battleships in high seas. Polish forces in total were the fourth largest of all Allied Forces and suffered the most per capita. Almost 20% of Polish population, over 6 million including 3 million Jews died. Another 17 million Poles were sent east as slave workers for the Soviets. Still Roosevelt and Churchill deserted the Polish government in exile and despite promises allowed Stalin and his Communist followers to gain power, undemocratically in Poland which led to the Iron Curtain. Only de Gaulle refused despite pressure from Stalin. No nation fought braver and

came Pearl Harbour, a sneak attack by the Japanese on American naval armada anchored there that provoked Roosevelt to declare war against the Japanese and then the Axis as they supported Japan[144]. The Japanese teamed up with the Nazis and the Fascists to create the Axis powers, the world divided and this lightening war broke out on almost every continent[145] that allowed the Nazi and Fascists to trigger the deadly and

receive less than the Poles. Read '*Poland*' by Adam Zamoyski (William Collins, 2009), '*Bitter Glory*' by Richard M. Watt (Simon and Schuster, 1979), '*The Jews In Poland and Russia, Vol. I 1350 to 1881*' by Antony Polonsky (The Littman Library of Jewish Civilization, 2010), '*The Jews In Poland and Russia, Vol. II 1881 to 1914*' by Antony Polonsky (The Littman Library of Jewish Civilization, 2010), '*The Jews In Poland and Russia, Vol. III 1941 to 2008*' by Antony Polonsky (The Littman Library of Jewish Civilization, 2012), '*The Poles*' by Stewart Steven (Macmillan Publishing Co. Inc., 1982), '*Poland 1939: The Outbreak of World War II*' by Roger Moorhouse (Basic Books, 2020).

144   From 1935 to 1939, the U.S. Congress passed four Neutrality Acts responding to the American public's isolationist sentiment. Americans were against intervention in what they considered European squabbles. The public and mass media was in synch. These Neutrality Acts tied Roosevelt's hands politically both against the Japanese led crisis with its invasion of China and Hitler and Mussolini's aggressive acts in Europe. Roosevelt attempted to 'quarantine' the Japanese in the Pacific, cutting off their oil supplies knowing the Japanese would attack and hoping the attack would untie his hands. Roosevelt expected, some historians opine, of the Japanese plans to attack American interests somewhere in the Pacific when Japan did, but chose to ignore the warnings. Meanwhile these same Neutrality Acts tied Roosevelt's hands to help beleaguered United Kingdom after it declared war against Germany and Italy in 1939. Lend Lease, the plan to lease American ships and armaments to the U.K. desperate for financial and armament support, was devised by Roosevelt and his inner circle of advisers to circumvent the Neutrality Laws to give the U.K. vital aid. Meanwhile, as in the prelude to World War I, the Germans sunk American ships in the Atlantic on the way to aid the beleaguered U.K. that helped turn American public opinion against Germany. These Neutrality Laws were not substantially repealed until 1941.

145   In 1941, at Babi Yar, at a scenic grassy ravine near Kiev that I visited when I assisted in monitoring Ukraine's democratic vote after the Soviet Empire dissolved, German troops and their Ukrainian collaborators slaughtered 33,771 Jews, the largest recorded one-day massacre, followed by another over 200,000 from then until 1944. Also in 1944, similar smaller massacres took place; in Odessa, a delightful Ukrainian sea-coast city once populated with a robust minority of Jews including doctors, writers, musicians, sailors, merchants, teachers and artists, where between 25,000 and 34,000 Jews were slaughtered and burned or dumped into the sea.

lethal Holocaust. The Holocaust was *"the worst episode in human history"* – Winston Churchill)[146, 147, 148, 149], two international conferences at Tehran

---

146 In 1984, three years after I became a Senator, Allan MacEachen, the Liberal leader in the Senate, invited me to join the Atlantik-Brücke, a small group of journalists, political scientists, businessmen and parliamentarians from Germany and Canada who met once a year in either Canada or West Germany for several days of discussions on foreign policy and transnational economic issues. The Marshall Plan after WWII fostered organizations like the Atlantik-Brücke (Bridge). These meetings I attended and rigorously participated in for twelve years. Only one participant, John Halstead, a friend and a former Canadian diplomat and gifted writer and academic, predicted the sudden fall of the Berlin Wall in late October of 1989.

During one such meeting in Munich, I had a free morning and decided to take a small walking tour of Munich, a beautiful city with the infamous Nazi past where Hitler started his diabolical rise to power.

I got a small city map from the hotel and went outside in the cold winter air to decide which direction to take. I was astonished to see the word Dachau located at the top of the map about 7 kilometres from the centre of Munich, the distance from King Street to St. Clair Avenue in Toronto. I had thought these death camps were located away from urban centres. I hailed a cab. The 35-year-old driver asked me where I wanted to go and I said Dachau. I never had the desire or curiosity to visit a 'death camp' though most of my father's and mother's vast cousinhood had perished in the Holocaust leaving all but three who had been sent to work camps in Poland and Auschwitz who later emigrated to Canada. The driver said he would wait. I said it wasn't necessary. No, he insisted, he would wait. As I disembarked from the cab, there were two buses full of young jostling teenagers with their two teachers entering the gates ahead of me. I decided to follow them through the camp. The youthful chatter slowly turned to silence as the teenagers walked through the wooden barracks and the gruesome pictures and artifacts. Once we arrived at the crematories, down a pleasant tree-lined path that it looked like a rustic red brick train station, there was a morbid silence. Finally when we emerged to catch our breath, I spoke to the two German teachers who told me that they did this with each class every year. The reaction of students was always the same – first cheerful exchanges, to silences, to tears and sobbing. When I left the gates of Dachau, I was exhausted, drained and speechless. My cab driver was waiting. As I climbed in the back, he looked at me and said, *"I knew that you would need a lift back to the hotel."*

147 Of the growing list of histories about the Holocaust was a recent one volume called *'In the Name of Humanity – The Secret Deal to End the Holocaust'* by Max Wallace (Allen Lane, 2017). This is a compelling tale of how one Orthodox Jewish woman living in Switzerland during WWII created a network of Jews and non-Jews to rescue Jews

and Yalta[150], the Allied invasion of Europe in June 1944[151], the island war in the Pacific that the war-weary Allies refused to accept only unconditional

---

destined for liquidation and the opposition she encountered from western governments and even Jewish community organizations to achieve her objectives.

148 By early 1943, clear evidence of the 'Final Solution' hatched at the Wannsee Conference near Berlin by Heydrich Reinhardt and Adolf Eichmann and other senior Nazi leaders in January 1942 flooded the west, Russia, especially in the United States and Britain. No action was taken. Delay was the order of the day. By the end of 1943, 4 million Jews were murdered by the Nazi and their collaborators especially in the death camps. By the middle of 1942, Auschwitz was re-engineered with far four new more efficient crematoria. 2,705 Jews were cremated every hour in Auschwitz alone. Meanwhile in the United States, a senior government official dismayed by proposed bureaucratic delays wrote a lengthy detailed memo to his superiors entitled 'The Acquiescence of the Government to the Murder of the Jews'. Finally President Roosevelt established the 'War Refugee Board' and 200,000 Jews were rescued by the end of the war with meagre government support. More Jews were killed in one day than all the Allied soldiers on the Beaches of Normandy. Could the Allies who had clear evidence including aerial photographs of Jews lined up to enter the crematories have done more? Could they have easily bombed the rail lines into the death camps? This answer seems clear. Yes. See '1944 – FDR and the Year That Changed The World' by Jay Winik (Simon and Schuster, 2015). General George Marshall, never considered a friend of Jews or Jewish aspirations to establish a Jewish homeland in what was then Palestine refused to allow Allied Forces to bomb the railways to the 'death' camps arguing it would be a diversion of military resources. Roosevelt agreed. Not really.

149 Recent calculations by researchers in Israel and elsewhere in 2019 have concluded that the six million Jewish victims was underestimated. The horrendous number of Jewish deaths is much greater, by a considerable magnitude. No doubt this research will continue. Before a leading Jewish historian Simon Dubnow was shot by the Nazis in World War II, he admonished his co-religionists "to record, record!"

150 Roosevelt convinced Stalin, playing the reluctant debutante, to meet him and Churchill first at Tehran and then Yalta to meet. Roosevelt's aim was to get Stalin to join the United Nations and to get Russia to declare war on Japan. Stalin by all accounts, the master negotiator ended up with Eastern Europe's hegemony. Meanwhile in Asia again by Roosevelt's miscalculations lost China and parts of Asia to Mao and his Communist cadres. Both were turning points in the history of the 20th century.

151 A most disputed issue still not clarified by history is the ramifications of the WWII quarrel between Churchill and Roosevelt who supported Stalin's early and incessant requests to relieve the Soviets on the eastern Russian front starting at the beginning of 1942 after the Soviet/Nazi agreement had collapsed when Hitler invaded Russia. Till then, Russia had occupied Poland and others parts of Eastern Europe. Stalin had

surrender. Other western nations exhausted by war chose to ignore Churchill's early warning of the fall of the 'Iron Curtain', in 1946. After the atomic bombs fell on Hiroshima and Nagasaki in Japan, these first atomic bomb attacks on civilian targets brought World War II to a sudden close in 1945[152, 153, 154, 155]. With the end of the war, a new lexicon entered the vocabu-

---

his strategic eye on Eastern Europe, the Baltics and the Balkans early in the war. Churchill was caught between Roosevelt and Stalin and the U.K. domestic leaders like Stafford Cripps who like others Churchill appointed in Britain who harboured Prime Ministerial ambitions. Cripps was an avid Soviet supporter as were other elements in Labour. This relatively unknown page in history is laid out with clarity in the magisterial book, 'The Maisky Diaries: Red Ambassador to the Court of St James's, 1932-1943' by Ivan Maisky edited by the English historians of Russian descent Gabriel Gorodetsky (Yale University Press, 2015). These diaries give new insights to the war time pressure on Churchill from the Soviet prospective and U.K. Soviet fellow travellers on both the domestic and international fronts. See also 'Ministers At War: Winston Churchill And His War Cabinet' by Jonathan Schneer (Basic Books, 2014). See also '1941: The Year Germany Lost The War' by Andrew Nagorski (Simon Schuster, 2019). Roosevelt became enamored by Stalin with disastrous post-World War II consequences while Churchill remained ever suspicious of Stalin's aims for world hegemony before, during and after World War II.

152   The only respite in this insanity was the Nuremberg Trials after WWII that brought individuals to account for their crimes against humanity and the world took a momentous turn for the better. Less remembered but equally important were the Tokyo War Crimes Tribunal that followed the Nuremburg precedent and brought Japan accused by 'aggressive' war and war crimes to justice. Still only a tiny fraction of complicit Nazis or Japanese extremists were brought to justice – a fraction of less than 1% of the Nazis SS. The International War Crimes Tribunal established in the Hague followed decades later and though important, demonstrates the thesis that the wheels of justice turn slowly, if at all. The sorry record of this International Tribunal needs exposure.

History continues to evolve as more facts about the Nuremberg War Trials convened in 1945 come to light. Called the International Military Tribunal it was convened by the four victorious nations, USA, UK, France and Russia, a pivotal historic event.

Russia suffered most from the German onslaught after 1941 when Hitler ripped up his treaty with Russia and quickly overran Poland, Eastern Europe and large areas of Russia ripping up what was called the Ribbentrop-Molotov Accord. In that agreement between Hitler and Stalin, Russia was ceded Eastern Europe especially Poland. The first war crimes trial was convened in Kharkov Ukraine then part of Russia in 1943 that set the first template from a war crimes tribunal.

lary of international law with the advent of the 'Nuremberg Trials' called 'Human Rights', 'Crimes Against Humanity' and 'Genocide'. International law began to change from the supremacy of state rights to minority rights to individual rights. Two events in 1947 combined to emphasize this

---

What emerges from a scintillating history in *Soviet Judgment at Nuremberg: A New History of the International Military Tribunal after World War II*' by Francine Hirsch (Oxford University Press, 2020). A much different narrative is described from the popular version of a popular movie called *'Trial at Nuremberg'* that displayed an American triumphant perspective of these monumental events.

We learn that the Soviets inspired by Aron Tussier, a Jewish Communist lawyer and legal adviser who influenced and transformed the approach of the Americans led by Mr. Justice Jackson. The Tribunal based its charges against the selected accuser for 'wars against peace', a 'criminal conspiracy' and 'genocide' of minorities mostly Jewish. It is a remarkable tale of the tangled legal and political debates fermented by Stalin and the Soviets to cover up the Soviet murders of Polish officers buried in Katyn in 1943. Until this issue was surfaced the Soviets held Nazi groups accountability for crimes of 'aggression' 'against peace' and 'conspiracy' that advanced the principles of international law. Any historian of the 20th century must put this book in their agenda as a must read. A fascinating tale of law the Soviets transformed and embedded crimes against humanity into international law.

153 In 1946 Russia surprised the world and the west when it tested its first atomic bomb, the second country to explode an atomic bomb after the American atomic bombing attacks in Japan on two mainly civilian targets in 1945. Soviet Russia gained access to the secrets of American 'Manhattan Project' that produced the American atomic bomb. A Soviet spy and scientific genius Klaus Fuchs, a Hungarian immigrant to Britain before World War II went to America and gave Soviets the Manhattan Project's ultra-secret advanced plans. Fuchs attended the 'Big Three' meeting in Yalta as an advisor treo the American delegation. Fuchs was discovered, tried and convicted in America in 1950. In 1959 released from prison Fuchs left for Communist East Germany, a puppet state of Soviet Russia, and was acclaimed as a hero. The Soviets never admitted Fuchs had been their spy. When Fuchs's died in East Berlin in 1988, a wreath was place on his grave by a delegation of Russians. In that delegation was a KGB officer serving in East Germany at the time, Vladimir Putin. Read *'Atomic Spy'* by Nancy Thorndike Greenspan (Viking, 2020).

154 Canada played a major role in the development of designs and export of uranium and plutonium and heavy water to the American 'Manhattan' project that developed the first two atomic bombs. It was Britain under Churchill, not the U.S.A., that started the race for the atomic bomb.

change. The establishment of the State of Israel and the Universal Declaration of Human Rights[156,157].

---

155 During World War II, Ursula Burton neé Kuczynski was a German-born English housewife living in the quiet scenic English countryside with her husband and three children, all from different fathers. As a Jewish teenager living in Berlin, she became a fanatic anti-Nazi and an equally fanatic Communist and was a top Soviet highly decorated intelligence officer who served in China, Poland and Switzerland before being assigned to Britain. An accomplished spymaster, courier, saboteur and bomb maker, Burton assisted Klaus Fuchs and other Soviet spies to smuggle vital secrets to Soviet Russia about the atomic nuclear bomb during World War II and the 'Cold War'. She was never apprehended, protected by other Soviet spies hidden in Britain. Her husband, Len Burton, was also a spy. History is still busy writing about the 'Cold War' and its unknown crucial players. Read *'Agent Sonya: Moscow's Most Daring Wartime Spy'* by Ben Macintyre (Penguin Random Books, Canada, 2020).

156 The emergence of six men in the post-World War II period with different ideologies and backgrounds helped create and promote this new human rights dialectic in the 20th century. Amnesty International and the first recognized NGO dedicated to Jewish refugees grew from this impulse. H.V. Lauterpacht, Jacob Blaustein, Peter Benenson, Maurice Pelzweig, Jacob Robinson and Raphael Lemkin who coined the phrase *'genocide'* were, each in their own way, 20th century originators of the 'human right's' movement. Read *'Rooted Cosmopolitans Jews and Human Rights in the Twentieth Century'* by James Loeffler (Yale University Press, 2018).

157 Post World War II, Canada also had its share of Communist spies and sympathizers. Most notable was Fred Rose, a Polish Jewish immigrant to Canada in the '30s. He started as a union organizer in Montreal and was a member of the Communist Youth. Rose ran for Parliament in 1943 as a Labour Progressive and narrowly won. In 1945, Rose ran as a member of Communist Party of Canada in the Cartier Riding, a poor area of Montreal, and won as the first Communist to be elected to Parliament. Rose introduced two bills in Parliament - the first anti-hate legislation and the first medicare legislation. In 1946 Rose was charged with breaches of the espionage act and was convicted and his citizenship revoked. In 1953 when released he was returned to Poland while appealing his loss of citizenship, He became editor of an English language magazine called 'Poland' devoted to Polish culture and civilization for western consumption. He died in Warsaw in 1983. During Diefenbaker's government, Ellen Fairclough, Minister of Citizenship and Immigration, passed an amendment to the Citizenship Act calling it the Fred Rose amendment that declared that Canadian citizenship could not be revoked. Allan MacEachen, a friend, colleague and mentor who at the time was Minister of Immigration acknowledged that the Prime Minister of the day, Mackenzie King in his voluminous diaries had missing pages dealing with the Fred Rose affair. The mystery continues.

Meanwhile in Asia, two nations with competing ideologies vied for economic progress in post-World War II – Japan and China. Under the U.S. mandate led by General MacArthur, Japan emerged from a war torn state to a successful democracy. China, after a crippling civil war, became the second most powerful Communist state after World War II. No one could predict how China still under the grip of Communism became the fastest growing economy in the world.

The 'Cold War' started, dividing east and west between Communist and democratic states[158] followed despite an early warning by Churchill coining the phrase 'The Iron Curtain'[159]. The race for weapons of mass destruction in the post-World War II continued. Civil war in Greece

---

Tim Buck, Secretary of the Communist Part of Canada, was a history teacher at London Central Collegiate Institute, a high school I attended in the early 1950's.

158 In 1946, Churchill, no longer Prime Minister and swept out of office though still Leader of the Opposition, spoke out at Westminster College in Missouri at the invitation of President Harry Truman about the 'Iron Curtain' descending across Europe. Truman, who at first agreed with Churchill's warning having read Churchill's speech in advance, later separated himself from Churchill's position. Still later Truman came to believe Churchill's admonition about Soviet expansionist aims in Europe, America and elsewhere. He was a stauncher antagonist to Communism than Roosevelt who felt he could handle Stalin or 'Uncle Joe' as he called him. Remember Yalta when President Roosevelt seeded the roots of the Cold War by yielding to Stalin's demands for Soviet hegemony in Eastern Europe and the Baltics, etc. It was the invasion of Poland in 1939 that triggered World War II fell under continued Soviet hegemony after Armistice. The 'free' Poles who fought brilliantly for the allies in World War II especially at Monte Cassino in Italy and with the RAF felt rightly that Poland's aspirations as a democratic were betrayed.

159 The end of World War II left Europe and the West deeply divided between the left and the right. See the 'Left Bank: Art, Passion and the Rebirth of Paris 1940–1950' by Agnès Poirier (Henry Holt and Co., 2018) that describes the vitriolic political deadlock between the left and the right especially in France, and most especially in Paris.

160 In 1946, President Truman was given only 40 days notice by the odious anti-Semitic Ernest Bevin, then British Foreign Secretary that Britain intended to withdraw military support from the democratic forces in Greece against the communist incursions. Truman decided to step in and send American economic and military aid (including 250 military advisors), an act of leadership, especially in war weary America anxious to turn away from Europe in 1945-1947, a startling act of Presidential leadership, going against popular opinion at the time. Meanwhile Bevin in England opposed

pitting the established order against the Communists in 1946[160], followed by the rapid Soviet takeover of Eastern Europe and in the Baltics, Balkans, the Caucasus, as U.S.A. and Europe withdrew[161], the Chinese Communist victory over the Nationalists as they escaped to Taiwan[162], the Soviet

---

the founding of Israel and he did his best to keep Jewish war refugees from entering the Mandate of Palestine then under British rule from 1945 to 1948. Bevin's sterling work as Minister of Labour in the U.K. during World War II in Churchill's Cabinet is seriously tainted by his later role as Minister of Foreign Affairs in the Atlee post World War II government as is the Atlee government, many of whom were early Zionist supporters. This core of anti-semitism within the British Labour Party was never excised.

161 In 1948, two turning points in European history were led by Harry Truman. First the Marshall Plan that gave billions of aid to kick start European economic recovery and second, the air relief to West Berlin encircled by Soviet forces led first by Britain. This in turn led to European recovery, the recognition of West Germany by the Allies and laid the foundation for the European Community. In turn the creation of NATO as a deterrence to Soviet expansion was a key to the demise of the Soviet Empire. For these acts of leadership, called the 'Truman Doctrine', Truman deserves his place in history.

162 From the monumental 'Long March' in 1934 that took 370 days where the Communists led by Mao Zedong and Zhou Enlai, when encircled by the Nationalists led by Chiang Kai-shek, escaped to the caves of Yunnan in south-west and then to north-west in China to survive and gained total power in China, the most populous country in the world, a little over a decade later in 1949 – a turn of events in world history which continues to amaze.

163 Stalin, autocratic, ever suspicious loner, confronting his mortality in the early '50s, a few years before his death in 1954, orchestrated a vicious purge against Jews, especially Communist leaders of Jewish extraction, in the Soviet Union and Czechoslovakia, Hungary and Romania followed with unleashing a deadly wave of anti-semitism, carefully planned and executed. First, Russian cultural organizations were 'cleansed' of artists of Jewish descent that included leading writers, composers, musicians, actors and dancers. Second, the infamous Doctor's Plot led to the torture and death of leading doctors of Jewish descent including the Kremlin's and the army's leading doctors. Third, show trials of Communist leaders of Jewish descent who were first tortured to provide the public with their confessions like Rudolph Slansky in Czechoslovakia and Ana Pauker in Romania, both lifelong Communist members. Finally a plan was underway to collect the names of all Soviet citizens of Jewish descent and then deport them to the Gulags. Massive new barracks were being built. These plans came to a halt with Stalin's miserable

Famine of 1947, the so-called 'Doctors Plot' in the early '50s unleashed by Stalin[163], the Korea War, the Algerian War that gave birth to the fearsome modern weapon of terrorism - 'suicide' bombing, the repeated cycle of Arab wars against Israel, the Cuban Revolution in 1959, the South Amer-

---

death in 1954. The thrust of anti-Semitism spilled over in Western Europe notably amongst strong communist parties in France and elsewhere. In France, two long time Communists who fought in the French resistance during World War II were kicked out of the Communist Party. Anti-semitism in these countries continued. A basis for this travesty was against Jewish citizens, in Western Europe and within the Soviet Empire was the Stalin concocted plot of Zionist plots with Israel and the incredulous charge of Jewish support for Fascism and Nazism in World War II. This canard, carefully prepared and executed, was so fantastic that it spread across the globe amongst Communists and their fellow travellers. Stalin before his death in 1954 was preparing another Soviet purge of Jews in Russia including the construction of camps and barracks in the far north. These plans were disrupted and discontinued on his death. See 'The Last Days of Stalin' by J. Rubenstein (Yale University Press, New Haven, 2016). A lesson learned about the recurring outbursts of anti-semitism in the 20th century. When innocent Jews are attacked, it is always as the scapegoats to distract from self-induced fissures or failures or loss of popularity in autocratic regimes and inevitably leads to the demise of those regimes.

164 The Vietnam War fought by America and its allies marked a major fissure in the United States by what Presidents Eisenhower, Kennedy and Johnson each considered the communist 'domino theory' that if unchallenged would lead to Communism hegemony over southeast Asia and beyond. Starting with Eisenhower, increased by Kennedy and then Johnson. United States sent troops to crush North Vietnamese home brewed Communism inspired and supported by Mao. The political classes and the military failed. Only DeGaulle of western leaders after the massacre of IndoChina stayed out. Recent history suggests the North Vietnamese were at the edge of a peaceful settlement before Nixon's horrific bombing policy. It almost worked. The far left, shattered by the revelations of Khrushchev of Stalinist horrors in 1957, was given new energy by the disastrous war against the northern Vietnamese. The student riots in Berkeley, California spread across university campuses and gave birth to the 'New Left' (see David Horowitz's book 'Prodigal Son: A Generational Odyssey' (Touchstone, NY 1998) for an insight to the ruptures in American politics and society that continues to this day.

165 In 1956 in the second Israel-Arab War triggered by President Gamal Nasser of Egypt who took possession of the Suez Canal that led to Britain, France and Israel agreeing to invade Egypt when Nasser blockaded Israeli shipping. All three States recognised Nasser's larger ambitions. The American intervention under President Eisenhower

ican coups, the Vietnam War[164], the Laos-Cambodia slaughter-houses, the endless violence in other Mid-East wars[165], wars against autocrats in South America and the breakout of wars in Africa amongst the Africans themselves, after the Colonial powers gave up and left their African colonies, the decade long Chinese Cultural Revolution from 1966 to 1976 when Mao Zedong died reputed to killing over 20 million Chinese and caused the dispersion of millions more – all elevated the 20th century into the record breaking massive slaughter house of innocent peoples or their forcible displacement to the highest level known in the long bloody history of mankind. The killing of innocents (over 250 million) numbed the public conscience while the elites, either intellectual or economic, failed to remain immune from the temptation of still more power and the escalating arms race.

An interesting counter narrative appear in the '30s to contest 'appeasement' of autocrats after World War II sweeping the west, the rise of comic books and super heroes like Superman, Captain Marvel and others. Superman was created by two young Jewish cartoonists, Schuster and Siegel. Siegel was born in Canada.

Two writers stand out against the tide of deep intellectual division between the right and the left that split the western intellectual world - George Orwell and Arthur Koestler. Orwell believed that lies and propaganda were the new pestilence of both the left and right that needed correction. Truth was the linchpin of democracy they both believed. The *'Animal Farm'* and *'1984'* were Orwell's works that remain relevant today and continue to resonate in this age of unrepented propaganda. Arthur Koestler[166] was a Hungarian-born Jew. His life trajectory reflected

who overruled his Secretary of State Dulles who at first was supportive, led to Prime Minister Pearson's leadership in the creation of the UN Peacekeepers and Pearson's Nobel Prize for Peace. Eisenhower's role in the Suez Affair led to collateral damage to stability in the Middle East which is still being debated.

166 *'Koestler The Literary and Political Odyssey of a Twentieth-Century Skeptic'* by Michael Scammell (Random House, 2009) is a must read for those interested in the chaotic intellectual history of the mid-20th century. Arthur Koestler's 2 volume autobiography is an insightful history of one man's journey from left to liberalism – *'Arrow In The Blue'* (Collins with Hamish Hamilton Ltd, 1952) and *'The Invisible Writing: The Second Volume Of An Autobiography, 1932-40'* (Collins with Hamish Hamilton Ltd, 1952).

the turbulent times of the 20th century. He travelled the political spectrum from the 1920's to 1980's from socialist to Zionist to communist to anti-communist. As a soldier, he was imprisoned several times and most memorably, in the Spanish War in the '30s. These experiences inspired him to become a prolific writer ranging from novels to polemics. He wrote *'Darkness at Noon'* that changed the world's attitude towards the far left and totalitarian Communist Russia after World War II and turned against the left especially Communist activists and fellow travellers against him[167].

Great American writers of the left (e.g. William Faulkner, John Dos Passos, Leo Santagora, Ernest Hemingway, Richard Wright, Rebecca West et al) dominated the literary crucible of economic disparity and who chronicled the ravaged American families starting in 1929 and the Great Depression that followed. John Steinbeck who wrote the *'Grapes of Wrath'* recounted these stories of the 'Great Migration' from the dust

---

167   Arthur Koestler famously supported Whittaker Chambers, a disenchanted American communist, against Alger Hiss (both State Department officials) who denied his previous communist affiliations. *'Witness'* by Whittaker Chambers Regency Publishing, Washington DC, 1952), the story of Soviet spies, Communist party members, fellow travellers in the United States in the '30s, '40s and '50s. The most famous was Paul Robson, star athlete, singer and political activist. Koestler believed Chambers and did not believe Hiss's denials upsetting many left sympathizers in U.S.A. and elsewhere in Europe against him. Canada had its own share of opaque communist sympathizers in government, academia and the media before, during and after World War II, and a comprehensive history of this period is still waiting to be written now that the archives are available to scholars.

Arthur Koestler, the Hungarian immigrant (who settled in London) and was an early Communist member and David Horowitz, born in the United States of progressive parents who both held Communist party membership, travelled the political spectrum from far left to right when they each became disillusioned with communist 'utopia' and undemocratic ideology – *'Radical Son: A Generational Oddysey'* by David Horowitz (Touchstone, 1998). Horowitz continued to expose leftist ideology, its impact at the American Supreme Court and the divisions in political classes in the United States. Read *'Dark Agenda: The War to Destroy Christian America'* by David Horowitz (Humanix Books, 2018). Horowitz traces the glaring split in the American society between secularists and citizens who were faithful Christians and others in 1960 of faith who held traditional beliefs. Canada was not immune to that same ideological draft.

belt in middle America to California, the region of hope and possible prosperity. Singer-writers took to the road. Woody Guthrie and Pete Seeger[168] were two iconic examples. Another considered the best writer in America by Ernest Hemingway and others was Nelson Algren. Born of leftist Jewish parents in Chicago in 1909, he left home penniless to wander across America in the '30s and became a new voice and created a new style of witty cutting realism, some called the 'new journalism'. His life was a chaotic series of ups and downs. Simone de Beauvoir, the intimate partner of Jean Paul Sartre[169] and ground-breaking feminist author, on a trip to America met Algren, fell in love and when he achieved literary fame, travelled to Paris in the '60s to continue their torrid relationship travelling together to Spain and other places. Algren, caught in the 'UnAmerican' craze' in Washington, refused, though once a communist member, to turn on his literary friends. America, the home of dreams and intellectual disasters continued as the nation of 'exceptionalism' increasing and expanding its thrust leadership in the 20th century, fractured as it was[170].

From the mid '50s to the assassination of Martin Luther King in 1968, no modern leadership was so unique or incredible as his leadership of Martin of the civil rights movement in the United States. From a middle class upbringing to a pastor in Atlanta, Georgia in his father's church, Dr. King's brand of leadership and non-violent philosophy gained from his studies of Gandhi and deepened on a trip to India, was different

---

168   When I served as Chairman of the Board of O'Keefe Centre in Toronto, the largest publically owned theatre in Canada, I suggested to the CEO Charles Cutts to book a concert with Peter Seeger, a celebrated folk song singer. When it came to negotiating the contract including ticket prices, Seeger insisted that the majority of the ticket prices be below $20. We reluctantly agreed. The night of the concert, I was surprised there were no cars in front of the theatre. I assumed the concert was a financial failure. I was surprised to discover a full house with standing room. The audience had mostly travelled by subway. Seeger understood and respected his audience.

169   Jean Paul Sartre is also considered as founder of the school of 'Existentialism', another forerunner of 'identity politics' in U.S.A. and elsewhere with disruptive negative results.

170   *'Never A Lovely So Real: The Life and Look of Nelson Algren'* by Colin Asher, W.W. Norton and Co., 2019

from every civil rights leader in racist America. From the strike against segregated bus service and boycott of businesses in Montgomery in 1955 before he was 30 to his march to Selma, to his pilgrimage to Washington DC joined by over 250,000 supporters – black and white, to his battles with a willing Lyndon Johnson for voting rights and equal civil rights, King was a unique leader of the 20th century whose influence resonated across the world for the rest of the 20th century[171].

Starting in 1956, two remarkable writers of Jewish origin, each published a best-selling novel that in its own way shocked America and influenced the world especially the Soviet Union – 'Atlas Shrugged' by Ayn Rand and 'Doctor Zhivago' by Boris Pasternak. 'Atlas Shrugged', a lengthy story of an iconclast architect that highlighted individualism against conventional wisdom, became the roots of modern conservatism in America. 'Doctor Zhivago' by the poet Boris Pasternak who refused to emigrate from Soviet Russia influenced Soviet Russia and communist fellow travellers around the world to begin to detach themselves from Soviet 'group think'. In 1956, Nikita Khrushchev, the newish Secretary General Communist Party but long time Stalin 'apparachnik' and new leader of the Soviet Union gave a secret speech to the Communist Party

---

171 Johnson and his legislative history of civil rights and social policies deserved repu-tation was overshadowed by his expansion of the Vietnam War and his bombing sorties that did little to dilute the resolve of the Vietnam leadership. No doubt, in time, Johnson's legacy will be restored to more balanced recognition. Read Doris Kearns Goodwin book on 'Leadership: In Turbulent Times' (Simon and Schuster, 2018) is an excellent history of Johnson's indelible contribution to civil rights in America. Robert Caro's second volume of Johnson's biography anticipated in the future will further elevate Johnson's reputation.

172 J.B. Salsberg, a union organizer and community activist and an old family friend who was the first elected Communist member in the Ontario Legislature in the '30s, and a devout believer in the Soviet Union and Communism finally broke with Communism in 1957 after hearing of Khrushchev's details of Stalin and his record as a savage Communist Leader. Khrushchev's remarkable speech given secretly to the Communist Party in the Kremlin in Moscow marks one of the turning points in the 20th century.

Joe had then what was known as a 'Kronstadt moment' – the term used when a Communist true believer lost his faith as the true nature of the Soviet regime is revealed and hits him like a thunderbolt. The 'Kronstadt moment' originated in

leadership that detailed the horrendous record of Stalin's human rights abuses went further[172].

The late '60s[173] and '70s witnessed the eruption of cultural wars in America and Europe[174]. The Vietnam War ignited the raging anti-war movement across university campuses in the United States that preoccupied the western democracies for the remainder of the 20th century and beyond. In 1972, Greenpeace was formally founded in

---

1921 when the Bolshevik army put down Russian sailors rebelling against Soviet rule in the port city of Kronstadt. Many early key adherents to Communism left the fold. The flourishing Communist movement in the United States in the mid 20th century was then exposed by the disruptive McCarthy hearings and split the American liberal community and pushed many liberals to the right. Neoconservatism in the United States stems in part from many of these disenchanted communist intellectual sympathizers. In Canada, communist spies were uncovered after WWII including a Member of Parliament who was also an early founding member of the Communist Part of Canada. This full history of Communist influence in Canada remains to be written. The Cambridge Communist cell in England and fellow travellers before, during and after WWII has been well covered. There remains much more to be told. Threads of this story continue to come to light. Eric Hobsbawn, one of England's leading historians who wrote through a Marxist lens died in 2002, still a devout Marxist. Other 'true believers' left the fold quietly but harboured utopian views about Marxism all their lives.

173 As a teenager my weekend music tastes were transformed in the early days by regular visits in the '50s to Detroit where I first discovered blues and rock and roll, soul, disco and songs like *'Earth Angel'*, *'Sha Boom, Sha Boom'*. This 'Motown' music was a turning point in popular 20th century music. Popular music was transformed by the arrival of the Beatles, a band made up for four young men from working class families in Liverpool in 1962. By 1964, they had fans in America and their career was given a gigantic boost by an appearance on the iconic Sunday Night TV show hosted by an inarticulate New York columnist Ed Sullivan. Over 73 million watched this show. The Beatles returned to United States for a tour a few years later and became world-wide musical pace setters. Frank Sinatra (1915-1998) was one of the most popular and influential singers of the 20th century whose music still haunts. Elvis Presley (1936-1977) called the 'King of Rock' also transformed popular music world-wide. Who can forget his voice or his movements!

174 In October 1970, Prime Minister Pierre Trudeau introduced the War Measures Act dealing a national shot of energy in response to kidnapping of a British diplomat and murder of Pierre LaPorte, a Provincial Liberal Cabinet Minister and acquaintance, by a handful Quebec supporters called 'FLQ' (Front de Libération du Québec).

Holland based on a Greenpeace group started in Vancouver, Canada to lobby against a nuclear bomb test in Alaska. This was spawned by members of the Sierra Club in Canada including Canadian Patrick Moore, and two west coast Canadian families, the Stowes and the Hunters. Greenpeace grew to be the leading ecology lobbyist in the world transforming norms in education, government and religion. Established norms and morals were upturned. The 'Flower Generation' joined forces and a vastly different perception of global reactions to the ecology and climate change took root transforming political dialetics social and economic policies[175].

To history and beyond, the dialectics of the 20th century might best be summed up in the 21st century shorthand of 'trigger' words. Words, 'trigger words', program we are told, our emotive behavioural responses. So conditioned, we react to align with our imbedded belief structures. Test your own reactions against these words:

- Imperialism
- Pogroms
- Congo
- Genocide
- Victoria
- Trenches
- Gas
- Tanks
- Communism
- Collectivization
- Purges
- Siberia
- Holomor

---

175 Whether tax measures such as carbon taxes will reduce global warming remains a 21st century question or will new and cleaner energy sources such as fusion, nuclear energy and tidal water power become better alternatives remains a potent question for policy makers and the public. Others believe climate change effects can be more effectively resolved by eradicating local polluted hot spots along our lakes, rivers and oceans. Some claim the biggest contributors to global warming are the increased births in Asia where tens of millions are born each year.

- Gulag
- Fascism
- Racism
- Nazism
- Holocaust
- Pearl Harbour
- Hiroshima
- Nagasaki
- Nuremberg
- Berlin Wall
- Airlift
- Baby Boomers
- Jets
- Fidel
- Missiles
- Feminine Mystique
- Vietnam
- Apollo
- Ethnic Cleansing
- Srebrenica
- Rwanda
- HIV
- AIDS
- Climate
- Jihad
- Facebook
- Apple
- Google
- Amazon

In 1997, Sunil Khilnani, a British historian of Indian descent, published *'The Idea of India'*, a must read to understand the world's largest democracy - applauding India's civil gains while denouncing its violent reactions. India felt the winds of peace as it withdrew troops from nearby Sri Lanka and enraged by violent outbreaks in Kashmir, sent troops towards its ever restive neighbour, Pakistan, to secure its border flanks. 'Border security' was and remains the Indian political mantra. Earlier in 1974,

India tested its first nuclear bomb. In 1998 under the leadership of India's Prime Minister, Atal Bihari Vajpayee, India tested three more nuclear bombs despite the world community banning them. A few years later, he bravely travelled to Pakistan as an act of peace.

Europe was different.

By the year 2000, a post national, cosmopolitan metamorphoses transformed the great historic cities of the European community – into 'open' cities. Of course there were rumblings of 'democratic deficit' as the unaccountable bureaucrats in Brussels spewed out endless regulations from cheese to the colour of cucumbers to enumerating beaches that were safe or unsafe for swimming – all propelled by the 'faux' notion that conformity equals to equality. The 'idea' of Europe with its highly regulated societies and high social net masked by the 'idea' of market commerce was needed for economic growth to fill and replenish its insatiable social demands.

Soccer, Europe's leading sport, demonstrated a dichotomy between nationalist fans wildly cheering for their home teams contrasted by the diversity of its players and management of each national team that originated from every corner of Europe and South America. Star soccer players reached a par with Hollywood movie icons. Gifted players received mega compensation, married attractive wives and were treated like royalty in the media. Managers were also lavished with mind-boggling salaries. Commercial contracts added to their pay and notoriety. This sports world became one large stage of 'celebrity'.

Intellectuals, especially on the left, in Europe struggled to find apt metaphors to encapsulate this new apotheosis.

THE 'COLD WAR' - THE '50S AND THE '60S

Politics started for many of my generation who were students[176] in 1959 when the first 'American Presidential Television Debates' between

---

176 The '50s was a crucial start on my pursuit at a higher education and as my career choice. At London Central High School in London, Ontario, while I was an average student, I was hyperactive in school activities ranging from extracurricular activities in plays and revues and tennis, basketball and football barely making the bench – and ran and won as class rep then to face defeat in my final year for election as School President. I graduated at seventeen. Summer times I worked at construction, road work, summer camps, door to door sales, and in the fall, at the Western Fair in London and then Canadian National Exhibition (CNE) in Toronto as a short order cook, a job I loved. In 1953 I was accepted for business at University of Western Ontario (UWO) undecided between law and business. A fanatic card and billiards player, I devoted much time gambling to help my working mother cover my share of family expenses. My mother did not know of my gambling activities. In November 1953 while at Western I decided to attend classes for the first time. The first class I attended was Economics 20 by Prof. Inman who wrote the text. I discovered that I knew nothing. Worse, statistics and numeric tables were a complete mystery. I panicked. I decided relying on my memory would be the only way to survive. So I took soft courses and doubled up in Psychology, History, English, and German (hoping my Yiddish would help. It didn't.).

The spring of 1954, a classmate I befriended from Hamilton, Norman Rosenblood convinced me that maybe we should become Rabbis. So we set off in his convertible and travelled to Cincinnati to Hebrew Union College, the Jewish Reform Seminary first. Then to New York City to the Jewish Theological Seminary and the home of Jewish Conservatism. Both week long visits were disappointments. We decided we both didn't have the calling except for chasing girls. I audited lectures at Yeshiva College and was mesmerized by Rabbi Joseph Soloveitchik, a Jewish scholar and teacher in the grand tradition. Yet most of his lectures flew over my head. Back at Western, I discovered that spring I had enough credits to get my degree in two years so I could hurry through Osgoode Hall, and return to practice criminal law in London, Ontario.

Fate had other plans. Western's Registrar, a Miss Allison, called me to her office. She advised that having seen my grades, the school authorities had some questions though, she added was I able to accumulate sufficient credits in two years to qualify for

Senator John F. Kennedy and Senator Richard Nixon was broadcast widely. Politics in the U.S. under Eisenhower in the '50s, who could not

---

a Bachelor of Arts that year. I explained as I was in a hurry to graduate from Osgoode Hall so I had used my student number and doubled up on all my courses. She smiled and explained a BA from Western required two years and two years of summer school with passing grades. However she might waive my summer in special circumstances when I told her about my desire to go to Osgoode Hall. If I agreed to visit Cecil Augustus Wright, the Dean at University of Toronto Law School who happened to be born in London, a graduate of my high school in London and Western and was considered the best law teacher in Canada, she would consider waving the second year summer courses requirement. I quickly agreed. All I had to do was take my car, a used 1947 Chrysler, to Toronto, have a brief visit with this Dean and she would allow me to go to summer school and if with passing grades, get my degree at Fall Convocation, which would allow me to go to Osgoode Hall for their 4 year law course.

A week later in early May, I travelled by car to Toronto to meet with Wright in his office at the small Law School then at the corner of St. George and College Streets. I arrived promptly at 10 am. Miss McLelland, the Registrar had arranged my appointment with Miss Allison. I climbed the rickety steps and knocked on the Dean's door. He bade me to enter and told me to sit while he finished working. After 20 minutes, 'Caesar' Wright – a lookalike of Franklin Roosevelt – asked me in his deep gruff voice if I knew the difference *"about the law is and what the law should be"*. I was dumbfounded. This was the first question I had been asked by any professor since attending Western. *"No"*, I mumbled. So 'Caesar' as he was called gave me a ¾ hour dissertation on his answer to his question. At the end, he said, *"Grafstein, Grafstein, I want you here."* And then without a word waved me out of his office while he returned to the papers piled on his desk. Stunned I walked down the stairs where Anne McLelland stood at foot of the stairwell and handed me an envelope. *"What's this?"* I said. *"It's your application to U of T Law School."* *"Who told you I wanted to apply?"* With a wink, she pointed to the Dean's office and these fatal words, *"He never misses."*

That summer I took two summer courses, worked on the assembly line at Kelvinators, got my degree and in September moved to a fraternity rooming house (BSR) on Willcocks Street and entered Law School. I was the second youngest in the class and the least prepared and desperate for help. Harry Arthur, who I knew from a summer camp experience, with Marty Friedland and Harvey Bliss had formed a study group. After my pleading they agreed to allow me to join their study group provided I didn't slow them down. Without their help, I would have never passed through law school. Harry Arthur went on to be Dean of Osgoode Hall at York and then York University President. Marty became Professor of Law and eventually Dean of Law and now University Scholar and historian. Harvey Bliss became a tough capable litigator.

put two coherent sentences together in his televised press conferences, was boring as were the amiable but equally boring televised speeches by Louis St. Laurent. Both Eisenhower and St. Laurent had attractive down to earth outwardly modest personalities but by and large were bland communicators. The' Cold War'[177] left the public cold, almost

---

After graduation, I married and I couldn't get a job. Though I had a satisfying standing in my class, I had to set out on my own as a criminal lawyer specializing in petty crimes, rapes, etc. Soon Ed Pivnick partner at a small firm Minden, Pivnick and Gross, approached me. By this time, I had tired of criminal law. Meanwhile every weekend the study group would meet on Sundays and for regular weekend dinners. My wife thought I should get out more in the community. One day a flier appeared at our small apartment in North York inviting all to attend a Liberal organizing meeting of the nearby North York Centre Liberal Association at the home of Jimmie Mizzoni, the Party Riding President. I went and that night my career arc changed. I met Keith Davey and Walter Gordon and Dick Stanbury and other key Liberals in Toronto. It was 1962. The Liberals under the master organizer Keith Davey were reorganizing the antique Liberal Party from the grass roots up. I was elected Young Liberal President of York Centre that night. Six months later I was elected Toronto District Young Liberal Association Young Liberal President and on the T&D Liberal Executive. Three months later, I was elected English Speaking Vice President of the Young Liberals of Canada in Ottawa. Then I was appointed to Liberal Party's National Campaign Committee and given a seat next to Mr. Pearson. My wife regretted her advice. As for me, my life changed and I never looked back.

In 1962 I met John Turner at a Liberal event having followed his rise in the Liberal Party from his participation at the Kingston Conference. I asked him if he was as good as he looked. I had read his speeches and thought he could do better. Three years later he hired me as his first chief of staff when he became a junior minister which set my career on a political arc.

177 During post World War II period from 1945 to 1965 the fangs of Stalinism reached out across the globe to claw impoverished nations led by Soviet supported agents and soviet weaponry to European nations like Rumania, Poland, the Balkans and Asian nations like China, Korea, Vietnam, the Philippines and Africa like Kenya, Nigeria, South and Central America, only to be opposed by American and British secret services whose efforts in turn were compromised by Soviet trained spies imbedded in their secret services. For a more comprehensive captivating book, read 'Small Wars, Faraway Places: Global Insurrection and the Making of the Modern World, 1945-1965' by Michael Burleigh (Viking Press, 2013), 'The Quiet Americans: Four CIA Spies at the Dawn of the Cold War--A Tragedy in Three Acts' by Scott Anderson (Penguin Random House (2020)

frozen while paying some attention to the first probe into space by the Russian Sputnik. The downing of American spy plane over Russia caused a ripple of angst amongst my generation but not much more. The Americans led by Eisenhower were confused and surprised that after Stalin's death, his small leadership clique continued to hold power as Soviet Russia's economic decay became increasingly visible. Nixon confronted Stalin's ultimate successor at a publicized meeting arguing which system of government democracy or communism was better for the masses. Even Khrushchev's 'secret speech' in the Kremlin ripping away the veil of Stalin's venal rule, was noted but did little disturb the calm of the '50s.

Suddenly this all changed with the first televised presidential debates in United States between John F. Kennedy - a youthful Senator who rose to public attention in his speech to the Democratic Party in 1956 Convention that nominated Adlai Stevenson, a so-called 'egghead' and beloved by liberals of all stripes, to run against the American war hero Dwight D. Eisenhower.

Canadian viewing of the first Presidential Debates were high especially amongst students who were generally not interested in politics or politicians.

In 1956 and 1957 Canadians got their first taste of disruptive politics when an unknown western politician upstart carrying the odd name of Diefenbaker surprised the Conservative Party and his followers and the Liberal Party when he won a minority government against St. Laurent dislodging the incredulous Liberals followed by Diefenbaker winning a huge majority government against a surprise complacent Liberal elite establishment led by Canada's Nobel Prize winner Lester (Mike) Bowles Pearson, an early hero of mine. Canada's establishment was shocked and surprised. So was the Canadian public.

Americans led be Kennedy helped bring Diefenbaker down when he refused Bomarc missing testing on Canadian soil while Pearson, initially opposed, agreed to do so.

In 1960, Interest in politics on both sides of the border had taken an upward swing. Every political wannabee in 1960 could not forget President Kennedy's mesmerizing inaugural speech in January which was repeated and quoted by every viewer. *"Ask not what your country can do for you - ask what you can do for your country"*.

At the same period, in 1959 another duo of youthful politicians caught worldwide attention and admiration – Fidel Castro and his erstwhile lieutenant Che Guevara. The remarkable revolution that took power in Cuba led by Fidel Castro, a failed lawyer and failed rebel who suddenly emerged, with the assistance of his carefully manipulated media profile, especially in the New York Times, whose ace reporter and editorialist 'Herbert' Matthews was duped by Castro into believing that Castro and his tiny band of radicals led a widespread popular uprising across Cuba against the autocratic corrupt leadership of President Emilio Batista supported by the American business interests. In truth, Castro led a ragtag army of less than 600, poorly armed volunteers, against a well-armed American trained Cuban army of over 32,000 who gave up especially after Emilio Batista, the American supported dictator fled to exile in Florida.

Castro, at first not a Communist, was rebuffed by the American government led by Kennedy and its advisors. The American leadership launched embargoes against Castro and Cuba. Only then Castro, influenced by his younger brother Raul Castro and Che Guevara who were both long-time committed Communists, did Fidel become a lifelong Communist believer. Together they built what became one of the world's top intelligence services in the world that protected their embryo Communist state especially against Americna spy services, American supported insurrectionists, and spread their branded Communist web across the Americas and Africa. With no alternative, Castro sought Soviet support. This led to the 'Cuban Missile Crisis of 1962' after failed attempts by Cuban dissidents encouraged secretly by Kennedy at the Bay of Pigs that ignited little popular anti-Castro Cubans support, despite American intelligence to the contrary. A small Cuban crew of counter revolutionaries was trained and armed in Guatemala by the C.I.A sailed on a small rickety yacht and landed on Cuban shores. Kennedy got cold feet. He refused to provide promised air cover for the rebels who were either slaughtered on the Cuban beaches or captured by the swift action of Castro and his Soviet supplied and trained army.

The 'Cuban Missile Crisis' led the world to the brink of nuclear war. Khrushchev had bet on Kennedy's preconceived weakness. The crisis was resolved by Kennedy agreeing not to invade Cuba and remove American missiles in Turkey aimed at Soviet Russia six months later, disconnecting the two agreements for Kennedy and Americans to save face.

Canadians felt hopeless watching a passion play staged by the youthful Americans, called the 'brightest the best' as they glorified themselves, led by Kennedy and his brother Robert, all manipulated by Joe Kennedy Sr. who sought to recast his reputation as a leading appeasing American ambassador to England before World War II to attempt a run against Franklin Roosevelt. On the other side was Khrushchev anxious to make his name as Soviet leader against the backdrop of Stalin's exposure of his egregious conduct to his presumed Soviet adversaries in 1957 by Khrushchev at a private meeting of Soviet leadership in the Kremlin. Fidel Castro and Che Guevara became global popular heroes and adored celebrities with Nikita Khrushchev their patron calling the shots. Threats of an invasion of Cuba diminished.

The balance of the '60s until the end of the 20th century was fragmented by two warring narratives. One was the 'freedom fighters' and 'revolutionaries' against the Imperialist powers, the western democracies led by the United States. The other about the necessity to protect democracies and the third world against communism. Castroism spread to Africa[178], South and Central America throughout the balance of the 20th century whilst the Americans became mired in Vietnam[179]. Canada became a quiet voice of reason against indiscriminate bombing in the Vietnam War led by Lester Bowles Pearson who urged President Johnson

---

178 Che Guevara, the committed Communist felt Fidel Castro lacked Communist fervour. Che replaced Castro as the darling of the Communists. Che decided to lead 35,000 trained Cubans to Angola when Portugal reluctantly withdrew from its West African colony. Liberia supported by South Africa and America became a western proxy for resisting the spread of Communism in West Africa that continued to the end of the 20th century fragmenting Africa into warring camps.

179 Ho Chi Minh, the tough Vietnamese Communist leader had been rebuffed by the Americans seeking self-determination at Versailles after World War I and never forgot the 'self determination' as professed by Americans was highly selective.

to give up 'carpet bombing', never a successful military strategy[180]. Johnson's abrupt resignation led to Nixon's return to power in 1972. As President Nixon skillfully withdrew America from Vietnam by carpet bombing along the Cambodian border and declared victory, Nixon became embroiled by his own egregarious conduct in the 'Watergate Affair' that led to his resignation. Nixon had vowed never to let Democrats steal an election from him as the Kennedy Democrats admittedly did in 1960, fuelled by Joe Kennedy's money that gave Kennedy a slight majority to win the 1960 election by a narrow margin. Corrupt Chicago headed by the old Democratic warhorse, Chicago Mayor Richard Daley, 'stole' that election from Nixon[181]. Therein lies the seeds of 'Watergate'. It was Lawrence O'Brien's office, then head of the Democratic Party, that was broken into. Nixon vowed never to let the Democrats 'steal' another election from him.

The '70s saw the rise and fall of Democrat Jimmy Carter starting when Ronald Reagan, former Democrat and Hollywood labour leader changed political horses and became the Republican Governor of California. Then, as triumphant President of United States, Reagan surprised everyone by bringing the 'Cold War' to a close when the Berlin Wall, the metaphor for the 'Cold War' came crashing down. Castro's Communist Cuba was one of few Communist countries that survived the retreat of worldwide Communism[182].

---

180 Hitler tried carpet bombing against Britain during the 'Blitz' and rather than cow the British, Britain became inspired to fight on led by Churchill's electrifying speeches and dramatic actions.

181 Lawrence F. O'Brien Jr., a top J.F.K. advisor admitted later that he used Joe Kennedy's cash to buy 'votes' in Chicago, even dead ones. Joe Kennedy had enlisted the Mafia to help in return for easing pressure on the mob. Robert Kennedy as Attorney General, broke his father's word and the Mafia leaders never forgot this broken bargain. Nixon never forgot either and therein lie the seeds of Watergate when O'Brien, then the head of the Democratic Party, had his office ransacked by Nixon operatives in the Watergate building, seeking Democratic election plans.

182 Cuba and Castro became an interesting backstage for Pierre Trudeau in 1974. Trudeau, a sympathizer of Communist leadership in Europe and China was especially intrigued by Fidel Castro. When Pierre Trudeau visited Castro in Cuba, his wife Margaret wore a tee-shirt bearing the Liberal logo that the Red Leaf Liberal Team

Schisms began to appear in the American Jewish community in the 1960's exemplified by the Democratic Party whose traditional support of Israel was undermined by the so called 'New Left' activists who began to denounce Israel's right to 'self defense' especially after Israel's success in the 1967 war. A leader of this movement was Noam Chomsky, a Jewish leftist professor. Many of these 'New Leftists' were so-called civil rights believers who forgot the history of Jewish activism in support of the Black civil rights movement before and especially under Martin Luther King who himself was always a staunch supporter of Israel. It was an American intellectual Lucy Dawidowicz working with Jewish organizations in Europe after World War II, who saved massive European Jewish archives, some of which had been hidden from the Nazi. Dawidowicz railed against the secularism of the 'New Left' *"who"* she wrote at that time *"have lived off the capital of traditional Judaism and have by now exhausted their patrimony"*.

---

that I led, had designed for the 1974 Liberal Campaign. Earlier Trudeau upstaged Nixon and Kissinger when he recognized Red China a day before the United States to Nixon's chagrin.

At a dinner party at 24 Sussex, the Prime Minister's residence after the 1974 Campaign, I offered Trudeau a Cuban cigar that had been made for me by two Cuban exiles in Miami. Trudeau refused my offer. Instead offered me a Cohiba cigar he drew out from a large wooden humidor given to him by Castro. I was dismayed. I had never heard of Cohiba cigars.

Later I discovered that Cohiba cigars were a special brand created for Castro's use that was carefully guarded from seeding to harvest to manufacture. Rumour had it that the CIA had tried to poison Castro's cigars. So a special brand of the finest Cuban tobacco was guarded especially for Castro's use. When I discovered this months later, I confronted Trudeau. I asked him, seriously, why he refused my cigar and preferred Castro's to our mutual laughter.

Later when Pierre Trudeau passed away, I met Fidel Castro for the first time who was standing a few feet away from me on the steps of the Cathedral in Montreal after Trudeau's funeral service. We were introduced. I told him this story. Castro then invited me to come to Cuba and promised he would provide me with a box of Cohibas. I never took up his offer. After I had retired from the Senate, Carole and I visited Cuba for the first time. We were greeted by the Speaker of Cuban Assembly, Sr. Alarcon. Regretfully by then Castro was old and infirmed and we did not meet. I bought Cohiba cigars in Cuba anyway. Much better than my own bespoke Cuban cigars.

In 1970, Yeshiva University, in New York City, appointed Lucy S. Dawidowicz to the first Chair in America dedicated to Holocaust Studies. This Chair started a counter-revolution at American universities as others followed and created Chairs, dedicated to Jewish studies. The influence of these Chairs and Departments created a quiet counter-narrative to 'New Left' secularism chocked with anti-Israel diatribes.

'TORONTO THE GOOD' – POST WORLD WAR II CANADA AND THE WORLD - THE '50S, ' 60S, '70S AND '80S

'Toronto the Good' in the mid 20th century was a misnomer[183]. True, major department store windows in downtown Toronto were curtained for the Sabbath. Liquor stores and restaurants licensed to sell alcohol were closed. Professional sports venues, live theatres and cinema were all closed for business. The 'puritan ethic' reigned supreme. All major hotels had colour bars. Blacks and Italians and Jews faced employment restrictions in large business, banking, legal, accounting firms and other professions. Hospitals restricted Jewish, Italian and black doctors, even if they ranked at the top of their profession, except for Mt. Sinai Hospital founded by Jews decades before[184]. Only in sports, entertainment, small businesses and local stock markets did Jews and Italians find a niche to prosper. Blacks across Canada faced higher barriers of discrimination in all walks of life. Elites of the city closed their private dining clubs and golf courses to all ethnic minorities.

---

183 After the advent of the mid 20th century, in the '50s something changed in social attitudes and tolerance of Toronto citizens. The roots of this change had deeper roots. William Peyton Hubbard, a black born in Toronto in 1842 and a leading orator nicknamed Cicero was elected a Toronto alderman from 1894 to 1903 and a controller 1989-1908 and was acting Mayor periodically in that period preceding over City Council. Hubbard after attending Normal School, became a baker inventing small commercial ovens that sold across America.

184 The Mount Sinai Hospital was founded in 1917 by members of the Jewish community in Toronto to provide health care but also to give Jewish doctors access to a hospital in Toronto for them and their patients which up until that time they were denied. My wife's paternal grandfather at the urging of her grandmother gave the first grant of land to build a small hospital on Yorkville Avenue to service Jewish doctors.

Suddenly step by step, visible and invisible barriers once challenged began to slowly dissolve. Yet blacks continued to be treated with the highest levels of restrictions[185].

The fascinating story about black racism and the blacks' struggle for equality of rights in Canada is little known. Once again there was a dichotomy of historic narrations. The Canada National Railways (CN) and Canadian Pacific (CP) were inseparable from history of Canada's origins and the emergence of Canadian national unity was linked from coast to coast in the 19th century. Hidden in the shrouds of the 20th century was the tale of black porters who fought for equal pay, promotions and working hours with little help from governments, the churches or the broader community. This lonely battle was led by George Grizzle, a black porter living in Toronto. Their erstwhile supporters in Toronto and Montreal included Kalmen Kaplansky, Sid Blum and Alan Borovay,

---

185 *They Call Me George: The Untold Story of Black Train Porters and the Birth of Modern Canada'* by Cecil Foster (Biblioasis, Windsor Ontario, 2019). This is forgotten fight led by Stanley Grizzle, a black railway porter, for fair employment practices in Canadian railways.

   Jackie Robinson when he came to play with Montreal Royals against the Toronto Maple Leafs in the '40s in Toronto, was refused accommodation at the Royal York and the King Edward and other major hotels as were musicians like 'Satchmo' Louis Armstrong or Miles Davis. They stayed at the Warwick Hotel, partially owned and managed by my late father-in-law, Harry Sniderman, himself a storied baseball and all-round athlete, where they were welcomed with open arms. Joe Lewis, and his softball team 'The Punchers' also stayed at the Warwick.

   This was the state of city and the nation in the mid 20th century. Irving Abella and Harold Troper in 1982 wrote a book entitled *'None Is Too Many: Canada and the Jews of Europe 1933-1948'* about immigration restriction against Jews during that period. The MS St. Louis, a ship carrying refugees from Europe were denied landing in Halifax at the onset of World War II. Many Canadian Italian immigrants were incarcerated or their movements restricted during World War II in Toronto as were Japanese Canadians citizens and even war veterans of Japanese descent of World War I who gained citizenship by their service and had their business and land appropriated and were incarcerated during World War II in Canada and more notoriously in the United States. Racism was alive and damaging to so many peace loving patriotic Canadian families.

who each were crucial actors in their struggle for these equal rights in the workplace, another tale not completely told.

A deeper dive back in Canadian history is enticing. In 1793, Lt.-Gov. John Graves Simcoe was sent by England to establish the first capital of Upper Canada. Simcoe travelled first to forks of the Thames River in my home town of London Ontario to establish Upper Canada's first capital[186], and then onto York, now Toronto. Simcoe directed the Executive Council and the Assembly of Upper Canada to pass an act that resulted in the gradual abolish of slavery. This act inspired 800 provinces and colonies across the British Empire around the globe to effectively eliminate slavery by court decisions and then legislation. In 1819, John Robinson, Attorney General of Upper Canada, promised that black residents who were slaves that were free that the courts would protect their freedom which they did. By 1834, Parliament in England passed the Slavery Abolition Act finally abolishing slavery in most parts of the British Empire effective August 1834. Slavery continued to linger amongst some aboriginal tribes across Canada beyond the end of the 19th century but for all effective purposes, slavery came to an end in all parts of Canada[187].

Upper Canada and Denmark became the first two governments in the world to outlaw slavery in 1797.

The first major turning point in 20th century in fair employment practices was the establishment of the Labour Relations Board under Leslie Frost, Premier of Ontario in 1951. The 1948 UN Human Rights Charter[188]

---

186 I became acquainted with life and times of John Graves Simcoe as my first public school in London, Ontario was called Governor Simcoe School, located on North Simcoe Street, the oldest public school in London at the time. Alas, only an empty lot remains today.

187 Another forgotten page in early Canadian history was how early Jewish settlers were denied free grants of land because they refused to sign the Christian oath to receive a small parcel of freehold. This was changed in 1803 when the Executive Council of Upper Canada allowed a Jewish immigrant Moses David, an early settler in the Windsor area (the County of Sandwich), and accepted his petition to receive his small land grant without the Christian oath. History moves slowly. Read 'Search Out the Land: The Jews and the Growth of Equality in British Colonial America, 1740-1867' by Judy Godfrey and Sheldon J. Godfrey (McGill-Queen's University Press, 1995).

188 The United Nations Human Rights Charter was drafted by a Canadian John P. Humphries, a lawyer and public servant supported by Eleanor Roosevelt.

accepted by Canada, incited the governments in Canada to extend its legal framework of rights to the domestic scene in 1960. Then came the Multicultural Act in 1970. Then Pierre Trudeau introduced the Canadian Charter of Rights and Freedom in 1982 following Diefenbaker's Charter of Rights passed in 1960 although limited to the federal sphere. This cascade of legislated rights to bring fairness and tolerance to the Canada workplace continued to end of century.

Seven men made a difference starting in the '40s, the '50s, the '60s and the '70s that integrated the transformation of workplace. A brief narrative of each of these men marks small turning points. Each in their own way, transformed the face of fairness, equity and equality of rights in the workplace that took concrete legal form.

Stanley Grizzle was the true exemplar as he led the black porters to outrage over treatment in their railway workplace which he himself experienced (the carriages of Canada' national railways). How symbolic tat Canada's national railway was rife with racial discrimination.

Louis B. Fine, a respected labour arbitrator in Toronto was approached by Premier Leslie Frost to lead the first Employment Practices Board established in 1951. Fine drafted the legislation, set the framework, and then established legal precedents to start the cleansing discrimination in the workplace and in unions, especially against minorities.

Ben Keyfetz, a World War II veteran, returned to his home in Toronto in the '40s. In the mid '50s Ben soon became head of the Joint Community Relations Committee (J.C.R.C.), an arm of the Canadian Jewish Congress in 1958[189]. With finesse, skill and soft-spoken effectiveness, he led this Community Committee of Jewish volunteers to respond to each daily egregious racist incident in the public square. The Committee met biweekly for a lengthy lunch and every Jewish Community organization was represented from labour to social workers to religious sects to fundraisers. Civic society began to take notice of to Ben's subtle yet powerful interventions, especially with police, civic officials and other religious denominations.

---

189 I was appointed representing B'Nai Brith at the JCRC and served on it for over decade until it was disbanded by the United Jewish Appeal which also led the way in disbanding the Canadian Jewish Congress to my endless regret.

Kalmen Kaplansky was an articulate key member of this Committee in the '50s, '60s and early '70s when we became allies on issues of anti-semitism and discriminations in business and unions and the professions in Toronto. A Polish immigrant in the 1920's, Kaplansky started organizing workers in the '30s, '40s and 50s. He quickly became a recognized leader in the Canadian labour movement. Ever the labour activist, starting with the Typographic Union in the '30s Kaplansky became head of the Jewish Labour Committee, helped organize a Human Rights Committee that became affiliated with the Canadian Labour Congress. Kaplansky went on to represent Canada in the International Labour Organization (ILO) in Switzerland. Kaplansky became a key supporter of the Pullman organization led by Stanley Grizzle, the activist leader, a black porter from Toronto while working on Canadian National Railway with his cohorts as he led the fight for fairer treatment, better pay and working conditions across Canada for pullmen, conductors and engineers in both national railways.

An associate of Kalmen Kaplansky, Sid Blum from Montreal, a labour activist began to work for the Canadian Labour Congress and quickly became head of Canadian Labour Congress Committee on Human Rights. Blum worked ceaselessly on the civil rights agenda during this evolutionary period until his premature death.

Lou D. Ronson, a Toronto businessmen, as head of B'Nai Brith Canada led the transformation of the Anti-Defamation League, an offshoot of the League on the U.S.A. to change its designation to the Canadian League for Human Rights in Canada. Under his leadership the League led fights against discrimination in all aspects of Canadian life, the workplace, the professions, as well as professional, civic and social organizations.

Sol Littman, an experienced American civil rights activist was hired by Ronson to come to Canada to advance a civil rights agenda, especially for the Jewish community.

Al Borovoy, a Toronto born lawyer of immigrant parents and a human rights activist in 1962, became head of Canada Civil Liberals Association and quickly emerged as an outspoken fighter for free speech and against bigotry in all its forms. Al was a brilliant organizer fighting discriminating practices especially against blacks. His work in Halifax and Dresden where shameful discrimination against blacks was rife in the workplace and in the communities in the '50s, '60s and '70s[190].

Without these men, the fight against discrimination of minorities would have been slower and less effective[191].

The early history of the 20th century was blotted by the 'head tax' placed on Chinese immigrants who built the National railway. 'The Chinese Head Tax' marks another sorry chapter in the history of Canada only to be rectified in the last decade.

Another chapter of bias ingrained in the Federal government during World War II was the treatment of Canadian citizens of Italian extraction that included naturalized Canadians of Italian extraction and landed immigrants from Italy.

---

190 Al was an advocate for absolute rights of freedom of speech. He strenuously argued against any limitations including 'hate' speech legislation.

191 As a young lawyer who got called to the Bar in 1960, I became of co-founder of Aaron Hart Lodge of B'Nai Brith in Toronto. This led to my appointment as a member of Joint Community Relations Committee (JCRC) of the Canadian Jewish Congress in Toronto over 20 years where I met Ben Keyfetz and Kalmen Kaplansky. Keyfetz was a community paid executive of the JCRC responsible for investigating anti-Semitic egregious discriminating issues in Toronto, coordinating with other similar groups across Canada. I was introduced to Louis B. Fine by my father-in-law Harry Sniderman. I never met Sid Blum, but his leadership and activism was recounted to me by Kalmen Kaplansky. Al Borovoy and I became sparring mates. I favoured 'hate speech' law reform. Al was a true believer in 'free speech'. History will determine who was right or wrong.

Sol Littman, Lou Ronson and I led the battle in Toronto to reduce the barrier to Jewish and Italian membership in Toronto's private men's clubs. One key incident bears repeating. Sol decided to target the Granite Club and a campaign was begun. Chairman of the Board at the Granite invited Sol Littman, Lou Ronson and me to meet with his Board at the Granite Club. The Chairman opened the meeting to announce that the Board had decided to open its membership to Jews and show us a short list of suggested members. My name was on the list. I told him that was excellent but why did he think I wanted to be a member which I did not. He laughed and said, *"Now I suppose you are a member of Oakdale Golf Club (that had only Jewish members) would open its membership to those not of Jewish persuasion."* Taken aback, I agreed. Immediately after the meeting, I called Bernie Herman, the President of Oakdale. He agreed to act. Within a few days, John Basset Sr. became a member of Oakdale. History advances by tiny steps.

In 1940 the Canadian government, right after the 1939 Declaration of War against Germany and Italy, put the War Measures Act into force. Citizens of Italian origin and Italian immigrants alike were considered fascist sympathizers and were put under surveillance. There were 112,000 residents and citizens, immigrants of Italian extractions in Canada. Thirty-one thousand were designated as 'enemy aliens'. Six hundred 600 were incarcerated and sent to remote prison camps. Over a third of the 600 were Canadian citizens or born in Canada. The 'rule of law' was ignored. The vast majority of those incarcerated were never charged with an offense. This tale should not be neglected or forgotten.

So, the early '60s, the ripples of human rights laws of reform of the '40s and '50s turned into waves washing over all aspects of the body politic and across Canada and reverberated in our political dialectics. No doubt John Diefenbaker's Bill of Rights Act passed in 1960 that applied only to the federal sphere triggered was a crucial fact in laying down the ground work for Pierre Trudeau's Charter of Rights and Freedoms in 1982.

In 1965 another reformist wave captured the media and public attention first in the U.SA and then Canada. Ralph Nader, son of American Lebanese immigrants, an army veteran and graduate of Princeton and Harvard Law rose to international prominence with the publication of the first of his book '*Unsafe at Any Speed*' that established Nader as the world's leading advocate for consumer rights.

And in 1965, I was serving in Ottawa as John Turner's executive assistant when he was appointed to the Federal Cabinet as Registrar General. He immediately undertook, with Mr. Pearson's blessings to transform that small department, responsible for patents, private federal corporations and related matters such as insolvency, into a modern department of government advocating consumer rights[192]. As Turner's assistant and

---

192 When the draft legislation reached the Federal Cabinet for approval, there was opposition mainly from the public service who argued that the department would raise expectations as its powers as consumer watchdog were limited to the federal sphere. Mr. Pearson overcame those objections and agreed to that the department should be called Consumer and Corporate Affairs rather than deleting 'Consumer' from the department's title. Turner and I had discovered that Mr. Pearson in the 1930's as a junior public servant was secretary to Borden's Royal Commission on "price spreads" that advocated a department of Consumer Affairs.

later as consultant, I was given responsibility to oversee the drafting and its passage in Parliament under Turner's leadership into federal law in 1967 - the first Department of its kind with consumer legislation - in the western world. To my chagrin, I watched as the Department was dismantled in 1993 and its responsibilities delegated to other departments. Alas.

Another quick look back at Government and the Canadian human rights experience. In 1944, Ontario passed the Ontario Racial Discrimination Act. In 1947, Saskatchewan passed Canada's first Bill of Rights. In 1947, Kalman Kaplansky led the Jewish Labour Committee to Combat Racial Discrimination and joined forces with the Canadian Labour Congress to fight discrimination. In 1948, the United Nations passed the Universal Declaration of Human Rights. In 1960, the federal government passed Canada's first Bill of Rights related to federal sphere of activity and Canada would; never be the same again. The UN Declaration of Human Rights which was finally implemented in Canada in 1976 which laid a framework for the Charter of Rights and Freedoms in 1982 that superseded Diefenbaker's governor's Bills of Rights legislation.

Of course the incarceration of Canadians of Japanese descent during World War II was by far worse an explicit example of racial discrimination. They were to sell their homes and businesses at bargain prices. Even World War I veterans of Japanese descent who were citizens had their property taken at unfair prices. Farmlands were confiscated and most families were sent to desolate incarceration camps – a rock solid tale of Canadian intolerance (read my maiden speech in the Senate on this issue reprinted in *'Parade: Tributes to Remarkable Contemporaries'* by Jerry Grafstein, Mosaic Press, 2017 - pages 19-37). Pierre Trudeau opposed any idea of apology or financial recompense. My maiden speech in the Senate was addressed to Pierre Trudeau[193]. Brian Mulroney finally

This report we brought to Mr. Pearson's attention just before Cabinet deliberated on this draft legislation. Pearson decided to overrule all objections.

193 I sent Pierre Trudeau a draft of my speech before delivery in the Senate. He told me he disagreed. When I handed him a copy of the speech recorded in the Senate Hansard a day later, Trudeau responded by saying he still disagreed. *"You can't change the past"*, he argued, *"You can only improve the future."*

atoned for this miserable Canadian historic record when he delivered a government apology in September 22, 1988 one month after Ronald Reagan made similar gestures. The Mulroney government apologized and established a compensation package to these Japanese Canadians. Nothing was given for those who died before compensation was finally paid out.

ENTER THE 1990'S: CANADA ON THE RISE – THE PIVOT TO THE 'NEW' MODERN

Meanwhile, with the entrance of the 1990's, we witnessed the Canadian economy shrug off its lethargy after the real estate collapse early in the decade. Canada's economy, reeling from endless deficits, enjoyed its first balanced budgets and experienced real growth fueled by 'free trade' by the end of the decade. Unemployment fell. There were blips along the way. Eaton's, Canada's largest and oldest retailer, went bankrupt after a century of growth and success. Creeds, the leading style pace maker boutique of imported women's high fashion in Canada dissolved in Toronto, after Eddie Creed, all-round athlete, community leader and a creative fashion genius, gave up the leadership of the storied store gained from his immigrant father 'Jack' who had founded 'Creeds' in the '30s starting as a fur designer of note.

Freer trade was on its way. It was the decade of the mighty explosion of free trade agreements in every part of the globe.

NFTA, the North American Free Trade Agreement, became a rocket booster to growing the Canadian economy and by the end of the decade, Canada was booming. In 1994, Unionism made a great leap forward with the passage of the North American Agreement on Labour Cooperation. While it levelled the playing field in Canada and the United States, Mexican labour costs continued to give Mexico an advantage especially in the auto sector. And, the 'new' modern burst forth with energy and diversity and the appearance of disruptive business models.

The government protected Canadian 'big banks' accelerated their expansion in the United States and abroad to pursue banking and trade opportunities.

No one road the high waves of 'free trade' in Canada more astutely than the remarkable and persistent Frank Stronach, an indigent immigrant mechanic from Austria, who built from his tool box in a garage in his small Toronto house an auto parts company that served the auto industry on both sides of the border before going on to become one of the largest international auto parts manufacturers conglomerates in the globe.

Globalism and the interconnectivity of the World Wide Web augured a new period of different kind of interaction between individuals and peoples with the expectation that interconnectivity would transform each of us into residents of a friendly 'global village' as McLuhan had predicted. The revamped Pearson Airport opened. Faxes spread. Workplace efficiencies increased with the faster inundation of the computer, email and the rise of mobile text and the ubiquitous cell phone. Work at home began. Everything was possible.

A large number Canadian newspapers were consolidated across Canada under the ambitious didactic Conrad Black whose media empire thrived in Canada, the U.S.A., and the U.K. and reached to Israel via the Jerusalem Post. Cable operators continued to consolidate into mega telecom companies as the division between voice and video disintegrated by regulatory fiat.

Our cultural scene took on a distinct Canadian-made flavour gaining wider popular acceptance. We heard new raucous sounds of bands like the Tragically Hip, the Guess Who, the Bare Naked Ladies and the Blue Rodeo flood the Canadian airwaves – all due to the change of FM regulations a decade before, mandating Canadian music to be played at higher levels of rotation. Their records became profitable and their concerts sold out.

In 1990, rock music in Canada began to pivot to 'hip-hop' and alternative rock. When Leonard Cohen[194], already an established song writer and singer, recorded his own song 'Hallelujah' several decades before, it received little recognition. But when the American singer Jeff Buckley

---

194 Leonard Cohen, a good acquaintance, wrote a poem for inclusion in my first published book, 'Beyond Imagination' (McClelland and Stewart, 1995). On his last tour across Canada, we met for the last time at a dinner in Toronto after his concert and Leonard took off his black fedora hat and gave it to me. I said I couldn't accept it. He said, "Take it. I give away dozens."

recorded '*Hallelujah*' in 1994 with a different beat, it instantly became and remains an iconic international song. Canadian women singers like Anne Murray and Celine Dion and K.D. Lang warbled to the fore. In 1997, Celine Dion album '*Let's Talk About Love*' made her the best-selling singer of all time. Alanis Morrissett and Shania Twain each sold an astonishing two million records in Canada alone while Avril Lavigne became an international star.

Robbie Robinson, born of a Mohawk mother and a Jewish father, on the Six Nations Reserve[195] outside of Brantford, Ontario near my home town of London, Ontario and leader of The Band issued their album '*One World One Voice*' in 1990 and then went on to found another band in 1994, the Red Road, a native American group to record native music that crossed over and gained wide acceptance in mainstream popular music and added yet another dimension to the '90s mix of exciting new sounds. DVD's made their appearance and the popular consumption of their unique music, lyrics and sound, changed the musical platform in Canada and America for the rest of the century and beyond.

In 1992, Garth Drabinsky, a boisterous Toronto lawyer, with his sanguine business partner Myron Gottlieb produced '*Kiss of the Spider Woman*' that opened in Toronto, then onto the West End in London and finally on Broadway in 1993.

---

195 The Six Nations Reserve near Brantford, Ontario was my first introduction to aboriginal issues. When I was taught poetry in primary school, I studied two poems of Pauline Johnson. My sister's name was Pauline, so Johnson's poems attracted my attention. I learned that Pauline Johnson was born on the Six Nations Reserve so as a teenager took my first visit to an aboriginal community. I also attended Tecumseh Public School located in London south in two primary grades. Overlooking the assembly hall was a large portrait of Tecumseh and his life became one endless fascination, especially his role in the War of 1812 that stopped the American annexation of Canada, a war that Britain and her North American cohorts, in Canada, won, despite American denials and heroic American paintings hanging in Congress.

Later I became fast friends with Chief Billy Two Rivers of the Mohawk Nation who lived in the Kahnawake Mohawk Territory in Quebec. Chief Two Rivers almost singlehandedly opposed the 1982 Constitution until Pierre Trudeau amended his legislation to recognize aboriginal rights.

On Broadway, dance musicals like '*Chicago*', '*Grease*' and '*Billy Elliot*' were the rage[196]. The recognition of 'gays' entered the mainstream via musicals like '*Kiss of the Spider Woman*', '*Victor-Victoria*', '*Rent*' and '*Madame Butterfly*' – all opened on Broadway followed by touring road-shows in American and Canada. '*Philadelphia*' hit the silver screen like a bomb shell and changed public attitudes towards 'AIDS', gays and gay rights. Who can forget the scene of the dying AIDS-ridden hero of this movie enraptured by Maria Callas singing a wrenching aria from the opera '*Andrea Chénier*'?

In 1992, Michael Ondaatje based in Toronto wrote the Booker Prize winning book '*The English Patient*' that in 1995 was made into a Hollywood movie that received seven Academy Award nominations, a first for Canada.

Challenges abounded and were overcome. Canadian female writers like Margaret Atwood and Alice Munro found larger audiences as their books steadily rose to prominence to fill Canadian and international bookshelves. Atwood as she continued to explore new literary forms in the '90s and produced a dazzling stream of published works from children's stories ('*Princess Prunella and the Purple Peanut*' – a children's novel) to poetry, artful prose and her first historical novel, a Victorian thriller – '*Alias Grace*' provoking the reader to grasp and glimpse at female amorality with new eyes. Atwood's first novel '*The Edible Woman*' brought her instant recognition. Munro published three new novels and was showered with international awards which led to her later Nobel Prize for Literature. Mavis Gallant, the 'expat' French Canadian writer living in Paris continued to draw rave international critical reviews with her stream of memorable short stories and each successive novel. At the same time, Carole Shield won the Pulitzer Prize, a first for a Canadian novelist, and in the decade was showered with a plethora of awards and international acclaim. Anne Carson, a novelist and modernistic poet, gained international recognition. All five female writers seduced male

---

196　These musicals followed in the footsteps of the 1900's to 1980's and the musicals and words and musicals from the gifted artists from Tin Pan Alley - singers like Eddie Centor, Al Jolson and composers like the Gershwins, Hart, Rodgers, Hammerstein, Cole and others that still reverberate across the globe.

readers to make a voyage of discovery into the female psyche from a feminine aesthetic.

Poetry 'slams' sprouted everywhere. I saw my private bill in the Senate to establish a Parliamentary Poet Laureate[197] to commemorate Canada's 125th birthday in 1992 pass into law after stiff vocal opposition on all sides to finally become a reality.

By 1990, popular rock music had been infiltrated by hip-hop and alternative rock pioneered by the breakout music of the REM. Hip-hop began to change the vernacular of popular music. Canadian Jazz musical stalwarts like Diane Krall, Peter Appleyard, Moe Kaufman and Guido Basso continued to attract growing loyal followers while Oscar Peterson led the small parade of top jazz musicians in the world. Leonard Cohen, a soft-spoken, genial acquaintance, the grand master or song and poetry won wider audiences with each delicate, carefully wrought, successive album. Leonard Cohen, from Montreal was deeply influenced by two great Canadian poets, A.M. Klein[198] and Irving Layton, both also from Montreal.

---

197 Under the Parliamentary Poet Act, the two Speakers of the Senate and House of Commons designate the Parliamentary Poet Laurette for a two-year term. From the five nominees selected by the heads of the federal cultural organization, one is selected by the two Speakers. The designated Poet has no responsibilities other than those he or she chooses and is remunerated with a modest annual stipend. The purpose was to indirectly influence Parliament with the grace of the spoken word, a work in progress. The Parliamentary history of this account, I set out in a book entitled '*The Making of the Parliamentary Poet Laureate: Based on a Senator Grafstein's Private Member's Bill*' published by the Porcupine's Quill in 2003.

198 I became familiar with the works of A.M. Klein, a friend and literary advisor of my uncle Max (Melech) W. Grafstein who from London Ontario published collected works of Sholem Aleichem and I.L. Perez, two of the greatest Yiddish writers, in English. A.M. Klein advised and contributed essays to both these collections. Klein was a Yiddish poet, who also wrote poems in English. He was an active Zionist in Montreal who edited a magazine on Jewish affairs for years in the '30s and '40s, the Montreal Jewish Standard. Klein's poetry influenced Irving Layton and Leonard Cohen, both Montreal poets. Layton received Canada wide recognition for his published poetry while Cohen received worldwide recognition for his songs, music and lyrics, and his novels, with an ever growing audience. Cohen's music and words for his song '*Hallelujah*' has become a global classic.

Music education, once a mainstay of primary and secondary education, but losing educators support, enjoyed a rebirth. 'El Sistema', a music learning system for youth created in Venezuela in South America developed across the globe after Jose Antonio Abreu, the founder became Special Ambassador to the UN. The 'El Sistema' network grew to 105 youth and 55 children orchestras led by the Simon Bolivar Symphony Orchestra which began to tour around the globe spreading the joyful gospel of music by young people for people of all ages.

In 1995, an appealing heartwarming Hollywood movie drama titled 'Mr. Holland's Opera' told a moving tale of a struggling music composer with a deaf son who gave up his dream to compose and instead became a high school music teacher who lavished his attention on student misfits through the window of music and in the process help revive the idea of teaching music in high schools as an essential part of a liberal education.

In the 1990's, there was an awakening of aboriginal politics as aboriginal rights were brought to public attention starting with the standoff on the Honoré Mercier Bridge leading to Montreal called the 'Oka Crisis'. The 1992 Charlottetown Accord added fuel to the fire of aboriginal rights. Two international treaties that were originated or propelled by Canada changed international norms. The Land Mines Treaty established by NGOs and non-state actors was supported by Canada[199]. The International War Crimes Tribunal, less a judicial body than a political actor, was approved by 120 countries and moved slowly after 2000. The reach and resources of this Court are limited as are its decisions.

The 1990's became the 'Decade of the Woman' in Canada.

Few women politicians have so quickly smashed through the political glass ceiling in Canada as quick-witted Kim Campbell who became the first female Conservative Leader and Prime Minister, while irrepressible

---

199 The citizen activists won the Nobel Prize for Peace for their efforts to gain state approval, one nation at a time. Lloyd Axworthy, a friend, who I brought to Ottawa to join me as another John Turner assistant, was Minister of External Affairs and was actively involved in this endeavour on Canada's behalf and influenced other nations. Lloyd's younger brother Tom became one of Canada's leading political thinkers and activists gaining his deserved reputation as Pierre Trudeau's advisor and favoured speech writer.

Sheila Copps of the Liberal Party became the first Deputy Prime Minister. No woman achieved more firsts than Kim Campbell – first female Justice Minister and Attorney General of Canada, first female Defense Minister of Canada and at NATO, first female Minister of Veteran Affairs, first female Leader of the PC Party and first Prime Minister born and raised in British Columbia.

In 1992, Micheline Rawlins became the first black woman to be appointed to the Supreme Court of Ontario.

In 1992, Rose Wolfe, a dynamic community leader, friend and wife of the late and lamented Rae Wolf, a leading businessman and an outstanding community leader, became the first woman and Jew to become Chancellor of the University of Toronto, the largest university in the Commonwealth.

The first female Canadian astronaut Roberta Bondar travelled into space. The glass ceiling began to crack wider.

In 1992, Juliette Payette became the second Canadian female astronaut. In 2017, she became the Governor General of Canada.

Also in 1992, Rosalie Abella, a daughter of Holocaust survivors, was appointed to the Ontario Court of Appeal becoming the first female immigrant and Jew. When she was first appointed a Judge at age 29 to the Ontario Family Court, she also became the youngest female and first pregnant female judge in Canadian history. Later she was appointed the first Jewish female to the Supreme Court of Canada in 2004[200].

The 1990's felt a surge of female participation in the work force. The public service in Ottawa and Ontario saw waves of talented, innovative and ambitious women rise to the highest ranks of bureaucracies. This change brought a great transformation in the male-dominated public services bringing not only bright new skills but wider sensitivity to the public workplace.

In 1991, Rita Johnson became the first female provincial Premier in British Columbia. She was followed by Catherine Callbeck in 1993 who

200 Irving Abella, Justice Abella's husband, together with Harold Troper, published in 1982, 'None Is Too Many: Canada and the Jews of Europe 1933-1948', a classic that disrupted Canadian's self-image of tolerance.

became the first female Premier of Prince Edward Island. Later Catherine became a Senator and friend whose contributions to the Senate were always tranquil, thoughtfully considered and sage.

This cohort of remarkable women and others now rising in the public service at all levels of government were independent and driven who juggled the exhausting demands of parenting, and homemaking with their equally demanding work duties bringing them closer to the stressed levels of the majority publics they served.

In 1994, Jocelyne Bourgon became the first woman appointed as a Clerk to Privy Council, the highest ranking public servant in Ottawa until 1999. There was a surge in female senior appointments to the public services, not only in Ottawa but in the provinces and municipalities. By 1999, the number of women in the federal public service became a majority for the first time. 'Pay equity' started to move in fits and starts in a fairer direction.

In 1993, Jean Augustine, a wonderful, genial friend and political colleague, became the first black woman to enter the House of Commons as Joyce Fairbairn became the first woman to become the Leader of the Senate. I joined the Liberal Women's Caucus in Ottawa to educate myself on the sense and sensibilities and concerns of inequality experienced by all members of the feminist movement. Each had an interesting narrative to share of their climb up the ladder to reach and participate in Parliament and render public service.

Lorna Marsden, a feminist leader, academic, author, sociologist and Senate colleague, left the Senate to become the first woman President of Sir Wilfrid Laurier University, and still later on in the decade became President of York University leading its mighty expansion program.

And in 1991, June Rowlands became the 60th mayor of Toronto and the first female office holder of that political office[201]. She served the City of Toronto with distinction until 1995.

---

201   I served as part of June Rowlands 'kitchen cabinet' of volunteer advisors along with Paul Godfrey who earlier joined me in my home one evening to convince June that not only should she run for mayor, but she would win. She kicked me off her 'kitchen cabinet' after I criticized her at a private meeting when she wondered about her age and told her that if she continued as Budget Chairman of Toronto Council and refused to go out and campaign, she was acting as an old woman and would lose her next election.

Paul Godfrey, an energetic young councillor from North York, son of an activist Conservative political mother became an innovative Metro chairman who helped innumerable politicos at all levels. Paul played a unique role in Toronto in the 1990's when he took over the helm of Sun Media, combining his talents as politician, sports enthusiastic, community leader and businessman to contribute to making Toronto the great city and sport centre it has become. He led to create Toronto's dome stadium later renamed by Rogers Centre by his efforts. He was an early CEO of the Blue Jays. He should work on his own autobiography.

Newspapers expanded its roster of female journalists like June Callwood and broadened the political spectrum with the refreshingly talented and insightful Barbara Amiel. At the Globe and Mail, Zena Cherry and later, Rosemary Sexton, ruled the social roost from their perch at that newspaper.

In 1997, Heather Reisman, an energetic entrepreneur who came from Montreal to Toronto opened her first book store in Burlington under the brand 'Indigo Books' that went on to be both the biggest and most innovative book store chain across Canada.

In 1993, the UN Conference on Human Rights in Vienna accelerated the rights of girls and women as female rights became part of the Universal Code of Human Rights.

In the 1990's, major legal advances continued to be made against gender bias under Kim Campbell as Minister of Justice. The Criminal Code was amended in 1992 supplanted the 'rape' offense with 'sexual assault' and redefined consent to a different, more gender sensitive basis by reversing the onus of proof from the victim to the alleged offender. The Supreme Court of Canada offered that the criminal defenses available to the rapists under the onus of proof on Crown rather than the alleged offender in that context was both inconclusive and unjust. As one acute observer later put it, *"No is no, but silence is not Yes."* By the 1990's, women in law schools across Canada gained more than parity with men altering the legal landscape forever. By 1996, over 56% of all university students were female. Gender bias was dealt the first of many serious wounds in public perception, especially amongst males. The 'rule of law' became more just.

In 1998, Gwen Boniface became the first woman Commissioner of the OPP and first female President of the National Association of Police Officers.

In 1999, Adrienne Clarkson became the first Canadian woman of Chinese descent to become the Governor General of Canada.

Led by the always persuasive, energetic and vivacious Frances Wright from Calgary, a Liberal activist and pal, who raised funds for a statue of the Famous Five - Nellie McClung, Louise McKinney, Henriette Muir Edwards, Irene Parlby and Emily Murphy – was unveiled on Parliament Hill in 2000. These five women had challenged the famous 'Persons Case' when the Supreme Court of Canada that held 'women' were not 'persons'. The Supreme Court of Canada case was overturned in 1929 by the Judicial Privy Council in the U.K. Cairine Reay Wilson became the first female Senator. A fine bust of Senator Wilson can be found in the outer chamber to the Senate[202].

The 'Decade of the Woman' reached another zenith when Beverley McLachlin became the first female Chief of Justice of the Supreme Court of Canada in 2000. Justice McLachlin's judicial career trajectory was instructive. She rose from County Court Judge, to BC Supreme Court, to BC Chief Justice to Supreme Court of Canada to Chief Justice of the Supreme Court in over a decade. Judicial gender parity was imbedded in Canada. Judicial decisions could finally be judged free of gender criticism. Reforms continued. McLachlan's free-wheeling stewardship as Chief Justice is still to be accurately measured and evaluated, particularly her decisions of aboriginal rights.

By the later '90s, Canada experienced the highest cable penetration in the world, about 70% and became a leading 'wired nation'. Canadians love to communicate and Canada became the highest user of telephones per capita in the world before the advent of the cell phone. Pay TV became a staple on cable TV adding dozens of new channel choices in the home. William Shatner leading in 'Star Trek' became a household name across the

---

202 Cairine Reay Wilson was the maternal grandmother of Joan Addison, wife of John Addison, who was MP for York North and who both were warm, wonderful and energetic friends.

world. Violence became more acceptable on the silver screen in Hollywood movies like 'Good Fellas', 'Fight Club', 'Carlito's Way', 'Reservoir Dogs', 'Bugsy', 'The Kralls', 'Pulp Fiction' and 'Silence of the Lambs'. Detective and spy thrillers headed the best seller lists with John Grisham and spy novels by John Le Carre, leading the way with Canadian authors following the trend.

The '90s experienced an outpour of Canadian crime, detective and science fiction books from authors like Peter Robinson, Gail Bowen and Kathy Reichs. Kyle Stone, later known as Sona Stone, brought scientific fiction with a Canadian twist to popular attention. Mordecai Richler, an inveterate iconoclast, continued to mesmerize his readers with his unique syntax all from a core Canadian context within a Canadian frame. Canadians recognized themselves in his books. A favourite Canadian author of mine was Howard Engel who created the bumbling, sweet, deceptively clever Canadian detective, Benny Cooperman, a Canadian version of the rumpled detective Colombo played by Peter Falk on the U.S. television.

Perhaps no writer caught the mood of the wary public at the start of the 1990's than my regular luncheon sparring mate, Morley Torgov. Morley, a lawyer/writer, who published 'St. Farb's Day', a tale of a back sliding lawyer involved in an egregious real estate deal at a time when the legal profession was riddled with similar cases at the beginning of the '90s and some were complicit in real estate crashes that rolled across Canada.

In 1996, Harlequin Books, owned by the Toronto Star, continued to publish streams of pulp romance books and became the first Canadian major publisher to greet the E-Commerce world with its e-books.

The long repressed memory of the Holocaust regained prominence via the silver screen with 'Schindler's List' and 'Sophie's Choice' joined by a tsunami of memoirs by Holocaust survivors that creased the public consciences and dredged up memories of the dreadful World War II replete with stories of unimaginable and unspeakable horror and trauma. Books by survivors began to flood bookshelves as repressed memories were unreleased[203]. The Holocaust Museum in Washington DC, opened

---

203 My cousin Abraham and his wife Chana Bleeman, both Holocaust survivors who married after World War II wrote a chilling tale of their experiences before World War II and in the camps called 'Survival and Revival" A Legacy for Our Children' (Mosaic Press, 2019) was self-published. They both lost their families and how head

in 1993, quickly became the most sought after tourist site in Washington and easily outstripped all other venues in annual attendance.

McClelland and Stewart, led by Avie Bennett[204], published my first book called 'Beyond Imagination' containing perceptions and insights of noted Canadian writers and poets of Jewish descent about the Holocaust who were not Holocaust survivors. Sir Alan Bullock, one of the world's leading historians, requested that his public lecture on the undeniable facts of the Holocaust be added as an afterword to my book when he first heard of its publication from Doug Gibson, my editor at McClelland and Stewart. Holocaust deniers were rebuffed, at least for a moment.

1996 marked the 200 year anniversary of the first publication of the 'Tanya' written by the Founder of the Lubavitch movement, Rebbe Shneur Zalman of Liadi, a small town located in present day Ukraine, AHL, a Chabad ('Gate') philosophic approach to 'Hasidic mysticism' and continues to sell thousands each year in different languages including English. The 'Tanya' means 'It is Taught' and details the meaning of Chabad 'the Gate' based on an acronym of three words – 'wisdom', 'understanding' and 'knowledge'. The 'Tanya' taught one cannot reform the world unless one reforms oneself. The mind was the route, a pathway as 'Deveikus' – emotional fervor – translating religious passion each day into a day of good deeds 'Mitzvot' – helping others[205,206].

---

a clan of over 40 naming their children and grandchildren and great-grandchildren for members of their deceased families. Their offspring married some of the leading Holocaust Jewish surviving families exclusively the Hofsteders and the Reichmans.

204 Avie Bennett was the son of one of the immigrant Bennett brothers who built the first malls in Canada starting with the Lawrence Avenue Mall at the corner of Lawrence and Bathurst in Toronto. I became well acquainted with Avie's father and uncle who were leaders in Canadian Jewish community who would frequently pick me up when I was waiting for a bus near my home to take me down then to my law office. Both were fascinating erudite men and staunch Zionists.

205 The most influential popular orthodox Jewish religious movement of the 20th century was the Lubavitch. Rebbe Shneur Zalman was the first of a line of Schneerson Rebbes ('Teachers') starting in 1796, a small village in Ukraine, as he gathered adherents to study and practice their faith in accordance with his strict adherence to biblical principles of conduct. He published his work in 1797 called the 'Tanya' – The Way that it translated into dozens of languages. Apparently he kept on his writing desk, a siddur (prayer book), written by my rabbinic ancestor, the 'Sheloh'.

Canadian business firms prospered, proliferated and expanded internationally in the wake of the 'free trade' agreements transplants in the '90s.

The Seventh Lubavitch Rebbe Menachem Mendel Schneerson who emigrated from Europe to United States in 1939 with his father-in-law, the Sixth Lubavitch Rebbe, settled in Crown Heights, Brooklyn. In 1951, after the death of his father-in-law, Menachem Mendel Schneerson reluctantly became the Seventh Lubavitch Rebbe and the last of the line. In his first public statement, he referred to the 'Sheloh', a direct ancestor of mine. He declared he was a 'Sheloh Yid', a follower of the Sheloh, a 17th century Hasidic master who published over 30 books of commentary, the most notable being *The Two Tablets of the Covenant*, hence the acronyms of his name. My material grandfather, Mirel Bleeman, was a direct descent of the 'Sheloh'. Rebbe M.M. Schneerson AHL is considered one of the most influential Jews of the 20th century. The Seventh Rebbe who I met privately on two occasions, believed in outreach to both Jew and Gentile alike. Under his leadership before he died in 1994, his emissaries had established Jewish centres and schools (called 'chabad') in all 50 states of the United States, across Canada and 80 countries around the world. He was posthumously granted the U.S.A. Congressional Medal of Honour for his good works. Unsung, he was a leader of the Russian dissident movement that helped bring an end to the Soviet Empire (Read *'Parade Tributes to Remarkable Contemporaries'* and my essay on the role of the last two Lubavitch Rebbes in the Russian Counter Revolution, pp. 95). Today the seventh Lubavitch Rebbe's legacy continues in over 5,000 active Lubavitch Jewish centres called 'Chabad' around the world and in over 185 countries. One centre is established across the world every two weeks. The word for these centres is 'Chabad'. Chabad is an acronym of three intellectual facilities – wisdom, understanding and knowledge. In the '80s, I had two lengthy meetings with the 'Rebbe' in Crown Heights, Brooklyn arranged through the good offices of Rabbi Zalman Grossbaum – an astonishingly energetic Lubavitch leader in Toronto and a great friend and advisor.

206 In 1991, through the efforts of the Rebbe and his Lubavitch adherents, a joint Resolution of Congress passed entitled 'Education Day' in U.S.A. Earlier in Canada, during a hotly contested by-election in Eglinton riding in 1979, Doris Anderson, a friend and leading feminist and writer, ran under the Liberal banner. Liberals needed all the support it could muster. Earlier I was asked by Rabbi Grossbaum, the Executive Director of the Lubavitch in Toronto, to arrange a meeting with Pierre Trudeau, then Prime Minister, to allow Lubavitch representatives from across Canada to present him with a Bible from the Lubavitch Rebbe to encourage Pierre Trudeau and the Liberals to promote education. The opportunity presented itself when the Liberals needed every vote in the Eglinton Riding and there was a sizeable Jewish vote in that

Seagram's Canada, one of the world's leading liquor and spirits firms that expanded globally after World War II first led by the dynamic Sam Bronfman, Canada's leading salesman and brand creator, took a dramatic shift. Seagram's, now headed by Sam's grandson Edgar Jr., moved Seagram away from spirits and real estate, from oil into chemicals with a major investment in DuPont and then pivoted again into the movie and faltering music business all to be merged with a French firm by the end of the century. Charles Bronfman, a thoughtful philanthropist, the son of Sam resident in Canada, financed short TV vignettes culled from Canadian history supervised by my friend Tom Axworthy to provide wider interest in Canadian history. Bronfman also helped with the annual 'March of the Living' when Jewish teenagers from around the world visit European death camps and Israel to teach them the lessons of history.

Norman Jewison was first a producer at CBC and then went on to direct iconic movies like 'Fiddler on the Roof' and 'A Soldier's Story' in Hollywood. While he continued his fine work in movies, he established the first centre for teaching film to young Canadians in Toronto, passing on his art forms to the next generation. Norman, an old friend, is a Canadian treasure[207].

riding. A meeting was arranged in Toronto with Mr. Trudeau that his staff previously had rejected. The meeting took place at a downtown hotel on Friday afternoon. This was difficult as Trudeau's time was limited and the Sabbath was fast approaching. The Lubavitch crowd needed to get back to the Lubavitch headquarters in North Toronto before the early evening when Sabbath commenced.

Trudeau became fascinated with the history of these bearded men and their Rebbe so the short meeting was extended for almost an hour as Trudeau, ever curious, sought more information about the Lubavitch and their legendary leader. Finally Jim Coutts, Trudeau's Chief of Staff, angered by the turn the meeting had taken, intervened to bring the meeting to a close. The Lubavitch raced to take their ride through the traffic clogged downtown Toronto streets to head to north Toronto. Immediately after the meeting, Trudeau asked me to stay behind to discuss the history of the Lubavitch to the chagrin of the time-sensitive Jim Coutts. Trudeau asked me more penetrating questions and wondered if I could arrange a meeting with the Rebbe in Brooklyn as the Rebbe never travelled far from his headquarters in Crown Heights. To my deep disappointment, that meeting never took place – alas.

207　After 9/11, a small group of volunteers and I led a large group of Canadians to visit New York City for a weekend as Mayor Giuliani had called for. More than 26,000 Canadians

'Big' Canadian movie sagas like *'The Bethune Story'*, the haunting *'Red Violin'* and the majestic *'Black Robe'* made it to the movie theatres. French Canadian cinema achieved its own record of 4 million in Canada sales with *'Les Boys'*. New wave directors like Atom Egoyan and Don McKellar joined the ranks of older established Canadian directors like Norman Jewison and Ted Kotcheff[208], Ivan Reitman and David Cronenberg whose films had all gained North American commercial success when they joined the ranks of Hollywood movie makers. Robert Lantos and Michael MacMillan, one a Hungarian immigrant and the other a homebred Torontonian, each built robust TV and movie production and distribution firms from scratch. By the end of the decade in 1998, their two firms, Alliance and Atlantis, merged into Atlantis Alliance, the biggest firm of its kind in Canada and a recognizable entity in the global entertainment business. Lantos went on to become an award winning movie producer with extraordinary film classics like *'Shine'* that displayed his Hungarian roots. Lantos produced a number of brilliant short films featuring aspects of people's lives effected by the Holocaust. *'The Statement'* is another evocative film about how the church helped a Nazi war criminal to survive. Lantos needs to work on his autobiography, an amazing story of survival and creativity.

The crossover of Hispanic music from Cuba and Mexico and then South America climbed the charts both in U.S. and Canada. Selena, Ricky Martin, Marc Antony broke through while Jennifer Lopez became the leading Hispanic movie star in Hollywood. The Hispanic fact was here to stay throughout North America and grow and transform entertainment 'pop' culture with zest and tantalizing rhythms.

---

showed up, in part due to a commercial that Norman volunteered to produce and which I arrange to play on TV screens across Canada and on large digital billboards in Times Square in the heart of New York City. Read *'Parade Tributes to Remarkable Contemporaries'* and my essay on this event entitled 'The Miracle on 52nd Street'. We called the weekend *'Canada Loves New York'*.

208 Ted Kotcheff of Bulgarian extraction had produced brilliant and effective 'free time' vignettes of Pierre Trudeau for television in the 1974 national election under the aegis of the Federal Liberal advertizing consortium that I led called 'Red Leaf'. Ted's breakthrough Hollywood successes included *'First Blood'* and *'Weekend at Bernie's'*.

The year 1994 saw the first major animated film of 'Batman', a superhero, start a trend that continues to flood movie screen around the world. Another radical breakthrough change in movies was launched by director Quentin Tarantino in his first film called 'Pulp Fiction'. It seemed that the film censors had given up containing blood, gore and obscene language which became acceptable for public consumption. Alas.

Canadian comedy stars lit up American and Canadian TV screens led by the Second City characters following the decades of earlier success of Wayne and Schuster on CBC who were invited on the Ed Sullivan Show gaining international fame and the star-studded footsteps of David Steinberg who became a staple on the John Carson Late Show. John Candy, Dan Aykroyd, Martin Short, Eugene Levy, Mike Myers and Jim Carrey and others who all became household names in America. All of them honed their talents with the great school of 'improv' at the Second City in downtown Toronto. 'Saturday Night Live' (SNL) created and produced by Toronto's own Lorne Michaels, a former stand-up comic, became and remains a perennial North American success[209].

In 1991, Ed and his talented son David Mirvish opened the first new 'live' theatre in Toronto in decades, the Princess of Wales, expanding their 'live' theatre universe.

The early '90s saw cheerful avuncular Al Waxman, a lifelong friend since college days, born of Polish immigrant family in the Kensington Market area in 1935, reach new heights as a critically acclaimed actor of stage, screen and TV as an award-winning artist. Al lost his hardworking father when he was nine. Ambition and success drove him. Al did it all – acting,

---

209 Lorne Michael's first comedic partner in Toronto was Hart Pomerantz, a lawyer, producer, comedian and short story writer. Together they started on a CBC show called 'The Hart and Lorne Terrific Hour' where both displayed busy hirsute mustaches. This CBC show was a progenitor of 'Saturday Night Live', the long playing comedy series televised weekly from NYC created by Lorne Michaels. Hart added a beard to his bewhiskered profile. Hart is married to Nancy, née Grafstein, a second cousin. My sister Pauline was married to Syd Wayne, a sometime CBC producer and younger brother of Johnny Wayne of Wayne and Schuster, the ground breaking Canadian comedians who starred on the Ed Sullivan show and who influenced Pomerantz and Lorne Michaels in their early years as stand-up comedians.

writing, producing for every entertainment venue. There wasn't a charitable cause that Al would not freely lend his time and talent. He was everywhere. He was the 'King of Kensington'. Al lit up any gathering, large or small. And it was Al who would, in jest, never cease to remind me that I was a failed actor and he was a failed lawyer, *"But who had the most successful career?"* he would exclaim! *"You, Al, you"*, I would respond to our mutual delight.

In 1993, the notorious '*M. Butterfly*', the cross-gender movie, directed by David Cronenberg debuted. Canadian live theatre thrived led by Livent, headed by the creative, notorious, energetic, high-tempered Garth Drabinsky, then the largest theatrical company in North America with hits like the 'Phantom of the Opera' and 'Ragtime'. Live theatre twinned with hockey as national preoccupations. Experimental regional theatre groups sprung up in Toronto (Soulpepper), Vancouver (Rumble), Montreal (Theatre Ex Mechanica) and Winnipeg (Radix and Primus) and the Maritimes whetting Canadian audiences with an increasing appetite for live theatre. Meanwhile Ed and David Mirvish expanded their theatrical empire to the U.K. to acquire and renovate a historic theatrical landmark in London, the 'old Vic'. They coproduced a stream of hits like '*Lord of the Rings*'.

After the real estate crash in the early '90s in Toronto, a remarkable crew of real estate developers composed of Italian immigrants and their sons, and Jewish Holocaust survivors and their sons, bounced back to rebuild their privately owned real estate development firms that came to rival and exceed the worth of many major public companies traded in the TSX. These ambitious, talented and driven men were creative builders, at times partners, but mostly competitors and sometimes, clients of my law firm who rose to prominence on each successive influx of newcomers that inundated Toronto and the GTA up to the '90s and beyond. They all worked feverishly to construct Toronto into a world class city with well-developed, well-designed homes, condos and commercial buildings.

Rising from construction labourers, carpenters, bricklayers, plasterers, electricians and sewage contractors, these small dynamic family groups first started building small homes themselves, then apartments and

commercial buildings and high rise condos to emerge as family-owned
real estate giants. Amongst the most notable were the DelZottos led by
taciturn, ever thoughtful Angelo Del Zotto and his brothers who became
the premier condo builders in Toronto called Tridel, the irrepressible Rudy
Bratty and his robust sons, elegant Freddie De Gasperis, his brothers,
sons and nephews, energetic workaholic Marco Muzzo and his brothers
and male offspring, Joe Zentil and family – mostly from Northern Italy –
the Province of Friuli[210].

The vast development around Pearson Airport was led by Orlando
Fidani and his family who became the major developer of commercial
and industrial space surrounding this ever expanding busy airport, the
largest in Canada.

These immigrant families were joined by Holocaust survivors from
Poland and other eastern European countries like my cousin Abraham
Bleeman and his partner, Alex Grossman and Joey Silver. Under the name
of Belmont and supported by their talented sons, Aaron and Nathan
Bleeman and George Grossman, they built triplex apartments, condos
and notably Regent Park. Sandy Hofsteder, a survivor from Hungary
and his sons led by Tommy Hofsteder all joined this stellar cast of immigrants and sons who transformed themselves from minor home builders
into master builders. It was the Hofsteders that premiered the REIT
as a vehicle for public investment. They were joined by another son of
Holocaust survivors and a distant relative of mine, the ever loveable and
entrepreneurial, Eddie Sonshine (whose surname reflects his personality), who started RioCan soon to become a leading North American
giant REIT specializing in shopping malls.

My favourite character and my first and lifelong client, first as a law
student and then a lawyer, was George Kalmar. George was an exuberant
positive person who loved Canada. George, born in Hungary, was a Holocaust survivor, first in forced labour escaped to become an underground

---

210   I was inducted to the Honourable Order of the Dukes of Friuli in Italy by Enzio Illy,
      the heir to the Illy Coffee Company who was first elected Mayor of Trieste and then
      the Governor of Friuli, when he visited Toronto for one of the annual dinners of the
      Furlane Society held in north Toronto at their capacious community centre.

fighter, came to Canada in 1948 with $1.50 in his pocket. Starting in real estate, he acquired the Constellation Hotel near The Pearson Airport and expanded it into over 900 rooms, the largest convention hotel in Canada. With his son Michael, he continued in the hotel business acquiring the Valhalla Inn and then the historic Old Mill. One of his young employees became one of Canada's leading chefs, Mark McEwan, who started as a kitchen helper at the Constellation Hotel when I first met him.

Another interesting sagas is the remarkable story of Sam Bresler, a Holocaust survivor who became a close friend with Elie Wiesel[211]. After the war, Sam went to Palestine, fought in the Israel War of Independence and then came to Canada, penniless. Sam built the Budget Rent a Car franchise from scratch at the Pearson Airport and a substantial business in real estate development, a remarkable tale of persistence and success aided by his energetic wife and family.

The Brookfield story is even more remarkable. Founded by the 'other' two Bronfman brothers, Edward and Peter, and commanded by Jack Cockfield, a South African immigrant accountant who together built a real estate international behemoth that grew around the globe and continues to expand and prosper with ownership of high-rise commercial towers in New York City and elsewhere, and roadways and infrastructure projects across the Americas, Europe and beyond.

Of course, the most unbelievable tale of the spectacular rise and the fall and rise again of the innovative Reichmann family headed by

---

211 It seems that Elie Wiesel, the Nobel winner for Literature, like me, was also a descendent of a 17th century famed Rabbi and writer, Isaiah Horowitz was called the 'Sheloh' after his 'magnus opus', 'The Two Tablets of the Covenant' as I am on my maternal side, which we discovered when we first met (see 107 on my relationship to the 'Sheloh'). Wiesel and I both attended an OSCE conference on anti-Semitism in Cordova, Spain, who spoke in his quiet thoughtful way and summed up the solution to anti-Semitism in one phrase, "You can teach a child to love or to hate". Later we met up again at another OSCE conference on the same topic held in the Reichstag, newly renovated in Berlin. Wiesel, ever the mesmerizing speaker, as his voice never raised above a whisper. This conference was held in the same room where Hitler harangued his Nazi Parliament especially his focus on anti-semitic laws and actions. I gave a brief speech on the same podium. Incredible.

resourceful Hungarian immigrant brothers, all devoutly religious, who escaped Nazism in Hungary to settle in Morocco with their parents and siblings during the war and then went on to resettle in Canada. The brothers started with a tile business in North Toronto. Then they built state of the art elegant high-rise buildings. Led by the astute reserved Paul and his equally talented and graceful brother Albert and their sons, they became one of Canada's greatest international builders of high rise architectural gems across Canada, Mexico and the U.K. First Canadian Place built in the heart of the Toronto financial district remains a white marbled graceful marvel built to meet their talents and taste. Then Canary Wharf in London, England. Bouncing back after the early '90s real estate crash, this ambitious family group (who were fiercely orthodox Jews[212]) and others propelled Toronto beyond Canada via family owned and operated real estate enterprises that rivalled and then surpassed the older largest holders of real estate in Canada. The story of their rise and fall and rise again and their remarkable impact on Canada's architectural profile remains an unrivalled story of historical proportions that few Canadians know.

The DelZotto clan from northern Italy, Friuli[213], led by the taciturn suave Angelo DelZotto who quit high school and a promising career as a hockey pro, to work for his immigrant father building contractor as a carpenter Angelo was the joined by his two younger brothers including an old Liberal friend Elvio. Later, their brand, 'Tridel', became synonymous with the highest excellence in condo building in Toronto. Rudy Bratty, also started in high school as a carpenter working for his immigrant dad (a contractor and small builder) and his uncle, went on to law school as he built small homes, later to be joined by his four talented and gregarious sons under the name Remington Homes. Marco Muzzo,

---

212 The Reichmans and their employees never worked on the Jewish Sabbath, Saturday, or the Jewish holidays in addition to other statutory holidays. Their employees were fully paid when Jewish holidays fell on weekdays.

213 While only about 10% of Canadians of Italian descent in Toronto originate from Friuli in Northern Italy, they number amongst the most successful, especially in business. The Columbus Centre that includes a home for the aged and is a physical tribute to their generosity, largely, by the Furlani.

an immigrant from Friuli, started as a plasterer with his family, while the bespoke tailored ever graceful Freddie De Gasperis, his brothers, sons and nephews built the largest sewage and water development service company in Canada and became major real estate developers and owners in the process. Joe Zentil, a tall, angular, physically fit immigrant who started as an electrician's helper, then electrical contractor and a devout tennis player, joined the ranks of these ambitious innovative builders.

Most of these developers were clad in immaculately tailored suits by Lou Myles, my next door neighbour who was also tailor to stars like Frank Sinatra, Telly Savalas and Tony Bennett in the U.S.A. Lou started as an immigrant shoeshine boy in the streets of Toronto and went on to international fashion fame and acclaim as a master designer and bespoke tailor.

Using the banner Belmont Construction, my cousin Abraham Bleeman together with Alex Grossman and their partner Joey Silver, all Holocaust survivors from the death camps of Poland, became major house then, apartment and commercial builders across the metro Toronto region and beyond into the U.S.A. and Israel. Their sons followed their fathers' footprints and expanded their family owned development business. Sandy Hofsteder, a devout Jew from Hungary aided by his talented sons joined this stellar cast of immigrants builders that made Toronto a world class city and who all survived 'the early 90's real estate meltdown to build, grow and thrive.

Children of Holocaust survivors became successful doctors, lawyers and businessmen. My distant cousin, Eddy Sonshine, a lawyer who built one of Canada's first REITs and with his elegant wife, Fran[214], who are both children of survivors, led in philanthropic endeavours in all directions.

Other immigrants, Frank Stronach, arrived in Canada from Austria after the war as a penniless mechanic starting in his backyard, built the largest auto part manufacturing firm in the world and went on to be the

---

214 It was due to Fran Sonshine's efforts that a monument to the Holocaust was created in Ottawa next to the war museum. Canada remains the only country in the western world without a museum dedicated to the events of the Holocaust despite a large number of Holocaust survivors who emigrated to Canada. My own feeble attempts in Ottawa and Toronto were not successful.

largest owner and breeder of race horses and race tracks in the world as he shared his magnificence first with his employees and then with countless charitable causes.

I have barely scratched the surface of these yet to be told fabulous tales of ambitious hard-working men who quietly propelled Toronto towards Canada's graceful skyline profile and boosted Toronto to world recognition as a world class city and architectural pacemaker in less than two decades.

The creation of all this new found wealth contained positive side effects for Toronto. Charitable giving and largesse became a required precedent for community recognition in Toronto on a massive, if unheralded, scale. My wife Carole aided and abetted by her small coterie of volunteer women like Catherine Nugent, Cathy Bratty, Anna Maria DeSouza rose to prominence on the social pages and used their prominence to lead charity balls, the most exciting of which was the Brazilian Ball, to support cultural entities like the Canadian Ballet and Opera companies helping them to become world class cultural icons. Staid volunteer committees were jolted into action. Other wannabee women rushed to join them. Then these hard-working volunteer women urged by my wife and her colourful circle of friends turned their attention away from Toronto's cultural institutions to the fight against breast cancer and to support medical research and hospitals (Mount Sinai, Toronto General, Princess Margaret, Sick Kids, et al) and old age institutions like the Baycrest Centre and the Columbus Centre. With her emphasis on taking the fight against breast cancer to every corner of Canada, the Women's Breast Cancer Foundation under her leadership and others was expanded across Canada and then created the Annual Run for the Cure and then the Walk for the Cure and in the process, raised tens of millions upon millions for cancer research annually. Then onto Princess Margaret Hospital, Mt. Sinai, Sunnybrook in the north end, Toronto Rehab, along University Avenue and then onto the old age home of Baycrest in Toronto's north end and then later the Bridgepoint, a rehab hospital built in the old Don Jail in the east end, helping make Toronto via the UHN (University Health Network) a leading centre of health care in all its aspects in the world today[215]. These dynamic resourceful women and their widening circle of friends quietly exceeded their male counterparts without fanfare in raising millions for health causes and their pioneering work continues unabated with creative annual funding events today.

On the sports front, Canada proved to be the home of fanatic and blindly loyal fans. Canada joined the ranks of North American baseball teams during the '90s. The Blue Jays played their first games at the Skydome in Toronto with record crowds of close to 4 million fans. The Expos in Montreal joined in. In 1992, the Blue Jays won the World Series followed up with a second World Series in 1993. Fans across Canada went wild. Vancouver and Toronto joined the NBA team expansion with the Vancouver Grizzlies via the Toronto Raptors. Basketball boomed, like hockey and baseball, becoming passionate Canadian pastimes aided by sports specialty channels. When public schools no longer provided after school sport teams, volunteer parents put together fully competitive regional basketball, baseball and hockey teams from primary to high schools to provide youth with a ladder to athletic prowess and path to the big leagues. CFL Football faltered due to the drowning coverage of NFL in Canada. Canada's own Steve Nash started in NBA career in 1986 and went on in the '90s to become an iconic star, twice becoming NBA's most valuable player and eight time NBA all-star. Canadian youth now actively vied for the 'big leagues' in all these sports.

While Toronto continued to be the leading hockey centre in North America and the Toronto Maple Leafs the richest hockey franchise in North America, my wife, a long-time fan who binges each Saturday night to watch Hockey Night in Canada, never ceased to be supportive as her beloved Leafs even as they failed to win the iconic Stanley Cup. Toronto fans just never give up hope.

Ted Rogers, a restless, kinetic, ambitious, visionary lawyer-businessman, who rose from the ownership of one radio station in Toronto, originally started by his late father, to combine cable, speciality channels,

---

215   UHN was led by brilliant entrepreneurial doctors like Robert Bell and Michael Baker. Robert Bell continued his sterling career as Deputy Minister of Heath in the Ontario government where he never failed to make a difference.

radio, magazines, cell phones and sport teams into a Canadian media behemoth while the established telecom leader, Bell Canada, the oldest and largest telco company in Canada, raced to mimic to catch up[216].

The Toronto Film Festival (TIFF) glowed with greater international notoriety and success under the creative leadership of Piers Handling. The Toronto Jewish Film Festival (TJFF) that quickly became the largest Jewish film festival in the world was founded and initially funded by the visionary amiable Helen Zuckerman. The Shaw Festival and the Stratford Festival attracted ever wider international audiences and critical recognition[217]. The 'true north' sparkled with the arts in every direction.

Higher education across Canada exploded with swamped registrations both at the established Universities and more so at Community Colleges[218] which experienced a flood of enrollments and wider course choices adding a new layer to prepare our youth for the 'brave' new and diverse job market.

Joe Rotman, ever energetic, cheerful, clever, college chum from Western, joined his Polish immigrant father Manny in his small thriving coal and oil home delivery business in Toronto. Joe expanded this small family owned enterprises into oil and mining and investment banking while donating large chunks of his wealth to the University of Toronto when the Rotman School of Management was established in 1990[219].

---

216 I knew Ted well from his earlier days as a cable pioneer and his trusted advisor Phil Lind when I acted for and against him in many contested CRTC hearings across the country. Ted Rogers, and Phil Lind, together with Geoff Conway and me cofounded YTV, a successful channel dedicated to programs for youth – the first of its kind

217 I served, for a time, on most those festival boards (e.g. TIFF, Shaw and Stratford) and came to know the artistic and financial challenges confronting their artistic directors and each board.

218 Premier of Ontario Bill Davis, serving as Minister of Education established Community Colleges that became the template for skills based post-secondary education across Canada.

219 Later in 2011, to my amazement, Joe invited me to attend his inauguration as Chancellor of University of the University of Western Ontario (UWO) where he and I were anything but great academic achievers at Western. At his inauguration, we both chortled at this surprising turn of events as we reminisced about our great times as wayward youth spent at Western.

Joe donated astutely to aid in brain research and other causes at Toronto hospitals. Meanwhile, his father Manny retired and went to university for the first time to renew his lust for learning in his seventies to gain the formal education he never received as a youthful penniless immigrant. Finally Manny settled on Israel to resume his education to round out a remarkable 'rags to riches' career.

The flood of major charitable donations from established Toronto families like the Thomsons led by always modest ever generous soft-spoken Ken Thomson and the Westons led by Galen – a graceful gentle-man's gentleman and a polo star – who in the '90s when his inherited food companies met with increased competition from American firms, suffered from retrenchment, and then later in the decade bounced back and expanded across Ontario and Quebec, returning his family food empire to profitability and never looked back. His wife, Irish born ever elegant Hilary Weston, became the Lieutenant Governor of Ontario, to cap her remarkable career as a style setter and charity leader.

Ted Roger's, a sometime client and partner, was the visionary pioneer of a sports behemoth that combined radio, cable, TV, cell phone, print productions and magazines like McLean's. He and his family made munificent gifts to hospitals and cultural and educational institutions especially to Ryerson University. The Rogers, Thomsons, Jackmans and others led the creators of the 'new' Toronto wealth like the MacEwans and Peter Munk, the O'Borns', Janice and Earle, and the Temertys' increasing their charitable gifts on a massive scale to Toronto's hospitals and higher educational institutions. The University of Toronto and York University and the hospitals that lined both sides of University Avenue and others all benefited from their largesse, as the street signage proclaims.

These gifts and others across Canada lifted medical research in Canada to new heights. The 1990's witnessed an explosion of advanced medical research into stem cells. In Montreal, Dr. Philip Wainberg and his team made the first breakthrough research for a cure for HIV and AIDS in the world. In 1992, Dr. Sam Weiss of the University of Calgary's discovered human neural stem cells. In 1993, Drs. Janet Rossant and Andras Nagy proved the pluripotency of embryonic stem cell research at Mt. Sinai Hospital. In 1994, Dr. John Dick isolated cancer stem cells in Toronto at the

Ontario Cancer Institute, University Health Network. In 2000, Dr. Derek van der Kooy discovered retinal stem cells. By 2000, Dr. Alan Bernstein became head of the Canadian Institutes of Health Research (CIHR). Canada was reaching the stars in science breakthroughs in stem cell research.

Vancouver, Montreal and other cities, following Toronto's lead, witnessed the accelerated vertical growth of condos and office towers transforming the skyline of Canadian cities in every region.

The Four Seasons luxury hotel chain originated with a small experimental 'luxury' motel on the Jarvis strip in downtown Toronto built by a Polish immigrant who became a budding contractor, Max Sharpe and his son Issie who went on to become a world leader in building and managing their brand of 'five star' hotels across the globe. The ever ambitious handsome 'Issie' Sharp assisted by his talented wife Rosalie, who were practiced ballroom dancers, then built the Inn on the Park in North Toronto, while it was Eddie Creed, a brother-in-law of 'Issie' Sharpe, who helped coin the name Four Seasons from a famous hotel in Germany called 'Vier Jahrzeiten' and along with Eddie's pal Murray Koffler became initial investors in the Sharp hotels that helped lift the Four Seasons expansion making it the leading Canadian owned international five star hotel brand.

Murray Koffler, an avuncular druggist and immigrant's son, started working in his father's two small drugstores near Kensington Market then merged them into a drugstore chain that was to become Shoppers Drug Mart, the largest in Canada. Murray went on to be a ground-breaking leading Canadian philanthropist in education especially at the University of Toronto, in health at Mount Sinai and in culture in North York. He was a leading Canadian supporter of the Weizmann Research Institute in Israel. Carole and I attended a visit to the Weizmann at Murray's insistence and were overwhelmed by Murray's philanthropic endeavours there. His early contributions to foster aboriginal entrepreneurs was a pioneering effort that still needs charitable help and leadership today.

Peter Munk, a delightful bon vivant and Hungarian immigrant landed in Canada as a penniless youth. After a few mishaps in varied businesses, he moved into mining. By 1990, he acquired control of American Barrick and changed its name to Canadian Barrick Gold. A series of acquisitions made Barrick Gold the third largest gold mining company in the world.

Peter quickly shared his new found wealth by large record-setting gifts to the University of Toronto and the Toronto General Hospital targeted to cutting edge new scientific advances in research and treatment.

Another dynamic mining developer, Seymour Schulich, who had moved from Montreal to Toronto, became a mining magnet and poured millions into York University quickly establishing its Business School as world class, and then shared his largesse especially aspiring University students across dozens of other communities endeavours including health and student support into the wider community which continues unabated.

In 1998, Toronto was amalgamated and became the fourth largest city in North America. After opposing amalgamation fiercely, Mel Lastman, the son of immigrants, a creative entrepreneur and then the popular mayor of North York became Toronto's first mayor after amalgamation[220]. By 2000, Toronto saw its first Italian immigrant police officer also from Friuli, Julian Fantino, become Police Chief of Toronto.

Ned Goodman, a restless mining engineer with a 'wanderlust' for far off mining opportunities, migrated from Montreal to build a thriving

---

220 Mel, a successful North York Mayor born of immigrant parents near Kensington Market, was reluctant to run for Metro Mayor, but Paul Godfrey and I joined forces to persuade him that he could not only win but only he could bring the amalgamated cities together, which he did. He finally agreed provided we helped him which we did. Almost at the end of the campaign, Mel, disheartened, considered quitting. Paul Godfrey called to inform me. I persuaded Al Waxman to take him on a tour of Kensington Market. Al was considered the King of Kensington because of his role in a CBC series of that name. Al and Mel were crushed by enthusiastic residents and Mel decided to stay the course and won.

Paul, as Metro Chairman, had earlier enlisted me to chair the O'Keefe Centre Board owned by Metro Toronto, the largest performing arts centre in Canada then facing a chronic cash losses of close to $2 million a year. In less than two years, O'Keefe Centre was cash positive and returning $1 million back to the city. Mel Lastman was a forceful vigourous member of the O'Keefe Board and supported my drastic measures to turn O'Keefe's finances around with the leadership and efforts of Charles Cutts, a talented low key accountant who became CEO and later head of Thomson Hall and Massey Hall with verve and cost-effective distinction. I served with Mel on O'Keefe's Board for over a decade and we both came to enjoy the variety of stage performers from musicals to opera to ballet, a taste that still lingers.

financial empire based in Toronto and went on to become a leading philanthropist with generous donations to education institutions like Brock University where he served as its Chancellor. Seymour Schulich, another mining engineer from Montreal amassed a fortune in the mining business and became one of Canada's leading philanthropists especially to secondary and higher education.

The 'Boomers' followed by the 'Millennium' cohort came of age and started to flood the work force with their reduced attachment to institutions and lifetime career jobs while consumed with the incessant use of texting to keep 'connected'. Clothing in the workplace changed from dresses and men's suits and ties to casual attire. There was a dress code revolution. Pant suits for women came into vogue. Casual Fridays entered the precincts of 'white collar' workplaces accelerated the changing styles. Tie manufacturers and wholesalers went out of business and travelling tie salesmen quit their decades old vocation for lack of business. Jeans and running shoes became acceptable in the work place. Running shoes became more expensive as they were marketed as style items for sports, recreation and work.

Starbucks having made its first foray into Canada joining Tim Hortons and in the process, transformed the public lust for coffee and company in a new coffee stop culture while espresso machines became common place in the home. Tobacco saw its first drop in cigarette consumption as 'Big Tobacco' was hit by a historic damage suit. Meanwhile exotic salads with nuts and cranberries, veggie burgers, and goat cheese joined the health craze of the palates of millennials and the food markets and restaurants in Canada raced to keep up. Canadians became 'foodies' and food labels were read with care from ingredients to calories as 'physicality' and 'health' became a prime preoccupation. Microbreweries sprouted up across the country expanding Canadian beer drinking preferences. Canadian wine production led by the wine pioneers like Don Ziraldo, my irrepressible buddy from Niagara who never failed to pepper me with the benefits to Canada of quality wines[221]. The Niagara Peninsula

---

221 Though many wines from Niagara Region have become world class, especially ice wine produced by my friend Gary Pillitteri, a one-time Liberal M.P., I collect and much prefer the wines of France. Oops.

quickly developed acceptable libations almost matching fine wines from France, Italy, Spain, California and South America. The Niagara region especially with its exquisite ice wines, one developed by another political pal Gary Pillitteri, made their mark with international and domestic connoisseurs. Saul Feldberg, a client of my law firm, another super successful immigrant who built a world class office furniture firm with the help of his talented son who worked for me as a young lawyer, developed first class wines and then amazing vineyard in Niagara.

New spicier food tastes invaded Canadian bland palates from 'TexMex' to exotic Indian, Jamaican, Ethiopian foods cruised through the changing taste buds of eclectic Canadians. Pizza, of course, became Canada's most popular food.

'Bollywood' with the large influx of South Asians to Canada burst into Canadian popular culture in movies and music, and in 1998 was granted a specialty cable channel in Toronto with East Asian movies and musicals spread across Canada amplifying the diversity in Toronto. Few knew that 37 languages including East Asian dialects were spoken at Toronto city hall. The world came to Toronto and Toronto became the world. India's Bollywood, the largest film producers in the world, led by legendary film-makers G. Dutt and Satyajit Ray, crossed over into North America with a unique beat, colourful costumes and scintillating music and Toronto led the way in distribution into North America.

The urban streetscape changed as sidewalk curbs were reduced as obstacles across Canada and became wheelchair accessible as did restaurants, stores, movie theatres and washrooms.

Science breakthroughs from America were felt with the start of mapping the genome, discovering a vaccine for HIV that offered relief from that vast deadly international epidemic, and of course, the introduction of Viagra with its obvious consequences reinventing concepts of aging.

Nintendo (*'Leave Luck to Heaven'*), a Japanese game invention, launched its products in North America in 1991. In 1992, Nintendo extended its market reach by opening shops and boutiques. By 1995, Nintendo had sold over 1 billion game cartridges, after dubbing 1994 'The Year of the Cartridge'. Suddenly joined by a flood of competitors, electronic games became an essential entertainment device and learning tool in children's and youth education preparing them for cyber age.

Canada was no longer the boring, invisible, snow-bound, sparsely settled, barren land of the North. In 1990, abstract paintings from regional centres across Canada came to fore as Canadian collectors turned in increasing numbers to acquire Canada art matched by the rise in the stock market's higher prices. There was an authentic sense of Canada's contribution to the art world as Canadian artists, painters and especially sculptors like our friend Anne Harris[222], less noticed that others, whose modern outsized works made it to the international art markets and public spaces in both Canada and the United States.

Canada, mimicking American knowhow as Canadians always do, benefited from innovations in America. In 1994, Yahoo, a pioneering search engine was launched in California[223]. Later in 1998, Google in Memlo Park joined the search engine flood that recalibrated the use of new personal technology, disrupting and transforming how we went about our jobs and how we reformulated our and conducted our daily personal lives. Texting disrupting home telephone usage emerged as a mainstay of daily communications. MARS (Medical and Related Sciences) in Toronto began to connect 'tech' start-ups with universities emulating the Silicon Valley experience instigated by Stanford University (the Stanford Research Institute), and the flood of transfer of technology organisms attached to universities like M.I.T. in Boston, then Oxford and Cambridge in England and all the universities in Israel as each began to commercialize and monetize science and 'tech' advances to the benefit

---

222 On a visit to Chongqing in China, I was given a maquette of the national monument to Zhou Enlai by the sculptor YaYu Shan. On my return to Toronto, I commissioned Anne Harris to do a sculpture which we entitled 'Flame of Friendship that is now in the Museum and School of Fine Arts in Chongqing led by Mr. Shan.

223 Robert Taylor (1932-2017), not the Hollywood actor, was an American internet pioneer who led the invention of the 'any key' and then on to search engines. Steve Jobs was deeply influenced by his work when he developed the 'Apple Computer'. Later, observing the 'three click' devices in a lab, he improved the awkward and expensive 'three click' devices to a cheaper 'one click' device that made his computers user friendly, a key innovation that led to Apple's success.

of both the academic inventor or discoverer, his department and his university and the private sector.

No Canadian university grew larger, became more innovative, more dynamic or achieved academic excellence faster than Ryerson led by Sheldon Levy, the most visionary and leading educational administrator leader in Canada. Ryerson grew to graduate more business students annually than all other Canadian business schools combined.

Privacy became an illusion. The 1990's began the systematic theft of privacy data. Privacy was stolen. Hacking became an art form practiced from credit cards to cell phones. Now everything was public and sharable. Facebook, Amazon and Google started, then grew into hegemonic monoliths that trafficked in private data. The 'digital divide' opened ever deeper chasms of turbulent interactivity.

Writers in U.S.A. continued as literary icons closely followed in Canada. In 1993, Edward Albee, America's foremost playwright brought 'Three Tall Women' to Broadway and opened the exposure to the interior lives of suburban women on the stage. Feminism was no longer a slogan.

Prolific writers like Philip Roth in 1995 published his abrasive work, now gaining renewed interest and readership, 'American Pastoral'. Isaac Bashevis Singer[224], now in his dotage, published his long awaited autobiography 'In My Father's Court' and Saul Bellow now nearing the end of his

---

224 I.B. Singer came to Toronto to sign his books at Edward's bookstore on Queen Street. I attended and acquired two books and asked Singer to dedicate them to my two sons. When he heard my name, he asked if my father was 'Simcha' Grafstein, my father's Hebrew name. As he signed the books, he groused, *"I didn't like him then and I don't like him now."* I was aghast. My father had died tragically decades before. My father was a quiet modest man. Singer repeated, *"Too bad. But I didn't like him then and I don't like him now."* Puzzled and upset, I persisted. *"What did my father ever do to you?"* Singer looked up from his chair and said that in the '20s, he and my father contributed small articles to the *Jewish Forward*, a leading Yiddish daily paper in New York. *"Your father once got $1.10, and I got $1. I didn't like him then and I don't like him now"*, he said with a twinkle in his eyes and a warm smile as he autographed two books. Whether it was true or not, the story endeared me to Singer, and as a result, I read almost all his tales of Yiddish life in Europe and America in English. I tried a book or two in Yiddish, but I stumbled and gave up. So I stuck to the English or English translations.

prolific career, presented his collective essays '*The Actuals*' in 1997 and his collection of short stories '*Something to Remember Me By: Three Tales*' and his essays '*It All Adds Up*'. John Updike continued to publish novels, prose and poems with variegated themes – '*Brazil*', '*In the Beauty of the Lilies*', '*Towards the End of Time*', '*Collected Poems*' and '*Collected Essays*' including '*Odd Jobs*' and '*More Matter*'. American writers led the western world in literary achievements and new genres.

In 1990's music tastes changed and the Beatles vaulted upon the global musical stage and new musical genres captured youthful attention that changed popular musical habits. And in 1998, as if to close another era of popular music in 1998 Frank Sinatra[225], the greatest crooner of the 20th century, died. Once you heard Sinatra sing a tune, you could never forget the words or music. Another musical genre epitomized by the music and persona of Elvis Presley waxed and waned.

In 1994, Black Rock was launched in New York, a private equity firm geared with complex algorithms to measure the ups and downs in the stock market. From an initial capital base of $600 million dollars, riding the 'ETF' wave, Black Rock grew to quickly become the largest equity firm in the world exceeding 15 trillion dollars in the next decade. Slower off the mark, as always, more fiscally conservative Canada gave birth to a new breed of smaller equity firms competing with the debt obsessed risk averse established 'big' banks and some satellites of the big banks altering the Canadian capital markets landscape forever and providing new channels of capital for smaller cap businesses especially 'tech' startups. 'Tech' displaced 'mining' on Bay Street as the new capitalist frontier on the Canadian markets. Blackberry, developed in Kitchener Waterloo in Ontario, and driven by two entrepreneurial dynamos

---

225 No movie in the '70s or the '80s achieve greater financial success called '*Saturday Night Fever*' and it introduced America and the world to the sounds of disco music. It seemed all the world was dancing to movements and musical score of that movie. Produced by the legendary Robert Stigwood it was based on musical numbers written by the Bee Gees who as young Australian performers moved to Miami to produce their unique music. The movie saw record world revenues of close to $200 million and earned its star John Travolta, an Oscar. Unforgettable. You can hear the beat!

(Mike Lazaridis and Jim Balsillie) spread across the world with its cell phones and unique text-based secure email offering and platform. First faxing and then emails began to replace mail as the Canadian Post Office suffered from this disruption. Faxing fell into disuse.

The Canada GNP after slumping at the beginning of the '90s grew to almost a trillion dollars by the end of the decade, fueled along by 'free trade'. Canada was on the way to capitalize on its economic growth and trade relations as its cities grew vertically as well as spread horizontally to the suburbs and beyond.

It was a coming of a new age for Canada and Canadians in all spheres of civic society. Opposition to 'oil' began to grow as the green 'generation' became more mature and vociferous and relentless. 'Global warming' entered the public lexicon. United States Congress passed a slew of climate protection acts on a bipartisan basis in the late 1980's. Canadian pioneering efforts in nuclear energy was left behind by the boisterous advocacy and influence of radical 'green' adherents while Europe and China built endless new 'nuke' energy plants. The 'green' followers attracted deeper financial support and upped their attacks on 'oil', 'coal' and 'shale', 'nuke' plants and pipelines and refineries. That contest hotly continues unabashed today. Meanwhile Canadian pioneer efforts in nuclear energy was thrown away by the political classes. A big mistake was made as other nations stole Canada's early world lead in clean 'nuclear' development! If we could leap forward to 'fusion' as a new energy source or harness the high water tides of James Bay as did we at Niagara at the turn of the century, this raucous debate would be modified and transformed in a more cost effective coherent way. Ontario could return to a low cost energy provider that made Ontario a manufacturing powerhouse. Perhaps it's still not too late.

The 1990's was the last decade before the public felt the multi-billion dollar onslaught of costs for security against terrorism, especially visible at airports (and now in commercial office towers) and public spaces, compounded by long lineups and flight delays that made travel by air time consuming, cost ineffective and fretful. The loss in productivity remains, untold and unmeasured, in our national economic measurements.

Still, Canada was on the relentless economic march upward.

EUROPE - EAST-WEST IN THE 1990'S

East Berlin, that I had first visited during Berlin's east-west division via Check Point Charlie in 1982 became overnight after 1989, a sparkling new addition to that vibrant reunited city with its bright neon lights, sleek coffee shops, stylish boutiques, especially along the 'Unter den Linden' boulevard in east Berlin, magnificent museums and compelling classical and 'pop' concerts, especially in Berlin's modernistic Concert Hall[226]. Europe was open to new ideas and rife with business and cultural exchange. Eastern European cities emerged from their dingy drab Stalinist landscapes like butterflies from their cocoons. In the '70s and '80s, I had visited dark Moscow several times but the most exciting was the opening of MacDonald's led by the always convivial ubiquitous George Cohen who invited his chums to celebrate with him and share this

---

226 I was invited by Mayor Diepghen of Berlin as a special visitor to the 750th anniversary of the founding of Berlin. An old Reichstag building called the Hans Gropius Bau was converted into a dazzling modern museum displaying the history of Berlin since its founding. The first artifact that preceded the founding of Berlin at the front door was a large irregular shaped pink marble slab with Hebrew lettering from the entryway of an old synagogue founded on the banks of the Spee Rivers coursing through Berlin built there before the founding of Berlin 750 years ago. A room in the museum was dedicated to Berliners of Jewish origin and their pioneering contributions to the business, media, medicine, science, publishing, marketing, education and cultural life of that city. The KWD was a decades old department store, the first of its kind and replicated around the world. Before World War II, a third of Berlin were German born Jews or immigrants from other parts of Europe. I visited East Berlin through 'Check Point' Charley, quite an experience in itself. Berlin became after unification a marvelous modern city, chocked full of cultural delights from music to art, museums, concert halls and vibrant universities that I visited. The Free University of Berlin was stimulating. I was asked to give a speech on Canadian politics and the Q and A following was a wonderful 'free for all' discussion.

historic moment[227]. George born in Chicago was the exuberant colourful marketing genius co-founder of McDonalds in Canada supported by Suzie, his astute Buffalo-born wife. In Moscow, we were feted to sumptuous dinners and even a dance in the historic St. George Ballroom in the Kremlin. We were delighted to hear the Russian Military Band play '*Hava Nagila*' as we danced with abandon in circles to this Israeli tune joined by bewildered bemedalled Russian generals and bemused Russian politicians. It was in Moscow during that visit, I started to collect the so-called '*Hidden Art of the Soviet Union*' – paintings by Russian and Eastern European artists (excluded from the official Soviet art echelons where artists were mandated to render their works only in social realism) that included versions of Impressionism, Expressionism, Post-Expressionism, Surrealism, Abstract and Cubism now liberated from Soviet State approved 'social realism'. These wonderful paintings were kept secret, privately exchanged between artists during the Soviet period, as artists who were compelled to paint social realism for a living, kept their artistic preferences hidden from public view and official criticism. These paintings ignited my lifelong obsession to collect some of these hidden and rarely seen artistic treasures.

Travelling in the early 1990's to Russia, I visited Leningrad, now open - free - and renamed St. Petersburg. I saw toppled Stalin statues in public parks under Prime Minister Boris Yeltsin and met the reformist Mayor Sobchuk. Sobchuk's staff at the time included a former KGB officer wearing a dark turtle neck sweater and dark leather jacket serving a foreign investment advisor called Vladimir Putin (who understood what I was saying in English) and a young well-dressed lawyer Dmitry Medvedev, later to become both President and Prime Minister of Russia. A political friend from the Russian Duma had arranged a meeting for me to discuss cable television prospects with the Mayor and his staff knowing of my past business experience in 'cable' in Canada, U.S.A. and the U.K. I quickly concluded that St. Petersburg's infrastructure was

---

227 Moscow was famous for long queues. The two longest queues I observed in Moscow in 1989 were for Lenin's Tomb in front of the Kremlin and MacDonald's new restaurant on Pushkin Square.

woefully inadequate and so 'cable' would be premature and the costs prohibitive. When I so informed the Mayor and his young advisers, I met with their collective chagrin[228].

However, a memorable delight was an exciting visit to the Hermitage (the greatest collection of art in the world) in the heart of the city on the banks of the Neva River, my third visit since the '80s. Catherine the Great's magnificent palace on the outskirts of St. Petersburg was then in the midst of restoration after its almost complete destruction in World War II. These meticulous restorations had now accelerated. The Hermitage's stunning modern art collection, some confiscated from Germany, was on partial display. Canadians like Robert Kaszanits had spearheaded efforts to provide funds for the renovation of the Hermitage in St. Petersburg especially for covering its windows to protect its artistic treasures from errant weather conditions, one of the greatest collections of art in the world[229]. It was breathtaking and a profound lesson in how much Russians prized their cultural institutions. Visits to the famed Ballet and Opera Houses jammed with adoring fans was rapturous[230]. Russia was successfully on its way back from its egregious past to cultural liberation and renewed international appreciation.

---

228 A decade later on President Putin's first state visit to Canada, he chided me in a brief encounter in Toronto, with a mischievous grin, what a business opportunity I had missed in St. Petersburg, Russia in 1994 when we met in Mayor Sobchuk's office, the reformist Mayor of St. Petersburg when Putin was his foreign investments advisor. I responded that Russia had also lost great sports opportunities as their top hockey players had immigrated to Canada and joined the N.H.L. to our mutual laughter.

229 In 2002, my cousin Bob Kaplan asked me to join the Canadian Board of The State Hermitage Museum Foundation of Canada dedicated to artistic exhibits, renovating the massive art collections structures in St. Petersburg and student exchanges. In 2013, I became Chair of its board. My cousin Joe Frieberg, Bob's uncle, an imaginative entrepreneur, philanthropist and pioneering investor in China and Russia, also served on the Board with vigour and distinction. Joe was a cofounder of Tennis Israel and other good works. Joe married my first cousin Budgie and raised a large successful clan, all with an artistic bent, in photography, art and film, of his own.

230 A modern new performing arts venue designed by Toronto architect and South African immigrant Jack Diamond was opened in St. Petersburg. Critiqued by some Russian fans longing for the older lavish décor did not deter them from filling this

In 1995, the French Assembly finally exonerated Alfred Dreyfus of all guilt of treason. While justice delayed is justice denied, it was a lesson in how the wheels of justice grind slowly and relentlessly. The historic record was finally put straight. Better late than never.

---

modern wood-clad space to capacity with its wonderful acoustics and sight lines. As Chair of the O'Keefe Centre in Toronto (Canada's largest publically owned performing arts venue with 3,400 seats) for over a decade in the '70s and '80s, I became an amateur expert on concert hall acoustics. I was given a wonderful backstage tour of this marvelous wood panelled structure.

MID-EAST – PEACE - IN THE 1990'S

In the 1990's, the Israel and the Mid-East turmoil continued as a constant almost irritating sore that wouldn't heal. In 1973, I had made my first visit to Israel, I was invited to join a small group of Torontonians led by my university school chum, David Dennis and businessman Jimmy Kay, who arranged for John Diefenbaker to inaugurate the John Diefenbaker Forest planted on a desolate piece of the land outside Jerusalem. The trip was organized by the Jewish National Fund in Canada.

A brief backstory to my unexpected relations with John Diefenbaker. In 1965, when I first arrived in Ottawa as the Executive Assistant to John Turner for my first stint in public service, I was anxious and green. While politically active and familiar with Mr. Pearson, most of the Liberal Cabinet and their senior appointed political staff, Parliament itself, the bureaucracy and how a government really worked was a mystery to me. I sought advice from Alistair Fraser, a knowledgeable Ottawa hand and top assistant to the irrepressible Jack Pickersgill. John Turner had been appointed to the Cabinet as an Associate Minister to Pickersgill, who dominated the Cabinet and held the powerful Minister of Transport, was considered the all-knowing political guru. Alistair who became Clerk of the House of Commons, a chunky short man from the Maritimes, was the 'go-to guy' about the workings of everything in government. He gave me a long precise lecture with a list of do's and don't's as a political assistant especially my relations with the senior bureaucrats and their aides who looked on all political staff as inferior and irritating. Ottawa under Pearson himself in formal Mandarin, was run by the Mandarin class of seasoned deputy ministers, their hand-picked associate deputy ministers and senior staff.

It was a closed elite bureaucratic circle that ran our federal government rather than the elected officials to my surprise and bewilderment. "*You had better learn to go along to get along*", Alistair admonished me.

Alistair then suggested I go and seek advice from John Diefenbaker who loved Parliament and knew the workings of government better than most and would give me a contrarian perspective as well as anyone. I was surprised. Diefenbaker was the avowed Liberal political nemesis. The Liberals had demonized him in the last two federal elections that gave birth to Pearson's Liberal minority. Now as Leader of the Opposition, the 'Chief' had time on his hands. *"Don't worry"*, Alistair advised, *"He would surely meet with you. Remember he has difficulty hearing his left ear. He gets irritable when he can't hear. Speak to his right side."*

I called Diefenbaker's office on the Hill and immediately got his secretary and heard Dief growl in the background demanding who was on the line. She shouted my name and I could hear him say, *"Well, tell him to come right over."* I was astonished. I timidly entered his quiet outer office and was immediately ushered into his large inner sanction. His large desk was a jumbled mess covered with clippings and notes. He waved me to sit down and asked what I wanted. *"Alistair Fraser had suggested that I ask you for advice"*, I blurted out.

John Diefenbaker, a tall ramrod straight broad-shouldered angular man, filled the room with his piercing fiery eyes that glowed like burning coals from deep dark sockets. He wore a dark bespoke double breasted suit, with a crisp white shirt, dark tie and a carefully folded white starched hankie. His manner of speaking surprised me – softer, less raspy, with a flashing wit. His tone was deep, quiet, resonant baritone. He was most convivial and quickly put me at my ease. *"I know who you are. You work for John Turner and you worked for The Truth Squad led by Judy LaMarch that flopped"*, he chortled. Indeed Keith Davey had asked me to do some research for his idea - The Truth Squad - led by Judy LaMarch which followed Diefenbaker on the 1962 campaign trail across Canada. It was set up to correct Dief's factual errors or mistakes about Diefenbaker's record and the Liberal governments, past and present. Indeed, Keith's idea had flopped quickly as Dief laughed it out of business. But Liberals won a minority government under Mr. Pearson, so maybe it had some effect.

In any event, Dief proceeded to give me a long list of 'do's' and 'don'ts' with quick quirky anecdotes about the Pearson Cabinet Ministers except

Paul Martin Senior who he held in high esteem. Later I found out why[231].
After praising John Turner as a 'comer' who he respected as a politician,
especially for Turner's fervent belief in the primacy of Parliament, a belief
Dief shared. I had held a grudging admiration for Diefenbaker as a law
student when he had introduced the first Bill of Rights Act that applied
to the federal spheres of power in his first government. Turner respected
him too. Later I discovered that Pierre Trudeau also admired Diefenbaker
for his Bill of Rights, passed in 1957 creating Canada's first Bill of Rights,
an oversight law that applied to the federal jurisdiction and for his
eloquent and passionate stand on 'One Canada', a belief Trudeau shared.
Diefenbaker, in his farewell address to the 1967 Conservative Leadership
Convention, where he posted a poor 6ᵗʰ place showing, to lose to Robert
Stanfield, railed against 'extremism' and the 'Two Nation' theory, then a
growing analogue to the 'separatist' movement that was spiking in political popularity in Quebec to the frustration of all federal parties, as if the
'Two Nation' theory would somehow better unite a divisive Quebec with
the rest of Canada.

Diefenbaker continued to sit in Parliament until the leadership contest
between Clark, Wagner and Mulroney. Though Mulroney was ahead,
he lost because he did not have a seat in Parliament unlike Joe Clark.
Diefenbaker gave a barn burning speech and sunk Mulroney's chances

---

231 Diefenbaker and Martin, though political antagonists, were close good friends,
spent private time together and held each other's talents in high esteem. Diefenbaker, a self-defined 'teetotaler' shared a glass of wine or two with Martin in private.
Both were life-long skilled successful politicians yet were never fully respected by
their party elites. Paul Martin, Sr. had an extraordinary career in public service
from the '30s to the '80s. Martin's remarkable two volume biography 'A Very Public
Life', published in 1983 and 1986 by Deneau, I consider one of the best of its genre.
Martin detailed his rise from humble beginnings, effected with childhood polio
and maimed for life to becoming the leading 'progressive' in the Liberal Party. He
introduced as Minister of Health the first stage Medicare in 1948 with grants and tax
credits, then aid to hospitals in 1956, threatening to resign if the St. Laurent government did not keep its election promises. Martin went on to be Secretary of State for
External Affairs and then High Commissioner to the U.K. government, and finally
Leader of the Senate – all in all, an astonishing 'progressive' 20th century record of
accomplishments.

by alluding to his lack of political experience. The riotous applause was a fitting conclusion to his long career. He preached 'One Canada' and ranted against hyphenated Canadians. Diefenbaker listed his accomplishments and his support for the diverse Canadian – his last hurrah!

'Dief' like Fraser's, most pessimistic yet insightful advice related to the bureaucrats, the Liberal Mandarins, who could slow down or derail any new reforms that they didn't own. *"Make sure they feel they own any Turner reforms and they might have chance"*, he advised with a mischievous gleam in his eyes. Then after more than an hour, I left 'Dief' thoughtful but invigorated.

During my time as John Turner's assistant, I would receive the odd hand-written note from Diefenbaker when I sat in the Common's Gallery listening to Turner deliver a speech I had helped draft. Diefenbaker always sat in his front seat in the House reading his mail and papers while listening to the Debates even during the evening Debates, when the House was almost empty. He would send me a note up to the gallery, delivered by a page boy with cryptic comments, *"Not bad, Chief of Staff"* or *"Missed the mark, Chief of Staff"*, and he would smile up at me as I read his note and nodded to him as he returned to intently listening to the Debates as he foraged through his small heap of notes, clippings and correspondence cluttering his Parliamentary desk.

Later in 1967 when Diefenbaker ran for Leadership at the Conservative Convention for the last time in Toronto at the Maple Leaf Gardens, I called 'Fast' Eddie Goodman, a Conservative stalwart and a key member of the 'dump' Diefenbaker movement led by Dalton Camp for two tickets. Eddy was the Chairman of that convention. He barked at me dismissively over the phone, *"No way"*, and that was that. I decided to call Diefenbaker's office. I immediately received two tickets seated several rows behind Dief in the Gardens. I attended with Carole. When Eddie spotted me as he raced about the packed audience, he shouted one of his creative expletives, *"What the ___ are you doing here?"* Diefenbaker, sitting a few rows below overheard Goodman's loud remarks, turned, stood erect, hands akimbo and then pointed to us, and then to himself and lip-synched, *"They are with me"* and smiled to Eddy's consternation. Nonplussed, Eddie shouted, *"Grafstein, you are impossible"*, larded with another of his stream of endless expletives. And so was 'Fast Eddie', I smiled to myself.

I shared in my admiration for Diefenbaker with the late and lamented Doug Fisher, a WWII vet, a lifelong NDP, an astute journalist, hockey fan, and the best political historian on the Hill. Doug had toppled C.D. Howe, the most powerful minister in the St. Laurent cabinet in 1958 and became an NDP MP at the Lakehead. Later he returned to Toronto to run against a Liberal, my cousin Bobby Kaplan, and was soundly beaten and whence he harboured a lifelong grudge against anything Liberal. That's how I first met Doug and we became lively sparring partners for the rest of his long storied career as one of Canada's best read insightful political journalists.

So when David Dennis, a University chum, a Conservative and loyal Diefenbaker supporter, wanted a bipartisan group to join the Diefenbaker visit to Israel in 1973, no other Liberal agreed to go. 'Dief' suggested David call me. David knew I was an active Liberal, but didn't know of my relationship with 'Dief'. David called me with some hesitancy and was surprised and pleased that I readily agreed to join the group to travel with Dief to Israel. The purpose of the trip was to inaugurate the John Diefenbaker Forest outside Jerusalem. So we travelled across the breath and width of Israel, from desert settlements to collective farms to Israeli towns to government sponsored events, watching Diefenbaker speak spontaneously to enraptured audiences from leading politicians to military leaders to 'Kibbutzniks'. We met the head of Knesset, the pint-sized Yitzhak Shamir, the celebrated underground fighter later to become a controversial Prime Minister who hit it off with Dief and then privately with Golda Meir, the outgoing Prime Minister who had just resigned who also was an obvious admirer of Dief, known as a staunch supporter of Israel.

It was a remarkable introduction for me to Israel and its leading personalities from Yitzhak Shamir, then Speaker of the Knesset, to Cabinet members to academia and artists. In Israel, Jimmy Kay, a Toronto businessman assigned to leading the delegation on behalf of the Jewish National Fund, introduced me to his friend Sir Marcus Sieff, a British Lord, Baron and owner of Marks and Spencer, a storied World War II hero and ardent Zionist who knew everyone in Israel. Sieff arranged for me to meet with taciturn Yitzhak Rabin, charming Moshe Dayan, the charismatic easy-going military icon, the preening Shimon Peres and sombre Menachem Begin, leader of Herut, the right wing Liberal Party who left me with the impression that he was in the mold of a prophet of old. Begin, a storied underground fighter and successor to Vladimir Jabotinsky, believed in 'One Israel'. Begin argued that the real Israel will return to the borders of biblical lands of old as prescribed in the 1917 Balfour Declaration envisaging Palestine on both sides of the Jordan as the Jewish peoples historic homeland. Jordan by this time was already home to a majority of Palestinians or their offspring. It is an historic messianic inevitability, some Rabbinic leaders proclaimed. Yitzhak Rabin, already an iconic military leader, was then a Minister in the Israeli Cabinet.

In a cramped building located in a cluster of jerry-built government offices in Tel Aviv, I had a lengthy encounter with Yitzhak Rabin, the Minister of Labour, who was taut, serious, with narrow steely blue eyes and a chain smoker wearing a light jacket and an open collar white shirt. Every word was weighted with care and precision. Rabin, in his deep rumbling baritone voice, predicted that there would be no peace for Israel until the Syrians decided to make peace. Syria had the largest standing army of Israel's adjacent neighbours and were fierce fighters. This conversation remained indelibly impressed on my mind.

Shimon Peres, also a Cabinet Minister, on the other hand seemed patronizing and self-absorbed. I had a desultory exchange that left me with the impression that Peres was most interested in Peres. The meeting arranged with Menachem Begin, former underground leader and then leader of the right wing party Likud was mesmerizing. Begin was an attentive graceful politician of the old school. Unlike both Rabin and Peres who wore open neck white shirts, Begin, always austerely dressed, wore a dark dress suit, dark tie and crisp white shirt. He spoke slowly, in a deep baritone voice, weighing and measuring every word, lawyer like. Thoughtfully studied, he was well versed in history, the Bible and an observant Jew. A law client of mine in Toronto, Nate Silver, who later immigrated to Israel, had been one of Begin's earliest and most fervent supporters for decades and had lavished me with tales of his extraordinary life as a Polish immigrant who became a devoted follower and successor to Vladimir Jabotinsky, the founder of the Revisionist Party and the founder of the Israeli self-defence force, the Haganah. Jabotinsky should be considered a founding father of Israel despite his premature death in 1940. His political ideas that shaped political Zionism lives on to this day. Jabotinsky believed that only armed revolt could dislodge the British Mandate from Palestine and hasten the founding of Israel.

One aside. When Begin, now the Prime Minister of Israel, made a state visit to Canada in the 1980's, a large community dinner was held in his honour in Toronto with Pierre Trudeau in attendance as his gracious host. Their mutual respect and wariness was evident.

Begin, on being introduced to me by Pierre Trudeau, recalled our chat during the Diefenbaker visit a decade earlier. Begin was warm, modest and gracious. In turn, I introduced him to Keith Davey as a great Canadian Zionist, which he was, to Keith's delight and Trudeau's laughter.

In the 1990's, the UN Assembly, the organized purveyor of partisanship, where over two-thirds of all Resolutions condemned Israel, the only democratic country in the war-torn Middle East, continued unabated. Yet there was a burst of sunlight even there.

Unleashed from the Soviet veto, in 1992, the Security Council held its first summit reaffirming itself to the original collective security objectives in the UN charter. A new UN office for Human Rights and a UN office for co-ordination of Humanitarian Affairs augured to take the UN in a new direction.

Back in 1979, UN Resolution 3379 had passed with 72 countries in favour, 35 against and 22 abstaining declaring 'Zionism is racism'.

In 1991, this invidious UN Resolution 3379 was repealed as the Soviet Union continued to collapse when the U.S. refused to participate in the Madrid Peace Conference convened by the host country Spain unless the new Russia agreed to abandon its support for the outrageous resolution 'Zionism is racism' - and so it was repealed. In 1991, the Madrid Peace Conference was then convened by the host country Spain. The Bush administration, triumphant after a speedy military victory in the Gulf War where Iraq was quickly expelled from Kuwait, used this window of opportunity to join with a weakened U.S.S.R. to bring Israel, Jordan, the Palestinians, Syria and Lebanon to the peace table. Only Syria and Lebanon refused to attend. With economic inducements as bait, Israel now under Prime Minister Yitzhak Shamir and the PLO led by Yasser Arafat[232] calling the shots from his fortified headquarters in Tunis agreed to attend.

---

232 Arafat was not a Palestinian. He was born in Egypt and was a cousin of the Grand Mufti of Jerusalem, Haji Amin al-Husseini, a street agitator who obtained this position by denigrating and undermining the moderate choice in the local elections in the late '20s. Then the Mufti assembled an extreme leadership clique concocted to promote his anti-Semitic philosophy. The Grand Mufti went on to support the 'Final Solution' by Hitler and the Nazis and Mussolini and the Fascists. He lived in grand style in Germany during WWII and in Egypt and was a key Axis collaborator. He advocated the 'Final Solution' devised by Hitler's henchmen led by Reinhard Heydrich and his top assistant Adolf Eichmann in a Reichstag style mansion on the shores of scenic Lake Wannansee just outside of Berlin in 1942 called the Wannansee Conference. This conference was started by Hitler's senior civil and military officials responsible for the concentration camps across Europe. Adolf Eichmann, later captured and tried in Israel, was Heydrich's top assistant at his conferard ignominious. After the Nazis occupied Czechoslovakia in 1940. Heydrich, appointed Gauleiter of Czechoslovakia, was next in line under Heinrich Himmler, head of the infamous SS. In 1942, Heydrich was assassinated in Prague by the Czech Resistance, the highest ranking Nazi in Europe to achieve this ignominious end. The Nazis who occupied Prague in 1940 decided to leave the ancient synagogues untouched - amongst the oldest in Europe - and began to accumulate the writings and artifacts of the Jewish community of Europe as a history of the Jewish people that the Nazi's intended to erase. Heydrich got the idea of building a Museum called the 'Museum of an Extinct Race' from an advisor that Hitler avidly supported as evidence of his plan to eradicate all Jews from Europe East and West. I visited Prague in 2018 and discovered the name of my maternal ancestor, the 'Sheloh', Isaiah Horowitz, who was Chief Rabbi in Prague in 1621 painted on the wall of an old synagogue. The synagogue was built by his family and originally called the 'Horowitz synagogue. It is now called the Pinkus Synagogue (renamed in 1780), considered the second oldest synagogue in Europe built in 1530. The 'Sheloh' had his first bar mitzvah there circa 1550. The names of many of the Jews slaughtered in World War II in Czechoslovakia are painted on the wall of this small synagogue. Much of this remarkable collection still exists in Prague and is accessible to the public. This divisive page of history has been forgotten by most modern 'progressive' observers when they stick to unwavering support for the Janus faced PLO and its murky extremist heritage. Seventy years of wars and defeats has not altered the PLO dream of one Muslim state in all of Palestine west of the Jordan – see their maps and read their school texts. Jordan now has a majority of Palestinian born or related citizens. Jews are prohibited from living or owning homes in Jordan, not even a condo in Jordan.

As noted earlier, I had met Shamir with Diefenbaker twenty years before where he was Speaker of the Knesset. The former underground fighter and later a leader in the Mossad was impressed with his quiet intelligence and toughness, not unlike the unforgettable stern Yitzhak Rabin or the powerful precise mind of Menachem Begin. In December 1991, the U.S.S.R. collapsed and so too the Madrid process which was to be overtaken by the Oslo Peace Process.

While there was a constant backdrop of violence in Gaza and on the West Bank, Israel opened doors to a multitude of Russian emigrants after 1990 - over 900,000 in one decade composed of highly educated doctors, teachers, engineers, physicists, mathematicians and scientists that added to the large nucleus of talented Israel which later helped launch the 'start up' nation of tech companies through the gateway of the internet using their technical skills, persistence and teamwork, they gained while serving and transferring via the Haganah, Israel's defence force into an agile military phenomenon. Thereafter, Israel became a technological world power, its astonishing economic growth rising quickly to the forefront of the 'tech' revolution.

In 1993, the UN convened its first ever but only several hours-long meeting to discuss 'anti-Semitism' based on an OSCE PA Resolution that American congressmen, German parliamentarians and I had helped craft and carry and pass at countless OSCE PA meetings convened in cities across Europe. The purveyor of this 'hate', the UN Assembly, was uncontested as over 67% of all its resolutions targeted and condemned Israel despite all the violence and aggression especially in the Middle East as well as Africa and Asia[233]. Finally, the UN digested this small antidote by a minor seminar of a few quick hours in New York. Better than nothing. The blowback from the crumbling of Soviet Union seemed to keep paying 'peace dividends'.

---

233 In the last 10 years, the UN Human Rights Committee and its successor, the UN Human Rights Council, issued 168 negative resolutions condemning Israel and 67 UN negative resolutions condemning all other member states. Members of this so-called Human Rights Council including the most egregious violators of human rights during the same period were rarely, if ever, castigated.

My own hopes to have these international resolutions to combat anti-Semitism because in my view, all discrimination is 'local', considered by a Committee of the Senate was dashed when the Committee's membership refused to complete its hearings or issue a report despite a clear mandate from the Canadian Senate for the first time in Senate history. Alas all was not liberal or perfect or tolerant in the Liberal dominated Senate.

In 1993, Yitzhak Rabin[234], former Chief of Staff of the Israel Defense Forces now Prime Minister of Israel, heavily pressed by Bill Clinton the United States, agreed to the Oslo Peace talks. Rabin, and Arafat, deemed a viable, if unreliable, partner, met in Washington to sign a historic Peace Accord between Israel and the P.L.O. Rabin reluctantly shook the smiling Arafat's hand, nudged by Bill Clinton, after signing the Oslo Peace Accords, all witnessed by the world on TV. Arafat, a brilliant negotiator, as was said, *"never missed an opportunity to miss an opportunity"*. Then the world was shocked by Rabin's assassination in 1995. My friend Eitan Haber, Rabin's Chief of Staff, gave a heart rendering eulogy holding a song sheet soaked with Rabin's blood he had taken from Rabin's pocket. World leaders attended his funeral in Jerusalem, most for the first time, as the Jewish world mourned. Jerusalem wasn't recognized as Israel's capital by the international community except when it came to attending state funerals.

The Oslo Accord Process petered out after Ehud Barak, Rabin's theoretical successor, agreed to even more concessions including sharing Jerusalem as a Palestinian capital in East Jerusalem while Arafat continued to renege on all previous written commitments despite being allowed into the West Bank to set up his government. Still the '90s brought hope for a final peace settlement between Israel and the PLO. 'Peace in our time' was the hope. In 1994, another breakthrough came with Rabin and Hussein of Jordan signed a peace accord joining Egypt as the second Arab

---

234 I met Rabin in 1973 on my first trip to Israel. He was the Minister of Education at the time. We had a private meeting for over two hours in his tiny office in Tel Aviv. He told me there would never be peace until an agreement was made with Syria. The Ger Rabbi in Jerusalem, not a fan of Rabin, disagreed with him on a visit to Jerusalem.

state to recognize Israel. Patience, Patience both the Lubavitch Rebbe in Crown Heights in NYC and the Ger Rebbe in Jerusalem advised me in the '90s. I will witness miracles in Israel that I never believed would happen. They were both right.

Meanwhile, 'apartheid' in South Africa, crumbled based on world-wide pressure including from Canada under Brian Mulroney, capsized by the sudden release of Nelson Mandela from his decades-long imprisonment by the Boer government. South Africa held its first democratic election of blacks and whites which saw the long imprisoned Nelson Mandela become President. Writers, long time advocates of freedom and equality, burst out on the literary scene. Nadine Gordimer, a South African Jew won the Nobel Prize for Literature in 1991. J.M. Coetzee, a South African Afrikaaner, won the Booker Prize in 1999 and Zakes Mda, a South African black, became well known in the West as a stunning novelist. Of course, Nelson Mandela himself a gifted writer noted for his own story of freedom was unmatched, as were his political polemics. The world was 'achanging'.

In 1990, the UN freed of its usual east/west deadlock swiftly condemned and repelled Saddam Hussein's Iraq's invasion of Kuwait anxious to take over their rich oil fields. Within a few months, Saddam had displaced the Kuwait government with a puppet government and ravaged Kuwait and its citizens. The 'unipolar world' now led by America quickly put together a coalition including U.K., Saudi Arabia, Egypt, France, Canada and Australia throwing back the Iraqi invasion with swiftness and limited casualties. America was back. The 'new world order' was alive and well!

The winds of optimism and peace making had never been harder against the entrenched parties to the Irish 'Troubles' that had wrecked death and havoc for more than a century in Ireland. The Catholic IRA and Ulster Orange protestors had been violently attacking and bombing each other in the IRA hope to gain Irish Hegemony over Northern Ireland, a British enclave with a Protestant majority. On Good Friday, the two warring sides led by Tony Blair and prodded by Bill Clinton (as Irish Catholic groups in New York, Boston and elsewhere supported the IRA) speed to an uneasy truce and then a peace agreement.

Peace tremors had lanced their egregious religious and political boil once again, the new world order of peaceful resolution to historic grievance had triumphed.

Pope John Paul II, the first Eastern European Pope from Poland, joined the international roster of luminous icons as his continued outsized missions of peace and hope throughout the '90s. Optimism was rampant. I had met John Paul II in the mid-1980's when he made his first visit to Toronto as Karol Wojtyła, Archbishop of Kraków introduced by Stan Haidasz, a doctor in Toronto's west end who became a friend, later MP and first Minister of Multiculturalism, who shared my Polish heritage of both my parents. Immediately after John Paul II became Pope (later a Saint), in his first meeting with John Emmett Cardinal Carter, an old friend of mine and one of the Pope's campaign organizers and staunchest supporters, he recalled our early meeting where we had shared reminisces of our fathers who had both served in the Pilsudski Brigades in the Polish War of Independence (1917 to 1921) and the historic Battle of Warsaw. On his return to Toronto, Cardinal Carter called and told me of his surprise first chat with John Paul II after his ascension to the Papacy. As a result, I was invited to five private audiences with His Holiness during his tenure as Pope, the last, eight weeks before he passed away in Rome. We always started our brief chats by the Pope insisting we reminisce about our fathers. The Pope spoke excellent English and passable Yiddish, much better than mine[235].

---

235 I have been a lifelong student of the Roman Catholic Church. I audited lectures at the Pontifical Institute of Medieval Studies at St. Michael's College while attending Law School at the University of Toronto in the late fifties. One of the most captivating leaders of the 20th century was Pope John XXIII. I took to reading Encyclicals after Vatican II in 1962. In that document, Pope John XXIII began to purge the Roman Catholic Church of its endless anti-Semitism. I admired Pope John Paul II and Pope Benedict XVI, both of whom I met later for extended discussions, continued to advocate the elimination of the sources of anti-Semitism within and without the Catholic church by their actions and encyclicals which I commend to all interested in this topic.

I was privileged to share a dinner with Pope Benedict XVI when he came as a Cardinal to speak at the Varsity Arena in Toronto. Pope Benedict XVI, then a Cardinal in Rome, and I had a long and fascinating conversation over dinner. My friend

The birth pangs of Islamist terrorism in America with foiled attacks in New York City was barely noticed nor the successful attacks on U.S. embassies and American military installations abroad. We all suffered from that potent blend of denial and great expectations. The 'new world order' was upon us as the ranks of democratic countries swelled. We believe devoutly that democracies do not make war against democracies. So the 'new world order' would flourish in peace and security, economic growth and the growth of democracy. The tremors of terrorism were barely felt. Perhaps I was under the spell of Maya, the Hindu goddess of illusion. But I thought that peace in the world was on its way for the final time.

The Hegelian dialectics of democratic exchange were back in fashion. Kant's classic essay *'Perpetual Peace: A Philosopher's Sketch'* published two centuries before in 1795 contributed the thesis and the rationale why democracies, popularly elected, chose not to engage in wars with other democracies. This thesis became the architectonic of my belief in democracy.

Then came 9/11 in 2001 and everything was dramatically transformed once again. The world re-entered a new more virulent phase of vicious largely asymmetrical wars. Welcome to the 21ˢᵗ century.

Dennis Mills arranged this dinner through the largesse of Frank Stronach. Father McConica, an acquaintance of my son from All Soul's College in Oxford and friend of Dennis Mills had got Dennis to help organize this dinner.

CANADA'S GREATEST ATHLETE IN THE 20TH CENTURY: FANNY (BOBBIE) ROSENFELD (1904–1969)

Certainly 'Bobbie' Rosenfeld was the most remarkable, all round, athlete in Canada in 20th century, on a par or exceeding the athletic career arc of the likes of Lionel Conacher, Al Rosen, Ted Reeves, 'Rocket' Richard, Larry Gaines[236] or even Tom Longboat. Unlike 'celebrity' sports figures in the latter part of the 20th century who star in one or two sports, Bobbie excelled in numerous individual and team sports. Setting records for athletic prowess in each sport she maintained a modest posture throughout her career on the playing field or off. Bobbie ignited an unparallel team spirit in each of numerous team sports she played, each in a leadership role.

'Bobbie' was a Jewish immigrant born in Ukraine and came to Canada as a youngster in 1905 and settled with her family in Barrie, Ontario. There her father earned a modest living as a junk peddler. Bobbie attended primary school and high school in Brampton and showed early athletic promise. When her family moved to Toronto near Kensington Market, she attended Harbord Collegiate, a hotbed of academic and sport skills for mostly immigrant children. Her modest demeanor and unrivalled skills quickly came to attention of her teachers and peers where she played every team sport and track and field and competed against men and women. She joined the Young Women's Hebrew Association (YWHA) where she became a leading star in all women's team sports including baseball, basketball and hockey. She could play any position in baseball

---

236 One of Canada's greatest boxers was Larry Gaines, a black Canadian born in Toronto in 1900. Gaines, a heavyweight drew global attention in the 1920's when he won the Canadian, British Empire and World Coloured heavyweight crowns. His career was restricted when he was barred from competing in the English Heavy weight title and kept from competing for the world heavyweight title because of his colour.

but shone as a softball pitcher leading her team to many championships. She even led in lacrosse and lawn tennis. No woman overcame more barriers or owned more all-round athletic skills than 'Bobbie' Rosenfeld. She gained the nickname 'Bobbie' for her short bobby-cut hairdo.

Bobbie first came to wider public attention after she graduated from Harbord Collegiate High and began to work as a stenographer in Pattison's, a well-known chocolate factory in Toronto. At a picnic, she was encourage to run the 100 yard dash defeating Canadian champion Rosa Grosse setting a national record. She soon set records in five different track and field events. She was a star in softball, basketball and hockey winning minor and major titles[237]. Playing on women's championships - baseball, hockey and basketball teams, she led her teams to city, provincial, national and international championships.

In 1928 Bobbie rose to global attention when women were allowed to compete for the first time in the Olympics in Amsterdam. The first event was 100 meters. After a number of false starts, Bobbie was beaten by the American star runner Betty Robinson by only 18 inches. The result was disputed to no avail. Bobbie was then the lead runner in the 4x100 metre relay, Canada won by a world record of 48.44 seconds.

Then Rosenfeld competed in the 800 meter to pace her teammate Jean Thompson, Thompson stumbled and Rosenfeld ran besides her to encourage her and let Thompson finish fourth while Rosenfeld finished fifth. Known as the 'Matchless Six' composed of Rosenfeld, Myrtle Cook, Jean Thompson, Ethel Catherwood, Jane Bell and Ethel Smith went on to win the team athletic event (based on total points) at that Olympics – a great moment in world sport history.

---

237 My father-in-law Harry Sniderman ('What a Man', Sniderman) - a joy to all who knew him, one of Canada's greatest softball players, was one of her coaches in baseball, basketball and helped in track and field. He introduced to her to Ted Reeves as he did to me who after a legendary football career became a famed sports writer for the Toronto Telegram. My father-in-law invited them to join him at the many spirited sports dinners where I shared the pleasure of both their company. Both were modest, quiet spoken and witty. Harry was a legendary fast ball hitter and pitcher who according to his high school Jarvis Collegiate website in their 200th anniversary listing Harry as one their top graduates and he invented the 'drop ball'.

When arthritis struck in the early '30s, Bobbie recovered to play hockey and softball until 1936 when her arthritic condition forced her to retire. In 1934, she was the coach of Canada's women's team at the British Commonwealth Games. In 1936, she started another career as a sports journalist first in Montreal, then in Toronto at the Globe and Mail becoming Canada's leading advocate for women's sports till her retirement in 1966.

Her awards were numerous and wide ranging. The City of Toronto established the 'Bobbie' Rosenfeld Park in 1991. In 1996, a Canadian stamp was issued commemorating her singular achievements. Each year the Canada Press honours Canada's top women athletes with Bobbie Rosenfeld Award. In 1949 she was inducted to Canadian Olympic Hall of Fame. In 1958, she was named Canada's Female Athlete of the Half Century. In 1955 in and Ontario Sports Hall of Fame in 1996. Canada's Sports Hall of Fame named her as well to that illustrious organization.

Bobbie was the greatest all-around athlete, male or female, Canada ever produced – the Canadian athlete of the 20th century.

---

238 The Volstead Act led by a Congressman by that name passed Congress in 1918.

THE ROARING '20S

No decade in the 20th century was more revolutionary in mores and morals across the globe than the 'Roaring Twenties'. Triggered by the Russian Revolution in 1917, the end of World War I in 1918, Prohibition - Article 18 Amendment to the United States Constitution in 1920[238] and the 'Spanish Flu' pandemic (1918-1919), deadlier than the deaths in World War I with estimates that range from 20 million to 50 million worldwide. Liberation was the vogue, liberation from past constraints on human conduct.

Everything was in flux. It was the age of the 'Flappers' and an explosion of womens' rights. Radical change was experienced in vocabulary, sexual morals, habits, art, books, both prose and poetry, music, stage, dance, clothing, hair styles, design, furniture, entertainment and of course politics. The rise of communism in 1917 and its softer sister – socialism permeated every political structure and corner of the world from the Americas to Australia to Europe, Africa and Asia. Each megacity was alive to a new beat and to florid, extravagant, styles. It was the beginning of the 'sexual revolution'.

The Volstead Act, passed in U.S. Congress in 1918, that prohibited the sale of liquor was quickly turned into the 18th Amendment of the U.S. Constitution in 1920 – one the fastest passages of any such amendment in American history. The prohibition of consumption and transportation of liquor opened the door to the rise of the new criminal cartels which amassed illicit wealth, and of course liquor barons[239]. No nation was immune from these cascading waves of change.

Liberation movements triggered by President Wilson advocating the right of minorities to 'self determination' sprang up around the globe

---

239 The traffic in illicit liquor especially from Scotland and the increase of manufactured liquor in Canada gave rise to large fortunes notably the Bronfman family in Canada and Joseph Kennedy in the U.S.A.

as a kindred harbinger of political revolution and change. From 1919 onwards, China experienced a state of perpetual revolution. New states proliferated led by 'minority' movements across the globe. Colonial states were upended. Some were ready for statehood, some not! History teaches that for every strong action there is an equally strong reaction. This period marked the beginning of the collapse of European Empires that had ruled the world for centuries[240]. So, it was!

Every aspect of life around the world was transformed with lightning speed in the '20s and was never the same again.

---

240 By the end of the 20th century and the collapse of the Soviet Empire in 1989, all other Empires had collapsed and only a shadow of their residues remained. New and different unbridled empires emerged in politics and commerce across the globe. Both marked turning points in history.

HOLLYWOOD AND THE MOVIES

As the 20th century ushered in the rise and spread of modern globalism, movies became its most powerful messenger.

From 1900 to 2000, from silent kinescopes to digital images, the movies was the mirror to the century. Darkened movie theatres became and remain that private space while one's imagination and dreams collide and emotions reach out and captivate the psyche. Thereafter visual images and memories reign, become indelible, and cannot be erased from our minds. Visions of memorable movie scenes and music and stars never leave us.

While Canada was a pioneer in movies as were other countries like England and France, it was Hollywood that soon led and still leads the world in how people from all walks of life and all levels of financial status view each other and the 'other'.

In 1900, the largest cinema palace in the world was built in Montreal in 1898. Movie pioneers, brought up in Canada like Louis B. Mayer and the Warner Brothers[241] became inseparable from rise of movie studios, movie making and movies as did early Canadian stars like Mary Pickford who was born in Toronto and Walter Pidgeon in Saint John.

The most notable change in movies took place in the '30s after the change from silent movies to sound[242] when immigrants from Europe and Nazi Germany began to flood Hollywood. A veneer of European

---

241 Louis B. Mayer was born in Russia in 1884, lived for a time in St. John's New Brunswick where his father was a scrap dealer. Later he moved to Boston in 1892. Jack Warner was born in London, Ontario (my hometown) in 1892 where his Polish immigrant father was a shoemaker and moved to Ohio in 1899. In the U.S.A., Mayer and later Warner together with his three brothers – Harry, Albert and Sam – found their way to Hollywood where Mayer co-founded MGM and Jack Warner and his brothers, the Warner Brothers Pictures whose brands still thrive today.

242 The first 'talkie' in the '20s was the *Jazz Singer* starring Al Jolson, the son of a Jewish cantor, who left home to become a popular singer and stage performer, that was the story line in the film.

sophistication appeared. Writers, directors, musicians, musical directors, set designers, actors, and actresses became the new creative energy to transform the Silver Screen into the premier artistic platform of the world and ushered in the golden age of movies.

Leaders across the political spectrum loved movies. Lenin, Stalin, Hitler, Mao, Churchill[243, 244], Roosevelt, (except for the Mullahs of Iran) all watched them obsessively and regularly. The Justices of the American Supreme Court weekly viewed pornographic movies. Political leaders deployed movies to spread their carefully manufactured messages. Eisenstein in Russia, Riefenstahl in Nazi Germany were engaged to make heroic movies to popularize ideologically based politics. Hitler and Goebbels, his propaganda chief, paid special attention to heroic movie production. Roosevelt encouraged the production of patriotic movies during World War II as did Churchill, Stalin and Mao all of whom were Hollywood film buffs. *Mrs. Miniver* staring Greer Garson and Walter Pidgeon, a story about England in war time that highlighted the citizens' rescue by small boats to Dunkirk to save the remnants of the British and French armies, was one of my mother and my favourite.

Canada led in nationwide cinema chains like Famous Players organized by Canadians. U.S. chains like Loew's and British owned Odeon Theatres followed suite. Independent Canadian owned theatres sprung up across every town or city in Canada. Classics took on new life and gained wide audiences. All genres like comedy, slapstick horror, westerns, drama, crime, detectives, spying, musicals and cartoons that spawned digital fantasies competed for audiences. Sci-fi's transformed the way movie fans began to see themselves in their own imagination. Heroes and heroines, villains and saints, crowded our brains, inspired new fashions, new hairstyles, hats, clothing, lovemaking, music, violence, family stories, tragedy, peace and war. Classic literary works were transferred to

---

243 Churchill's favourite movie was a biopic of Nelson and his tragic death at the naval Battle of Trafalgar that saved England at the time. Churchill watched the movie a number of times during World War II and could quote Nelson's dialogue.

244 In the 1920's in Soviet Russia, 85% of all films exhibited were American movies. Stalin's favourites were westerns.

the screen – *The Hunchback of Notre Dame, The Count of Monte Cristo, Little Women, Richard The Third, Henry IV, Hamlet* to name a few. Literature came alive on the screen. Movies held centre stage in our imagination at the beginning of the century as they did at the end of the 20ᵗʰ century.

Theatres were designed to imitate imperial palaces. In more difficult economic times, movie business were reconfigured to sharing unadorned multiple small rooms clustered under one roof. Theatres marked the march from grandeur to practicality. Movies have enjoyed more revivals than life eternal.

Language, sexuality and violence was unleashed as the censor's morality controls loosened. In turn, this changed the cultural landscape of politics as politics and coarse language in the public square followed. People began to interact with each other in unexpected and uninhabited ways.

Movies, so easily deeply buried in our psyche required small effort to excavate the contours of our movie memories, so indelible and inseparable from our thought processes.

Recall your first movie, your favourite movie or movies – scenes, images of actors, even songs and sound tracks spring effortlessly to mind.

Consider just a few... *Snow White and the Seven Dwarfs, Over The Rainbow, Bugs Bunny, Fantasia, Mary Poppins, April In Paris, The Sound of Music, Casablanca*[245], *Gone With The Wind*[246,247], *Citizen Kane, The Big, Bad*

---

245 Released in 1942, *Casablanca*'s cast and production crews were almost entirely composed of exiles or foreign born with the notable exception of Humphrey Bogart ('Rick' in the movie) and the piano player Arthur 'Dooley' Wilson remembered as 'Sam' who played the unforgettable theme song '*As Time Goes By*'. To read the title to the song, the lyrics and music immediately spring to lips and mind. The director Michael Curtiz was a Jewish Hungarian immigrant who had directed 68 movies. *Casablanca* was his only Oscar winner. Jack Warner had been nominated eight times for an Oscar finally winning *Casablanca* for the Best Picture... all this after a troubled and consistent problems with the script and production.

246 Ben Hecht helped write screen scripts for classic movies like *Gone With The Wind, The Front Page, Gilda, Foreign Correspondent*. Born in Racine, Wisconsin in 1908 of Polish Jewish immigrant parents where his mother owned a small dress shop. Hecht started as a journalist and became a novelist, stage play writer (*The Front Page*) and screen play fixer and writer, contributing or writing over 140 screen scripts that hit

and Ugly, Bullet, The French Connection, Jaws, April in Paris, Chinatown, The Paths of Glory, The Manchurian Candidate, The Godfather trilogy, *The Longest Day, The Bond* series, *Goodwill Hunting, The Bourne* trilogy, *Philadelphia, Saturday Night Fever*[248] - the list is endless.... Yet each transformed individual imagination and public opinion.

---

the silver screen. Called a 'genius' by the French director Jean Luc Godard, Hecht labelled himself '*a child of the century*'. Paulin Kael, American's most outstanding movie critic not noted for hyperbole called Hecht "*the greatest American screen writer*". Hecht, a non-practising Jew, changed by events in World War II and the Holocaust. Hecht began to raise funds for arms for Menachem Begin and the Irgun in Palestine ('*Ben Hecht: Fighting Words, Moving Pictures*' by Adina Hoffman, Yale University Press, 2019).

I first heard of Hecht from my father-in-law, Harry Sniderman, co-owner of a small hotel in downtown Toronto who help organize an event where Hecht spoke in Toronto right after World War II. Harry led the Jewish owned hotel and liquor sector to contribute to this cause. While my uncle 'Moishe' helped raise funds from the Jewish own textiles sectors. My father was a supporter of the Agudas Israel, a coalition of orthodox groups led by the Ger while my uncle Melech was a leader of supporters aligned with David Ben-Gurion and his socialist party the Mapai.

247   One forgotten Hollywood story was the lonely heroism of Olivia de Havilland, an actress who starred in '*Gone With The Wind*'. She was one of my mother's favourite actresses. De Havilland was beseeched by Hollywood Communist sympathizers to condemn President Truman and later Senator McCarthy for their extreme anti-communism stances. Rather than follow their advice, de Havilland told a Hollywood audience set up to criticize McCarthy made up of a coalition of so-called 'progressive' forces who had supported the Roosevelt New Deal from 1932 to 1945. But now she proclaimed reactionary forces have driven a wedge in the liberal coalition taking orders from Moscow and following the party's line. The only answer was to distance themselves from Stalin and his followers. "*We believe in democracy, not Communism.*" She was a brave actress who put her principles before her career. De Havilland also transformed Hollywood run by movie moguls like Jack Warner. Under contract to Warner, she refused parts in movies she felt were inappropriate for her. She broke her contract, fought a legal battle and started a trend in Hollywood of independent companies owned by the talented actors themselves to decide what roles and what movies they would participate in. She was a strong and determined star that unlocked the studio system created and run by movie moguls. Read her biography '*Olivia de Havilland and the Golden Age of Hollywood*' by Ellis Amburn (Lyons Press, 2018).

248   *Saturday Night Fever* was based on the 'disco' music of the Bee Gees that broke world gross revenue records for a film in the '80s.

Evoking the name of a favourite movie brings instant recall. Movies become inseparable from how we imagine the world around us throughout the 20th century.

Movies like life itself, ever changing, yet always the same – all viewed in a quiet dark room where dreams are discovered and relished. Watch the movies and discover where society is traveling next.

THE GOLDEN AGE OF MOVIES[249]

No recent history in Hollywood casts the spotlight on the Golden age of movies better than '*The Sun and Her Stars: Salka Viertel and Hitler's Exiles in the Golden Age of Hollywood*' by Donna Rifkind, Other Press (2020). It centres on the life of a Galician born Jewish minor actress Salka Viertel (who had a minor part in Garbo's film *Catherine the Great*) and who emigrated to Hollywood in the late '20s and became the hostess and network builder of exiled actors, actresses, producers, directors, set and costume designers, writers, musicians who created the utopia of America displayed on the silver screen that they each dreamed about. From her comfortable home in San Diego, near the Pacific Ocean, she threw parties to bring these talented artists together. Attendees included Bertolt Brecht, Greta Garbo, The Mann Brothers, Arnold Schoenberg, Franz Werfel and Gustav Mahler. Other exiles from Europe included directors like Ernst Lubitsch, Michael Curtiz, Fred Zinnemann, King Vidor, Walter Wanger, George Cukor, William Wyler, Billy Wilder and stars like Paul Henreid, Hedy Lamarr, Peter Lorre, Charles Boyer, Otto Klemperer and Marlene Dietrich. What these talented driven artists projected on the screen was their own imagination of the perfect world populated by elegant sophisticated actors tailored clothes, exquisite manners, witty repartee, beautiful homes that manufactured beautiful dreams for everyone to enjoy leaving their difficult lives, striving for a better life.

---

249 A corollary to making movies was animation shorts that morphed into full length feature animated films. The leader was Walt Disney whose firm continues to lead the world in animation. Nowhere is this area of popular culture better described than in '*Wild Minds: The Artists And Rivalries That Inspired The Golden Age Of Animation*' by Reid Mitenbuler (Atlantic Monthly Press, 2020). The theme of rivalries between artists was a major driving force in both artists and producers in the golden age of films and animation. It continues.

Nowhere around the globe can one find anyone young or old who does not watch the movies to uplift their lives. Salka Viertel became known as the 'mother of exiles' and an animating spirit of the Golden Age of movies. She helped create a break for exiles in the hostile environment of the Hollywood studio system. She kept a diary of her remarkable exploits and her theatrical experiences as a budding stage actress in Vienna, Munich, Dresden, Berlin and Prague. Arriving in Hollywood in 1928 and settling in a house in Santa Monica steps from the Pacific Ocean, as an exile herself from Galicia, Salka's crackling warm personality enticed fellow exiles to meet and socialize in her welcoming home where she hosted an endless series of weekend parties. Here this largely exile creative community came to eat and drink, network and break through to the silver screen, pushed open the door to Hollywood star system and changed the Hollywood production system.

Throughout the 20ᵗʰ century, Hollywood continued to reign and frame popular culture in each corner of the globe, as other countries followed suite. New young directors from Europe especially England, Poland and Germany introduced a new wave of film experiences telling compelling tales set in every day working class experiences. The beat goes on.

THE GREATEST CANADIAN ACTOR IN THE 20TH CENTURY - CHRISTOPHER PLUMMER (1929-2021)

No actor, not even Laurence Olivier, could match the range, quality or depth of the acting art practised by Christopher Plummer. Olivier did not translate well from the stage to movies with rare exception (e.g. in the 1960 movie *The Entertainer*, where Olivier played Archie Rice, a seedy vaudeville performer to perfection). Olivier's speech, heavily accentuated and punctuated seemed more suited the stage[250], while Plummer could adapt his stage voice to plain flat Canadian tones on the screen. Nevertheless Olivier was acclaimed as the greatest English actor of the 20th century.

Plummer excelled in over 50 films in every media - radio, stage, television, movies, audio guides and books, whether alone as 'Barrymore' or with ensembles as in the Sound of Music and Shakespearean companies. Born in Toronto, raised in Montreal[251], he was first noted for a stage performance in his Montreal high school by the Canadian theatrical critic Herbert Whittaker and later lionized by the incomparable Nathan Cohen of the Toronto Star. Plummer first wanted to become a concert pianist but chose acting he said because "*it was easier*"[252]. Plummer was transformed into a mesmerizing character in each of his Shakespearean roles especially as King Lear. He could act, sing, dance and fence with equal dexterity. Renown on stages in New York, London

---

250 To be fair Olivier's voice over used in some British propaganda films during World War II were pitch perfect. Olivier in the movies as Henry V, Hamlet and Richard III were in the classic mode. He won the Academy Award for '*Hamlet*' in 1949. '*That Woman Hamilton*' released in 1941 where Olivier portrayed Lord Nelson was Churchill's favourite.

251 Plummer was descended from Canada's third Prime Minister Sir John Abbott (1891-1892). His grandfather was born in rural Quebec.

252 Plummer befriended Oscar Peterson, the great jazz pianist while a youth in Montreal.

and then revered in Hollywood he transformed every performance into a memorable experience. He could calibrate his voice from stage rants to radio whispers. His movements were subtle, nuanced, carefully 'bespoke' to each role.

I first saw Plummer perform at the Stratford Shakespearean Festival as Henry V in 1956 with my mother. It was the role, he agreed, catapulted him to stardom[253]. Later when I served as a member of the Board of the Stratford Festival, I learnt more of his storied career and still later when we met at a dinner in Toronto. A noted bon vivant like his acting pals Richard Burton, Peter Finch, Albert Finney, Sean Connery and Michael Caine[254], Plummer never let his private pleasures deter him from clearing his head and concentrating on the preparation for each role. Plummer, blessed with a classic profile and reeked with athletic masculinity, was gentle almost feminine in one to one conversation. Surprised and unaffected by his fame, modest, soft spoken, witty and always attentive to the person he engaged with, as if he was concentrating on not only what was said but how it was said.

My favourite roles where Christopher Plummer breathed life into each character and subtly turned each into an exquisite performance was as the aging Russian writer Leo Tolstoy in the movie *Last Station;* as the lawyer Henry Drummond in the stage play version of *Inherit the Wind*[255] in New York City. Another later masterpiece was as John Marshall Harlan,

---

253 Plummer won every acting award in Canada, U.S.A. et al and finally the Oscar for best supporting actor for *'Beginners'* in 2012

254 In the '80s, I met Michael Caine in his restaurant on Lincoln Road in Miami where I was introduced him as a Canadian Senator. *"Oh"*, he chortled, *"I know a Canadian, Christopher Plummer."*

255 *Inherit the Wind* was a fictionalized version of the Scopes Trial. Known as the State of Tennessee vs Thomas Scopes and called the Scopes 'Monkey Trial' it was based on an American law case brought in 1925 against a school teacher for teaching Darwinism evolution when the State law allowed teaching only about the biblical version of creation. The two actual protagonists were Clarence Darrow and an American Presidential candidate William Jennings Bryan. Scopes was convicted. Plummer played Henry Drummond, the defendant's lawyer. Drummond's true life character was Clarence Darrow, the socialist leaning attorney who's autobiography I devoured as a law student called *'Attorney for the Damned'* (University of Chicago Press, 2012).

the liberal Supreme Court of United States Justice who changed his mind persuading other recalcitrant justices not to convict Muhammad Ali as a 'conscientious' objector who refused to be conscripted during the Vietnamese War in an HBO special called '*Ali's Greatest Fight*'.

I doubt we will never see the likes of him again. Christopher Plummer was like a star burst in each sculpted performance. One of a kind. He remains the quintessential Canadian.

THE RISE OF THE WIRELESS AGE
AND THE CENTURY OF COMMUNICATIONS
AND COMPUTERS

Nothing was so disruptive or transformative as the advent of the 'wireless' age that burst across the world just before the birth of the 20th century.

Radio waves, called 'Hertzian waves', were first identified by a German scientist Heinrich Hertz in 1886. Improvised radio transmitters and receivers were then quickly developed first by an Italian Guglielmo Marconi in 1896.

What began as 'wired' changed to 'wireless' telegraphy. Radio waves were transmitted called telephony, first by line at the start of the century and then by wireless.

In 1900, a Brazilian priest Roberto Landell transmitted human voices via a public experiment in Sao Paulo, Brazil a distance of five kilometers. From this modest beginning radio communications erupted around the globe. From radio to telephony to television to satellite to digital, the 20th century became the century of communications. Every aspect of social exchange, work, commerce and entertainment was transformed. People connected with each other and in groups, large and small, attracted by a common interests.

The 'Great Depression' in the '30s witnessed the rise of religious programming and 'talk' radio led by radical extremists in America like Canadian born Father Coughlin[256] and American humourists like Will Rogers, or 'gossip' mixed with sculptured news called 'news flashes' by the unmistakable voice of Walter Winchell (1897-1972) backed by the sound

---

256 Father Charles Coughlin (1891-1979), a Detroit based priest, at first a vigourous supporter of Roosevelt's original New Deal turned to spew hatred and anti-semitic rants reached over 40 million listeners at the height of his radio career.

of ticker tapes[257] - the pioneer who mixed gossip with hard news. Disc jockeys (DJ's) propelled music bands and singers from every genre, classics to popular dance, blues to hip hop to folk, western to Latin. Opera was reserved for Saturday afternoon from the 'Met' in New York City. Families were glued to their weekly favourites and youth to their brand of music.

Powerful private corporations grew quickly out of these electronic platforms in radio, television and cable company that combined entertainment with 'news'.

The age of the 'attention economy' arrived. And with it[258] the unlimited accumulation of political power that proliferated beyond the reach of governments. The age of 'Big Brother' arrived.

Parallel to the explosion of communications was the rise in computers from calculating machines to mammoth computing rooms to miniaturization of elements, especially chip transmitters and memory cells that became the building blocks to digital electronics to mobile computer devices, table top laptops to mobile phones. Digital cameras began to proliferate especially on phones, making the world the most photographed in history.

Instant calculations driven by every complex coded algorithms heralded a power lightning fast way of instant communications. Charles Babbage (1791-1821) considered the father of computers, an English mathematician and mechanical engineer who hand wrought machines that originated the concept of a digital programmable computer.

---

257 Winchell started as a gossip columnist in New York in a Hearst paper column then expanded by the King Features Syndicate. At the zenith of his career, he was read by 50 million and heard by 20 million on radio. He was a staunch anti-communist and supported Senator McCarthy. He was the first major newspaper columnist to attack Hitler and appeasement rife in America in the '30s.

258 In 1997 Michael H. Goldhaber, an American consultant and writer, lectured in Cambridge, Massachusetts on the 'The Attention Economy and the Economics of Digital Information' – a pivotal point in the 20th century. The world first took notice with the work of Ronald Coase (1910 -2013). Coase, born in Britain, received the Nobel Prize in 1991 in Economics and was a pioneer in this field while teaching law and economics at University of Chicago. A course should be a mandatory subject for each student of law.

With the advent of electricity that allow for increasing scope, power and speed, the next turning point in the 20th century for the invention of coding and decoding machines was during World War II.

Led by Alan Turing[259] who was enlisted by Churchill's German born scientific advisor – Frederick Lindemann (later 1st Viscount Cherwell)[260] to build a decoding machine to decode Nazi military codes during World War II. This secretive project called 'Enigma' was based on Alan Turing's 1938 paper where he detailed the theoretical basis for a stored program computer. It was a turning point in history. Without a working understanding of 'coding' no one can be considered educated in the 21st century[261].

---

259 Alan Turing (1921-1954) was an English genius, mathematician and cryptoanalyst who developed with others the Turing machine dubbed Enigma to decode secret Nazi military codes. Churchill later divulged that he believed Turing and his small group of colleagues at Bletchley Park outside of London changed the course of World War II and accelerated the Allied victory.

260 By accident I visited his elegant villa in Italy where he hosted Winston Churchill.

261 At one time early in the century there was a widely held belief that the knowledge of how electrical turbines worked was not necessary to be educated. To enjoy the fruits of electricity was enough. Not so with 'coding'. Coding is necessary to understand how quickly communication is transforming everything civilization does.

THE RADIO AND TELEVISION ERA

The Global Village

Radio and television that originated in the West converted the world to the 'global village'[262]. Radio transmitters spread like wild fire to the loneliest regions of the globe. Adults and children lusted for radio shows that brought news, local and international, sports, weather, music and entertainment to wherever there was a pair of ears to hear.

Most American radio programs caught national and international attention from musical reviews[263], band concerts, operas, crooners, comedy, westerns, dramas, sleuths, and super heroes like Superman, Batman, Green Hornet and "who knows what lurks in the hearts of men.... the Shadow knows".

Radio while popular continued to thrive it was overshadowed by television, first in flickering black and white then colour. Radio and television brought families together to listen to their favourite programs especially on the weekend.

Sports like baseball, football, hockey, soccer and even cricket became national and international pastimes shaping nations competitive spirits.

---

262 It was Marshall McLuhan, a Professor at University of Toronto in his books 'The Gutenberg Galaxy: The Making of Typographic Man' (University of Toronto Press, 1962) and 'Understanding Media: The Extensions of Man' (McGraw Hill, 1964), a Canadian who coined the phrase 'global village' that united the world by telecommunications into a single community. I audited McLuhan's lectures, I watched him on TV interviews and met him a number of times. Actually, at first, I could not understand what he was saying or comprehend the broad ramifications of his thoughts.

263 For me and my family, our favourite radio and television programs were comedies led by Jack Bennie, the Bumsteads, the Goldbergs, on radio and the Jackie Gleason Show and 'Show of Shows' by Sid Caesar and his comedic ensemble on television. Of course, Sunday TV night with Ed Sullivan Show was an ingrained habit, Monday night radio with Cecil B. DeMille from Hollywood, as was Saturday Hockey Night in Canada with the memorable rasping voice of Foster Hewitt.

The televised Olympics broaden the public's interest in track and field, male and female. Horse racing results created betting networks.

The era of radio and television arrived and with the addition of cable and satellite that followed, changed the way we reflected on the confusing jolts of wars, famines, natural disasters that fragmented the chaotic world around us.

CANADA'S TWO 20TH CENTURY GRAND MASTERS: GLENN GOULD (1932-1982) AND OSCAR PETERSON (1925-2007)

Crouched on busy Front Street in downtown Toronto, outside the sterile glass covered high rise headquarters of the Canadian Broadcasting Corporation, sits a remarkable, lively, statute. There we discover a realistic sculpture of Glenn Gould, captured in darkly brushed bronze, slouched on a park bench wrapped a heavy overcoat, cap and thick gloves. No artifact could represent Glenn Gould better. Gould was Canada's foremost classical musician in the 20th century. As one observer noted, Gould and the word 'piano' became inseparable. Think piano and one thinks of Glenn Gould.

A classical pianist and composer, Glenn Herbert Gould was born in Toronto in 1932 and passed away prematurely in 1982. A child prodigy, Gould quickly rose to become one of the best known and revered classical pianists of the 20th century. No one could surpass his technical prowess nor the clarity of his definitive contrapitual renditions especially his Bach concerto versions, called the 'Goldberg Variations'. More than a musical wizard, Gould was a brilliant polymath. He was a deep student of history and political affairs. Known for his eccentric behaviour, his slouch at the keyboard and away from the piano, his disheveled appearance, clad in a thick cap, gloved fingers, scarf and heavy overcoat which Gould favoured in all seasons. Gould had handsome aquiline features with pale skin, a shock of thick brushed back dark brown hair and a flashing pixie like broad smile. His persona exuded a pent up magnetism. Glenn Gould, attractive to female and male alike, vital, despite his eccentricities, remains the man for all seasons who brought alive all the classic masters - Bach, Beethoven,

Chopin, Haydn, Schubert, Tchaikovsky, Rachmaninoff and others as never heard before[264]. Hearing Gould once in concert is to never forget his speed, clarity, precision and his rhapsodic renditions and, as he went on to recreate the grand masters on discs for eternity.

No serious student of the piano or, for that matter music is not influenced by the compelling artistry of Glenn Gould[265].

The age of jazz, a musical genre created and popularized from the outset of the 20th century, transformed the musical ear to become addicted to this unique blend of lyrical sounds, harmonies and rhythms that originated in the American south. Rhythm and blues then emanated from the original jazz masters. When I first came to Toronto in 1955 to attend law school, I visited three jazz havens, the King Cole Room in the Park Plaza Hotel on Bloor Street West, the Colonial Tavern downtown on Yonge Street, and later the Westover Hotel on Dundas Street West. It was in the King Cole Room I first heard the xylophone artistry of Peter Appleyard and Canada's grand master of jazz himself, Oscar Peterson.

No one was Oscar's equal on the piano playing the great jazz riffs and many of his own composition. Each grand master of jazz, Louis Armstrong, Duke Ellington, Miles Davis, just to name a few, all consider Oscar the most original and leading jazz pianist of them all. Ellington

---

264 My former law firm, Minden Gross, then known as Minden Gross Grafstein Greenstein, acted for Glenn Gould. His lawyer was my late partner Morris Gross. When Morris passed away, Steve Posen, a most congenial partner and friend, became Gould's trustee and acted for the Glenn Gould Trust. My personal exchanges with Gould, at times, took on the comedic. Gould did not relish physical contact of any sort and I would pat him on his shoulder to greet him when I encountered him in our law offices. He wore his cap with his scarf wrapped around his neck, his overcoat buttoned up for meetings in our law offices and reacted to this form greeting with obvious distaste. My humour wasn't his! At other times, Gould was animated and intensely interesting. He was a marvelous conversationalist interested in politics, astute and acerbic in his acute analyses of political trends and personalities.

265 Many concert pianists were inspired by him but no one could reach his mastery of Goldberg's Bach Variations as performed by Gould. Not even Lang Lang who came close.

referred to Peterson as the 'Maharajah' of the keyboard while Armstrong called him 'the four-handed piano player'. While Oscar became a renowned global musician as pianist and composer, he was less known for his deep commitment and involvement with the Martin Luther King in the civil rights movement in the United States. Paterson composed the '*Freedom Hymn*' that became the anthem of the civil rights movement. For this he derived the greatest pleasure and pride, always modest in his unequalled accomplishments. Once you hear the hymn it lingers in your mind. With his passing, an era of the musical greats in jazz in Canada came to an end[266].

---

266 When I first heard Oscar play with his trio, I believe in the King Cole Room at the Park Plaza Hotel (the home of the incomparable Peter Appleyard and his trio) in Toronto in the late '50s, I became mesmerized by the sounds, his lyrical renditions of the classic works of jazz and his own compositions. I introduced myself and I followed his career with intense admiration. When I travelled to Europe, I visited jazz spots in Frankfurt, Germany and always visiting the shrine of jazz in London –Ronnie Scott's that Oscar first suggested I visit. In 2005 during the Tsunami disaster in Asia, I decided to approach CBC to broadcast a musical telethon. CBC was interested but had no budget for stars. I convinced them that stars would participate without compensation. They were unconvinced. I decided to call Oscar who was I believe in concert in Montreal. I asked him if he would come and perform for this event. In a second, he agreed. Afterwards it was easy to convince others stars to participate. Oscar had a heart and soul bigger than his outsized body.

Another Toronto jazz artist was the flutist Moe Koffman who played with his group for years at the Westover Hotel. Moe's son married a distant cousin of my wife. I enjoyed his artistry especially his riffs of Klezmer music- an unusual blend of dazzling music that originated in Eastern Europe popularized in America by Benny Goodman, the great jazz clarinetist and band leader and later made famous by *Fiddler On The Roof*, a Broadway musical transformed into movie masterpiece directed by Canadian and Torontonian Norman Jewison, a much admired long-time friend. Norman created a film school in north Toronto for budding movie actors and technicians. Every year, the Toronto Film Festival holds a crowded outdoor event at Norman's School. Norman's artistic beat goes on, a tribute to his cinematic genius.

ALWAYS IN BLOOM: HAROLD BLOOM (1930-2019)

No doubt the leading critic and advocate of literature in the 20th century was Harold Bloom (1930-2019) who burst onto the public stage in the latter half of the 20th century with his elegantly written, popular, stimulating books and equally engaging university and public lectures and revelatory conversations in the media. Harold Bloom was the ultimate advocate of reading for its own sake and the connoisseur of the printed word. A lifelong student and teacher, Bloom was a true believer in the imperative of the humanities and the study of literature as the touchstone to a higher education. No leading author or religious figure or thinker missed his attention or recalibration.

It was said of Bloom that he read everything and understood everything and remembered everything. Bloom once described himself as a 'monster reader'. He could read a thick book in an hour and quote back passages. He loved to quietly quote long chunks from 'Dante's Inferno' or other master poets. Meanwhile he energetically excavated and extracted the wisdom from the canons of religion - Judaism, Christianity, Mohammedanism, Buddhism, Shintoism, Confucianism, Bahá'í - the leading faiths in the world, finding connectivity and relationships between ideas of the wordsmiths of religion and literature who, read together, propelled civilization ever forward.

For Bloom, the forces of religion and literature were inexorably bound to the progress of mankind. Poetry in all forms mesmerized him which he was delighted to share with his devout readers. Art and music were also pursued and explained to plant their imprint onto the aspiring liberal mind.

No serious work of literature or philosophy or art or music was overlooked. Bloom could spin a rich tapestry for his readers from Plato to Shakespeare to Montaigne (his favourite) to James to Freud. Every celebrated playwright, essayist, novelist and poet, new or old, caught his critical, loving and creative attention. Of course he had his favourites.

He plumbed the depths and contours of the thought of philosophers, new and old. His own books on his conception of the authors and editors of the Old Testament read like breathless detective stories. He had a gift of relating the Bible, old and new, to literature and life. Almost alone, he ushered in a delicate sensibility and unity to all literature and philosophy combining the canons of religion into a majestic whole while promoting the humanities as a lifelong avid reader and teacher at Yale University. No one could match the power and the depth of his sheer intellect nor the scope of his literary extrapolations in the 20th century as he mined literature, philosophy and religion, and then made all come alive in his vivacious, popular and capacious books. To gain an education in the humanities in the 21st century, any erstwhile student should start with reading Bloom's books and never stop[267].

---

267 My favourite Bloom books are *:
- *Possessed by Memory: The Inward Light of Criticism*, Knopf (2019) *
- *Macbeth: A Dagger of the Mind*, Scribner (2019)
- *Iago: The Strategies of Evil*, Scribner (2018)
- *Lear: The Great Image of Authority*, Scribner (2018)
- *Cleopatra: I Am Fire and Air*, Scribner (2017)
- *Falstaff: Give Me Life*, Scribner (2017)
- *The Daemon Knows: Literary Greatness and the American Sublime*, Spiegel and Grau (2015)
- *The Shadow of a Great Rock: A Literary Appreciation of The King James Bible*, Yale University Press (2011) *
- *The Anatomy of Influence: Literature as a Way of Life*, Yale University Press (2011) *
- *Till I End My Song: A Gathering of Last Poems*, Harper (2010)
- *Fallen Angels*, illustrated by Mark Podwal, Yale University Press (2007)
- *American Religious Poems: An Anthology* by Harold Bloom (2006)
- *Jesus and Yahweh: The Names Divine* (2005) *
- *Where Shall Wisdom Be Found?* New York (2004) ***
- *The Best Poems of the English Language: From Chaucer Through Frost*, New York (2004)
- *Hamlet: Poem Unlimited*, New York (2003) *
- Genius: A Mosaic of One Hundred Exemplary Creative Minds, New York (2003) *
- *El futur de la imaginació (The Future of the Imagination)*, Barcelona: Anagrama/ Empúries (2002)

A close second to Bloom as the 20th century's leading critic who shared many of Bloom's opinions was George Steiner (1929-2020). Born in France with his Austrian born parents, Steiner fled to New York City in 1940, received his French Baccalaureate in 1947, attended University

- *Stories and Poems for Extremely Intelligent Children of All Ages*, New York (2001)
- *How to Read and Why*, New York (2000) *
- *Shakespeare: The Invention of the Human*, New York (1998) *
- *Omens of Millennium: The Gnosis of Angels, Dreams, and Resurrection*, New York: Riverhead Books (1996)
- *The Western Canon: The Books and School of the Ages*, New York: Harcourt Brace (1994) *
- *The American Religion: The Emergence of the Post-Christian Nation*, Touchstone Books (1992; August 1993)
- *The Gospel of Thomas: The Hidden Sayings of Jesus*; translation with introduction, critical edition of the Coptic text and notes by Marvin Meyer, with an interpretation by Harold Bloom, San Francisco: Harper San Francisco (1992)
- *The Book of J: Translated from the Hebrew by David Rosenberg; Interpreted by Harold Bloom*, New York: Grove Press (1990) *
- *Ruin the Sacred Truths: Poetry and Belief from the Bible to the Present*, Cambridge, Mass.: Harvard University Press (1989) *
- *The Poetics of Influence: New and Selected Criticism*, New Haven: Henry R. Schwab (1988) *
- *The Breaking of the Vessels*, Chicago: University of Chicago Press (1982)
- *Agon: Towards a Theory of Revisionism*, New York: Oxford University Press (1982)
- *The Flight to Lucifer: A Gnostic Fantasy*, New York: Vintage Books (1980)
- *Deconstruction and Criticism*, New York: Seabury Press (1980)
- *Wallace Stevens: The Poems of our Climate*, Ithaca, N.Y.: Cornell University Press (1977)
- *Figures of Capable Imagination*, New York: Seabury Press (1976) *
- *Poetry and Repression: Revisionism from Blake to Stevens*, New Haven: Yale University Press (1976) *
- *Kabbalah and Criticism*, New York: Seabury Press (1975) *
- *A Map of Misreading*, New York: Oxford University Press (1975)
- *The Selected Writings of Walter Pater*, edition with introduction and notes, New York: New American Library (1974)
- *The Anxiety of Influence: A Theory of Poetry*, New York: Oxford University Press (1973); 2nd ed. (1997) *
- *The Ringers in the Tower: Studies in Romantic Tradition*, Chicago: University of Chicago Press (1971)

of Chicago, then Harvard and into Oxford as Rhodes Scholar at Balliol College Oxford. His thesis published as *The Death of Tragedy* in 1955 led to a doctorate in English Literature in 1955. A polymath like Bloom, editorialist, writer, lecturer finally at Cambridge where he taught for the rest of his life, with stints lecturing in Geneva, New York City and at Harvard as Professor of Poetry for a short period. Like Bloom, Steiner felt that reading especially the literary giants was a moral imperative. He essayed the impact of barbarism, especially the Holocaust in the search for meaning in literature, culture and humanity. Steiner brought a profound European nuance to literary criticism. Reading Steiner in conjunction with Bloom is to grasp at least the full contours of humanism in 20th century[268].

- *Yeats*, New York: Oxford University Press (1970)
- *Romanticism and Consciousness: Essays in Criticism*, Edited with introduction, New York: Norton (1970)
- *Walter Pater: Marius the Epicurean*; edition with introduction, New York: New American Library (1970)
- *The Literary Criticism of John Ruskin*, Edited with introduction, New York: DoubleDay (1965)
- *Blake's Apocalypse: A Study in Poetic Argument*, Anchor Books: New York: Doubleday and Co. (1963) *
- *The Visionary Company: A Reading of English Romantic Poetry*, Garden City, N.Y.: Doubleday (1961), Rev. and enlarged ed. Ithaca: Cornell University Press (1971)
- *Shelley's Mythmaking*, New Haven: Yale University Press (1959)

268 His books include:
- *The Poetry of Thought: From Hellenism to Celan*, New Directions (2011)
- *Ceux qui brûlent les livres*, L'Herne (2008)
- *A cinq heures de l'après-midi*, L'Herne (2008) (fiction)
- *Les Logocrates*, L'Herne (2008)
- *George Steiner at The New Yorker*, New Directions (2008)
- *My Unwritten Books*, New Directions (2008)
- *Le Silence des Livres*, Arléa (2006)
- *At Five in the Afternoon*, in Kenyon Review and Pushcart Prize XXVIII (2004) (fiction)
- *Nostalgia for the Absolute*, House of Anansi Press (2004)
- *The Idea of Europe*, Nexus Institute (2004)
- *Lessons of the Masters*, Harvard University Press (2003)
- *Grammars of Creation*, Faber and Faber (2001)

Finally to add to this list of daunting literary critics in the 20ᵗʰ century is Northrop Frye (1912-1991), a curmudgeon of a Canadian who joins this tiny illustrious group of original critics and advocates of the humanities adding his own narrative from a Canadian perspective. Frye brought a Canadian nuance and sensibility to this 'troika' of profound critics.

- *Errata: An Examined Life*, Weidenfeld and Nicolson (1997)
- *The Deeps of the Sea, and Other Fiction*, Faber and Faber (1996)
- *No Passion Spent: Essays 1978-1996*, Faber and Faber (1996)
- *Homer in English*, Penguin (1996) (Editor)
- *What is Comparative Literature?*, Clarendon Press (1995) - an inaugural lecture before the University of Oxford, U.K. on October 11 (1994)
- *Proofs and Three Parables*, Faber and Faber (1992)
- *Real Presences: Is There Anything in What We Say?*, Faber and Faber (1989)
- *Treblinka* (1986)
- *A Reading Against Shakespeare*, University of Glasgow (1986)
- *The Portage to San Cristobal of A.H.*, Faber and Faber (1981)
- *Antigones*, Clarendon Press (1984)
- *George Steiner: A Reader*, Penguin (1984)
- *The Uncommon Reader* (1978)
- *On Difficulty and Other Essays*, Oxford University Press (1978)
- *Heidegger*, Fontana Modern Masters (1978)
- *Has Truth a Future?*, BBC, 1978 -The Bronowski Memorial Lecture (1978)
- *Contemporary Approaches to English Studies*, Heinemann Education 1977)
- *Why English?*, Oxford University Press (1975)
- *After Babel: Aspects of Language and Translation*, Oxford University Press (1975)
- *Nostalgia for the Absolute* (1974)
- *The Sporting Scene: White Knights of Reykjavik*, Faber and Faber (1973)
- *Extraterritorial: Papers on Literature and the Language Revolution*, Faber and Faber (1972)
- *In Bluebeard's Castle: Some Notes Towards the Redefinition of Culture*, Faber and Faber (1971)
- *Poem Into Poem: World Poetry in Modern Verse Translation*, Penguin (1970)
- *Language and Silence: Essays 1958-1966*, Faber and Faber (1967)
- *The Penguin Book of Modern Verse Translation*, Penguin (1966)
- *Anno Domini: Three Stories*, Faber and Faber (1964)
- *Homer: A Collection of Critical Essays* (1962)
- *The Death of Tragedy*, Faber and Faber (1961)
- *Tolstoy or Dostoevsky: An Essay in Contrast*, Faber and Faber (1960)
- *Fantasy Poets Number Eight*, Fantasy Press, Eynsham (1952) (Seven poems)

Born in Sherbrooke, Quebec, educated at Victoria College and Emmanuel College at University of Toronto and Merton College, Oxford, Northrop Frye taught at Emmanuel College at University of Toronto. Frye is considered one of the most influential literary critics and literary theorists in 20th century. Deeply influenced by the Italian Giambattista Vico (considered the modern world's first political scientist[269]), Oswald Spengler, William Blake and F.R. Leavis, Frye cut his own path through the forest of humanities to illuminate the importance of culture in our lives.

His books deeply influenced writers like Margaret Atwood and Harold Bloom himself.

His first book, *'Fearful Symmetry'* (1947) about the poetry of Blake is a must read for any budding writer or poet. In *'Anatomy of Critics'* in 1957, as he set the framework of 20th century literary criticism. Bloom called him at the time *"the foremost living student of Western literature"*. Frye, a cultural and social critic, attracted a school of followers everywhere. Northrop Frye was a dour man with a pixie smile, slow of speech, careful with each word. Frye's writing style was less accessible than the others yet illuminating in its own careful considered way. To leading 20th century literary critics, Harold Bloom and George Steiner, Northrup Frye must be added.

Read each of their works and consider oneself educated[270]. One clear lesson of history emerges from their works. Familiarity with the humanities has preceded liberalism and progress.

---

269 Once rummaging through a fine second-hand book store in London, England, I came across a first edition of Giambattista Vico's magnum opus and principle work *'Principi di scienza nuova'* (1668-1744). I donated it to York University in the hope that it would inspire my friends in Toronto of Italian origin to build a collection of these early works that led to the study of modern political science.

270 I first encountered Frye as a CRTC Commissioner when I appeared before the Canadian Radio and Television Commission numerous times. Once at Keith Davey's suggestion, I called on Frye at his booklined office at Emmanuel College after the clouds of Quebec separatism burst across the Canadian political firmament to seek his sage advice. He listened patiently to my rant about separatism and what we should do about it. Frye responded quietly, *"This too shall pass."* He was perceptive as always.

MARSHALL MCLUHAN (1911-1980) -
IN A WORLD ALL HIS OWN

Marshall McLuhan burst on the world stage like a projectile fired from, as Fern Cadeaux once opined, an electronic cannon in the '60s. He was Canada's premier disrupter in the 20th century. Born in Edmonton, a graduate of University of Manitoba and the University of Cambridge before finally moving to teach at the University of Toronto in 1946 at St. Michael's College that became his main base for his extraordinary career arc as a thinker, writer, lecturer and celebrity. Born a Protestant, he converted to Catholicism and practiced his new found faith. McLuhan stunning described the coming world of media and its impact or society, coining phrases that reverberated around the globe - "Medium is the message" and "the global village." Alone he navigated the waves of this confusing electronic universe and first predicted how the web would meld culture, economics and politics into a sterile embrace. In the process, he predicted the social media would drown old norms and transform society into small groups then into new tribal members where the border between morality and immorality would diminish beyond recognition.

Pierre Trudeau closely followed McLuhan's work and sought his advice when Prime Minister. McLuhan changed the way we looked at ourselves and the world around us forever.

One cannot grasp the contours of McLuhan's thoughts and, at times, arcane prose without recalling he was a student of medieval languages. Nor can one fully ingest his published works without the easier study of the lucid prose of Harold Innis (1894-1952) who with McLuhan and others made the University of Toronto a leader in communication thought which McLuhan acknowledged in his book 'The Gutenberg Galaxy' how the book 'The Fur Trade' – influenced by Harold Innis, his friend, colleague, and critic, had influenced and shaped his intellectual ideas and world view.

In 1930, Innis published perhaps the most influential book in Canadian history that grasped the interplay between history and communication in

Canada and beyond. A pioneer in media theory, Innis's seminal research brilliant exposed in his books, and articles, and lectures, how staples such as the fur trade, fishery, lumber, wheat, minerals and coal shaped Canada's economic and cultural development along east and west lines rather than north and south lines towards the United States prior to its founding in 1789. His book on the fur trade in 1930 (*'The Fur Trade in Canada: An Introduction to Canadian Economic History'*) was followed by *'Empire and Communications'* in 1950 (Clarendon Press, Oxford, 1950) and *'The Bias of Communications'* in 1952 (University of Toronto Press) each succinctly demonstrated how oral and written communications contributed to the advance of civilization. Innis acted as an earlier warning system who foresaw how western civilization was threatened by media obsessed elites and early 'cancel culture' advocates that erased elements essential to understanding history and civilization's humane adaptations.

Innis also warned that Canada was becoming a subservient colony to the overpowering influence of America especially through the media. He was amongst first to warn against influence of American advertizing that was a source of American economic and political economic imperialism. Without Innis lucid prose or McLuhan's disruptive ideas on media the history of Canada's is incomprehensible. Innis taught the importance of independent universities, tolerant to all viewpoints as the hinge to western civilization.

Two original thinkers changed the way we looked at our world.

Marshall McLuhan was in class all his own and predicted a world that no one else yet recognized[271,272].

---

271 I first met McLuhan in his office at St. Michael's College on the inspiration of Pierre Trudeau. Trudeau was unique in Prime Minister who cultivated thinkers, teachers and writers like McLuhan who describes Trudeau as 'cool' because of his TV appearances. To be candid, I didn't understand a thing he said. Later I laboured over his books and began to only slightly grasp the power of his insights into the media that became the focus of my business career.

- *The Place of Thomas Nashe in the Learning of His Time* (doctoral dissertation); published as The Classical Trivium in 2006 (1942)
- *The Mechanical Bride: Folklore of Industrial Man*; 1st Ed.: The Vanguard Press, NY (1951); reissued by Gingko Press (2002)

- *Report on Project in Understanding New Media*; National Association of Educational Broadcasters, U.S. Dept. of Health, Education and Welfare (1960)
- *Explorations in Communication* edited with Edmund Snow Carpenter; Beacon Press, Boston (1960)
- *The Gutenberg Galaxy: The Making of Typographic Man*; 1ˢᵗ Ed.: University of Toronto Press (1962); reissued by Routledge and Kegan Paul
- *Understanding Media: The Extensions of Man*; 1ˢᵗ Ed. McGraw Hill, NY (1964); reissued by Gingko Press (2003)
- *The Medium is the Massage: An Inventory of Effects with Quentin Fiore*, produced by Jerome Agel; 1ˢᵗ Ed.: Random House (1967); reissued by Gingko Press (2001)
- *Verbi-Voco-Visual Explorations*; Something Else Press, NY (1967).
- *War and Peace in the Global Village* design/layout by Quentin Fiore, produced by Jerome Agel; 1ˢᵗ Ed.: Bantam, NY (1968); reissued by Gingko Press (2001)
- *Through the Vanishing Point: Space in Poetry and Painting* with Harley Parker; 1ˢᵗ Ed.: Harper and Row, NY (1968).
- *Counterblast design/layout* by Harley Parker; McClelland and Steward, Toronto (1969)
- *The Interior Landscape: The Literary Criticism of Marshall McLuhan 1943–1962 selected*, compiled and edited by Eugene McNamara; McGraw-Hill, NY (1969)
- *Culture is Our Business*; McGraw Hill/Ballantine, NY (1970)
- *From Cliché to Archetype* with Wilfred Watson; Viking, NY (1970)
- *Take Today: the Executive As Dropout* with Barrington Nevitt; Harcourt Brace Jovanovich, NY (1972)
- *The Violence of the Media*, The Canadian Forum (1976)
- *Inside on the outside, or the spaced-out American*, Journal of Communication (1976)
- *Seminar on Myth and Media*, University of Toronto (1976)
- Misunderstanding the Media's Laws, Technology and Culture (1976)
- *City As Classroom: Understanding Language and Media* with Kathryn Hutchon and Eric McLuhan; Book Society of Canada, Agincourt, Ontario (1977)
- *Laws of the Media*, with Preface by Paul Levinson, et cetera, June (1977)
- *Laws of Media: The New Science* with Eric McLuhan; University of Toronto Press (1988 1992)
- *The Global Village: Transformations in World Life and Media in the 21ˢᵗ Century* with Bruce R. Powers; Oxford University Press (1989)
- *The Medium and the Light: Reflections on Religion* edited by Eric McLuhan and Jacek Szlarek; Ginkgo Press (2003)
- *Understanding Me: Lectures and Interviews* edited by Stephanie McLuhan and David Staines; The MIT Press (2004)
- *The Classical Trivium: The Place of Thomas Nashe in the Learning of His Time* (first publication of McLuhan's 1942 doctoral dissertation); Gingko Press (2006)
- *Media and Formal Cause* with Eric McLuhan; NeoPoiesis Press, LCC (2011)

272 The first Presidential TV Debates in 1960 between Kennedy and Nixon triggered
a deeper interest in politics. While Kennedy won the TV debate, Nixon won the
radio version. Each media has its own characteristics, I learned. The political landscape was charging. Then in 1962, early in my political activism, I read Marshall
McLuchan's ground-breaking work, the *Gutenberg Galaxy*, then *Understanding
Media* 1964. I thought I would grasp how this new thinking on media would impact
politics. Not so easy. Then in 1966, Bud Estey attended my office in Ottawa in the
hope that I could influence John Turner when I served as his Executive Assistant
about the new Broadcast Act being developed in the public service under Judy
LaMarsh. Bud and I were acquaintances. One of Canada's leading lawyers, skilled
in litigation, tax and corporate law, Bud was a master of all aspects of the law especially administrative law. With a visible war arm injury he received while serving
in the air force, he was knowledgeable about the technical aspect of airplanes and
everything else. At the time, he was Chairman of Canada's largest cable system
controlled by Charles Bluhdorn, a mogul who headed Gulf and Western, an American conglomerate based in New York City. Bud described to me the growing
importance of cable television. I barely grasped what he told me. Shortly thereafter
on a whim I attended a hearing in Ottawa before the Board of Broadcast Governors to watch Ken Sobel, a distant relative of my wife, present his imaginative plan
to expand his small independent TV station Hamilton (CHCH) across Canada via
satellite. I was bowled over. I decided then and there that I would seek a career as a
communications lawyer when I returned to my practice in Toronto. In 1968, the new
Broadcast Act was introduced and the new Canada Radio and Television Commission (CRTC) was established. In 1969, I began to receive retainers from small clients
to appear before the CRTC. Pierre Juneau was the Chair. Other Commissioners
included Harry Boyle, a writer, Roy Faibish, a polymath, and Northrup Frye, Canada's eminent literary critic. Each CRTC hearing was an intellectual delight and I
prepared my cases carefully to attempt to appeal to these Commissioners' intellectual and literary interests.

 During this early period, in 1971, I was approached by Phyliss Switzer, a broadcast consultant, to assist her in her application for a low powered UHF television
start up in Toronto. The idea was the brainchild of Sruki Switzer, her husband and
one of Canada's most imaginative broadcast engineers. I refused because of her
programming plan and financial backer which I believed would not be approved by
the CRTC. Six months later, she appeared in my office to again to invite me to join
her in a new application as her financier had backed out. In the process, I became
a co-founder of Channel 79 with others I approached, that later became City TV.
Around the same time, I was approached by Geoff Conway. Geoff was a friend who
had gained notoriety as one of Walter Gordon's outside advisors in Gordon's first
disastrous federal Budget. Geoff, an economist and gold medalist in accounting,

was a brilliant financial analyst who had done a study of cable for Paul Desmairais. I suggested to Geoff that he get Desmairais's permission to use the study which Desmairais did gladly as he was not interested in pursuing regulated cable opportunities.

Together Geoff and I developed a scheme to connect all the high rise apartments in Toronto to a new cable system. Eph Diamond, the head of Cadillac, a major developer of high rises in Toronto, encouraged me in this idea. Geoff and I knew the idea would not gain approval as it would over wire all the existing cable systems in Toronto. At the same time, we applied for cable licence for Scarborough in the east end of Toronto. Geoff came up with the idea to get Rochester TV added to the carriage to attract greater consumer interest. Our small cable company, I named Cable Utilities Communications (CUC) grew to the fifth largest cable company in Canada. Charles Allen, an accounting whiz, joined us and became a cofounder with us in cable systems in California, Windsor, and then especially in northern Ontario which we called Northern Communications Company. There we invited Baxter Ricard, a Sudbury businessman and owner of a faltering French language radio station, and others to combine CTV, CBC TV outlets with other losing northern French Radio Stations with Cable into one company. When Geoff died, I led the charge with Charles Allen to gain a cable license for the Thames Valley in England becoming the first to offer telephony with cable television in the U.K. When British Telephone pulled out, we replaced them with Telus of Canada who continued as a solid and positive partner.

Later I was invited to co-found another cable venture in Sao Paulo, Brazil financed by Bell International by Ali Nazerali and Omar Grine and a Brazilian partner - Brazilian print mogul Roberto Civito and Roberto Longo, a Brazilian advertizing and marketing expert whose wife was one of Brazil's greatest painters. This was not a successful venture, though imaginative in concept. I coined the name Canbras for that company. Later with Ali, we set up wireless cable systems in parts of Ecuador.

Back in Toronto, on channel 79, City TV multilingual programs were added on Saturday produced by Dan Iannuzzi who owned an Italian language paper in Toronto. When Dan's programing growth outstripped his Saturday slot, he was replaced by City TV's new controlling shareholder Alan Waters of CHUM radio fame. With everyone's consent, I joined Dan in co-founding another UHF channel – channel 47 that became Multilingual Television (MTV) and now is OMNI TV. When Ted Rogers took over faltering MTV, he asked me to continue to serve on that board which I did for over 20 years along with Joe Sorbara and later John Tory. Together with Ted Rogers and Geoff Conway, we co-founded with Phil Lind YTV, a specialty channel focused on youth that continues to flourish and was a success story from the outset.

From Canada to U.S.A. to South America to Europe, my broadcast investment career continued to amaze my shocked wife Carole. To broadcast, I added print to my interests. Geoff Conway encouraged CUC to acquire a chain of urban magazines called Calendar Magazine. In the process, we merged faltering Calendar with Toronto Life headed by Michail DePencier. The merged Toronto Life/Calendar magazine became instantly profitable. The merged magazine thrived under the creative leadership of Debbie Gibson. At her insistence, we launched Toronto Life Fashion – a women's magazine then with Tim, Blank, we started Toronto Life Fashion File, a syndicated TV show dedicated to world fashion with CBC. It was a global wonder – broadcast in over 120 countries. To this day, I continue to work at high tech start-ups with younger entrepreneurs in Toronto and Ali Nazerali in Vancouver. The world keeps turning and it is still not time to jump off.

THE AGE OF IMAGINATION – THE CONQUEST OF AEROSPACE, OUTER SPACE AND EXTRATERRESTRIAL SPACE

From balloons to aeroplanes to rockets to jets to missiles to space capsules to UFO's[273], the conquest of space became national obsessions in the 20th century.

What lay beyond the oxygen bubble of mother earth captured civilization's imagination since Nicolaus Copernicus, a Polish Catholic scholar (1473-1543), mathematician and astronomer who, over 500 years, first formulated a model from his observations through his rudimentary telescope that the sun rather than earth was the centre of our universe. Copernicus was, at times, a rent collector, managed a brewery, a bakery and cared for the medical needs of other canons. He taught *"To know that we know, and to know that we do not know what we do not know, that is true knowledge."*

In turn Copernicus influenced Johannes Kepler, Isaac Newton, Leonardo da Vinci and others.

Johannes Kepler (1571-1630), a German astronomer and mathematician, delineated three laws of planetary motion – (1) planets move in elliptical orbits with a sun as the focus, (2) time to traverse any planetary arc is called 'area law', (3) there is an exact relationship the squares of the planets periodic times and cubes of the radii of their orbits called 'harmonic laws'. These reflected Kepler's belief in God's design for the universe. In turn Kepler's ideas led to Sir Isaac Newton (1643-1727),

---

273 Theories include laser powered sun sails, string theory, supersymmetry, multiuniversies and black light and black holes et al. *"The absence of life evidence"*, one scientist opined, *"is not evidence"*. Read *'Extraterrestrial: The First Sign of Intelligent Life Beyond Earth'* by Avi Loeb (Houghton Mifflin Harcourt, 2021). The first so-called 'ecoplanet' capable of life was discovered in 1995.

the English mathematician, physicist, astronomer, theologian and author, and his laws of motion and law of universal gravitation. Enter Einstein, the German Jewish mathematician, physicist, astronomer and theorist who disputed Newton's gravity theory with his own theory of relativity early in the 20th century.

With the advent of aviation as the American Wright Bros started in 1903 the race for the conquest of aerospace with powered flight followed in Europe with the first aerial dog fights between the British, Canadian[274], Australian and French and later the Americans against the Germans in World War I. In 1924, Charles Lindbergh drew international attention in the 30s as he travelled from America to Europe alone in a single engine plane. Mail carrying airplanes followed[275]. Commercial air travel across

---

274 Billy Bishop, a Canadian air pilot in World War I, was credited with 72 victories making him the top Canadian and British Empire ace in that war. He was awarded the Victoria Cross, the Croix de Guerre, other honours, and later became Air Marshall in RCAF. Bishop in his later years lived for a time in the second floor duplex apartment near the Casa Loma where my uncle Morris resided on the first floor. We were introduced in 1955 when I came to Law School and at my uncle's urging Bishop reminisced about some of his exploits during World War I – an amazing modest man.

275 Airplanes and the advance of human history are inseparable. Airplanes and small aircraft companies led by pilot entrepreneurs sprung up around the globe. Nowhere was this more evident than in the outer reaches of the globe where trains and highways could not advance to supply and connect people.

History, like a large onion, has many succulent layers until its core is uncovered, and, then you find there is much more to be uncovered. History is a collage of countless individual stories that form a tapestry of many strands, textures and colours.

Air travel transformed the world's social economic sphere from its rickety early profile at start of the 20th century. The time lines of the globe were shrunk.

A fascinating, little known, story is recanted in 'The Business of Tomorrow' by Dirk Smille (Pegasus Books, 2021) who lays out the visionary trajectory of financier Harry Guggenheim. Guggenheim, a member of a storied financial family, transformed aviation into a viable commercial enterprise with growth around the globe. Friend and supporter of the iconic Lindbergh, he financed airlines and rocketry. Harry Guggenheim became Lindbergh's lifelong friend and supporter as Guggenheim with the Guggenheim networks and finances and personally financed, planned and supervised the construction of the iconic Guggenheim Museum, in New York City, designed by Frank Lloyd Wright, replicated in 21st century in smaller museums in Europe.

the Atlantic with the BOAC in the lead was quickly followed by others. With the explosion of World War II came fighters, bombers, and the first supersonic jets. Of course, the 'blitz' of London and other cities included German made V2-'buzz bombs'. After World War II, the Americans enlisted the German scientists who designed the German 'buzz bombs' to build space jets, that led to space capsules. The race for the conquest of space was on.

In 1961 the 'Sputnik' the first manned space capsule was launched by Soviet Russia with pilot Yuri Gagarin. This was quickly followed by American astronauts, first Alan Shepard and then John Glenn. The first man on the moon in 1964 was Neil Armstrong who radioed the world as he stepped on the moon's surface, "a giant leap for mankind" and others quickly followed. Further steps in conquest of space accelerated. The private sector became interested.

The history of aviation cannot be fully appreciated without the essential vision work of Harry Guggenheim.

In the late '70s and early '80s I witness this phenomenon up close in western northern Canada, land of aboriginals, miners and energy exploiters, all dependent on the bush pilots for most of their needs. I was retained as a lawyer by Bob Engel, a giant of man, an American pilot who came north to Yellowknife in the Northwest Territories to start a small airline to supply the far north up to the Arctic coastline. I travelled to Calgary and then to Yellowknife where I was promptly made a member of the Northwest Territories Bar by a travelling judge from Calgary, Judge Parker. I was there to attend a hearing of the Canadian Transport Commission. I was invited to dine with pilots at 'Herc' village next to the Yellowknife airport. There, accompanied by copious spirits, I tasted bison steak for the first time. Interesting. Engel's small airline was competing to gain approval to site a cargo plane, the largest in the world, the Lockheed Hercules developed by Lockheed to supply the U.S. military in Vietnam. These expensive planes became available for commercial acquisition and use after the Vietnam War. Up to that time, Engel, starting with the workhorse Sea Otter that could regeared from wheels to pontoons to skis to fly into the north, acquired second hand DC47s, Lockheed Electras, and wanted to take a leap forward to compete with other airlines such as Pacific Western located in Vancouver led by Don Watson, a former air ambulance pilot in Saskatchewan and Wardair led by the legendary Max Ward. At Max's suggestion, I flew several times in Wardair's daytime flight to London. The service was superb. I became well acquainted with all these men during long competitive 'air' hearings. Finally I was successful gaining for

Unidentified flying objects (UFO's) had a different yet impressive trajectory starting in the earliest days of observation and conjecture.

Mathematical odds suggest that there was and is life beyond earth in the universe.

UFO sightings were not new to the 20th century. Used to describe sightings of alleged extraterrestrial objects or called by some observers 'space craft' early reports include Haley's Comet first recorded by Chinese astronomers in 240 BC. In the 4th century, Julius Obsequens a Roman wrote a work called *'Prodigiorum Liber'* (*'Book of Prodigies'*) that triggered intense interest in moving flaming objects visible across the skies. In 1561 over Nuremberg, in 1566 over Basel, sightings were called 'miracles' and 'sky spectacles'. In 1878 an American farmer reported the sighting of a flying object called a 'flying saucer'. In 1897 observers in Canada and United States reported seeing 'airships'. In 1904, 1916 and 1926 across United States, rows of lights and other flying objects were reported. During World War II, metallic spheres of light appeared over Pacific and Europe theates of war were spotted by pilots. In 1948 Swedish authorities advised the USAF that their investigators believe the objects seen there were 'extraterrestrial' in original. Sightings accelerated after

---

Engel the rights to site a Hercules in Yellowknife. Bob's small company never looked back. During that time I flew with Bob across the far north as he taught me the perils and challenges of flying in the far north. In the Senate I became fast friends with Charlie Watts an Inuit born in Fort Chimo, from James Bay in Northern Quebec who was a hunter, public servant and pilot who ran a small airline, Inuit Air, in northern Quebec at the time. I befriended Willie Adams, an Inuit from the Northwest Territories and Senator who told me of the challenges of daily life in the far north. Together we worked to get my private members bills passed in Parliament to alleviate the horrific saga of bad drinking water plaguing aboriginal reserves across the north and Canada. These bills were never approved by both houses of Parliament despite over 10 years of effort. They both regaled me with their experiences flying in small planes in Canada's far north in all kinds of weather.

It was these airplanes and their pilots in the north that became the lifeline that connected us together as a people across Canada's far flung landmass, the second largest in the world.

World War II. Movies, comic books and documentaries that popularized theories of alien life visiting earth. In the 21st century observations and theories exploded with interest around the globe.

No doubt science fiction will turn to reality. Will this field of investigation change human behaviour? Probably yes. Copernicus was not wrong (500 years ago) when he wrote the earth is not the centre of the universe nor was Carl Sagan and others who popularized the idea of life in space.

21st century theories include measured and observable sights and sounds that scientists are beginning to believe could only have come from intelligent life – welcome to the future.

THE CHINA ARC

1980

In 1980 my wife gave me a surprise gift for my 55th birthday. Carole knew of my deep interest in all things Chinese, an interest I gleaned from a mentor Roy Faibish, an 'old China hand'[276]. She arranged a trip to China, well before the floodgates of tourism had opened. Accompanied by our two young sons, Laurence and Michael, we followed Marco Polo's ancient trading route called the 'Silk Road' that originated in Italy, then Europe and continued west entering China at its farthest northwest corner where its border intersects with Pakistan. Launching from Urumqi, a small town in northwest Xinjiang Province, we would follow the 'Silk Road' as it leisurely transversed the desolate northern plains and then crisscrossed down through the south west into the heartland of China following the wide, languid Yangtze River, teeming with junks and boats of all sizes. We travelled by plane, bus, car, boat, bicycle, pony, rickshaw and even at times, by horse driven two wheeled carts. Mostly we travelled by train – all the while, marveling at the changing geography of China first along the broad steppes of the arid northern deserts across the desolate vastness of Xinjiang Province bordering on Mongolia with its majestic pink and lavender snow-capped mountain ranges dotted with isolated empty yellow plaster-coated mosque relics in this northwest region[277] then, down along the broad, meandering, basin valley of Yangtze River drifting along its dark waters through narrow gorges surrounded by wedge-like high cliffs and strange towering rock outcroppings into the broad expanse of its dense flat populated centres of China.

---

276 Roy Faibish as advisor to Diefenbaker led to export grain to China in the late '50s. In the early '60s, Roy admonished me that I was too Europe-centric in my political focuses. The future of world politics was especially China.

277 Xinjiang Province is the largest province in size in China and the only officially bilingual province of China - Uyghur and Mandarin.

Along the way, we visited collective farms, villages, towns and crowded cities. China was in throes of a remarkable transformation, politically and economically. Everywhere, people of all ages, were hard at work whether stooping over in endless muddy rice paddies or thrashing wheat fields, or in numerous small brickworks or primitive factories or grimy workshops. China was and is diverse. Each region enjoys its own dialect, cultural interests, folklore and especially its own cuisine.

One memorable stop was in Changsha, the capital of Hunan Province situated in the middle of China – in the middle of the 'Middle Kingdom'. There we visited the Ordinary 1st Normal School[278] and took turns sitting at the tiny wooden desk reputed to be used by Mao Zedong as a student in the small plain classroom encased in blackboards. It was in this school for teachers that Mao's intellect and leadership qualities first came to wider attention. Mao imagined himself as a teacher as he embarked on his astonishing political career first as a revolutionary, organizing and teaching in coops for workers, community groups, political organizations, writer (poetry and dialectics), news editor, then military strategist and warrior and finally undisputed leader of China in 1949. We viewed his drab lodgings in Changsha, the capital of Hunan Province, where he was said to live as a student. Mao was born to a well to do though illiterate landowner in rural Hunan Province which Mao covered up as he made his ascent from co-founding the Chinese Communist Party in 1919 to full time political activism. Because of this short visit, we all became fascinated by the tale of this remarkable leader who arose from these humble surroundings with numerous setbacks to become the undisputed leader of a united China in 1949, the most populous state in the world, on the cusp of becoming one of the world's largest economies[279].

---

278 The Changsha First Normal School, a teacher training school, was considered one of the finest schools in China. Carved over the entrance were these words, 'Seek Truth From Facts'. These words became the bedrock of Maoist thoughts. Mao spent five-and-a-half year here emerging as a leading student. He graduated at age 25 years and plunged into his unparalleled career as a journalist, pamphleteer, editor, teacher and talented union and political organizer.

279 Changsha and Hunan Province was where Mao cut his teeth as an organizer of co-op schools, small community organizations, political activist and union organizer.

Meanwhile, China in 1980 was still trembling in the flickering aftermath of the 'Cultural Revolution' provoked by Mao, the great disrupter,
a decade earlier that he instigated with the help of the so-called 'Gang of
Four' (including his third wife) in 1966 that lasted in full force till 1972.
Many young Chinese we encountered on streets still wore the plain khaki
or blue Mao tunics of the Red Guard, with red arm bands, enameled pins,
wide pants and a smallish bright red gold trimmed star on their matching
peaked caps. Mao died, still revered in China in 1976, while his cult of
leadership, his dialectics and his fanatic followers and the Communist
Party leadership elite, rumbled on and kept his legacy burning brightly
in every corner of China.

Once during our visit, as we were strolling down a narrow street
of a small provincial city, we were jostled along in a wave of crowded
spectators marching to reach a small drab public square attended by a
large packed cohort of sullen onlookers, many shouting slogans, some
carrying long narrow banners. There was a reason. On the raised wooden
platform in the centre of the packed square was a slight, middle age
man, on his knees, with a large sign painted with bold Chinese characters hung around his neck covering his concave chest. He was a teacher,
we were told. The frightened man faced a set of young stern looking,
enraged, uniformed youth who apparently were both accusers and
judges. Most in the packed crowd, we noted carried little red booklets
containing Mao's thought which they waved to accentuate each charge
of crime shouted out against the frail man. Others waved their narrow
large character covered banners. In 1966, Mao, surprising even his closest
advisers (except the 'Gang of Four' that included his fourth wife), had
single handedly ignited the flames of the 'Cultural Revolution' to rekindle
Communist fervour hoping to lift the Chinese from what he perceived
was their apathy[280]. Mao, the ceaseless revolutionary disruptor, felt even

---

Mao was a master organizer throughout his rise to power. He served as the first
Secretary of the small Communist Party in Hunan Province in the 1920's as a step-
ping stone into leadership of nascent China Communist Party and ultimately known
as Chairman Mao.

280 Mao was a disrupter in direction and action. In the 30s and 40s, he preached thought
control and practiced 'rectification' campaigns to induce his Party faithful to

the Party elderly leaders, some of whom accompanied him on the 'Long March' in the '30s, were lacking their early Communist fervour especially amongst the elder upper elitist ranks of the Central Committee and the Communist Party that filtered down into the Party and the general population. Zhou Enlai, Mao's most devoted advisor, barely escaped the fangs of the Cultural Revolution as he sought to ease the burden of those shipped to rural regions. His fanatic, grim-faced youthful followers waving Mao's little Red booklets containing Mao's concise declarations of precise conduct coupled with shouting, screaming, slogans and repeating chants, while some were carrying narrow and large characters signs while both male and female Red Guards were clad in plain identical tunics with the small Red Star emblazoned on their matching caps that became the visual hallmarks of the Cultural Revolution.

Later, in a capacious bookstore in central Shanghai, I acquired a set of Lu Xun's collected stories and essays translated in English[281]. Lu Xun was Mao's liberal minded favourite writer and longtime friend, some say conscience, who was not a Communist. There I bought a large poster of Einstein emblazed with Chinese characters declaring his importance as the world's leading scientist. The Chinese leadership admired Einstein. He served as a beacon in China to the brave new world of science and technology. Surprising to me, Einstein was a revered figure of China, almost a godlike icon. Another dramatic large poster portrayed Norman Bethune, a Canadian doctor who attended Mao's army during the latter part of the iconic Long March in the late '30s that meandered north through the heart of China as Mao and his cadre of close advisors escaped with his ravaged rag tag army to caves in Yan'an - northwest China – harassed by the endless attacks of the Chinese nationalist militias, seeking to encircle and destroy the rag tag Communist army, led by Chiang Kai-shek who was supported in turn by the Russians, the Nazis and by America. Bethune became and remains a revered hero in the pantheon of Chinese

---

continually rekindle their Communist spirit and closely follow Mao's ever changing ideas and the flood of his latest stream of edicts, pithy slogans and different renditions of the Party line.

281   Later I acquired the 19th century woodcut paint of Lu Xen from the old artist, the first of which was owned by Mao.

icons. America, led by Franklin Roosevelt and his envoy General Marshall and then Lt. Colonel Hurley, had chosen to support the corrupt Chiang rather than Mao, both fighting the Japanese invaders, who was at the time lusting for American support[282]. Roosevelt and Marshall lost China.

As we sped across the hinterlands of China and the endless marsh paddies alive with slender green rice shoots and then lush golden wheat and corn fields, we witnessed the economic miracle as villages and rural collectives being transformed from mud huts to clusters of small brick houses surrounded by low brick walls, while fragile electricity poles reached up like fingers across these remote rural areas connected by electrical lines, swaying in the gentle breeze. We noted endless gangling electrical towers being erected. We visited one small village classroom where young children were being taught on rudimental computers. The writing was on the wall. Change directed by Mao via the disruption of the 'Cultural Revolution' had sent Communist Party adherents especially elderly, senior members of the Central Committee like Deng Xiaoping accompanied by their families and surrounded by fanatic urban youth to distant rural areas to work at menial rural tasks as they became re-educated, reindoctrinated and hopefully to reignite their Communist fervour. The early selflessness of the Communist Revolution when Mao and his fervent followers took over China in 1949 was being recalibrated and replayed to the disruptive new tunes of the aging restless Mao. Mao upended Marxist and Leninist thought by teaching that revolution would be first ignited in backward rural areas via the outnumbered Communist Army and their political Commissars and local rural activist groups, rather than by workers and radical intellectuals in urban regions. Mao's ragged army on its historic 3,000 mile 'Long March' from the south to north west China was a model in treatment of poor rural workers along the way, paying for the food and supplies they commandeered enlisting their countless rural poor's devotion as Mao built the Communist Party

---

282 Early in his career, Mao became a devout admirer of George Washington interested in how Washington had led a beleaguered American militia to defeat the more powerful British against hopeless odds in the American Revolutionary War almost two centuries before.

from the bottom up! Mao decided to replace Confucian ideas[283] with his own which he did once he became ultimate leader.

Mao's shadow palpably covered every level of society. From local, provincial and federal governments to rural villages, from city squares to schools to public buildings to Tiananmen Square in Beijing. Mao's familiar face caught on gigantic coloured picture posters was everywhere. In massive Tiananmen Square, his oversized portrait was on display over the ornate gateway to the Forbidden City. And there, in the centre of the vast Square sat a lone ornate Chinese lacquered two-storey building. Inside we discovered a gigantic two-storey high statue of Mao sitting in an overstuff armchair all in encased in gleaming white marble alone in a cavernous room[284]. In the equally adjacent oversized room, his preserved life-like body was displayed like Lenin - Kremlin style. People formed long quiet respectful lines to catch a glimpse of Mao in his open casket and then his monumental statute as they slowly filed out of the building.

During the Cultural Revolution that erupted in 1966 and began to ebb a decade later, Mao mandated via regular Party edicts to teachers to encourage schools children to turn against their parents and report any minor misconduct if their parents failed to strictly adhere to the Party line. The 'Cultural Revolution' was still alive at every level of society. It allowed us to catch a cursory glimpse how Mao had transformed China and the daily lives of the Chinese people under his autocratic rule from the bottom up. Each street and each neighbourhood had committees

---

283 Confucian philosophy had culturally bound the divided 'Middle Kingdom' together. His teachings were based on principles of morality, respect for autonomy, beneficial non-maleficence, honesty of conduct, propriety and respect for elders. He preached the 'Golden Rule' – "*What you do not wish for yourself, do not do to others*". Confucius lived from 551 to 479 BCE.

284 Later on a mission to twin Toronto with Chongqing in the '90s, I met and befriended YaYu Shan, the handsome young sculptor who as a reward for winning the right to sculpt Mao's massive statue in Mao's mausoleum in Tiananmen Square became head of Chongqing's art museum and school. He gave me a gift of his small maquette of Zhou Enlai, Shan's beloved mentor who had chosen Shan from over 50,000 other contestants to sculpt Mao's statue, which I cherish and holds a position of pride in my home library.

of Party officials monitoring ordinary Chinese daily for any breach of the precise practices of Party line of the month. 'Big Brother' with loud messages over public loudspeakers was at work daily.

North Korea, North Vietnam and Cambodia, Malaysia and others in Asia, Africa and the Americas followed Mao's revolutionary lead. The Party leaders of each of those neighbouring countries, taking their cue from Mao, gain full control over the lives of their inhabitants. Maoism first spread across China, then Asia, then Europe, then Africa and finally, Central and South America, Mao left the largest footprint of any leader in the 20th century. For my 55th birthday, my wife arranged a trip across China accompanied by son's Lawrence and Michael was one of the most remarkable trips of my life. Mao's influence continues unabated to this day[285].

---

285 See 'Leadership and Failure of Leadership In the 20th Century' that outlines how Mao and Maoism left the greatest impact of any leader on 20th century compared to Roosevelt, Churchill, de Gaulle or Stalin. This book by the author is scheduled for publication in 2022-2023.

PANDEMICS AND EPIDEMICS
IN THE 20ᵀᴴ CENTURY

The 20th century marked a turning point in the fight against unexpected global pandemics and regional epidemics. Before the 20th century, starting in mid 19th century, governments began to recognize the need to address public health issues arising from impoverished sanitary conditions. Then, like a rising tide, throughout the remainder of 19th century began Public Health officers began to appear. City Committees, then regional, provincial, then federal government boards and federal and provincial and city departments began to spring up, usually based on a local health crisis. Britain took the lead to legislate then implement public health policies. United States followed this revolution in public health. Starting 1848, a British Public Health Board was established. Universities like McGill, and Trinity in Dublin in 1871 and later Yale in 1914 established leading departments of health to train doctors and public health officials. This plethora of actions turned into cascade across the civilized world. Sanitization became the trigger as urban sanitary systems began to be built. Medical leaders alerted governments to the pressing need for public sanitation and health as public health agencies began to address the visible growing problem of the health of all levels of society. The neglected broke through the public conscience. Ninety-nine percent who fell under periodic epidemic outbreaks were under 65 years old. Periodic epidemics continue to break out around the globe. Most continued to be deadly until the late 1940's. And only after the end of 20th century were effective vaccines available for most viruses and bacillus. Widening of public awareness to obtain recommended even mandatory inoculation did not become common place until the 21st century.

THE PLAGUE

In 1947 Albert Camus, the French Nobel Prize winner in Literature, a favoured essayist, published an existentialist classic novel called 'The Plague' ('La Peste'). Camus had introduced the world to the notion of 'the absurd' – how absurd conduct becomes commonplace - that continues to this day. Camus tells the tale of an epidemic sweeping the capital of Oran in French North Africa. This fascinating book some critics say was also an allegory of fascist politics that had infected the world up to and during World War II. More directly, it was a metaphor for the Nazi occupation of France in World War II. Camus illuminates the human condition, high-lights how mankind reacts to epidemic crises. First denial, then slowly, facing the reality and finally always too late, necessary actions to curb these modern plagues. Camus describes how society is transfixed then transformed. First paralyzed then focussed - as society returns slowly to normal. The vulnerability of humanity is explored. While progress continues he described how there is no escape from human frailty. Does the absurdity of life lead to despair? The plague, Camus asserts, never dies but invisible, it waits to emerge again. Camus recognized, what mankind refuses to acknowledge - that *"everyone has it inside himself – therefore no one... no one is immune."* The question he raises is whether civil society learns from these disruptions to human life. Or whether history is doomed to repeat itself – a major unanswered question of the 20th century.

Here is a partial list of pandemics and epidemics (mostly regional) in the 20th century:

Tuberculosis from 1900 into 1923

Cholera	1899-1923
Bubonic Plague	1900-1904
Typhoid	1906-1907

Polio	1916-1955
Influenza[286]	1918-1921, 1957 and 1968
Diphtheria	1921-1925
Small Pox	1924-1937
Typhoid Flu	1968
Small Pox	1972-1974
Legionnaires Disease	1976
Measles	1981-1991
Whooping Cough	2010-2014
Zika Epidemic	2015-2016
HIV/AIDS	1981-2000

No cure has yet been found for this disease, only the alleviation of symptoms

Crisis management expertise to gain necessary data and the will to initiate actions to curb and arrest these epidemics remained scarce and hard lessons learned were easily forgotten throughout the 20th century. One of greatest mistakes in Canada in the 20th century was the little published sale and dissolution of Connaught Laboratories in Toronto established in 1914 that was one of the world's leading research facilities for infectious diseases and vaccines. Absurd but predictable!

---

286 Each influenza was identified by their presumed regions, Spanish Flu H1N1, Asian Flu H2N2, Hong Kong Flu H3N2. The 1918 outbreak of Spanish Flu considered the most deadly in human history killed an estimate 50 to 100 million.

THE RISE OF THE 'RULE OF LAW' IN THE 20TH CENTURY

"Fragile as reason is and limited as law is as the institutionalised medium of reason, that's all we have between us and the tyranny of mere will and the cruelty of unbridled, undisciplined feelings."

- Quote by Justice Felix Frankfurter repeated by Dean Cecil 'Caesar' Augustus Wright at the opening of the University of Toronto Law School on Queens Park Crescent

"The life of law is not logic, it is experience". "Young man, the secret of my success is that an early age, I discovered I was not God." [287]

It was in the fall of 1955 that I first came to Toronto to attend the University of Toronto Law School. I was twenty, armed with a thin two year Bachelor of Arts degree from The University of Western Ontario (1953-1955) animated by high expectation and higher anxiety. Suddenly, I discovered a new world. The life of the law[288]. And my life changed forever. Law was called a profession. Law had all the benchmarks of a 'calling'. With hard work, I slowly became a devotee and member of a secular priesthood. Like religion, the study of law is complex and multi-faceted. Both require endless study. Both slowly shape one's belief structure. Each aspect of the law is endlessly retooled, like a combustible engine. One part is no less important than the other for the legal engine to run effectively. Law school, law teachers, law students, practicing lawyers, legal societies, judges, judicial councils, prosecutors and defenders in criminal law,

---

287 Oliver Wendell Holmes, Jr.

288 Without my study group at Law School composed of Marty Friedland, Harry Arthurs and Harvey Bliss which met for several hours every Sunday, I would not have overcome the rigours of my legal studies.

litigators in civil law, adjudicators in administrative tribunals, legislators (federal, provincial or municipal), legislated laws and regulations, judge-made common law, open and fair democratically elected law making bodies each with their own checks and balances, popularly elected governments, departments of justice and police, a free fair and informed media, are all essential parts of a well-tuned and well maintained legal infrastructure to uphold the 'rule of law'.

The practice and processes of law, like democracy, are not perfect. Both demand endless monitoring to repair the cracks and renovate the fissures. The principle of the 'rule of law' remains the best we have to protect us against autocracy and chaos that lies waiting to erupt and disrupt near the heart of every political system and civil society.

Words, like democracy[289] and the 'rule of law', have been constantly used and abused to justify the legitimacy of those who seek to exercise power over their citizenry.

The miserable 'ism's' of the 20ᵗʰ century, Communism, Nazism, Fascism, Islamism – all used the 'rule of law' and the trappings of law to gain credibility, legitimacy and allegiance amongst its subjects and citizens. Autocratic leaders and their followers used patently flawed legal processes to obtain and maintain power. The abuse of law is the foundation of autocratic power.

Law is inseparable from words. Words are important and imperfect. Words can kill[290]. More can be killed by an order, ostensibly based

---

289 A democracy is a system of government by the whole of the population with fairly elected representatives to exercise state power on eligible members of the state to exercise power by fairly elected representatives. According to Freedom House there was not a single liberal democracy with universal suffrage in the world in 1900 that could be called democracies. There were 19 constitutional monarchies with regularly elected assemblies and ostensible government by 'rule of law'. Only 11 had regularly elected assemblies. By year 2000, 164 could be loosely considered democratic governments. The definition of democracy remains complex without clearly agreed principles.

290 The great Hasidic master 'Sfas Emes' (the Mouth of Truth) who died in 1905 taught that the careful use of words and the truth of words are the foundation leading to a moral life. He warned that words are more dangerous than lethal weapons because orders from afar can kill more people, more quickly. *"Take care with words you speak or write"*,

on law, than can be done at close at hand by knife or a handgun. So law starts with words - the plain meaning of words. A law student learns that words can be ambiguous, unclear and uncertain. The search for the clear meaning of words lies at the heart of any just legal system.

Francis Bacon (1561-1626), lawyer, judge, writer and thinker, a devout Anglican believer wrote in his search for meaning: *"The greatest sophism of all sophisms is the equivocation and ambiguity of words and phrases."*

John Dryden (1631-1700), the English and England's first Poet Laureate in 1668, writer, poet, dramatist and literary critic, replicated the same idea in verse:

> *"As long as words a different sense bear*
> *And each may be his own interpreter,*
> *Our airy faith will no foundation find,*
> *The words a weather cock for every wind."*

With the imperfection of vocabulary, few words have a precise or definitive meaning except perhaps mathematical or scientific terms. Some even argue scientific terms are imprecise and are ever changing as science evolves and new scientific principles are waiting to be uncovered.

Hence the need for care in the use of words. Law is power wrapped in words. John Locke (1682-1704), English attorney, physician and philosopher, regarded as a 'father of liberalism', in his *The Epistle to the Reader* wrote, *"there are not words enough in any language to answer all ideas..."* This problem should not be a hindrance from resisting patent abuse or intentional misuse of words. The fight against obscurity or confusion of meaning is never ending[291]. To seek precise and clear use of the plain meaning of words and language is the object of law, under the rubric

---

he admonished his followers. My grandfather Israel Bleeman became his student before he emigrated from Poland to Canada and thereafter one of his erstwhile followers.

291 In the 20th century a leading philosopher, a Jew born in Austria who emigrated to Britain, Ludwig Wittgenstein (1884-1951) who taught at Cambridge became one of the most original thinkers of the 20th century based his analysis on the meaning of words in each theory.

of the 'rule of law'. At times, even common sense meaning of words seems uncommon. Locke also was an advocate of separatism of powers in government and limited powers. His treaties on civil government are still relevant.

'Democracy' has many meanings. At its core, democracy requires an open, rules based, infrastructure based on fair, transparent, monitored, supervised regular election processes. A democratic legislature, needs built in checks and balances on its members, the government, its public servants, independent courts and an independent court system itself with legal practitioners to ensure the implementation of 'rule of law'. The public became unsatisfied with the slowness of Parliamentary processes and the work of Parliamentarians and government oversight. Parliamentary ethics officers, budget officers began to proliferate. Lawyers and judicial councils, at first, self-regulated, began to open their governing boards to outside experts and independent oversight.

Examples of blatant abuses of the 'rule of law' in 20th century by nations include Nazi Germany, Soviet Russia, Cuba and Iran. All had so called elected legislatures and appointed courts. None were democratically elected nor independent of their autocratic leadership. Autocratic leaders need these controlled agencies to gain, exercise and sustain their power. The dictatorship of the autocratic led party is the hallmark of autocracy.

The 'rule of law' with its long evolutionary history was shredded beyond recognition in the 20th century and still, like a bipolar experience, witnessed extraordinary changes in society.

Advances in the 'rule of law' in the 20th century became inseparable with progress.

'Rule of law' to operate fairly requires a democratically elected legislators. No election is perfect. Elections need independent oversights. If an election is markedly flawed, the democratic system fails as it loses its essence - the infrastructure of the 'rule of law' and ultimately trust and confidence of the electors.

The 'rule of law' origins are found in the Bible. The origins of western law can be traced to the Ten Commandments, still the most concise statement of 'rule of law' under God and man. Moses, the great law giver, taught that people will only obey the law if the judges believe in justice and are fair minded. *"Justice, justice shall you pursue"* dictates the Bible. 'Justice' is mentioned twice. Many interpretations of this phrase has come down through the ages. One interpretation is that one reference to justice applies to the nature of law itself and the second to judges who adjudicate disputes based on the law.

From time immemorial while 'war' was considered a means to exert national rights over neighbouring states[292], the early Biblical prophets and philosophers like St. Augustine (343-430 AD) and Thomas Hobbes (1558-1679), each sought rules to differentiate 'just' war from 'unjust' war. Recall that honour codes, in early centuries between warriors and warrior classes, began to set limitations of violent conflict, even 'just' wars. Carl von Clausewitz (1780-1831) opined that *"war"* is an extension *"of politics by other means"*. Sir Henry Bannerman Smith (1836-1908)[293], a Prime Minister of England, and one of the leaders of the Liberal Party during the Boer War in a famous and oft quoted speech said, *"When is war not war? When it is fought by methods of barbarism."*

---

292 The roots of international law can be found in the laws of the sea. Ancient Roman Codex were expanded by the Hanseatic League in the post medieval period. Boards of arbitration were set up to establish disputes between city states and between ship owners.

   With advent of train travel rules of carriage were established. With telegraphs internationally recognized rules of utilization were developed. When cars proliferated, rules of the road were deemed necessary for safety. With air travel came rules for airplane in the air and rules for landing and take-off. With the advent of radio then television came rules for regional spectrum management to prevent congestion which were drawn by users and legislation to gain ownership of spectrum was adhered to. Finally international crime gave birth to international organizations designed to stem the flow of illicit crime. Each new activity had its own set of rules and its own international institutions to govern and adjudicate specific rules: trains, telegraph, radio and T.V. spectrum, autos and air just to name a few.

293 Sir Henry Bannerman Smith was a direct ancestor of my late friend and political cohort, Senator David Smith who never failed to regale us with anecdotes about his distinguished forebearer.

The 20th century, a century of wars, witnessed world wars, regional wars, civil wars and finally asymmetrical wars. Meanwhile growth of international law by the League of Nations after World War I and finally its successor the United Nations after World War II attracted a host of international thinkers and lawyers who began to place limits of war. The Geneva Accords, at the turn of the century dealt primarily with treatment of prisoners of war and began to broaden the scope to theories of 'appropriate' responses to unlimited attacks by others. Public assent narrowed the acceptable rules of violence between combatants (outlawing gas attacks), treatment of war prisoners and circumscribing 'collateral' damage to innocent citizens.

International law was rooted in the rise of the ancient and evolutionary laws of seas agreed to by seafaring states dealing with their ships and their cargoes sailing in what became known as 'national' and 'international' waters. International agencies of enquiry and arbitration were established to settle disputes about ships, passengers and cargo.

Under the 1982 UN Convention of the Law of Seas, coastal water boundaries were clarified and expanded to 12 nautical miles (22 km, 14 miles) open to navigation of all ships of 'innocent passage'. 150 states joined. A new designation of territorial waters extended to water boundaries to 200 nautical miles (370 km, 230 miles) that gave each coastal nation the right to claim these areas as exclusive economic zones (EEZ). Disputes could be settled by international arbitration reducing the uncertainty of competing economic interests. The 'rule of law' applied.

By the end of the 20th century, a host of domestic and international laws, and institutions devoted to peace, placed curbs on the conduct of 'just' wars by states even based on 'self defence'[294]. 'Appropriate response' to attacks by 'self defense' began to be circumscribed by legal oversight, international agencies and wider public awareness through

---

294 The Geneva Protocol banning the use of poisonous gas and other like chemical weapons was signed in 1925. The first treaty, forgotten by history, was the Strasbourg Agreement of 1675 between France and the Holy Roman Empire led by the Habsburgs in response to the use of poisoned bullets. This was following by the Hague Agreement of 1899 that banned chemical weapons such as the use of projectiles capable of spreading deleterious gas or chemicals.

the growing media. Armies retained lawyers to ensure all actions were approved under rules of international jurisprudence that began to expand. 'War crimes', 'crimes of aggression', 'crimes against humanity' and 'genocide' gave birth to international Courts of Justice culminating with the Treaty of Rome in 1998 when 40 nations agreed to establish the International Court of Justice at The Hague that came into effect just after the beginning of the 21st century. The United States did not join this Treaty concerned that its military might be open to prosecution based on criminal charges marinated in political motivation rather than law. Even those states, not bound by the Treaty, began to practice care in the use of force. Notwithstanding, the international 'rule of law' continues to grow, at a slow if meandering steady pace.

Philosophers like St. Augustine preached importance of the just application of the 'rule of law' in wars between states. 'Just wars' ('*jus in bello*') were based on the 'rule of law' according to St. Augustine (354-430) and later St. Thomas Aquinas (1224-1274) and then Hugo Grotius (1583-1645).

The ideas of these thinkers to limit war between states and establish rules of war percolated throughout 20th century and led to the rise of international courts adjudicating between against states and laterally against individuals. International courts expanded the contours of international law to adjudicate disputes under transparent legal processes and act as an undulating safety valve against 'unjust wars'.

This cascading trend started at the turn of the 20th century, The Hague became the locus of the Geneva Conventions to adjudicate rules for the treatment of war prisoners and the codes of conduct that originated initially during the American Civil War.

With the establishment of League of Nations after World War I, international courts continued to be a venue to settle disputes between nations. The reach of these courts largely failed as the League of Nations dissolved with the advent of World War II. Meanwhile the Geneva Conventions continue to be recognized for treatment of war prisoners during World War I and World War II and then, beyond. With the establishment in 1944 of the United Nations, the first Nuremberg War Crimes Tribunal at Nuremberg composed of ally appointed judges and prosecutors was convened to try a handful Nazi leaders for 'aggressive' war crimes[295]. Trials in Tokyo followed against a few Japanese war leaders. Some were convicted and some dismissed. Others were incarcerated and all but one ultimately released.

These international war crime courts penalized individuals based their crimes of 'aggression' first defined in the League of Nations articles to avoid the charges of that this was a retrospective law and in itself and breach of the 'rule of law'. Eventually, these tribunals gave birth to the International Court of Justice established in 1998 by the Treaty of Rome acceded to by 40 states that could prosecute crimes of 'genocide', war crimes and 'acts of aggression'.

This Court was tethered by jurisdictional disputes. States that did not join like the U.S.A. refused to be convinced that 'war crimes' under the Treaty of Rome against their soldiers in foreign wars would only be charged with alleged crimes saturated by political motivations rather than law. Still when finally enacted in 2002, the Court of International Justice commenced its work. Few leaders were tried or convicted. Still the world began to evolve slowly to new level of the 'rule of law'.

The roots on the limits of the 'divine' rule of English kings was the Magna Carta signed in Runnymede, England in 1215 between an English king and feudal lords. Of course, King John reneged yet it was a start. The Magna Carta survived King John's perfidy. The sanctity of the 'person' and the 'rule of law' began to take shape. Trial by jury of peers was a key. The writ of Habeas Corpus was created. The English common law, settled, case by case, required judges who slowly exercised independence and began to exercise restraint. Step by step, the 'rule of law' came to be understood and accepted by the public, by its rulers, its law makers, the courts and the prosecutors as states began to implement equality of treatment under the umbrella of the 'rule of law'. The 'majesty' invested in the crown was transferred to majesty of the courts of law.

Great thinkers of these tenets followed Moses. Aristotle, St. Augustine, Montaigne, Blackstone, Locke and Hume and others who all promoted the

---

295 Less than half of one percent of the tens of thousands of Nazi activists were tried and the few convicted were released after short stints in prison. A few were hung after being convicted. Göring took his own life by poison before he was to be hung.

'rule of law' as a means towards a 'just' society as the idea of the 'rule of law' bore fruit that all could digest by the 20th century. This notion served as a fluttering check on the vagaries of unlimited political power and the barbarity human condition. Everyone who breached the 'rule of law' could be brought to justice so 'show trials' were adopted to teach an example to politicians and the public to obey the so-called 'rule of law'. 'Justice' became a word by autocrats to legitimize their aberrant behaviour.

The 20th century witnessed an explosion in the growth of democratically elected assemblies. With the growth of the 'rule of law' by these popularly elected assemblies came a proliferation of political institutions and principles to preserve and protect the full and fair exercise of the law.

The 20th century gave birth to the passage of laws by elected multiple assemblies, first like a trickle, then a spring, then a strong and steady flow, then cascades and finally a flood of laws and regulations that covered every aspect of human and even animal activities.

With the flood of laws came the endless call for rights of every kind – natural rights, civil rights, minority rights, women's rights, transgender rights, gay rights, and human rights. The call for *"Rights"*, *"Rights"*, *"Rights"* turned into a mantra. Pierre Trudeau, worried that this one sided demand for 'rights' would eviscerate 'responsibility'. *"There can be no 'rights' without 'responsibilities'"*, he admonished us. This latter point was drowned out by the megaphone insistence on 'rights'[296]. Easier to scream for rights than define or activate responsibility[297].

---

296 Lawsuits against government for tortious acts by government officers or public servants started in 1887 in Canada when the Exchequer Court of Canada issued a judgment of damages against the federal government. In 1953 the Crown Liability Act was passed setting out the legal frame work for such legal actions. By 1985 this aspect of law was updated as Crown Liability Act RSC 1985 C50. Since then the federal government and provincial governments who followed the federal lead on allowing civil claims have been flooded with lawsuits. The public is unaware of the escalating costs to the taxpayers. By end of the century, the costs direct and indirect ballooned to the billions. Should all taxpayers be penalized for egregious acts of public officials? This remains an open question in the 'rule of law' in 21st century for democracies. Respect for the taxpayers' dollars was eviscerated by the end of the 20th century.

297 No doubt Pierre Trudeau gleaned his concept of the duopoly of rights coupled with responsibility from Max Weber's 1919 lecture on *'Politics As A Vocation'*

With the flood of 'rights' and laws came problems. 'Ignorance of the law' was deemed no excuse. With the rising flood of laws came delays in the courts. *"Justice delayed is justice denied."* So the law's delay brought increasing civil disobedience. Critics of the laggardness of the courts and the legislators and governments to change obvious injustices flagged a parallel loss of respect for legal institutions. Still in the 20th century, the 'rule of law' was directly tied to the advance of 'progress' and equality.

In 1929, Lord Hewart – the Chief Justice of England – published a devastating critique called *'The New Despotism'* (Ernest Benn Limited, 1929). Hewart focused on the growth of agencies of government that were given the power to issue regulations to deal with an increasing complex society without judicial oversight. With these prolific agencies came a plethora of regulations. Lord Hewart in his classic *'The New Despotism'* published in 1929, complained that these agencies acted with all the powers of government and remained beyond the purview of the courts. This critique was somewhat ameliorated by regulatory oversight committees. Over regulation became a valid critique that grew throughout the 20th century. Regulations were issued at times for the sake of bureaucrats to justify their offices and slake their thirst for oversight. Legislators who came to be paid and serve full time, with funded ample staffs needed the passage of laws and regulations to defend against criticism from a disengaged public. Special interests began to utilize both law and regulatory making to shape both to their advantage. The 'tyranny of the minorities' came to usurp popular power. Mindless 'red tape' became a clog on freedom of action at times and a needless check on liberty and human activity.

The 'rule of law' has many reiterations and definitions. The architectonics of the 'rule of law' require a constitution where equality is the lynchpin, a regularly democratic election of an assembly, legislation passed transparently, careful choice of the judiciary, free and independent of political pressure, lawyers who serve as officers of the court in criminal trials as prosecutor and defender and plaintiff and defendant council in civil trials. Judges are admonished to exercise judicial restraint

---

where Weber emphasized the imperative of the *"ethics of responsibility"* in leaders' actions.

and refrain from allowing their views and belief structure to taint their conduct or their decisions. Following England and the British Empire traditions, the ideology of respect for the Crown was in part transferred and entrenched in the courts. Judges preside on a raised dais clad with robes as do lawyers in most states to demonstrate their mutual respect for the majesty of the 'rule of law'.

In the United States, the appointment of Supreme Court judges became an open transparent tradition as federal judges are nominated by the President, after vetting by legal groups and other groups. The 'advice and consent' of the Senate in open televised hearings is required as these appointments are life time appointments designed to enhance judicial independence. Oliver Wendell Holmes, Louis Brandeis (my favourite)[298], Louis Cardozo, Felix Frankfurter, and Earl Warren, Thurgood Marshall, Antonin Scalia, Ruth Bader Ginsburg were but a few of these iconic judges. Each held the 'rule of law' sacred. Each was assiduously engaged in the search for the truth by weighing each material fact to render 'just' decisions. Easier said than done. Each were a 'master' or 'mistress' of the law[299].

---

298 Holmes and particularly Brandeis by their decisions (or especially by their dissents, often called the 'Great Dissenters), began to erode the right to property to open a 'progressive' window on a spectrum of issues. It was Brandeis who co-wrote in the Harvard Law Review (4 Harvard LR 193 (Dec 15, 1890) *The Right to Have Privacy*', primarily as a 'right' to be left alone' that was not in the U.S. Constitution but used a basis for women's rights to abortion in Wade versus Roe 410 US 113 decided Jan. 22, 1973.

Perhaps Holmes most far reaching dissent was in 1919 in the case of Abrams and the United States. This case was a group of immigrants were prosecuted under the 1917 Espionage Act for distributing pamphlets opposing U.S. intervention in Russia. They were convicted. Holmes dissented by defining 'free speech' as an open marketplace of ideas that led to expanding protection for expressing controversial views and opinions – the heartbeat of American democracy. Justice Brandeis known as the 'People's Attorney' was considered a leading 'progressive' writing a tract in 1919 called *Other People's Money*'. Brandeis believed in small government closer to the people and railed against commercial monopolies' excessive power. The word 'progressive' became the obverse in modern political dialectics.

299 No American lawyer in the 20th century, relatively unknown, could match the mastery of Benjamin V. Cohen (1894-1983), a lawyer born of Polish Jewish immi

The American courts early became divided between 'originalists' who clinged to the notion that judges should restraint themselves to notions of the founding fathers and those who believed the U.S. Constitution should be seen as a 'growing tree doctrine' to meet changing conditions and complexities in society and became at times an unelected legislature of last resort.

University of Toronto Law School, reputed as the leading law school in Canada brought a radical reform to teaching law in Canada when Cecil Augustus 'Caesar' Wright[300] after a dispute in 1947 about legal education with the Benchers of Upper Canada in Ontario who ran Osgoode Hall, resigned and left Osgoode Hall with three law teachers to become Dean and the key teaching staff at University of Toronto Law School in 1949. 'Caesar' adopted the Harvard 'case' method of teaching law based on case by case, fact by fact analyses opening new vistas of legal comprehension.

---

grant parents in Muncie, Indiana. Cohen went on the University of Chicago gaining a doctorate in jurisprudence, considered to be the most brilliant mind ever to attend Chicago Law School, and then a doctorate in juridical science from Harvard Law where he encountered Felix Frankfurter who became his mentor, and then a protégé of Justice Louis Brandeis. He first worked for US Shipping Board in World War I and then advised the National 'Consumer' League.

He helped Frankfurter draft a minimum wage bill for women, advised American Zionists in the '20s, and then became the key architect behind Roosevelt's 'New Deal'. He drafted a dizzying array of legislation including the FCC (Federal Securities Commission), TVA, the Tennessee Water Authority, FHA (Federal Housing Authority), Rural Electrification Act, Social Security, Fair Labour Standards Act and Wage and Price Controls. During World War II, Cohen wrote a legal opinion that allowed legislators to overcome the American Neutrality Laws that prohibited the sale of war materials to the Allies especially Britain and later he helped draft the Lend-lease legislation to allow America to lease war ships to Britain. After the World War II he was involved in drafting the United Nations Charter at Dumbarton Oaks. He attended as an advisor to Truman at the Postdam Conference. He helped draft the Marshall Plan in 1947. Later he helped the Johnson administration draft landmark Civil Rights legislation. No lawyer, modestly, did so much to advance the 'rule of law' through domestic and international law in America that had an impact around the globe.

300 Cecil Augustus Wright, born in my home town, London, Ontario, graduated from University of Western Ontario, then Osgoode Hall and went on to Harvard to study law, became the first Canadian to earn a Doctor of Judicial Science (J.D.S.) and returned to lead and teach law at Osgoode Hall and then as the University of Toronto Law School.

Legal education under his leadership changed in Canada for ever. All other Canadian law schools followed 'Caesar's' lead.

My teachers at University of Toronto Law School included 'Caesar' Wright (torts)[301], Jim Milner (contracts), Bora Laskin (constitutional and real property)[302], Albert Able (administrative law), Eugene La Brie (international law) who taught malleable minds to search for the facts of that should determine to outcome of each legal dispute[303]. 'Facts', 'facts', 'facts' was the daily mantra taught in each of their classes. 'Facts' are truth. Case law collected in regularly printed legal reports expanded exponentially in every democratic legal system. It was almost impossible to keep up the 'case law' and the study of law. To parce legislation that flooded the bookshelves became even more difficult.

Canada was blessed with superb legal practitioners, some of whom I became acquainted first as a student then as a member of the Bar in Ontario when I was admitted in 1960[304]. Each were noteworthy for their legal scholarship, courtroom rhetoric, wit, skills and character. John J. Robinette was Canada's articulate exemplar[305]. Joseph Sedgewick,

---

301 'Caesar' Wright became my mentor after Law School when I visited him biweekly or so for advice. When I was offered a job by John Turner, a newly appointed junior Federal Cabinet Minister in 1965, to work in Ottawa as his Chief of Staff, 'Caesar' convinced me to accept it.

302 Bora Laskin became the first Jew appointed a Supreme Court Judge to the regressive Court of Appeal of Ontario due in part to my efforts. See 'A Leader Must be a Leader' by the author (Mosaic Press, 2019) starting on page 70. Later he was appointed to the Supreme Court of Canada and then Chief Justice by Pierre Trudeau.

303 The only top mark of my class I received at Law School was in international law taught by Eugene La Brie. I applied and gained a modest scholarship to the Academy of International Law at The Hague. To my regret, I didn't go.

304 I was appointed Queen's Counsel, the youngest in my class, in 1970 by the Bill Davis Conservative government. Regretfully this practice of designating lawyers for excellence was dropped as it was considered too politicized.

305 J.J. Robinette taught a course in ethics to first year law students at University of Toronto Law School. I recall our first class. Robinette asked our class to whom does the lawyer owe his first duty. We all said "to our client". "No", Robinette admonished us. "A lawyer's first duty is to himself, as an officer of the court." Robinette refused to be appointed a Supreme Court of Canada judge. Robinette believed that the highest calling in life was the practice of law.

counsel par excellence in the English common law tradition, G. Arthur
Martin, Canada's preeminent criminal lawyer, Charles Dubin, a superb
all round counsel later to become a Supreme Court judge, and Arthur
Maloney, a first class criminal lawyer as was Austin Cooper and a top
notch litigator who was elected by lawyers as Treasurer, chief bencher,
in Ontario, Syd Robins. Each of these I audited when they argued in the
courts of Ontario. No one could match the diverse legal skill sets in every
aspect of civil law, criminal law, the laws of the air and sea, tax corporations and administrative law of Bud Estey, a close friend and mentor,
later to be appointed by Pierre Trudeau to the Supreme Court of Canada.
What a gruelling education.

'Caesar' encouraged his students to take the time to go to the courts
to listen and learn from those masters of the Bar.

Arthur Maloney, a leading criminal lawyer, fought against the death
penalty and for its abolition as did Larry Pennell, also a criminal lawyer
from Brantford, Ontario who became Solicitor General of Canada. Pierre
Trudeau and John Turner, both skilled lawyers before becoming Members
of Parliament[306], were instrumental in convincing Parliament to abolish
the death penalty in Canada. Kim Campbell, a well trained lawyer both in
Canada and England, as Minister of Justice, changed the onus in crimes
pertaining to assault on women. A law school classmate John Sopinka
became the first Canadian of Ukrainian origin to be appointed a member
of the Supreme Court of Canada, Frank Iacobucci, a law professor at
the University of Toronto's Faculty of Law (1967-1982) as well as Dean
of the law faculty (1979-1982) and Vice-President and Provost of the
university (1983-1985), adorned the Supreme Court of Canada (1991 to
2004), with his kind balanced thoughtful approach as a judge. Martin
Friedland and Harry Arthurs, my classmates and key members of my law
school study group, each were important players in the 'rule of law' in
Canada in the 20ᵗʰ century as law teachers, Deans of their law schools,
legal writers, arbitrators and advisors to governments – Marty, mostly

---

306 See 'A Leader Must Be a Leader: Encounters with Eleven Prime Ministers' by the author
     (Mosaic Press, 2019). Trudeau was a civil rights and labour specialist and Turner an
     expert in navigation and international law.

in criminal law and evidence, Harry in labour law where both published widely respected books on their specialities. Earle Cherniak, a friend and law school roommate became one Canada's outstanding counsel. Julius Isaac a quiet contained witty classmate went on to become the first black Justice of the Federal Court and then Chief Justice of the Federal Court of Canada who set a lively example as a devout believer in the 'rule of law'. The founding partner of my firm was Arthur Minden, a genius at real estate[307]. My late law partner Morris Gross was a solicitor's solicitor bringing calm and common sense to all tangled legal problems[308]. No lawyer work harder or for longer hours at the profession of law than Bernie Chernos, a top student at law school and a leading civil litigator. No one was more feared or respected. Each were friends and taught me to respect 'rule of law'.

Slowly, the public in the 20th century came to understand the traditional processes of law making and the equally complex legal steps to legal adjudications by the courts.

---

307 When I joined Minden, Pivnick and Gross in 1960, I was the fifth lawyer of the firm. When I became a partner after Arthur died, the firm for a while was called Minden Gross Grafstein Greenstein. My specialty was Criminal and Civil litigation and then Communications and Administrative Law. Art Minden, the diminutive senior partner took me under his wing and ask me to assist him on his real estate projects. He put together a project to rent 480 feet from Victoria University and with two partners built the Colonnade, the first multiuse building (residential, offices and stores) in Toronto on 360 feet. He sold off a portion of the land lease next door on 120 feet that became an office tower. The design was imaginative. He asked me to come up with a name. I did. It was called the Colonnade. Arthur's son George, took over an old hotel nearby called Windsor Arms owned by his father. George redesigned it into an elegant boutique hotel that included the 'Three Small Rooms' - two dining restaurants and one wine bar, the first of its kind in Canada, all of which were wildly successful. George introduced me to collecting fine French wine that continues to this day.

308 Hartley Nathan, a law partner and friend, was not only co-author of leading law books on how to conduct corporate meetings, but is a global expert in the fictive detective stories of Sherlock Holmes by Arthur Conan Doyle. Steve Posen, a law partner and friend is one of Canada's leading real estate leasing experts and adviser to the Glenn Gould Foundation.

Checks and balances began to proliferate on law makers and law practitioners as a wide array of specialized tribunals emerged. Tribunals for employment practices and human rights grew like grass in this well-tended legal garden.

Distrust of Parliament, Parliamentarians, government and the public service and failure on Parliamentary oversight of budgets triggered by what David Smith, one of Canada's leading constitutionalists called the rise of the 'Fourth Branch' of government, the other three being the House of Commons, the Senate and the Crown. The first Parliamentary officer nominated by the government and appointed by a vote in Parliament established the office of Auditor General for a term of seven years. The Auditor General is required to table an annual report to Parliament. This appointment was followed by a cascade of other independent offices of Parliament, now an active fourth branch of government has emerged as a post constitutional development each officer with broad investigative powers.

Others officers include:

- Chief Electoral Officer
- Commissioner of Official Languages
- Information Commissioner
- Privacy Commissioner
- Conflict of Interest and Ethics Commissioner
- Commissioner of Lobbying
- Public Sector Integrity Commissioner
- Parliamentary Budget Officer

The 20ᵗʰ century saw the rise of Ombudsman to ensure that judges and public servants acted in accord with the web of laws, parliamentary rules affecting their conduct[309]. Ombudsman officers began to proliferate in Canada in almost every department of government – federal, provincial and municipal[310]. The complexity and sloth and cost of the traditional

---

309 The idea of the Ombudsman in the modern era started in 1804 in Sweden.

310 The Ombudsman concept was developed in Scandinavian countries before the advent of the 20th century. But the idea of Ombudsman took root in the 1960's in Canada.

legal processes made the public dissatisfied with the 'rule of law' by legislation and courts. The office of Inspector General attached to each federal department of government in U.S.A. was another check on aberrant behaviour by public servants, not always successful.

So the 20th century witnessed the descent of trust and credibility in Parliamentarians to do the job they were elected to do. The arduous task of oversight in key areas was delegated to this unelected 'Fourth' branch of government. The 'rule of law' continued to oscillate between attention and benign neglect while Parliamentarians became distracted by a host of other media grabbing topics. 'Gotcha' politics reigned supreme.

Beware of those who seek to take on the trappings of the 'rule of law' by abuse of words like 'Democratic' which continues unabated. For example,

- The Democratic Republic of Algeria[311]
- The Democratic Republic of Congo
- Democratic Republic of Afghanistan

Abuse of 'words' by autocratic states seeking a mantle of legitimacy continues. The United Nations run, to a large measure, by autocratic nations continues these patent abuses. The UN Committee on Human Rights is a farce controlled by autocratic nations who have regularly singled out Israel as the most egregious offender in the world, while Israel continues to be the most transparent, relentlessly democratic nation in the Middle East.

The 'rule of law', used and abused, became a mantra that thundered throughout the 20th century.

---

311   The Algerian War of Independence (1954-1962) set the platform for acts of intentional harm against innocent citizens by Algerian revolutionaries to gain independence from colonial status under France. These numbers are not fully confirmed. Over 600,000 citizens in public places were targeted and bombed and killed during this bloody war. These successful terrorist actions laid the seeds for the advent of suicide bombers in Lebanon in 1981 and for the rest of the 20th century especially against Americans but others as collateral damage was wrought to mostly innocent bystanders.

The diminishment of 'rule of law' began to be accompanied and augmented by aggressive polling of selected segments of the public. At best polls were one flawed snapshot at one short time period.

The 20th century experienced the sharp rise and power of pollsters and polling that began to shape public attention and action on every issue and utilized by leaders, parties and special interests on every political issue and especially on political leaders popularity.

In the '30s, an American advertizing executive - George Gallup - refined early crude techniques to measure public attitudes on consumer issues with the goal, like advertizing itself, to begin to manipulate political behaviour. Elmo Roper was another early American pioneer in this art of gauging public attitudes and desires. By the end of the 20th century, every political leader, political party, those seeking public office, and businessmen leading larger corporations and even larger charities, employed pollsters to shape their decisions, language and actions. What was right became supplanted by what was popular!

These new crafted policies injected with special interest came to dominate public discourse and public policy, economics, politics, culture and media in the 20th century. Driven by a particular belief structure or preconceived notions of fairness made it difficult for a voter to exercise his own independent views for the good and bad aspects of civic society. Polling results began to take precedence over the 'rule of law'.

My own experience with innards of polling started with zeal in 1974. I was approached to become volunteer head of Red Leaf a consortium of advertizing executives to work for the Liberal Party during election cycles by Keith Davey and Pierre Trudeau. Keith Davey, my political friend and mentor, in the early '60s had retained an American pollster Louis Harris to bring his expertise to Canada. Keith Davey, the political campaign advisor, first to Mr. Pearson and then to Pierre Trudeau urged Trudeau to set up this new advertizing group and to appoint me President of Red Leaf, a consortium of advertizing, marketing experts and pollsters who came together to assist the Liberal Party in each election cycle. All that expertise (and new 'focus groups who opine on words and policies supplanted the opinion of elected officials) I garnered from 1974 to 1986 was overtaken by this obsession with polling that continued to expand exponentially by the end 20th century with newer and intensive polling and marketing techniques[312]. Pierre Trudeau, different from other leaders, I observed, decided on a course of action and then used polling to help him persuade the public. He refused to use polling to decide what course he should follow or what policy he should adopt.

No idea in politics or art is original. Red Leaf was adapted from the successful model called the 'Big Blue Machine' that the Conservatives first organized under the leadership of Alistair Grosart and later Dalton Camp and his brother-in-law and my Senate colleague Norman Atkins.

The 20th century saw the rise of the 'fifth estate' in politics – the lobbyists. The 'rule of law' now acquired highly paid gatekeepers. Access to members of Parliament, the Cabinet and the public service narrowed as now the keys to this kingdom are held by lobbyists. No major or minor legislation was or is beyond the lobbyist's reach, attention or purview. Today we find lobbyists covertly behind each major and minor political decision, law or regulation. Public access to the 'rule of law' has become a keyhole open to highly paid lobbyists. Lobbyist reform is imperative if we are to recapture the 'rule of law' for the benefit of the public good[313].

The 'rule of law' spread like wild fire within and across national boundaries in the 20th century transformed by instigators against 'unjust' laws. The 'right' of peaceful assembly to protest law was incorporated into the constitutions of democracies. Civil disobedience against 'unjust law' grew, fermented by the cry for 'rights' of every variety, 'natural rights', 'civil rights', 'equal rights', 'human rights', 'labour rights', 'women's rights', et al became a rolling 20th century mantra. Protests exploded. Strikes proliferated. The marriage between 'rights' and the expansion of media infected every society from autocracies to democracies.

By the end of the 20th century, polling and protests amplified by the media became the prime instigator of political conduct and legislation.

---

312   For a fuller history of my experience as the head of Red Leaf, read *'A Leader Must Be a Leader: Encounters with Eleven Prime Ministers'* by the author (Mosaic Press, 2019)

313   Lobbyist reform could include a mega registry where the name of each person –politician or public servant, the requested lobbyist contacts, on every cause, when each meeting occurred, on each issue, on each policy file, all made readily open to public scrutiny online, and kept up to date on a daily basis.

Public protests, mostly lawful, grew by leaps and bounds, were mostly peaceful (Vietnam, Tiananmen Square, etc.) all with the purpose of upholding the 'rule of 'just' laws' and 'unjust wars'. In Canada we experienced in '60s and early '70s violent protests[314].

The human condition and its proclivity for violence continued unabated yet became somewhat muted for short periods as the 20th century drew to a close[315].

A final note about judges and 'rule of law'. Too often judges, secure in their tenure of judicial appointment cannot resist the temptation to 'legislate' rather than adjudicate especially cases of wide public interest. Judicial restraint became rarer, in inverse proportion of the number of judges, and increased as the 20th century moved to a close.

The essence of judicial restraint lies in the self-imposed discipline to cringe from striking down laws, unless the laws under judicial review are so glaring and so compelling in their clear meaning that they transcend the Constitution. Better to give legislatures time to rethink and perhaps change the law than for the judges to become legislators themselves.

Some judges found it difficult to restrain from voicing their opinion on politics outside the court, which in itself may be an 'abuse' of power.

---

314 In Montreal, Quebec separatist inspired violence led by a small band of about 35 extremists broke out. In October 1970, a British diplomat was kidnapped and then Pierre La Porte, a provincial Cabinet Minister was assassinated. Prime Minister Pierre Trudeau instituted the War Measures Act putting Canada in a state of National Emergency only brought into force three times – during World War I, World War II and October 1970. Then Minister of Justice John Turner was away from Ottawa when the Federal Cabinet approved the 'state of emergency' and hundreds of sympathizers were rounded up and imprisoned including Claude Ryan, a friend and editor of Le Devoir. At the time I thought this action was overkill as civil liberties are curtailed. After two weeks, Turner ensured that the 500 or more arrested were released without a criminal record. A handful were convicted on minor charges. Later Brian Mulroney introduced a modified, more limited Emergencies Act that finally became law in 1988. By then, as a senator I participated in committee hearings and Senate debates.

315 Read 'Just and Unjust Wars: A Moral Argument with Historical Illustrations' by Michael Walzer (Basic Books, 1977) for an excellent exegesis on 'war'.

'*Stare decisis*' (following established precedent) is another venue of temptation overwhelming some judges to overturn existing established case law.

Olive Wendell Holmes repeatedly described the need for judicial restraint that he argued lies at the heart of the 'rule of law'. Bora Laskin echoed Holmes as did another famed American Justice, Ruth Bader Ginsburg who admitted to herself and others that 'measured motions' are preferred to 'breakthrough' judicial decisions. Bora Laskin abhorred judges making 'political' speeches.

The 20th century was, on the whole, bereft of human restraint or moderation in all things and especially when it came to the 'rule of law'[316].

---

316 Cultural outlooks, art and literature, shaped a nation's belief in the 'rule of law'. See '*The Free World: Art and Thought in the Cold War*' by Louis Menand (Farrar, Straus and Giroux, 2021)

KEYNESIAN ECONOMICS OVERTAKES POLITICS IN THE 20TH CENTURY: JOHN MAYNARD KEYNES (1883-1946)

Economics was called by the 'dismal science' by the English historian Thomas Carlyle. Carlyle purloined the phrase from T.R. Malthus, the philosopher who worked on the growth of population and its impact on society. Malthus predicted the growth of the population would outstrip the food supply leading to poverty and hardship. Both were wrong. Economics was and is not a science. Their predictions were dead wrong. Poverty in the 20th century was massively reduced. The global food supply exponentially increased.

Most economic predictions in the 20th century failed. Economics is an art form, not a science. Economics and its self-anointed gurus continue to influence government policy and human activity. An economist is sought as a source to enhance a writer's credibility when writing about politics in the economy that are the two twins of the 20th century wrapped in at times a sterile embrace.

Three men shaped economic debates in the 20th century. First, Adam Smith's thesis on the wealth of nations who pointed to criteria for a 'laissez-faire' capitalist system. The 'Invisible hand of Capitalism' would recycle and expand economic growth. Second, the Karl Marx argument that 'class warfare' was necessary to equalize and redistribution of wealth. This could only be imposed by the State from the top down led by a small self-appointed one party clique of leaders. This was the antithesis to the thesis of capitalism.

These two seminal thinkers were not economists. Rather they were mathematicians or historians who posed as social philosophers. Each wrote books to advocate their radical ideas about the impact of economic ideas on their citizenry. Adam Smith's 'Wealth of Nations' (1776)[317] and Karl Marx 'Das Kapital' (1867).

Suddenly in 1914, along came a young Cambridge mathematician with ideas that radically shaped the debate about the power of economics to shape the size of each nation's prosperity. National debt loomed on the national front from the onslaught of World War II. Money unleashed from the Gold Standard could gear economic growth, he argued. His name was John Maynard Keynes. Keynes almost single handedly wrestled major economies off the Gold Standard and laid the foundation of 20th century economic theory.

Smith promoted capitalism as a synthesis countering with Marxism as an antithesis. Keynes and his radical ideas emerged as the most influential economist in the 20th century and whose writings became the economic synthesis to Smith and Marx. As President Nixon famously noted once, "We are all Keynesians now".

Keynes' book on 'The Economic Consequences of the Peace' (1919) made him an instant celebrity. His investment acumen brought him personal wealth and independence. Keynes' scathing sketches of leaders, especially Wilson, Lloyd Georges and Clemenceau had consequences. Wilson's Democrats were defeated. Georges' Liberals in England lost power and never regained it for the balance of the 20th century. Clemenceau's influence evaporated.

Keynes' predictive models were built on probabilities. The inputs of human activity into probability models are so wide, complex and so variable that economics continued as an art, and not a science. Models, complex as ever, had changing inputs determine why outcomes and accurate predictability remains low. Guesswork, thoughtful guesswork, determines all the shapes and ideas about fiscal and monetary policy. The Keynes ideas are usually taken out his precise context. Keynes was the father of 'Macro-economics'. The infinite aspect of inputs are almost impossible to capture – a work still in progress at the end of the century.

---

317 'Wealth of Nations' is a short form for Smith's book 'An Inquiry into the Nature and Causes of the Wealth of Nations'

Economics was not considered an academic discipline until 1903 when Cambridge University established the first department of economics under the leadership of Alfred Marshall, a teacher and writer, who Keynes considered his most important influence. Economics became the bridging language of the 20th century for public policy and politics. Economic staples like GDP, employment and unemployment rates, interest rates, public debt, budgetary deficits were phrases used to elect and defeat governments. Politics and economics became inseparable in the 20th century.

In Keynes' most influential work, '*The General Theory of Employment, Interest and Money*' (Palgrave Macmillan, 1936), he wrote:

A large proportion of our positive activities depend on spontaneous optimism rather than on a mathematical expectation, whether moral or hedonistic or economic. Most, probably, of our decisions to do something positive...can only be taken as a result of animal spirits - of a spontaneous urge to action rather than inaction, and not as the outcome of a weighted average of quantitative benefits multiplied by quantitative probabilities. Enterprise only pretends to itself to be mainly actuated by the statements in its own prospectus... Only a little more than an expedition to the South Pole, is it based on an exact calculation of benefits to come. Thus if the animal spirits are dimmed and the spontaneous optimism falters, leaving us to depend on nothing but a mathematical expectation, enterprise will fade and die - though fears of loss may have a basis no more reasonable than hopes of profit had before[318].

Markets were guesses are more social than mathematical. Economics is less science rather than guesstimates and probabilities. The 20th century hinged its measurements of progress on these probabilities.[319, 320, 321]

---

318 '*The Price of Peace: Money, Democracy, and The Life of John Maynard Keynes*' by Zachary D. Carter (Random House, New York, 2020)

319 His books and publications include the following:
- *Note on rents, prices, and wages*" (Economic Journal, 1908)
- *The method of index numbers* (Adam Smith prize essay, 1909)
- *The Recent Economic Events in India* (Economic Journal, 1909)
- *Review of Borel's Eléments de la Théorie des Probabilités* (Mathematical Gazette, 1910)

- *Review of Webb's Rupee Problem* (Economic Journal, 1910)
- *Correspondence: Influence of Parental Alcoholism* (J of Royal Statis Soc., 1911)
- *Principal Averages and Laws of Error which Lead to Them* (J of Royal Statis Soc, 1911)
- *Review of Irving Fisher's Purchasing Power of Money* (Economic Journal, 1911)
- *Review of Morison's Economic Transition in India* (Economic Journal, 1911)
- *Review of E. Czuber's Wahrscheinlichkeitsrechnung, v.2* (Mathematical Gazette 1911)
- *Review of W.S. Jevons's Theory of Political Economy* (Economic Journal, 1912)
- *Official Papers: Report upon the Operations of the Paper Currency Department of the government of India during the Year 1910-11* (Economic Journal, 1912)
- *Obituary - Gustave de Molinari* (Economic Journal, 1912)
- *Review of Huan-Chang's Economics of Confucius* (Economic Journal, 1912)
- *Review of McIlraith's Prices in New Zealand* (Economic Journal, 1912)
- *Official Papers: Tables showing for each of the Years 1900-1911, the estimated value of Imports and Exports of the United Kingdom* (Economic Journal, 1912)
- *Official Papers: Report of Departmental Committee on matters affecting Currency of the British West African Colonies and Protectorates* (Economic Journal, 1913)
- *Indian Currency and Finance* (Macmillan and Company, 1913)
- *Review of Barbour's Standard of Value* (Economic Journal, 1913)
- *Review of J.A. Hobson's Gold, Prices and Wages* (Economic Journal, 1913)
- *Currency in 1912* (Economic Journal, 1914)
- *Review of Fischel's Le Thaler de Marie-Thérèse* (Economic Journal, 1914)
- *Review of Morison's Economic Transition in India* (WWA, 1914)
- *Review of Ludwig von Mises's Theorie des Geldes and Bendixen's Geld und Kapital* (Economic Journal, 1914)
- *Review of Innes's What is Money?* (Economic Journal, 1914)
- *War and the Financial System, August 1914,* (Economic Journal, 1914)
- *The City of London and the Bank of England, August 1914* (QJE 1914)
- *The Prospects of Money, November 1914* (Economic Journal, 1914)
- *The Trade of India in 1913-14* (Economic Journal, 1914)
- *The Works of Bagehot* (Economic Journal, 1915)
- *The Economics of War in Germany* (Economic Journal, 1915)
- *Frederick Hillersdon Keeling (1886-1916)* (Economic Journal, 1916)
- *The New Taxation in the United States* (Economic Journal, 1917)
- *Note on the issue of Federal Reserve Notes in the United States* (Economic Journal, 1917)
- *The Economic Consequences of the Peace* (Harcourt, Brace and Howe, 1920)
- *When the Big Four Met* (The New Republic (U.S.) 1919)
- *Europe after the Treaty* (The New Republic, 1920)

- *The present state of foreign exchanges* (Manchester and District Bankers' Institute Magazine, 1920)
- *How to mend the Treaty* (The New Republic, 1920)
- *Discussion - Suggested Remedies* (The Famine in Europe, 1920)
- *Review of Hawtrey's Currency and Credit* (Economic Journal, 1920)
- *Review of Shirras's Indian Finance and Banking* (Economic Journal, 1920)
- *The Peace of Versailles* (Everybody's Magazine, 1920)
- "Economic Readjustment in Europe", (Farm & Home, 1920)
- *America at the Paris Conference: A delegate's story* (Manchester Guardian, 1920)
- *The Economic Consequences of the Paris 'Settlement'* (Manchester Guardian, 1921)
- *Dr. Melchior: a defeated enemy* (Two Memoirs, 1921)
- *The latest phase of reparations* (Manchester Guardian, 1921)
- *Will the German mark be superseded? Reasons why permanent recovery is unlikely* (MGCRE, 1921)
- *The proposed occupation of the Ruhr* (Manchester Guardian, 1921)
- *The new reparation proposals* (Manchester Guardian, 1921)
- *Mr Keynes as a prophet* (New Republic, 1921)
- *A Treatise on Probability* (Macmillan and Company, 1921)
- *Europe's Economic Outlook* (Sunday Times, 1921)
- *Record depreciation of the mark: how speculators are more than paying the indemnity?* (Manchester Guardian, 1921)
- *Reparation payments. The suggested moratorium, time to drop the 'make-believe'* (Sunday Times, 1921)
- *The stabilisation of the European exchanges: A plan for Genoa* (Manchester Guardian, 1922)
- *On the way to Genoa: What can the conference discuss and with what hope?* (Manchester Guardian, 1922)
- *The conference gets to work* (Manchester Guardian, 1922)
- *Currency reform at Genoa* (Manchester Guardian, 1922)
- *Getting back to a gold standard* (Manchester Guardian, 1922)
- *Rubbish about milliards - the facts of the Russian reparation struggle* (Manchester Guardian, 1922)
- *A Plan for a Russian Settlement* (Manchester Guardian, 1922)
- *The theory of the exchanges and the 'purchasing power parit'* (MGCRE, 1922)
- *The forward market in foreign exchanges* (MGCRE, 1922)
- *A chapter of miscalculations at the conference* (Manchester Guardian, 1922)
- *Letter to the Editor* (NY Times Book Review, 1922)
- *The reparation problem at Genoa* (Manchester Guardian, 1922)

- *The financial system of the Bolsheviks* (Manchester Guardian, 1922)
- *Financial results of Genoa* (Manchester Guardian, 1922)
- *The Russian rouble and the basis of future trade* (Manchester Guardian, 1922)
- *The proposals for Russia* (Manchester Guardian, 1922)
- *The Reconstruction of Europe: A general introduction* (MGCRE, 1922)
- *The Genoa Conference* (MGCRE, 1922)
- *Introduction to the Series* (in D.H. Robertson, *Money*, 1922)
- *Introduction* (in M.E. Robinson, *Public Finance*, 1922)
- *Introduction* (in H.D. Henderson, *Supply and Demand*, 1922)
- *A Revision of the Treaty: Being a sequel to the economic consequences of the peace* (Harcourt, Brace, 1922)
- *Economic Section President's Speech* (in R. Pierpoint, ed, *Report of the Fifth International Neo-Malthusian and Birth Control Conference*, 1922)
- *Reparations and Inter-Allied Debt* (Essays in Liberalism, 1922)
- *Russia* (MGCRE, 1922)
- *Inflation of currency as a method of taxation* (MGCRE, 1922)
- *The consequences to society of changes in the value of money* (MGCRE, 1922)
- *A moratorium for war debts* (Westminster Gazette, 1922)
- *An economist's view of population* (MGCRE, 1922)
- *Germany's difficulties: how the mark will go* (Manchester Guardian, 1922)
- *German people terrified by uncertainty* (Manchester Guardian, 1922)
- *Is a settlement of the reparation question possible now?* (MGCRE, 1922)
- *Speculation in the Mark and Germany's balances abroad* (MGCRE, 1922)
- *The stabilization of the European exchanges - II* (MGCRE, 1922)
- *The need for a constructive British policy* (Manchester Guardian, 1922)
- *A Tract on Monetary Reform* (MacMillan & Co. 1923)
- *The reparation crisis: Suppose the conference breaks down?* (Westminister Gazette, 1923)
- *The underlying principle* (MGCRE, 1923)
- *Europe in decay* (Times, 1923)
- *Mr. Keynes on the economic outlook* (Times, 1923)
- *Letter to the Editor* (Times, 1923)
- *Professor Jevons on the Indian Exchange* (Economic Journal, 1923)
- *Some aspects of commodity markets* (MGCRE, 1923)
- *Statement of policy of The Nation and Athenaeum* (Manchester Guardian, 1923)
- *Editorial Forward* (N&A, 1923)
- *British policy in Europe* (N&A, 1923 and New Republic, 1923)
- *The German offer and the French reply* (N&A, 1923)
- *The suggested German reply to Lord Curzon* (N&A, 1923)

- *Mr. Bonar Law - a personal appreciation* (N&A, 1923)
- *The international loan* (N&A, 1923)
- *The German loan delusion* (New Republic, 1923)
- *The diplomacy of reparations* (N&A, 1923 & New Republic, 1923)
- *Is credit abundant?* (N&A, 1923)
- *Bank rate at four per cent* (N&A, 1923)
- *Bank rate and stability of prices - A reply to critics* (N&A, 1923)
- *Mr Baldwin's prelude* (N&A, 1923)
- *The Measure of Deflation - An Inquiry into Index Numbers* (N&A, 1923)
- *Is a settlement of reparations possible?* (N&A, 1923)
- *Mr. Baldwin's task* (New Republic, 1923)
- *The American debt* (N&A, 1923)
- *A reparations plan* (New Republic, 1923)
- *Currency policy and unemployment* (N&A, 1923)
- *What can Great Britain do?* (New Republic, 1923)
- *The legality of the Ruhr occupation* (N&A, 1923 and New Republic, 1923)
- *Population and unemployment* (N&A, 1923)
- *Lord Grey's letter to the Times* (N&A, 1923)
- *[Anon] The inflation bogey and the moral* (N&A, 1923)
- *How much has Germany paid?* (N&A, 1923 and New Republic, 1923)
- *Is Britain overpopulated?* (New Republic, 1923)
- *The Liberal Party* (N&A, 1923)
- *Free Trade",* (N&A, 1923)
- *A Reply to Sir William Beveridge" (on Population and Unemployment)* (Economic Journal, 1923)
- *Free Trade and Unemployment* (N&A, 1923)
- *Free Trade for England* (New Republic, 1923)
- *Gold in 1923* (N&A, 1924 and New Republic, 1924)
- *The French press and Russia* (N&A, 1924)
- *The Prospects of Gold* (N&A, 1924 and New Republic, 1924)
- *The speeches of the bank chairmen* (N&A, 1924)
- *France and the Treasury: M. Klotz's charges refuted, Mr Keynes's reply* (Times, 1924)
- *A Comment on Professor Cannan's Article* (Economic Journal, 1924)
- *The Franc* (N&A, 1924 and New Republic, 1924)
- *Mr J.M. Keynes's Speech Unemployment in its national and international aspects* (ILO conference, 1924)
- *Newspaper finance* (N&A, 1924)
- *The experts' report I: The Dawes report* (N&A, 1924)
- *The experts' reports II: the McKenna report* (N&A, 1924)

- *How can the Dawes Plan work? A British view* (New Republic, 1924)
- *The meaning of 'bonus'* (N&A, 1924)
- *Investment policy for insurance companies* (N&A, 1924)
- *Does unemployment need a drastic remedy?* (N&A, 1924)
- *Discussion on monetary reform* (Economic Journal, 1924)
- *Note on Robertson's Real Ratio of International Interchange* (Economic Journal, 1924)
- *A drastic remedy for unemployment: reply to critics* (N&A, 1924)
- *The policy of the Bank of England* (N&A, 1924)
- *The policy of the Bank of England: reply* (N&A, 1924)
- *The London Conference and territorial sanctions* (N&A, 1924)
- *Wheat* (N&A, 1924)
- *Debt payments from ourselves to American and from Germany to the Allies* (Daily Herald, 1924)
- *Foreign investment and national advantage* (N&A, 1924)
- *Alfred Marshall, 1842-1924* (Economic Journal, 1924)
- *The Dawes scheme and the German loan* (N&A, 1924) & *What the Dawes Plan will do* (New Republic, 1924)
- [Anon] *Notice on the movie Tess of the D'urbevilles* (N&A, 1924)
- *Defaults by foreign governments* (N&A, 1924)
- *The balance of political power at the elections* (N&A, 1924) & *The balance of power in Great Britain* (New Republic, 1924)
- *Edwin Montagu* (N&A, 1924)
- *Bibliographical List of the writings of Alfred Marshall* (Economic Journal, 1924)
- *The inter-allied debts* (N&A, 1925 and New Republic, 1925)
- *Some tests for loans to foreign and colonial governments* (N&A, 1925)
- *The Balfour note and inter-allied debts* (N&A, 1925)
- *The return towards gold* (N&A, 1925 and New Republic, 1925)
- *The bank rate* (N&A, 1925)
- *The problem of the gold standard* (N&A, 1925)
- *Is sterling over-valued?* (N&A, 1925)
- *The gold standard* (N&A, 1925)
- *Is the pound overvalued?* (N&A, 1925)
- *An American study of shares versus bonds as permanents investments* (N&A, 1925)
- *The gold standard: a correction* (N&A, 1925)
- *England's gold standard* (N&A, 1925)
- *The Committee on the Currency* (Economic Journal, 1925)
- *The Gold standard Act* (Economic Journal, 1925)
- *The arithmetic of the sterling exchange* (N&A, 1925)
- *Unemployment and Monetary Policy* (Evening Standard, 1925)

- *The Economic Consequences of Sterling Parity* (1925) later re-titled *The Economic Consequences of Mr. Churchill*
- *Am I a Liberal?* (N&A, 1925)
- *Our monetary policy: rejoinder to Lord Bradbury's recent article* (Financial News, 1925)
- *Letter to the Editor* (N&A, 1925)
- *Discussion on the National Debt* (Economic Journal, 1925)
- *Great Britain's 'Cross of Gold'* (New Republic, 1925)
- *Soviet Russia* (N&A, 1925)
- *Relation of finance to British industry* (MGCRE, 1925)
- *The French Franc: an open letter to the French minister of finance (whoever he is or may be)* (N&A, 1926)
- *The French Franc: an reply to comments* (N&A, 1926)
- *Review of Wallis Budge's Rise and Fall of Assyriology* (N&A, 1926)
- *Some facts and last reflections about the franc* (N&A, 1926)
- *Germany's coming problem: the prospects of a second Dawes year,* (N&A, 1926)
- *Liberalism and labour* (N&A, 1926)
- *Broadcast the budget!* (Radio Times, 1926)
- *Obituary: Francis Ysidro Edgeworth, 1845-1926* (Economic Journal, 1926)
- *Bagehot's Lombard Street* (Banker, 1926)
- *Trotsky on England* (N&A, 1926)
- *Coal: a suggestion* (N&A, 1926)
- *Back to the coal problem* (N&A, 1926)
- *The need of peace by negotiation* (New Republic, 1926)
- *Review of Stock Exchange Official Intelligence for 1926* (N&A, 1926)
- *The control of raw materials by governments* (N&A, 1926)
- *Letter to the Editor* (N&A, 1926)
- *The first-fruits of the gold standard* (N&A, 1926)
- *Letter to the Editor* (N&A, 1926)
- *Mr Baldwin's Qualms* (N&A, 1926)
- *The franc once more* (N&A, 1926)
- The End of Laissez-Faire (N&A, 1926)
- *The End of Laissez-Faire* (Hogarth Press, 1926)
- *Laissez Faire and Communism* (Hogarth Press, 1926)
- *Obituary: A.A. Tschuprow (1873-1926)* (Economic Journal, 1926)
- *The progress of the Dawes Scheme* (N&A, 1926)
- *The Autumn Prospects For Sterling: Should The Embargo On Foreign Loans Be Reimposed?* (N&A, 1926)
- *The position of the Lancashire cotton trade* (N&A, 1926)

- *The prospects of the Lancashire cotton trade* (N&A, 1926)
- *Will England restrict foreign investments?* (N&A, 1926)
- *The Cotton Yarn Association* (N&A, 1926)
- *Clissold* (N&A, 1927)
- *McKenna on Monetary Policy* (N&A, 1927)
- *Letter to the Editor* (N&A, 1927)
- *Mr Churchill on the War* (N&A, 1927)
- *Are books too dear?* (N&A, 1927)
- *Liberalism and industry* (in H.L. Nathan and H. Heathcote Williams, eds, Liberal Points of View, 1927)
- *The coming crisis on reparations* (New Republic, 1927)
- *A Note on Economy* (N&A, 1927)
- *The Colwyn Report on Debt and Taxation* (Economic Journal, 1927)
- *A Model Form for Statements of International Balances* (Economic Journal, 1927)
- *The British Balance of Trade, 1925-27* (Economic Journal, 1927)
- *The financial reconstruction of Germany* (New Republic, 1928)
- *Note on the British Balance of Trade* (Economic Journal, 1928)
- *Lord Oxford* (N&A, 1928 and New Republic, 1928)
- *He's a relation of mine* (New Republic, 1928)
- *A London view of the war debts* (New Republic, 1928)
- *The Stabilisation of the France* (New Republic, 1928)
- *Amalgamation of the British Note Issues* (Economic Journal, 1928)
- *How to Organise a Wave of Prosperity* (Evening Standard, 1928)
- *The United States Balance of Trade in 1927* (Economic Journal, 1928)
- *Review of F.C. Mills's Behavior of Prices* (Economic Journal, 1928)
- *Postwar Depression in the Lancashire Cotton Industry* (J of Royal Statistical Society, 1928)
- *The Great Villiers Connection* (N&A, 1928)
- *The French Stabilisation Law* (Economic Journal, 1928)
- *The War Debts* (N&A, 1928)
- *The German Transfer Problem* (Economic Journal, 1929)
- *Review of Warren and Pearson's Inter-Relationships of Supply and Price* (Economic Journal, 1929)
- *A Rejoinder to Ohlin's Reparation Problem* (Economic Journal, 1929)
- *A Reply by Mr. Keynes* (to Rueff and Ohlin) (Economic Journal, 1929)
- *Can Lloyd George Do It?* An examination of the Liberal pledge, with H.D. Henderson (Nisbet & Co. 1929)
- *Winston Churchill* (N&A, 1929)
- *Mr Churchill on the Peace* (New Republic, 1929)

- *The reparations crisis* (New Republic, 1929)
- *The bank rate* (The Listener, 1929)
- *A British view of the Wall Street slump* (NY Evening Post, 1929)
- *Unemployment* (Listener, 1930)
- *The question of high wages* (Political Quarterly, 1930)
- *Ramsey as an Economist* (Economic Journal, 1930)
- *Obituary: C.P. Sanger (1872-1930)* (Economic Journal, 1930)
- *The London Artists' Association: its origin and aims* (Studio, 1930)
- *The draft convention for financial assistance by the League of Nations* (N&A, 1930)
- *The draft convention for financial assistance by the League of Nations II* (N&A, 1930)
- *The League and the Underdog* (Saturday Review, 1930)
- *Review of the the Stock Exchange Official Intelligence for 1930* (N&A, 1930)
- *A dupe as hero* (N&A, 1930)
- *The Industrial Crises* (N&A, 1930)
- *Obituary: the Earl of Balfour, Arthur Balfour (1848-1930)* (Economic Journal, 1930)
- *A.F.R. Wollaston (1875-1930)* (N&A, 1930)
- *The future of the rate of interest* (The Index, 1930)
- *Fine Gold v. Standard Gold* (Economic Journal, 1930)
- *A Treatise on Money, two volumes, vol. 1 - The pure theory of money, vol. 2 - The applied theory of money* (1930).
- *Economic Possibilities for Our Grandchildren* (N&A, 1930)
- *Review of G. Glasgow's English Investment Trust Companies* (N&A, 1930)
- *Sir Oswald Mosley's manifesto* (N&A, 1930)
- *The Great Slump of 1930* (N&A, 1930)
- *Economist analyses year* (Christian Science Monitor, 1930)
- *The Problem of Unemployment II - Saving and Spending* (The Listener, 1931)
- *An Economic Analysis of Unemployment* (in Quincy Wright, editor, *Unemployment as a World Problem*, 1931)
- *Credit Control* (in E.R.A. Seligman, editor, *Encyclopaedia of the Social Sciences*, 1931)
- *A Rejoinder to D.H. Robertson* (Economic Journal, 1931)
- *The Pure Theory of Money: A reply to Dr. Hayek* (Economica, 1931)
- *On the Eve of Gold Suspension* (Evening Standard, 1931)
- *The End of the Gold Standard* (Sunday Express, 1931)
- *After the Suspension of Gold* (Times, 1931)
- *Proposals for a Revenue Tariff* (NSN, 1931)
- *Some Consequences of the Economy Report* (NSN, 1931)
- *The World's Economic Outlook* (Atlantic Monthly, 1932)
- *The Prospects of the Sterling Exchange* (Yale Review, 1932)
- *The Dilemma of Modern Socialism* (Political Quarterly, 1932)

- *Member Bank Reserves in the United States* (Economic Journal, 1932)
- *Saving and Usury* (Economic Journal, 1932)
- *The World's Economic Crisis and the Way of Escape* with A. Salter, J. Stamp, B. Blackett, H. Clay and W. Beveridge (1932)
- *A Note on the Long-Term Rate of Interest in Relation to the Conversion Scheme* (Economic Journal, 1932)
- *A Monetary Theory of Production* (in G. Clausing, ed., *Der Stand und die nächste Zukunft der Konjunkturforschung: Festschrift für Arthur Spiethoff,* 1933)
- *Mr. Robertson on Saving and Hoarding* (Economic Journal, 1933)
- *The Means to Prosperity* (Times, 1933)
- *National Self-Sufficiency* (Yale Review, 1933)
- *The Multiplier* (NSN, 1933)
- *Essays in Biography* (1933)
- *The Means to Prosperity* (1933)
- *An Open Letter to President Roosevelt, 16 December* (New York Times, 1933)
- *Commemoration of T.R. Malthus* (Economic Journal, 1935)
- *The Future of the Foreign Exchange* (Lloyds Bank Review, 1935)
- *William Stanley Jevons* (JRSS, 1936)
- *The Supply of Gold* (Economic Journal, 1936)
- *General Theory of Employment, Interest and Money* (MacMillan & Co., 1936)
- *Fluctuations in Net Investment in the United States* (Economic Journal, 1936)
- *"The General Theory of Empoyment* (QJE, 1937)
- *Professor Pigou on Money Wages in Relation to Unemployment* with N. Kaldor ((Economic Journal, 1937)
- *Alternative Theories of the Rate of Interest* (Economic Journal, 1937)
- *The Ex Ante Theory of the Rate of Interest* (Economic Journal, 1937)
- *The Theory of the Rate of Interest* in Lessons of Monetary Experience: In honor of Irving Fisher (1937
- *Some Economic Consequences of a Declining Population* (Eugenics Review, 1937)
- *Comments on Mr. Robertson's ` Mr Keynes and Finance* (Economic Journal, 1938)
- *Storage and Security* (NSN, 1938)
- *The Policy of Government Storage of Foodstuffs and Raw Materials* (Economic Journal, 1938)
- *Mr. Keynes's Consumption Function: A reply* (QJE, 1938)
- *Mr Keynes on the Distribution of Income and the Propensity to Consume: A reply* (RES, 1939)
- *Adam Smith as Student and Professor* (Economic Journal, 1938)
- *Introduction to David Hume, An Abstract of a Treatise on Human Nature,* (with P. Sraffa, 1938)

- *James E. Meade's Consumers' Credits and Unemployment* (Economic Journal, 1938)
- *The Process of Capital Formation* (Economic Journal, 1939)
- *Professor Tinbergen's Method* (Economic Journal, 1939)
- *Relative Movements of Real Wages and Output* (Economic Journal, 1939)
- *The Income and Fiscal Potential of Great Britain* (Economic Journal, 1939)
- *The Concept of National Income: Supplementary note* (Economic Journal, 1940)
- *How to Pay for the War: A radical plan for the Chancellor of the Exchequer* (1940)
- *The Objective of International Price Stability* (Economic Journal, 1943)
- *El Plan Ingles* (El Trimestre Económico, 1943)
- *Mary Paley Marshall"* (Economic Journal, 1944)
- *Note by Lord Keynes* (Economic Journal, 1944)
- *The Balance of Payments of the United States* (Economic Journal, 1946)
- *Newton the Man* (Newton Tercentenary Celebrations, 1947)
- *The Collected Writings of John Maynard Keynes* (D.E. Moggridge, editor) 1971-1989
- *v.1 - Indian Currency and Finance* (1971)
- *v.2 - The Economic Consequences of the Peace* (1971)
- *v.3 - A Revision of the Treaty* (1971)
- *v.4 - A Tract on Monetary Reform* (1971)
- *v.5 - A Treatise on Money, v.1* (1971)
- *v.6 - A Treatise on Money, v.2* (1971)
- *v.7 - The General Theory* (1973)
- *v.8 - Treatise on Probability* (1973)
- *v.9 - Essays in Persuasion* (1972)
- *v.10 - Essays in Biography* (1972)
- *v.11 - Economic Articles and Correspondence: Academic* (1983)
- *v.12 - Economic Articles and Correspondence: Investment and Editorial* (1983)
- *v.13 - The General Theory and After: Part 1 - Preparation* (1973)
- *v.14 - The General Theory and After: Part 2 - Defence and Development* (1973)
- *v.15 - Activities 1906-1914: India and Cambridge* (1971)
- *v.16 - Activities 1914-1919: the Treasury and Versailles* (1971)
- *v.17 - Activities 1920-1922: Treaty Revision and Reconstruction* (1977)
- *v.18 - Activities 1922-1932: The End of Reparations* (1978)
- *v.19 - Activities 1922-1929: The Return to Gold and Industrial Policy, Part 1 & 2* (1981)
- *v.20 - Activities 1929-1931: Rethinking Employment and Unemployment Policies* (1981)
- *v.21 - Activities 1931-1939: World Crises and Policies in Britain and America* (1982)
- *v.22 - Activities 1939-1945: Internal War Finance* (1978)
- *v.23 - Activities 1940-1943: External War Finance* (1979)
- *v.24 - Activities 1944-1946: The Transition to Peace* (1979)

John Maynard Keynes, the most original economic thinker of the 20ᵗʰ century[322], was born in Cambridge of a comfortable academic family.

- *v.25 - Activities 1940-1944: Shaping the Post-War World: the Clearing Union* (1980)
- *v.26 - Activities 1941-1946: Shaping the Post-War World: Bretton Woods and Reparations* (1980)
- *v.27 - Activities 1940-1946: Shaping the Post-War World: Employment and Commodities* (1980)
- *v.28 - Social, Political and Literary Writings* (1982)
- *v.29 - The General Theory and After: A Supplement* (1979)
- *v.30 - Bibliography and Index* (1989)

320 *'The Price Of Peace: Money, Democracy and The Life of John Maynard Keynes'* by Zachary D. Carter (Random House, New York, 2020) is an excellent review of John Maynard Keynes's impact on economics including the rise and fall and renewal that continues from 1914 to the end of the century.

321 *'The Essential Keynes'* by John Maynard Keynes (Penguin Books, 2015) is an excellent collection of excerpts of John Maynard Keynes articles, letters, essays and books.

322 I was a dunce when it came to economics. At university, I avoided economics courses like a plague. Political activism changed that. I came to understand that politics was economics under a different name. So I began to read books in economics which I found impenetrable. Finally I became interested in the works of John Galbraith. I felt a kinship to him when I discovered he was born in south west Ontario and studied at Ontario College of Agriculture (now University of Guelph) specializing in agricultural policy. I discovered his father and my father were grassroots Liberals who both admired Mitch Hepburn, the populist Premier of Ontario. When I founded and edited the Journal of Liberal Thought in 1965, a modest attempt to galvanize portentous self-proclaimed Liberal policy thinkers and Liberal activists to read widely and to think, I wrote to Galbraith at Harvard to ask him to contribute an article. Galbraith quickly responded and informed me that he was busy with his commitments but to write to Barbara Ward in England and mention his name. She quickly agreed and sent the lead article in the first issue of Journal of Liberal Thought in 1965. Galbraith kept in touch, I met him again when he came to Ottawa to advise Pierre Trudeau on 'wages and price' controls. Trudeau, fought the 1974 against Stanfield's policy of imposing 'wage and price' controls, Trudeau was reluctant to introduce those measures while Galbraith was an enthusiastic advocate to pummel rampant inflation. A decade later, I was surprised to get an invitation to attend Rideau Hall when Galbraith was awarded the Order of Canada. Less than a dozen attended and only two active Liberals, Charles Caccia and me. I was honoured. Galbraith always considered himself a 'true grit'. Galbraith believed the power to improve the plight of the poor was the prime purpose of politics. Galbraith

His father was a Professor of Moral Sciences at Cambridge. Schooled at Eton where he led his class in academics, Keynes chose mathematics when he entered Cambridge. Again led his class, graduating with firsts in mathematics. He did not distinguish himself in economics. Quickly he became a leader of the Cambridge Union and the University's memorable debates. At Cambridge he was selected to join the 'Apostles', a secret society made up of the leading minds laced with homosexual habits. These young men were brilliant leftist socialists and communists in their political belief and mostly pacifists. Five became spies for Soviets after World War II including the Queen's senior art advisor who was never charged or convicted.

After graduation from Cambridge, Keynes became a close member of the Bloomsbury set in London, an elite circle of writers, artists, philosophers, leftist activists and pacifists where he easily fitted in taking on several male lovers. All were tainted by the polite endemic anti-semitism of the elite classes in England at the time. Keynes decided to join the British Civil Service where his brilliant conversations and memos quickly drew the attention of U.K.'s leading public servants. In 1914 at the outset of World War I, he was summoned to London and began his career and swift rise as an influential public servant.

He fell out with his pacifist circle – the Bloomsbury set - when Keynes began work as a leading public servant advising the Lloyd George government on economic policy.

At thirty-five, he fell madly in love with Lydia Lopokova, an emigrant Russian ballerina, and was married. Lydia became his lover, wife, adviser and active advocate. She encouraged Keynes to pursue his ideas as she understood his genius and originality.

Keynes wrote brilliant essays on leading public figures and personalities. He became wealthy and used that wealth to acquire a magazine called the *Economist* magazine which he revived and served as editor and lead writer. While he was open minded about politics and studied Marxism-Communism with diligence, he was and considered himself a lifetime adherent to U.K.'s Liberal Party.

---

had another facet that endeared him to his followers, unusual for economists. He always admitted to his mistakes.

He served for a time as Lloyd George's top advisor and wrote Liberal Party policy papers. Keynes was a leading opponent of the peace settlement cobbled together at Versailles after World War I believing that beggaring Germany would lead to greater unrest. In this, he was right. The harsh war reparations imposed on Germany led to inflation and set the table for the rise of Adolf Hitler. Keynes wrote his summary opposing Versailles Treaty called 'The Economic Consequences of the Peace' (Harcourt and Braces, 1920).

He became a leading figure at the Bretton Woods Conference in the U.S. after World War II that devised the post-World War II architecture for global economic cooperation that remained largely intact to the end of the 20th century.

John Galbraith[323], a Canadian by birth became one of his best known advocates who popularized Keynes' ideas by his scintillating best-selling books on politics, public policy and economics including *The Affluent Society, A Theory of Price Control, The Great Crash, 1929, Economics and The Public Purpose, Money: Whence It Came, Where It Went, Annals of an Abiding Liberal, Economics in Perspective: A Critical History, The Culture of Contentment and A Journey Through Economic Time: A Firsthand View.*

Keynes' ideas changed lives. He remained convinced that government can expedite polices that lead to reduction of poverty and economic progress if carefully instituted and more carefully monitored and adjusted. To him, economic policy could not be separated from morality.

He died suddenly from exhaustion in April 1946 at Sussex, U.K.

Keynes' ideas continue to reverberate throughout the 20th century and beyond.

The 20th century was blessed with a quartet original thinkers who disrupted and transformed our way of looking and drawing meaning from the mysteries of human behaviour.

---

323 Keynes and Galbraith had a curious first meeting in Washington in the '30s. Galbraith, a lowly economic researcher in F.D. Roosevelt's 'New Deal' administration was surprised when Keynes came to visit him to the bowels of the public service where he served as a researcher on the agricultural policy to a U.S. federal agricultural board. Keynes, unannounced, visited Galbraith in his tiny office, introduced

Einstein in quantum physics, Freud in psychology and Keynes in economics, each brought a different vocabulary to their chosen fiend, disrupting the previous way observers saw the essence from their deliberation and influence.

Ludwig Wittgenstein, an Austrian born Jew became the disruptive English philosopher who focused on 'words' and the meaning of words as the foundation of philosophy. He and Keynes were well acquainted. Without comprehending what words mean one cannot understand our existence.

Keynes uncovered and invented a host of words and phrases that became an intrinsic part of language, economic discourse with the wider public. Macro-economics, indirect employment, money, economic growth, price police, GDP – gross national product, employment rates, unemployment rates, interest rates, debt, deficit, multiple employment are just a sample of this 20th century vocabulary.

Keynes fell in and out of fashion in the 20th century as an original and useful economic policy maker. Still by the end of the century, Keynes ideas and his vocabulary continue to be the grammar of economic debates across the globe.

The major idea that always attracted me to Keynes was that art and culture both had intrinsic, essential value that contributed to the public good, public wealth and civic society. Keynes was right then and he is right now.

So called economic principles as practiced after Keynes rest on generalized predictions of 'growth', wealth and jobs which fail to be accurate, as the national economy is made up of small, fragmented, local and regional market forces. Keynes warning on this front – that generalized assumptions are most inaccurate - is still not heeded, but spewed out that often and mislead policy makers and the public.

---

himself and had detailed knowledge of Galbraith's reviews and publications. Both men were about 6'4" in height. Small room for two big men. Galbraith became an acolyte yet never failed to criticize Keynes' errors in judgement and the ineffectiveness of some of his own ideas. A rare quality for any economist. Both Keynes and Galbraith owned this quality, rare for economists.

CANADA'S GREATEST WRITER IN THE 20ᵀᴴ CENTURY - MARGARET ATWOOD

Canada was blessed by writers acclaim all around the globe. Margaret Laurence, Alice Munro (the Nobel Prize winner in Literature in 2013), Morley Callaghan on a par with his pal Earnest Hemingway and more honest, and Leonard Cohen just to name a few. French Canadian writers like Gabrielle Roy, Anne Hébert, Marie-Claire Blais or Marie Laberge (just a few of French Canada's writers who made a contribution to 20ᵗʰ century literature), became famous in the Francophone world.

Canada published more books of poetry per capita than any nation in the world and made more telephone calls per capita. Canadians crave contact and devour literature.

No writers in the world captured the literary imagination in the 20ᵗʰ century like Atwood. Her more than 50 works have been published in more than 45 countries. Her first published novel, 'The Edible Woman' (1969) was like a clap of thunder to male and female readers alike. She awoke and changed minds and attitudes.

Born in Ottawa in 1939, both her parents were scientists and she was homeschooled until 12 years. Her father Carl a forest entomologist allowed her to accompany him as he travelled and worked through northern Quebec and Ontario. Her family moved to Toronto where she attended Leaside Collegiate and then Victoria College at University of Toronto where she fell under the spell of Northrup Frye, Canada's eminent literary critic. Frye encouraged her to attend Radcliffe College at Harvard University for her M.A. Her theses was entitled 'The English Metaphysical Romance'. Frye influenced her interest in literary criticism. She never completed her doctorate.

She demonstrated precocious signs of brilliant writing at six years old and owned a remarkable imagination and curiosity. Atwood is a polymath and multi-talented novelist and writer. No genre of literature escaped her interests. She is a novelist, poet, essayist, critic, teacher, lecturer, activist and inventor (she invented the LongPen – an electronic device that allowed her to autograph her books from afar).

Nowhere did Atwood more elegantly demonstrate her deep knowledge of literature coupled by profound insight and respect for another great American author E.L. Doctorow than her magical review of Doctorow's novel '*Loon Lake*' in her critical essays '*Second Words: Selected Critical Prose 1960-1982*' (Anansi Press, 1982).

Atwood published books on historical fiction, science fiction, speculative fiction, children's stories, dystopic novels, even a comic book. At university, she wrote scripts for musical and comedic revues. She is an award winning poet. Atwood bridged the cerebral with the popular.

Her numerous literary awards followed her astonishing output. These include:

- The Booker Prize for fiction
- The Carl Sandburg award for poetry
- The Franz Kafka International Literary Prize
- The Giller Prize
- The Arthur C. Clarke Award for best science fiction
- The Governor General's Award for poetry, and the list goes on

Atwood possesses an imagination impossible to define its boundaries. Each of her sentences in every topic is polished and placed in the exact cadence as the reader races to catch up to her surprising insights. She possesses the gift of candescent writing that illuminates each prose. Like an explorer, she dives into the interior landscape of her memory to illuminate the hidden crevices of mind, emotions and imagination.

Each of her works demonstrates an endless search for meaning. Like Hasidic Jews who believe that each being owns a good and evil side which each struggle for mastery, hoping to practice a moral life. She recognizes and describes the deep fissures in the human condition.

A confession: I have purchased each of her books. Try as I might, I could not easily fathom or penetrate her novels with each purchase. Each time, I began to read her historical novels, I read the first chapters and then raced to the last chapter to capture her meaning. The breadth of her language is astounding. Like J.R. Tolkien, she created her own language. She invented syntax language to transport her message. Though rooted in the past much is metaphor for the present.

When it came to her memorable poetry and prose, each book was read and reread and underlined. Her insights into politics is astounding and each page vibrates with startling insights. Each paragraph is a surprise. Her poetry and that of A.B. Klein, Irving Layton, Anne Carson and Leonard Cohen persuaded me while in the Senate to launch a bill called The Parliamentary Poets Act that passed Parliament in 2001 to establish the position of Parliamentary Poet Laureate. The Poet Laureate has no statutory duties but may do what the poet chooses to do.

I first encountered Margaret in 1957 at Camp White Pine in the foothills of Haliburton. I was the Senior Boys Section Head ('Jerry Gnu') while Margaret was as a specialist in arts and crafts and nature lore.

Joe Kronick ('Joe Joe' to his legion of admirers) in 1955 purchased an old lodge the wild acreage in Haliburton to establish a summer camp for youth on the banks of Hurricane Lake that Joe had mischievously renamed Lake Placid.

Joe had an intrinsic talent for attracting a diverse crop of counsellors from different backgrounds, each with their own specialty. Margaret was attractive diminutive, quiet rather shy and reluctant unlike most of her boisterous peers. Our exchanges were limited mostly about troublesome campers. Those who chose to work with her respected and adored her quiet charm and wit. Atwood left an indelible impression on many. Like all of us, she loved the nature around us, Lake Placid, the water and water sports especially canoeing in which she was confident and capable and the forests that surrounded the camp.

Atwood's range of talents unleashed her writing and her imagination to millions. Though some consider Atwood to be a feminist writer, this is far too narrow a quality to define her.

While Atwood's political assessments were at times too harsh for me, her graceful and magnanimous reviews of other writers' books was never surpassed, when her friend, the celebrated American author John Updike, published one of his last, of over 25 superb novels –

'*Toward the End of Time*' ravaged by reviews by New York Times critic Michiko Kakutani and David Foster Wallace, a rising American novelist, Atwood elegantly wrote, "*As memento mori and its obverse, carpe diem, 'Toward the End of Time' could scarcely be bettered.*"

No author in the 20th century has had such limitless influence and scope that she exhibits in each of her works[324]. She remains a work in progress.

Margaret Atwood, I predict will soon win the Nobel Prize for Literature as she remains in her prime, demonstrated by the instant and enthusiastic reception to each of her new publications. Her books have been adapted into popular films and TV series gaining her an ever wider audience. An acute observer of the human condition, she remains relevant, scintillating and insightful. No writer in Canada in the 20th century could match her range or her writing gifts.

---

324 Her novels include the following:
- '*The Edible Woman*' (1969)
- '*Surfacing*' (1972)
- '*Lady Oracle*' (1976)
- '*Life Before Man*' (1979)
- '*Bodily Harm*' (1981)
- '*The Handmaid's Tale*' (1985)
- '*Cat's Eye*' (1988)
- '*The Robber Bride*' (1993)
- '*Alias Grace*' (1996)
- '*The Blind Assassin*' (2000)
- '*Oryx and Crake*' (2003)
- '*The Penelopiad*' (2005)
- '*The Year of the Flood*' (2009)
- '*MaddAddam*' (2013)
- '*Scribbler Moon*' (2014)
- '*The Heart Goes Last*' (2015)
- '*Hag-Seed*' (2016)
- '*The Testaments*' (2019)

THE GREATEST DEMOCRATIC LEADER IN THE 20TH CENTURY – CHARLES DEGAULLE (1890–1970) AND 'THE IDEA OF FRANCE'[325]

Who can fail to fall in love with Paris - the 'City of Love', the 'City of Lights'? This was and is the city where Charles de Gaulle lived as a youth, went to school, became an army officer, war veteran, teacher, writer,

---

325 One definition of the greatest democratic political leader is the leader who overcame existential threats to his nation and thereafter rose to pre-eminence without bloodshed earning the respect and admiration of his fellow citizens while transforming the ideals of citizenship and patriotism into everyday life, all by democratic means. Great democratic political leaders include Winston Churchill, Theodore and Franklin Roosevelt, Lloyd George, David Ben-Gurion, Nelson Mandela, Helmut Kohl, J.F. Kennedy, Lyndon Johnson, Golda Meir, Menachem Begin, Margaret Thatcher and Ronald Reagan whose storied histories as iconic leaders were subjects of my study and admiration. Charles de Gaulle towers over all as he became the very personification of France and remains so to this day. De Gaulle sought and became inseparable from the 'Idea of France'. See 'A Certain Idea of France: The Life of Charles de Gaulle' by Julian Jackson (Random House U.K., 2018). See earlier book in French by Michael Cazenove 'De Gaulle, Une Certain Ideé de la France' (Critterion Press, Paris, 1990). His idea of France meshed the grandeur of its history into the living present.
    Why choose de Gaulle over Churchill as the 20th century's greatest democratic leader? Churchill was first Prime Minister from 1940 to 1945. He was chosen by his party leadership affirmed by his established party with a majority in Parliament. Almost at the end of World War II he was soundly defeated by the opposition Labour Party. He continued as Leader of his Party and was re-elected in 1951 as leader and Prime Minister until 1955 when he retired. While he was a memorable leader during World War II, he was a lacklustre opposition leader occupied by writing his histories and when returned to office for his second term, chased for influence on the global stage, leaving a lacklustre economic record on the domestic front. No doubt Churchill alone raised international consciousness about Soviet designs and became the first 'Cold War' warrior.
    De Gaulle, alone with only one aide and one British liaison officer, left France in 1940 for England, 10 months after World War II started, even leaving his wife

senior bureaucrat, left in 1940 as a Brigadier General and returned in 1944 as leader of the French nation. De Gaulle and Paris are inseparable.

From the turn of the century Paris led the world in culture, futuristic exhibits and planes, cars, couture, art, literature, china and tableware, clothing, facial and body products, perfumes (men and women), paintings, glass, sculptures, furniture, popular music and dance like the tango, cabarets, ornate street lavatories, theatres, concert halls, museums, book stores, 'haute' cuisine, restaurants, bistros, wine, accoutrements, table and glassware.

Paris became a second home for budding writers (Irish, English, Canadian, American, South American and others) and it was the preferred refuge for radical Asian leaders including Ho Chi Min, Zhou Enlai, Deng Ziaoping and Muslim leaders like Khomeini and the last Shah of Persia, even Arafat's billionaire widow. Nehru spoke French and spent time in France in the '30s and was influenced by the ideas of the French Revolution and later by de Gaulle's leadership especially during war time[326].

Through Paris slowly flows the majestic River Seine into the English Channel at Le Havre with its elegant river boats ('bateaux mouches'), tastefully designed cobbled river embankments decorated with historic bridges[327] that make strolls a pleasurable pastime. Along the

---

and three children to find their own way to England later. He also left behind his aged mother. Despite obstacles from friend and foe alike, he gained power, almost alone, with a tiny circle of admirers, insisting on the democratic means by the French Consultative Assembly for approval. He gathered a small team, mostly from his leadership circle in the 'Free French' and rehabilitated France's weak divided image of itself, economics on the domestic front and influence on the chaotic world scene. And as described herein, he led the way in constitutional reform to reduce the divisive party, political system, transformed the political domestic and economic status and became the founding father of the Fifth Republic of France. He created a political movement called 'Gaullism' which continues to this day. De Gaulle left an indelible revered imprint in the minds and hearts of his fellow citizens, respected by most leaders after World War II and the post-World War II era.

326 Ghandi in his autobiography describes his visit to Paris and the Eiffel Tower as a young lawyer in the 1890's.

327 De Gaulle as a youth fell in love the most beautiful beaux art style bridges across the Seine and in particular the Pont Alexandre III named after Tsar Alexander III who

upper banks tiny huts brimmed with antique and secondhand books, magazines and maps, prints, posters, stamps, coins - a book lover and collector paradise.

With its grand boulevards, artfully manicured trees and gardens, Paris is a storied 'flaneur's' delight. The 18th century five storey residential buildings combine ateliers on the roof and bakeries, offices and elegant shops and each neighbourhood contains bistros, coffee shops, bakeries, flower kiosks, food stores, newsstands, stationary (pen and ink), shoes, open markets, art galleries all with elegantly arranged windows at the street level giving each passerby a treat for the eye and the nose. The worlds' leading department stores are located on one central area while outdoor markets dot the city on the weekends especially at Porte Clignancourt at the Marche aux Puces (flea market).

Iconic hotels like the Ritz on Place Vendome, the Bristol on Rue St. Honoré, the Crillon on the corner of massive Place de la Concorde and the George V on Avenue George V off the Champs-Élysées led the world in style, service and food. The 'Left Bank' attracted French and international literary lions who habituated storied bistros – Le Deux Maggots, Café Flore and across the street, Brasserie Lippe and, further on, Le Select and La Closerie Des Lilas on Avenue Mountparnasse. Michelin starred restaurants like Laurent, Lassere[328] or superb hotel cuisines at the Ritz and the Bristol were and are gourmand delights.

Historic statues populate each spacious square especially the corners along the Champs-Élysées, to accentuate the long history of France, its leaders and its cultural figures. Avenues are named after famous foreign leaders like Wilson, Roosevelt and Churchill. The Louvre, Jeu de Paume, l'Orangerie, The Pompidou, Quai D'Orsay, Rodin's home, and sculpture garden, and Picasso's Paris home and workshop, 'Les Invalides' where

---

concluded the Franco-Russian Alliance in 1892. Hence de Gaulle's deep interest and understanding of Franco-Russian relations.

328 My preference is Lassere on Avenue Franklin Delano Roosevelt, where I was inducted into Lasserre Club de la Casserole by Rene Lassere himself shortly after I became a Senator. Across from the Senate of France is a hotel particular that houses the Senate's private dining room. I was a guest there for lunch several times and is rightfully reputed to have the best chef in Paris.

Napoleon's majestic tomb is located are but a few temples dedicated to art, culture, and history.

Perhaps the most beautiful library and meeting rooms in the world are found in Cardinal Richelieu's residence where in 1635 he founded the Académie Française dedicated to the French language, literature and science. The members are limited to forty and are called the 'Immortals'. Maurice Druon (1918-2009) and I became acquainted when he came to Toronto to teach for a period at Glendon College part of the University of Toronto. Druon, one of France's most distinguished novelists, was elected Secretary Perpetual of the Académie Française (1985-1999). In that capacity he hosted me on a tour that was a living lesson about France's commitment to language, literature[329], science and distinguished French men and women including cultural, political leaders and military leaders like Phillipe Petain who was later removed.

From its grand capital and stories past and present, Charles de Gaulle[330], emerges as its most revered political leader in French history. Charles André Joseph Marie de Gaulle legacy overshows even Napoleon

---

329 Once in the Senate, a former Speaker of the Senate and also a friend of Druon, Maurice Riel (a descendent of Louis Riel) challenged me in a speech when I referred to Albert Camus without pronouncing the 's'. We wrote to Druon for adjudication. Druon agreed with me and then Maurice gracefully corrected himself in the Senate Hansard.

330 I briefly encountered Charles de Gaulle once in 1966 at a Defense Minister Conference in Paris where I attended with the Canadian Minister of Defense, Leo Cadieux, at an elegant reception at the Elysees Palace on Rue St. Honore in the heart of Paris. We were introduced. He towered over me. He was a presence yet he was pleasant and interested about my job. I noticed his graceful hands. Later I was upset when he snubbed a visit to Ottawa and instead made speeches in Montreal and Quebec City after sailing from France to Canada in a French naval warship and then disembarked and travelled along the historic St. Lawrence road route to delirious crowds along the way exclaiming Vive Le Quebec while Canada was besieged by Quebec separatism. Mr. Pearson fumed and saved his vitriol for a speech at a farewell luncheon in de Gaulle's honour in Quebec City. According to Maurice Sauve, the Canadian Cabinet was divided on Canada's response to this incident. Pierre Trudeau and Jean Marchand changed Mr. Pearson's mind and urged him to take a strong public stand in de Gaulle's presence.

Bonaparte[331]. Only one street in Paris is named after Bonaparte while de Gaulle's footprint is visible everywhere especially the second most iconic sight in the world (after the Eiffel Tower), the towering twin arches (The Arc de Triomphe) over the Tomb of the Unknown Soldier called the Etoile was renamed Charles de Gaulle Place shortly after his death in 1970 set at top of the Champs-Élysées, the most famous avenue in the world.

By the end of the 20th century, Charles de Gaulle became the most revered figure in France outstripping Bonaparte in countless polls. More streets, squares, monuments across France are named after de Gaulle than any other historic figure. The modernist Paris airport was named after de Gaulle immediately on his passing.

How did this most unlikely leader rise to such monumental heights by the end of the century? De Gaulle's story is one of the most remarkable climbs to power that one could imagine. He became by his own design the personification of France.... and the very idea of France[332].

As a youth I recall my father reading accounts in the newspaper and radio reports of De Gaulle's visit to Ottawa, I believe in 1945, where he was rapturously received as he shouted at public events *"Vive Le France, Vive le Canada"*[333]. Later I discovered de Gaulle had a deep admiration for

---

331 Napoleon Bonaparte is buried in a majestic tomb at the rear of L'Invalides, the military hospital for veterans. I visited there regularly. To the left of the rear entrance is a small photo museum dedicated to the Resistance. I once attended and contributed to a glittering event to raise funds for repairs to the roof of Napoleon's tomb.

332 *'A Certain Idea of France: The Life of Charles de Gaulle'* by Julian Jackson (Penguin Random House U.K., 2018); *'De Gaulle: Une Certaine Idée de la France'* by Michael Cazenave (Criterion, 1990).

No doubt de Gaulle's surname meaning 'from the ancient region of Gaul' inspired de Gaulle's powerful patriotic bonds to France as a sovereign nation.

333 My father was a fan of de Gaulle as de Gaulle served as military liaison to the Pilsudski Brigades in the Polish War of Independence (1918 to 1921) when my father served there. De Gaulle could be easily identified by his white gloves, French uniform and French style helmet. In 1919 when my father, a non-commissioned officer rejoined the Pilsudski Brigades he trained at Rembertow, a large training camp just north of Warsaw (now the site of Poland's leading military academy). De Gaulle continued to have a fixation with clutching and wearing fine white gloves. His portrait on his World War II memoirs shows him holding his white gloves. De Gaulle, with a rank

Prime Minister MacKenzie King due to Canada's unwavering support for him and the Free French during World War II.

Charles de Gaulle, from a large well-adjusted family became a brilliant student, trained by Jesuits, an elegant writer, with a phenomenal memory[334] who early chose a military career and was educated as a soldier[335]. During World War I, he was seriously wounded three times and once left for dead at the Battle of Verdun[336] and imprisoned throughout

---

of commandant, as a liaison to the Pilsudski Brigades served there that year as well. No doubt de Gaulle with his towering height dressed in his French uniform French helmet wearing white gloves would have been noticed. Mea culpa. I first became interested in France and Napoleon when I came across of book in my father's library in Polish about Napoleon during his time in Poland. The book contained Napoleonic prints that I began to collect especially of Napoleonic battles across Europe. My father told me Napoleon was the first leader to grant citizenship to Jews. In a small museum dedicated to Napoleon in Israel south of Tel Aviv, I came across a copy of a declaration given by Napoleon in 1799 when he continued his battles there especially at Acre. In the declaration Napoleon called for Palestine to be the 'homeland of the Jews'. This declaration predated the 1817 Balfour Declaration by 118 years.

For over four decades I travelled regularly to France and across almost all regions by car, train and bike especially the Bordeaux and Provence wine regions. In the '90s together with my business associate and friend Charles Allan and others we applied for a contested cable license for the port city of Le Havre. We won. Regretfully we could not gain the promised financing and so we returned the license. Meanwhile, I visited Napoleonic battlefields of Waterloo on Dutch lands near the Belgium border and then on a bike trip to the Battlefield of Marengo in northern Italy. Regularly Carole and I would visit friends in Paris and along the southern coast in the Cote d'Azure in St. Tropez, the Film Festival in Cannes, Nice, Menton and Cap d'Antibe. During the summer the small towns and cities each hosted cultural events to attract nearby neighbours and tourists like us. Each town specialized in different cultural events in choirs, classic music concerts, popular music, dance, art and food, a treat for the eye, the ear and the stomach. The diversity of French accents, food and drink in each region continues to amaze us.

334 As a youth de Gaulle trained himself to read words backwards to sharpen his concentration and memory.

335 De Gaulle could trace the military roots of the De Gaulle family and his military ancestors back through the centuries of the history of France and ancestors to Ireland who were also early warriors for independence.

336 When his father was first advised of his death, he asked, *"Did he do his duty?"*

the balance of World War I and escaped imprisonment. Later as a French officer, he served as liaison to the Polish army in Poland after World War I during the Polish War of Independence in 1919 to 1921. Again he was wounded, imprisoned for two years and then escaped endlessly only to be recaptured. Along the way he learned to speak German and Polish (and while in London during World War II he perfected his English). On his return to France he taught at Saint-Cyr, the prestigious French military academy. He failed to gain entry to L'Ecole de Guerre, the prestigious military officer's school. His mentor Marshall Phillipe Petain[337] (who as a World War I hero was idolized in France) upset with the school administration who as Marshall of the army then arranged for a lecture by de Gaulle there, where he pushed de Gaulle ahead of him to enter the lecture hall. This led to de Gaulle giving being invited to give a lecture at the Sorbonne, again stunning his audience and gaining public attention. De Gaulle owned a romantic notion of France personified by his icons - Joan of Arc and Saint Louis. Proudly he wore the unique double barred Cross of Lorraine throughout his career as leader. To him it was more than a symbol, it represented his deep belief in France and its grandeur as a sovereign nation. De Gaulle quickly became a formidable teacher, writer, historian, military and political strategist, who wrote over 15 books, 5 books of speeches, over 3,500 letters[338], articles and essays on military strategy, especially modern tank warfare studies read by Hitler, Stalin and their generals, as well as English and Israeli military leaders[339]. Churchill was a careful student of de Gaulle's revolutionary military tank tactics.

---

337 De Gaulle early sought and cultivated the attention of influential mentors like Petain who assisted him in his climb to leadership.

338 Only de Gaulle could match the literary output of Churchill as a 20th century democratic leader except Theodore Roosevelt who wrote over 80 books. Of the World War II leaders, only de Gaulle was, at times, a teacher. Eisenhower was also, at times, a teacher.

339 There remains a debate about who was more influential as a tank strategist de Gaulle or J.F.C. Fuller, a British military theoretician – a Chief of Staff of British Tank Corps in World War I who led the first surprise mass tank assaults in history and whose books written in 1920 'Tanks in the Great War' and later in 1928

De Gaulle almost single-handedly formed a political movement called Gaullism, two political parties[340] and was a meticulous author of the renewed French constitution that led to the establishment Fifth Republic of France in 1958[341]. Exhausted by political party divisions, he insisted on stronger powers be granted to the President. A contrarian, he followed his own drummer and in the process rehabilitated France and the patriotic spirit of its citizens after World War II transforming the enfeebled French psyche into one infused with national pride and patriotism that reverberates loudly today.

Students of leadership have described the essence of leadership in variations of this trinity. *"Some are born to lead, others are destined to lead and still others are thrust into leadership."* De Gaulle fit all three categories.

De Gaulle, of all World War II leaders, was the tallest, towering over 6'4". Only he and Churchill experienced military action in World War I, where each was wounded, but de Gaulle saw action in World War II in 1940 before the fall of France and led successful tank attacks against the Germans, the only French general to do so at the time.

'*On Future Warfare*' before de Gaulle wrote his books in the '30s. Many of Fuller's ideas were later attributed to de Gaulle. Both Fuller and de Gaulle overlooked the advent of air power that the Nazis deployed in their blistering attacks. German Stuka bombers had screeching devices to frighten their targets.

340 De Gaulle created a movement around himself as the personification of the 'idea of France'. At times he even referred to himself as 'France' especially to Churchill and his colleagues. When his first party (Rally of the French People – RPF, 1955-1958) failed to gain a majority in the Assembly it sputtered, lost traction and ran out of financial support. The second effort to build a party (Union of the New Republic - UNR, 1962-1967) succeeded. The key were his party barons' and loyalists who called themselves 'Gaullists' that lingers to this day. No other democratic leader accomplished this feat of political affirmation. De Gaulle inculcated his principles of French governance into his party and leaders, which principles survived him.

341 If de Gaulle can be called the 'Founding Father' of the Fifth Republic, Michel Debré could be called the 'Founding Mother' who added depth to the detailed study they each did of the U.S. separation of powers with a strong President and the U.K. Parliamentary system which controlled the public purse as was granted to the National Assembly. Both agreed that the President should appoint the Prime Minister and the Cabinet.

No leader kept his own counsel so closely that even his own small coterie of advisers could not predict what he would do[342]. One exception was his wife whose judgement he trusted implicitly. They enjoyed a long and happy marriage. Most often his advisors were surprised. Before any major decision he would seek peace and quiet to consult only his own mind. Of all leaders he maintained a tight circle of advisors, who were more loyal admirers than advisors. Mostly they were members of the entourage who joined him in London as leader of the 'Free French'. Even then he preferred the company, in London, of literary figures as he did in Paris when President of France, over others, especially politicians. He continued throughout his political career to maintain regular contact with members of his early entourage in London, noted by all for his rapier wit.

De Gaulle's tastes were simple. He consciously preferred a simple khaki uniform and the French 'Kepi'[343]. Often he refused the 'cheese' course as it took much time. While his drinking habits were modest, he maintained a taste for fine French wine. His preferred champagne was Drappier made near his country home. Addicted to cigarettes and a chain smoker, he preferred a Gold tipped expensive brand of cigarettes and during the war, American cigarettes. He enjoyed cigars especially in the company of Churchill. Owner of an iron will, he suddenly decided to quit smoking, which he did. He was an avid excellent bridge player. He enjoyed soccer games, especially later on TV[344]. Unlike Roosevelt, Churchill or Stalin he was religious - a devout Catholic and attended mass regularly[345].

His greatest joy was to spend time walking and playing with his challenged younger daughter and when she predeceased him, he was unconsolable. When she died, he set up a foundation in her name to help simi-

---

342 Throughout his long career de Gaulle considered himself a 'loner'. When President of France, he was once asked who are his close friends. De Gaulle responded this he had one friend....decades ago.

343 De Gaulle was trained by Jesuits and maintained a close connection to Jesuit trained clergy.

344 As a youth he was an avid soccer player.

345 As President he favoured a dark black worsted suit, a crisp white shirt and dark tie.

larly challenged children. When the foundation needed capital, he took out a loan on his country home. Then he directed royalties of his books to this fund.

De Gaulle was honest to the end and parsimonious with money. He did not benefit economically from his time in public office. In that sense other than Harry Truman, he was unique. Churchill derived his main income from largely tax exempt royalties from his books after World War II as did de Gaulle whose royalties however were not tax exempt. He refused a Presidential pension. He lived on his military pension and revenue from his farming acreage[346]. De Gaulle survived many assassination attempts, over 90 is one guesstimate, yet he was oblivious to danger, fearless and refused extra protection unlike all other World War II leaders except Churchill, and perhaps, Roosevelt aboard ship at sea. De Gaulle refused to be driven in a bullet-proof limousine unlike Roosevelt, Churchill and Stalin. De Gaulle had another girl and a boy. His daughter married a military officer who worked as an aide to de Gaulle. His son Phillipe as a teenager joined the French Navy and on his own talents became Admiral[347].

Of all the leaders, de Gaulle's own country home was the most modest by comparison. He purchased the small property 90 miles (144.9 kilometers) south of Paris near a tiny village called Colombey-les-Deux-Églises[348] when a young officer in the French army. Both he and his beloved daughter are buried in the cemetery of the small church in the tiny nearby village. Only plain grey granite pillars marked their graves. He insisted

---

346 When de Gaulle abruptly left public office soon after World War II, he received only a Brigadier General's pension. When colleagues sought to increase it to at least a full general's or even a marshal's salary, de Gaulle rejected the offer saying it was 'ridiculous'. In addition he returned to the government the Cadillac and DC4 airplane that Roosevelt had gifted him. Instead he acquired a small French car for himself and his family.

347 Few great leaders leave accomplished offspring. Roosevelt, Churchill, Stalin and Mao did not. De Gaulle was the exception. His son Phillipe joined the French Navy in London in World War II as a teenager. He served with distinction in both ground and naval battles during World War II and thereafter became Admiral by his dint of his talents and presence.

THE GREATEST DEMOCRATIC LEADER IN THE 20TH CENTURY

on a simple funeral and was buried in a simple casket. A grand funeral in Paris organized by the French government was attended by 63 world leaders from around the globe.

Unlike most other leaders de Gaulle abhorred the phone or large meetings. He preferred one on one meetings and he especially enjoyed lengthy meetings with cultural figures and others rather than politicians. At the Élysée Palace, an antique clock behind his desk warned visitors to keep within their allotted time. His favourite colleague was Andre Malraux who became his Minister of Culture[349].

Of all the world leaders only Churchill and de Gaulle would exhibit talented literary pretentions – Churchill of course more richer and voluptuous in style while de Gaulle more elegant and sparse. De Gaulle's multi-volume World War II memoirs considered on a par with the classics written by Julius Caesar on the Gallic wars and Thucydides on the mythic Greek battles. His first volume of memoirs after finally leaving office became an instant best seller.

---

348 On a hilltop over this village is a towering Cross of Lorraine erected in 1972 dedicated to de Gaulle.

349 Malraux was a leader of the 'Free French' in France during the war and didn't meet de Gaulle until after. He was before and after the war a leading political activist and author, leaning during the 30s to the left and participating in Spanish civil war. He was a pilot and considered a natural leader who was captured and luckily escaped torture during World War II. His autobiography called in English the 'Anti Memoirs' was like no other. The Malraux philosophy which he shared with de Gaulle was different. "...art is man's supreme way of escaping his fate and ever dominates it." "Is there any meaning to the idea of man" Malraux was once asked. "...Essentially our art is a way of humanizing the world", he responded. "Though digging under a variety of cultures, under divergent myths through different myths through different structures we can isolate the single factor that is valid throughout the world, valid throughout history." Malraux became, after his first meeting with de Gaulle, one of de Gaulle's closest advisors. He was Minister of Information in the de Gaulle first Cabinet and then when de Gaulle returned to power the world's first Minister of Culture helping with de Gaulle's party organizing events and introducing him. Pierre Mendes France after one meeting in London was equally impressed. Though a Radical on the left and later a French Prime Minister, Mendes France's never lost his respect and admiration for de Gaulle. Malraux like his friend and writer Arthur Koestler travelled from 'left' to 'centre' in the political spectrum after World War II.

De Gaulle was an early advocate of a Common Market with Germany[350]. Yet he opposed the U.K. entry as he felt it gave the United States with its 'special relationship' with U.K. a door into Europe, believing as he did, that Europeans should govern their own affairs and sovereignty was the essence of independence and nationhood. A war time colleague, Jean Monnet (who though in London for a period during the war never joined the 'Free French'), became a bitter political and ideological foe in a clash of their views over the wider bonds with Common European Market. De Gaulle would have applauded Brexit and abhorred the bureaucrats in Brussels. As a contrarian, not a believer in NATO, he withdrew French membership as again he believed that NATO would undermine 'détente' with Russia because of America's overwhelming influence. Even Dean Acheson though he disagreed, understood de Gaulle's view that NATO was more political than military.

When De Gaulle picked up the reins of power in France in August 1944, Nazi forces still lingered in Paris, he boldly marched up the Champs-Élysées with his cohorts. He understood that the French Resistance and the labour unions, were mostly Communist during and after World War II. France became home to one of largest Communist parties in Europe. Brilliant in his handling of Communist politicians, he showed a deft hand when it came to dealing with Stalin directly, and Mao from a distance, who both held him in high regard.

De Gaulle invited Maurice Thorez, the Communist leader into his first Cabinet as Deputy Prime Minister with three other Communist leaders. Thorez and his cohorts in Cabinet never defied de Gaulle and supported his programs.

De Gaulle faced the existential threat to France and stood alone after opposing the Nazi occupation with successful tank attacks during the onslaught of World War II in 1940. On June 5, 1940, then a senior French military bureaucrat (Under-Secretary of Defense), he suddenly flew to London alone with one assistant and an English liaison officer. On June

---

350　De Gaulle only once entertained a foreign leader in his plain country home – Konrad Adenauer where they bonded, and by friendship and by agreed joint actions, dissolved over a century of French-German animosity.

22, he launched a series of BBC radio broadcasts (six programs in total) with a modest amount made available to him by Churchill's government (one million pounds)[351] and with Churchill's approval, though under Churchill's watchful eye. De Gaulle insisted on drafting the text for each broadcast without outside interference.

De Gaulle became, in the early darkest period of World War II, the voice and the personification of the French resistance and scattered 'Free French' forces who slowly began to rally behind him in London, France and the French colonies in Africa and elsewhere. No one elected him leader at that time. He meticulously created his own 'celebrity' and by the force of his will, his eloquent words, his carefully modulated voice, his modest uniform and his actions transformed the 'Free French' into a major power in World War II, more power in perception than reality.

In his first radio address on BBC, de Gaulle denounced the French Cabinet's Armistice with Germany and announced the formation of a French National Committee urging Frenchmen everywhere in France and the colonies to continue to resist and fight and then announced the formation of a Free French fighting force and appealed for volunteers. On June 23, the Churchill Cabinet recognized this committee but renamed it in Churchill's words a 'Council of Liberation'. This recognized de Gaulle only as the military leader leaving wiggle room about political leadership. Churchill was well acquainted, admired and would have preferred at that time Georges Mandel[352], French Minister of Finance who opposed the Vichy's armistice with Germany, refused to leave France and was later captured and executed by the Nazis. At various times, Generals Catoux, Weygand and Giraud were considered secretly by the Allies to be French leader while de Gaulle protested. In August 1940 the Free French Army consisted of 140 officers and 2,109 men. A few months later this force had grown to over 17,500. De Gaulle insisted that the Free French

---

351 Later a substantial cache of French currency was discovered and allocated to de Gaulle and the 'Free French'.

352 Georges Mandel, a French Finance Minister and a Jew, who adopted his mother's name was born in Alsace-Lorraine. My paternal grandmother's parents came from Alsace-Lorraine, who were also named Mandel, not a common name there.

forces stay under his control unlike the Poles, Greeks, Dutch, Norwegians and others who served under Allied Command.

While England earlier broke off relations with the racist Vichy government and Marshall Petain, the United States and Canada continued to recognize Vichy until November 1942. Roosevelt continued his correspondence with Petain referring to Petain as "my warm old friend" delivered by Admiral Leahy, Roosevelt's hand chosen representative to Vichy. These secret exchanges and equally secretive roadblocks to de Gaulle was due to two ideas – one that Petain felt de Gaulle was a 'traitor' and secondly that Roosevelt felt he could keep Petain's Vichy forces ,especially the formidable French navy from attacking the Allies, a deluded strategy, which Churchill early recognized. Halifax, the rabid appeaser who Churchill sent off to America as Ambassador, colluded with the State Department who reasoned against de Gaulle with two diametrically opposite views – one, de Gaulle, surrounded in London by socialists and Jews, leaned left and the other that de Gaulle was a fascist style leader who leaned to right. Neither view was correct.

On November 8, 1942, as noted, Roosevelt's personal letter to Petain delivered by hand, started with "My dear old friend". The letter advised Petain of 'Operation Torch', the pending Allied landing on the Algerian and Moroccan Mediterranean coasts stating the U.S. had 'no territorial ambitions', all with a view to convince Petain not to deploy Vichy naval or military forces against the Allies. De Gaulle was not advised of this letter. Churchill ordered firing on French warships when they refused to stand down, sinking at least three ships and losing well over 1,000 French sailors. De Gaulle approved.

With meticulous planning and visits the African French colonies began to rally to his cause. In North Africa, a Free French tank corp led by General Koenig refused to surrender to Nazi forces though surrounded until a breakthrough occurred. Churchill labelled this 'one the greatest military feats in World War II'. De Gaulle then renamed the Free French to 'Fighting France'.

Dogged in his determination to succeed, de Gaulle made small incremental moves, step by step, to gain independence of action supported by elements at his 'Free French' movement in Algiers, West and Central

Africa and other French colonies. He deployed 'Free French' forces to Greece and Egypt to assist the Allies. He sought to establish relations with South Africa, the Belgian Congo and other National Committees in London for his provisional government. He sought to inject French interests in the Allies' Pacific war plans. Meanwhile these efforts were continually hampered by both British and American officials.

These acts of obstruction by the Allies slowly changed. In 1942 de Gaulle knew little of the resistance in France. The Resistance in France was divided. When a leader of one group Christen Pineau (later to be a Prime Minister) arrived in London he spent hours with de Gaulle describing the situation. The Resistance was divided into three major groups – the largest and best organized were the Communists. George Bidault (also later to become Prime Minister) led a third group. Jean Moulin, a former French public servant, who had joined de Gaulle in London and who under de Gaulle's orders in 1941 de Gaulle chose to build an umbrella group to unify these disparate groups. Moulin parachuted into France, united the groups under his elected leadership, was captured, tortured and died in 1943 on a train to Metz prison.

De Gaulle created a new French Order – The Order of Liberation with the Cross of Lorraine as its decoration. Only Churchill, though he exasperated from time to time, was steadfast in his belief and support for de Gaulle as both a military and political leader[353]. Eisenhower was one of the only two major Americans who held de Gaulle in high regard. The other was Nixon. No so General Marshall.

De Gaulle was a thorn in the side of Roosevelt. Churchill admired him and put up with his antics. De Gaulle, powerless in London, used his intransigence as the most powerful weapon in his limited arsenal. He rallied the French colonies starting with his visits to St. Pierre, then Miquelon – both small islands in the St. Lawrence[354]. Then he traveled to French colonies in Africa and elsewhere. On all these visits, he was

---

353 In October 1943 Churchill wrote to Duff Cooper the British liaison with the FCNL in Algiers "*I do not wish to overlook the good qualities of de Gaulle, and I certainly do not underrate the smouldering and explosive forces in his nature or that he is a figure of magnitude.*"

354 Roosevelt and his state department opposed de Gaulle's takeover at St. Pierre and Miquelon while Mackenzie King supported him for which for a time de Gaulle was

besieged by the local French speaking population. The failed attempt by Allies to secure Dakar, a seaport on the coast of Africa, was quickly blamed on de Gaulle by Roosevelt. Churchill was more even handed and blamed both the Allied and 'Free French' forces for the fiasco at Dakar[355].

In the spring of 1944, with the prospect of the liberation of France. Roosevelt had come to despise de Gaulle for what Roosevelt deemed his autocratic methods, intense nationalism and renewed colonial aspirations. This view was held by Cordell Hull, Secretary of State, his State Department and Admiral Leahy, Roosevelt's representative of Vichy. Only Henry Morgenthau, Roosevelt's Secretary of the Treasury supported de Gaulle and France especially with financial aid due to the efforts, in part, of Jean Monnet. Roosevelt even ordered that Eisenhower be given responsibility for governing France as the Supreme Allied Commander at liberation. Eisenhower demurred. He briefed de Gaulle on D-Day plans just before the invasion. He even sought de Gaulle's advice about when to launch the invasion delayed due to the inclement weather conditions. De Gaulle told him that was this decision was Eisenhower's alone but added, sooner was better. The Allies prepared a radio speech for de Gaulle to give to France right after D-Day. De Gaulle refused and instead wrote and delivered his own speech. When Bayeux, the first French city was liberated, Eisenhower allowed de Gaulle to go there on June 17ᵗʰ. De Gaulle was besieged by the rapturous French inhabitants of Bayeux as pictures of Petain were hauled down and trashed. The French citizens' reaction to de Gaulle justified Eisenhower's confidence despite contrary orders from Roosevelt. Eisenhower used his authority as Supreme European Commander to read his orders in a way to allow de Gaulle freedom of movement.

---

grateful. Canadian and American public opinion supported de Gaulle. Churchill in speech to the Canadian Parliament praised de Gaulle and the Free French that increased support for de Gaulle in Canada and especially in Quebec. United States still recognized the Vichy government and Petain after the U.S. entered World War II as an ally until November 1942. Later the Nazis took over Vichy territory in France. Vichy forces fought the Allies in Lebanon and Syria influenced by Nazi Muslim collaboration led by the Grand Mufti of Jerusalem.

355 De Gaulle suffered, as Churchill did, from periodic bouts of depression. Dakar triggered one such bout.

Most historians of World War II after the 'Overlord' Normandy landings in the spring of 1944 recounts, on film and in the history books, from the perspective of the Allied invaders. Rare is a history written about what happened in France from the start of those Allied landings in early June 1944 until France was fully liberated from both the Vichy government and the Nazis by May of 1945.

The Normandy landings triggered anarchy and chaos across France. Like minor fireworks there were explosions in every region of occupied France. Into this maelstrom strode Charles de Gaulle armed with only with the legitimacy as the leader of a provisional government barely recognized by the Allies seeking to restore order. Armed forces of the 'Free French', French Communists, other resistance groups, militias, Vichy loyalists, local police forces, and retreating Nazis armed forces displayed a chaotic and confusing picture across France. Retribution and vengeance was taken out on Vichy officials and Nazi collaborators. De Gaulle, denied by Allies participation in the planning of the Normandy invasion, intruded himself to gain prominence and to carefully pick up the slender threads of power to restore order and unify the nation as the enemy forces chaotically retreated.

After the Normandy invasion, De Gaulle finally persuaded Eisenhower who changed his mind to make the liberation of Paris a priority. De Gaulle recognized that power and legitimacy historically radiated from the French capital. While gunfire was still evident, de Gaulle raced ahead with the French led liberating forces to arrive in Paris in August of 1944 with limited personal protection. His intelligence sources kept him abreast of the situation in Paris and across France still mostly occupied by the Nazis who had recently occupied Vichy controlled areas in the south. A pincer movement by Allies called 'Operation Dragoon' landed on France's Mediterranean coast which aimed to increase the division and push back of retreating Nazi forces. The Allies, after much debate, had decided to invade the French south coast to gain control of the shipping port of Marseille and to divide Nazi forces.

When de Gaulle arrived in Paris in August 1944 joined by elements of his 'Free French' cadre from London and France, he and his entourage marched together boldly up the Champs-Élysées to the Tomb of the Unknown

Soldier[356] then to the Mayor's office for a speech that started the myth that France had liberated herself, and then to the Notre Dame Cathedral for prayers. De Gaulle immediately settled into his old Military Defense offices, took command of situation, insisting those Ministers of the Provisional Government in Algiers return at once to take command of their government departments in Paris. He quickly took control of the Police Forces to restore public order. Asking from more military support from Eisenhower to remain in Paris to help restore order who gave him a fraction of his request, de Gaulle demanded a public review of all the military forces requested even though most of these Allied and French forces just marched through Paris to the front lines as a visible sign of peace and order.

The major challenge confronting de Gaulle's provisional government were the Communists who had fought valiantly with and were the major element in the 'Resistance' and were now organizing into armed militias in Paris and across France. De Gaulle arranged in January 1945 to visit Stalin in Moscow and agreed with Stalin to a 'Soviet France Pact'. This led to de Gaulle to allow Maurice Thorez the leader of French Communists to return to France from his refuge in Moscow. Thorez agreed to exhort the Communist militias that were forming around France to disband and join the police forces now controlled by de Gaulle. Thorez and other Communist leaders were invited by de Gaulle to join the Provisional Cabinet as Ministers. De Gaulle's objective was to form a union cabinet made up of representatives from all major parties of the former French Assembly except Vichy. In this he was influenced by the make-up of Churchill's all party war cabinet.

Meanwhile de Gaulle continued to direct French Army forces working with the Allies to liberate the rest of occupied France, city by city, region by region.

Powerless, de Gaulle used the appearance of power to restore calm under democratic government to unify a divided France. By his actions

---

356 I obtained from then Mayor Jacques Chirac a large poster of this historic event that I proudly hung in my Senate office in Ottawa and one of de Gaulle and his closest advisor Andre Malraux that were hung on high lighting posts along the Champs-Élysées in Paris to celebrate the 100th anniversary of de Gaulle's birth in 1990.

and speeches, de Gaulle reignited latent patriotism in the French population then confused, cowed and divided. Many were still loyal to Vichy. These were all acts of singular surgical leadership.

Raymond Aron[357] in his fact filled book '*De Gaulle: Triumphant – The Liberation of France August 1944 – May 1945*' (Putnam & Co. Ltd., 1964) described how de Gaulle showed himself to be rigidly intransigent, refusing every concession to the Allies that might militate against French independence or sovereignty. He succeeded in persuading the Allies to recognize a French government of his own making and made certain his Government would be the only one in power in France at Liberation. Still he insisted it be recognized by the French Assembly. This result he created not only based on his personal prestige and remarkable determination but by detailed preparation and instructions to his political, administrative and judicial cadres who were destined to quickly erect a new facade of democracy and order on the ruins of the Vichy government.

In this way, Aron goes on, De Gaulle won the support of the remnants of the armed forces and "*in the hearts of all the French, who without being adherents of his, that had nevertheless not betrayed their country*".

No democratic leader with less resources did more to earn a singular place in history of the 20th century.

Despite his challenges with the French Communists[358], the faltering French economy[359], the divided political scene, he transformed France into a modern economy and personally oversaw the creation and

---

357 Raymond Aron, during World War II fought in the Resistance in France, was arrested by the Gestapo, escaped in 1942, fled to Algiers where he worked for the provisional government formed by de Gaulle and General Giraud. Once in London, Aron edited a daily newspaper for 'Free French'. After the war, he became a journalist, writer, teacher and a spark plug in the efforts to rewrite the French Constitution. A critic of de Gaulle especially with respect to De Gaulle's stance in Israel after the Seven Day War in 1967, Aron was considered one of the leading intellectuals of France.

358 The French Communist Party (PFC) emerged as the largest Communist Party in the western world. The PFC controlled 12 daily newspapers, 47 weeklies including the *Liberation* that had a daily circulation of over 100,000. The PFC held mastery over the post liberation media.

359 He named Rene Pleven a close Free French colleague and Pierre Mendes France to his first Cabinet. Pleven was a free market advocate while Mendes France believed

passage of the French Constitution imbuing the President with broad central powers with the establishment the Fifth Republic. He overcame the bloody 'Algerian' separation from France with purpose and persuasiveness and brought a troubled peace to North Africa. All the while, diehards opposed him and sought to assassinate him. No other democratic leader was faced with armed military insurrection domestically in both France and Algeria. De Gaulle, the ultimate democratic abhorred military disobedience to democratic civil control. Brilliantly, in a series of visits to the military rank and file, with passionate speeches, he won over the rank and file as loyalists from their insurrectionist military leaders. In a series of television and radio speeches to France in a Referendum on separation from Algiers he won overwhelming public support. These speeches were simple, persuasive as he engaged intimately with his French audience forging a bond, their trust and their emotional support in acts of pure statecraft. Only Churchill could match this connection with the public when they spoke as people across the land were glued to their words on radio.

In all things he undertook he was a master meticulous organizer, interested in culture and architecture, and developed a superb team of technocrats to implement his ideas. It is said that he never forgot a slight. Yet, any slight did not cripple him. He quickly emerged as a respected European leader when Europe was slowly recuperating from the severe ravages World War II as he slowly restored French power in Europe.

De Gaulle's activities with Canada in '60s were purposefully nefarious. Before his state visit to Canada in 1966, he confided to his colleagues that he had to share common cause with the Quebec separatist movement then raging in Quebec. He studiously avoided a visit to Ottawa. Instead he travelled across the Atlantic by a French naval ship to Quebec City, disembarked, spoke to the Quebec Legislature then took a leisurely car tour along the old historic land route on the north shore of the

---

in a planned economy. When their disagreements reached a peak, de Gaulle met alone with both for hours and then sided with Pleven. Mendes-France contemplated resigning from de Gaulle's Cabinet but chose to remain at his post. Though de Gaulle disagreed with Mendes France, Mendes France never lost his respect or admiration for de Gaulle.

St. Lawrence where he was besieged at every stop by Quebec admirers. Both in Quebec City and Montreal, he shouted, *"Vive Le Quebec Libre"*, the slogan of the Quebec's separatists without consulting Prime Minister Pearson who was furious. He purposely avoided at meeting in Ottawa. At a farewell lunch hosted by Prime Minister Pearson in Quebec City, he lacerated de Gaulle who quietly deflected the criticisms later saying he didn't mean to infringe or interfere with internal affairs yet never regretted his unwanted intervention and later confessed he could no other. On his return to Paris, his Cabinet was silent, stunned by his report. Even Andre Malraux, his cultural advisor and friend thought de Gaulle was wrong about his interjection into Canada politics and sovereignty as did others like Raymond Aron. De Gaulle's Prime Minister Georges Pompidou was also disappointed. Giscard d'Estaing, a lifelong Gaullist loyalist left de Gaulle's party, as a sign of his disagreement.

No political leader wrote with greater self-effacing literary skill or elegance. Each of de Gaulle's books are considered classics of their genre. What shines through is the lucidity of thought, concision and elegance of expression and the simplicity of argumentation. No extra verbiage dilutes de Gaulle's advocacy. In that sense, he is Hemingwayesque or rather like Camus.

His first thin book written in 1932 later translated into English called the '*The Edge of The Sword*' gained de Gaulle an instant reputation as a military thinker and strategist. The chapter headings laid out his thinking. The Conduct of War, of Character, of Prestige, Doctrine, of politics, and the soldier.... There is he notes, *"A vague sort of attraction does exist between the rulers and the generals. Seeing one another on opposite two path of the same river, endlessly harnessed to the ship of their ambitions, impassioned champions of authority are conscious of the mutual respect that the strong feel for the strong. Enlightened views.... cannot be drawn from acquired knowledge.... These are markers of intuition and character...."*

Throughout his life, from his earliest writings and lectures, de Gaulle emphasized leadership qualities that included ability', intent, 'character' and 'mystery'. De Gaulle agreed with the 'great man' theory of history.... *"Nothing great will be achieved without great men and then only if they are determined to be so... such men should never be drawn to despair, or become victims of disappointments."* These simple words guided de Gaulle while he arose from obscurity to regain for himself and France, a historic position in the world.

De Gaulle had a series of mentors in the military. The most influential was Marshall Petain, the military hero of World War I. Petain early took him under his wing, saw to his promotions and got de Gaulle out scrapes of insubordination always choosing to do his own thing. As noted when de Gaulle, to his despair, was refused entry to L'Ecole de Guerre, the top school for military officers, Petain as Marshall of the Army announced a lecture to be given there by de Gaulle overturning a decision of the school administration. At the lecture Petain pushed de Gaulle into the lecture room ahead of himself. De Gaulle stunned and mesmerized his audience. This led to an invitation to lecture at the Sorbonne which in turn brought de Gaulle to wide public attention. When de Gaulle wrote, the *'The Army of the Future'* in the late '30s, he dedicated it to Petain and asked Petain to write a foreword. De Gaulle then rewrote Petain's foreword in a more favourable light. Petain was furious and de Gaulle promised to change the foreword in his next edition which didn't happen as World War II intervened. Petain felt de Gaulle had stolen some of the ideas in de Gaulle's book without proper attribution. Petain felt that de Gaulle deserting France when he did, was a traitor. Later de Gaulle, after the war, agreed to Petain's trial for treason. De Gaulle then commuted his death sentence but Petain was imprisoned on an island till his death. Petain kept a copy of de Gaulle's *'The Edge of The Sword'* with him.

De Gaulle believed in 'balance of power' theory – balancing one major power against another to maintain stability and peace, as a lifelong student of power. Hence he accelerated France's goal to gain a nuclear bomb ('le force de frappe'), later with the help of Israeli scientists. He dreamed up the idea of a Directorate of democratic nuclear powers - United States, U.K. and France. Both U.S.A. and U.K. not just rejected but were dismissive of this idea. Successive Americans led by Truman, Eisenhower, Kennedy and Johnson and British leaders Churchill, Atlee, and MacMillan in the U.K. also dismissed this de Gaulle idea.

At the same time, de Gaulle sought to balance Europe and Russia against American power, and, China against Russia. In this he was misunderstood especially by America as he was perceived to curry favouritism with Communists both domestically and in foreign relations. In this sense he was a believer like Kissinger in 'realpolitik'. Unlike Kissinger, he was a deep practitioner of democratic principles and a devout believer in 'rule of law' by constitutional law and legal principles. Kissinger on these subjects was nuanced at best. Kissinger who met de Gaulle several times, wrote of Zhou Enlai with whom he also engaged in lengthy discussions, that no one had a greater grasp of world events than Zhou except de Gaulle. Kissinger also wrote that Mao, after their lengthy meetings in China, had *"raw distilled concentrated will power"* like de Gaulle.

Few Americans understood de Gaulle better than Henry Kissinger[360]. In his book *'White House Years'* (Little, Brown and Company, 1979), Kissinger titled his reflection *"The Colossus of de Gaulle"*. De Gaulle, he wrote was the spokesman of the nation – state and European autonomy distinct from the United States. *"Washington dreamed of an international structure that made physical action physically impossible..."* De Gaulle insisted that *"co-operation would be effective only if each partner had a real choice"*. *"...The world is full of opposing forces...."* de Gaulle argued. Americans stressed partnership dominated by them while de Gaulle emphasized 'equilibrium'.

"Intentional life, like life in general is a battle". The battle can unite and not divide...*"to liberate and not to dominate"*.

Kissinger argued de Gaulle could not accept this American conviction of the obsolescence of the nation state therefore European unity required that the national state not be subservient to "a federal supernational superstructure. To de Gaulle nation states *"were the only legitimate source of power"*.

The most complicated and perhaps least understood was de Gaulle's attitude towards Jews and Israel.

---

360 Hans J Morganthau, a leading American scholar opined on de Gaulle's contrarian views of Europe that *"de Gaulle design is rational, not devoid of audacity and even grandeur."*

The de Gaulle family were outspoken Dreyfusards, especially his father, as was de Gaulle himself. His father and he both agreed that the French military were anti-semitic in principle and in practice with which they both vehemently abhorred. De Gaulle was critical of Vichy's anti-semitic laws and practices. His niece and another close relative were survivors of death camps[361]. His first mentor a Col. Emile Mayer was Jewish as were numerous of his supporters like Maurice Schumann and Rene Mayer, the second Jewish Prime Minister of France. Others like Pierre Mendes France, a left wing member of his provisional government and future French Prime Minister always held him in the highest regard. He had great admiration for Georges Mandel, the Jewish French Minister of Finance from Alsace-Lorraine, who rejected Vichy. De Gaulle begged him to join him in London. Mandel, captured by Vichy in France, imprisoned, died murdered by Vichy Police in 1944 after refusing to flee to England to join de Gaulle[362]. De Gaulle had good relations with Leon Blum the first Jewish Prime Minister of France in the 1930's though Blum was a leading socialist. Other friends and associates who were Jewish like Rene Cassin and Michel Debre, a convert, but whose grandfather was Jewish was one of de Gaulle's longest advisors. His lifelong doctor and confidante was Jewish Frenchman Andre Leibevitz. When de Gaulle learned of the death of Mme. Mendes France he sent Mendes France a handwritten two page letter of condolences. So in all his personal relations he was free of any taint of anti-semitic views. On the contrary, he admired Jews in politics, business, the arts, science and the military.

When it came to Israel his attitude was more complex. David Ben-Gurion and de Gaulle held each other in high mutual esteem and wrote

---

361 When de Gaulle paid a state visit to Poland, he included a tour of Auschwitz. At the end of the tour, visibly upset, he was asked to sign the visitors' book with his thoughts. For the longest period de Gaulle paused, with tears in his eyes, undecided what to write. Finally he wrote ever so slowly, "*Quelle tristesse, Quelle pitie.*" Finally before the word "*Quelle tristesse*", he wrote, "*Quel degout*". Then added an exclamation mark. Then after another long pause he wrote, "*Quelle Esperance Humaine*". Then signed his name and date.

362 For some still unknown reason de Gaulle later pardoned Mandel's convicted killers.

each other regularly[363]. Ben-Gurion was warmly greeted in Paris by de Gaulle in a state visit in 1960[364]. When it came to the Suez Affair in 1957, de Gaulle was out of office. He was supportive of France's participation but felt France did not utilize enough military force to achieve its goals.

In a conversation with Claude Guy in 1947, de Gaulle remarked: *"In the Palestine business my preference goes to the Jews. The Arabs don't deserve to be helped: they are over-excitable. In 1930 when I went to Palestine for the first time, I remember having seen the orange trees cultivated by the Arabs: they were shriveled, their fruits were bitter and small. The Jews on the other hand cultivated theirs remarkably successfully. These fanatical individualists, doubtless because they were working on what they had a sense of being the land of their birth, these former merchants from Poland and Germany, were ready to do the toughest work in the fields. During the war, when I returned to Palestine, the progress the Jews had made was amazing. That is why we need to help the Jews and we should hurry because anti-Semitism will reappear in its virulent form."* ('A Certain Idea of France: The Life of Charles de Gaulle' by Julian Jackson (Penguin Random House U.K., 2018)).

In November 1967 at a massive press conference when asked about the Jewish-Arab conflict at the time he concluded.... *"an exceptional dominating people, sure of themselves"*[365]. Was this a compliment that he would ascribe he also to himself and the French people? His admirers

---

363 Both de Gaulle and Ben-Gurion were voracious readers. Both were gifted linguists in English, French, Polish, Russian, Latin and Greek.

364 During Ben-Gurion's state visit to France de Gaulle inquired of Ben-Gurion if more could have been done to save Jews during the Holocaust. Ben-Gurion was surprised when de Gaulle promised to defend Israel if Nasser destroyed Tel Aviv. De Gaulle continued, *"it would cause a world war"* (A State at Any Cost: The Life of David Ben-Gurion by Tom Segev (Picador, 2019)).

365 De Gaulle warned Israel's representatives especially its Foreign Minister Abba Eban that Israel should not fire first in the 1967 war when Israel's was threatened by Egypt, Syria, Lebanon and Jordan. Israel decided to attack and wipe out the Egyptian air force and later its tank forces and encircle its army. De Gaulle was miffed that his advice was not accepted. After Algeria, de Gaulle shifted support to Arab positions to neutralize Muslims in Algeria, especially French speaking Arabs there and elsewhere. Yet he was not surprised and admired Israel's military prowess against greater Arab forces.

and detractors took up opposing positions[366]. No doubt Israel's reliance on United States, always a critic of American influence, de Gaulle found questionable as he did with other powers especially the U.K. It was U.K.'s self-proclaimed 'special' relationship with America that caused him to object to their entry in the Common Market. The fact that Jews in Algeria found common cause with O.A.S. the anti-Algerian independence group led by Jacques Soustelle who found common cause with Israel did not affect de Gaulle's attitude. Soustelle, according to a leading Jewish journalist, who remarked while in Israel, there was 'imbalance' in de Gaulle thinking on this and other matters. De Gaulle himself was surprised by the avalanche of criticism he received in France. De Gaulle no doubt tilted towards the Arabs after Algeria but he never curried favour for the Muslim vote in France[367].

This 'imbalance' also was found in de Gaulle's capacious ambitions that didn't match France's limited means.

And while de Gaulle criticized Israel's closeness with America, de Gaulle wanted to unite French speaking people in Canada, Switzerland and Belgium and French speaking states and enclaves in Africa, Madagascar, Haiti, Vietnam, Cambodia and Mauritius – even Lebanon and Syria. De Gaulle was coherent in his own mind, but raised questions amongst with his critics and colleagues about his inconsistency of thought. Yet all agreed, his 'character', his force of personality and his deep perception of how he sought to lead France to address the fissures in the world through powerful acts of leadership cannot be denied.

---

366 Raymond Aron, French Jew, colleague of de Gaulle and leading French journalist and intellectual during World War II in London and later an activist promoting the new Constitution of the Fifth Republic castigated de Gaulle for this statement with a blistering criticism in his book '*De Gaulle, Israel And The Jews*' (Routledge Press, 2002).

367 No doubt de Gaulle forgot how Vichy forces opposed the Allies led by the Australians and Free French forces in Lebanon and Syria. Yitzhak Rabin and Moshe Dayan were chosen by David Ben-Gurion leader of the Jews in wartime Palestine to lead youthful Jewish fighters behind the lines in Lebanon to cut down telephone lines. Rabin succeeded. Dayan encountered Vichy forces and lost is eye in a pitched battle which later made him recognizable by his black eye patch.

Except for Roosevelt and Truman[368], Churchill, Stalin, Ben-Gurion and other noteworthy leaders like Eisenhower, Kennedy, MacMillan, Nehru and Mao, all held high opinions of de Gaulle as a leader. De Gaulle had a low opinion of Roosevelt. The feeling was mutual. As for Churchill, though they often quarrelled, and Churchill at times was exasperated with de Gaulle, both held each other in affection and high esteem. Churchill once whispered to de Gaulle in 1940 on a meeting in France that he was 'a man of destiny'.

De Gaulle's pithy thoughts on Roosevelt while instructing an emissary to America, said, "Don't forget that Roosevelt is a 'faux temoin' (false witness)." Roosevelt from his perspective felt de Gaulle had too much personal ambition and little aptitude for following orders. Hmm![369] In June of 1944, de Gaulle was invited to visit the White House by Roosevelt believing his charm would overwhelm de Gaulle as he had with Churchill. After came a triumphant visit to New York City organized by Mayor Fiorello Le Guardia, a Republican who after a tickertape parade with millions in attending in Manhattan, de Gaulle made an impressive speech to the New York elite. Earlier de Gaulle had arrived to Washington in plane gifted by Roosevelt for a state visit with Roosevelt at the White

---

368 Truman's Secretary of State Dean Acheson shared the American State Department dislike of de Gaulle. Acheson wrote his pompous memoirs 'Present at the Creation: My Years in the State Department' (WW Norton and Company Inc, 1969) where every one of numerous references to de Gaulle's were dismissive. Later Acheson changed his view of de Gaulle when he was delegated by Kennedy to inform de Gaulle of Kennedy's decision to blockade Cuba. De Gaulle immediately agreed without examining the evidence especially photos Acheson brought. De Gaulle felt if Kennedy decided to do this, he didn't need evidence.

369 When Roosevelt and Churchill met in Casablanca in January 1943 to review plans for the invasion of France they invited de Gaulle and General Giraud who previously had met Roosevelt in Washington. De Gaulle had never met Roosevelt. When de Gaulle sensed of a plot to displace him as leader of Fighting France with Giraud, de Gaulle demurred. Pressured both Americans and British and his advisors who persuaded him to attend. Roosevelt plan was to place Giraud in command of Fighting France and put de Gaulle as his second in command leaving open the political leadership. De Gaulle refused upsetting both Roosevelt and Churchill who wanted not to displease with Roosevelt.

House. Roosevelt ever the astute politician in a Presidential election year noted de Gaulle's popularity and sought to deploy his charm to smooth de Gaulle's ruffled feathers as Roosevelt had not yet recognized de Gaulle's provisional government which he continued to avoid. While de Gaulle was impressed with Roosevelt and his visit to Washington's Arlington cemetery and the Lincoln Memorial, he still did not trust Roosevelt and nor did Roosevelt like him. After the visit and his lengthy discussions with de Gaulle, Roosevelt confided in his advisors that de Gaulle was *"nuts"*. After de Gaulle's triumphant visit to New York City, Roosevelt changed course and gave de Gaulle's provisional government limited approval to handle the administration in France. Later when de Gaulle was given a confidential letter describing Roosevelt's views of him as an 'egoist', de Gaulle noted - so was Roosevelt.

Churchill described de Gaulle as *"the most autocratic forthright determined stubborn undiplomatic haughty unbending ruthless yet brilliant leader I ever met."* De Gaulle reciprocated these feelings about Churchill. He understood how alone Churchill had been in the darkest days of World War II as was he! Churchill once referred to him as the notorious

---

Roosevelt turned on his charm. De Gaulle would not agree to the communique but reluctantly agreed to a photo, grimly shaking hands with Giraud. De Gaulle gained three allies. Harold MacMillan, British resident in Algiers, and two Americans – Harry Hopkins, Roosevelt's closest advisor and Robert Murphy, Roosevelt's point man in Algiers. Both concluded that de Gaulle was a better choice leader for the Fighting France. Roosevelt back in Washington described de Gaulle as *"arrogant, argumentative, egocentric and close-minded'*. He quipped that de Gaulle thought he was Joan of Arc and Georges Clemenceau at once. Meanwhile Churchill fumed but continued to support de Gaulle as both military and political leader of France. Walter Lippman, the iconic American journalist, once compared de Gaulle and Mao incarnates of their nations.

Roosevelt's future plans for Europe were clearly misguided and not realistic. Armaments should be concentrated in the hands of Britain, United States and Russia. Then Roosevelt argued *"The smaller powers should have nothing more dangerous than rifles ... the three powers should police Europe....a new state called Wallonia should include the Walloon parts of Belgium with Luxemburg, Alsace Lorraine and part of north France."* demonstrating Roosevelt's bias to his Dutch roots and German preference as no part of Germany was included his grand scheme of European divisions. Roosevelt had little sympathy for France and none for de Gaulle.

'Scarlet Pimpernel' who arranged for Frenchman to flee England from the turmoil of the French Revolution. De Gaulle religiously followed Churchill's addresses on radio. He exclaimed about Churchill after these speeches, "*What an actor, what an actor*" in French.

Stalin had a high regard for de Gaulle. When in Moscow de Gaulle refused to recognize the Soviet puppet Polish leaders ('Lublin Government') unlike Churchill or Roosevelt who both broke their word, Stalin told de Gaulle, "*I didn't know they still made Frenchmen like you.*"

Ben-Gurion despite de Gaulle's criticism of Israel felt that anti-Jewish criticism by de Gaulle was greatly exaggerated. Ben-Gurion publically tabled their very long correspondences to demonstrate Ben-Gurion's and de Gaulle's mutual admiration for each other and described de Gaulle as a friend of Israel and a world leader. One ironic footnote. When Israel invaded Lebanon to which de Gaulle was attached because of its French speaking population, de Gaulle unilaterally canceled a paid contract with Israel for five missile ships (called the 'Boats of Cherbourg'). On December 24, 1969 with the assistance of French officials the ships secretly left France for Israel, first two, then the three remaining. By then, in retirement, de Gaulle was miffed but not surprised.

De Gaulle warned President Johnson that Vietnam war "*would be an entangled web*" to Johnson's dismay. De Gaulle's unhappy experience with French Indo-Asia had scorched into his brain. De Gaulle early believed that Vietnam should be reunited[370].

---

370 De Gaulle and Churchill both had the same political objective in World War II – to retain each of their nations' far flung empires. This political objective was not shared by the Americans especially Roosevelt who were anti-colonists when it came to the British and French empires. Indochina-south east Asia - (Cambodia, Leo, Vietnam et al) held de Gaulle's attention from almost the moment he became leader of the 'Free French'. Perhaps not only became he was a believer at that time in the French colonies but also because they were not only French speaking officially but also many of the native officials were Catholic.

In 1940 Japan had ruthlessly overrun French Indo China, a strategic gateway to China, slaughtering thousands of both French and native troops but French women and children. Japan maintained their dominance until 1945. This was the only region where de Gaulle sought to work with Vichy French officials and the military.

Khrushchev highly respected de Gaulle. Khrushchev planned move on Berlin may have changed because of the strength and convictions he noted in de Gaulle in their lengthy meetings in Moscow.

Ho Chi Minh, the energetic leader of the Viet Cong, spoke French, had lived in France as a worker for seven years (1917-29), was a Marxist Leninist and member of the French Communist Party then led Vietnam's independent movement starting in 1941 combatting the Japanese. At first Ho was deemed 'progressive' by the Americans who supported him with military training arms and materials to assist in his struggles against the Japanese. Ho adapted de Gaulle's ideas calling his group the "National Liberation Committee'. When the atomic bombs were dropped on Japan in 1945, de Gaulle with French military leaders thought the time was propitious to recoup French hegemony in south east Asia.

After de Gaulle abruptly left office in 1946 this policy continued until 1954 when French forces were soundly defeated in Dien Bien Phu 1954. Ho Chi Minh had spent time in China with Mao and spoke and wrote fluent Chinese, who, together, contrived to ignite the Korean War. Mendes-France then Prime Minister promptly made peace with Ho Chi Minh at Geneva and the French politicians relinquished political control as they withdrew their military forces. De Gaulle while he maintained his interest in the region changed course. His belief in the sovereignty and the nation state prevailed.

He became an advocate for neutralization of this entire region and withdrawal of all foreign forces. De Gaulle warned the Americans especially Kennedy and Nixon against the quagmire Vietnam had become. In 1966 as part of a world tour de Gaulle visited Cambodia and addressed a rapturous crowd of over 200,000 advocating the withdrawal of all foreign troops from the region.

The Americans immediately publically disagreed. Johnson was furious and refused to heed de Gaulle's advice. Johnson later refused to run again for President as he had lost public support for his Vietnam policies. This chapter in history and America's failed policies in the region require much broader historic analysis. The best recent account can be found in 'The Quiet Americans: Four Cia Spies At The Dawn Of The Cold War – A Tragedy In Three Acts' by Scott Anderson (Penguin Random House Canada, 2020).

One postscript to America's loss in the Vietnam War came to light in 1995. In a Wall Street Journal interview, Bui Tin, former Colonel in the North Vietnamese army stated that its leadership listened daily at 9 am to world news. They carefully followed the media's coverage of the anti-war movement in America. Visits to Hanoi by Jane Fonda and former attorney General Ramsay Clarke gave the Vietnamese leadership confidence to hold on in face of battlefield reverses. The role of media coverage, rarely examined, appeared to be a factor in America's military loss.

All notable democratic leaders, Roosevelt, Churchill and others in the 20th century inherited the reins of an existing democratic party, and an existing democratic constitutional structure. Charles de Gaulle alone with only a small entourage established himself as a leader in dark days of World War II, founded a democratic political movement, created a democratic political party, insisted on loyal affirmation of his leadership and recognition from other states of his provisional government and oversaw the drafting of a new democratic constitution and assured that the constitution was democratically passed into law. He was a profound believer in the democratic 'rule of law'. For these acts alone, de Gaulle can be considered the greatest democratic leader of the 20th century. Was de Gaulle perfect?[371] No. Which leader is?

Politics always suddenly springs surprise full scenarios. It is not the unpredictable surprises that continually erupt in politics, rather its political leader's responses to those surprises that forge a leader's mettle.

In 1968 de Gaulle was visibly aging, hard of hearing, with faltering eyesight, gaining a visible paunch, a stoopy slow gait and above all bored with the routine of his high office.

Suddenly de Gaulle and his Cabinet were confronted with extraordinary challenges to public order. It was the era of student protests ignited in America by the Vietnam War. Disruptive university campus scenes incinerated by violent government responses were televised around the globe.

A copycat element pervaded the electronic 'global village'. Student protests became the vogue. It was also the time of the 'sexual revolution'.

These combustible elements combined in France. A student protest had erupted at Nanterre a provincial university. Students decided males should be allowed in female dorms and a swimming pool. De Gaulle's Minister of Education attempt to take command of the situation were rudely rebuffed. University administration space was occupied. Student

---

371   No doubt de Gaulle believed he was the reincarnation of the glory of French history. No doubt he contradicted himself at times. Systemic in his thinking he believed in his own consistency and came to considered conclusions relying on his own thought process what to do in virtually all situations.

protests quickly spread across France and to Paris. A radical German student Daniel Cohn-Bendit attending Nanterre leading the protest was dubbed 'Danny the Red' due to his radical views and wild red hair becoming an instant global celebrity. He travelled to Paris to join the student protests there at the Sorbonne[372]. Students occupied the Sorbonne administration space and refused to leave.

De Gaulle and his Cabinet were caught off guard. De Gaulle appeared to lose his usually deft handling of this public crisis. The student protests were joined by worker unions armed with their own grievances against de Gaulle and his government. Protestors marching in Paris and across France grew to over 10 million, the largest such protests in French history. Police and military called out to put down these protests were reluctant to use violent means.

Suddenly de Gaulle uncharacteristically disappeared from public view. Secretly without his Cabinet knowledge, he went missing. De Gaulle flew by small plane to Baden in Germany to confer with an old colleague, General Massu who was stationed there with French troops. As he did during the Algerian military insurrection where Algerians sought to separate from France, he sought to ensure that French troops would remain loyal to his civil oversight.

On his return to Paris, a massive counter protest was organized by Malraux and other loyal Gaullists who led millions in parade marching down the Champs-Élysées declaring loyalty to de Gaulle. De Gaulle soberly addressed the French nation seeking support to establish public order. Meanwhile Cohn-Bendit was expelled from France.

This was quickly followed by a national election where de Gaulle's support in the French Assembly was still strong but slipping. The writing was on the wall.

This was the prelude to de Gaulle's last act that led to his resignation – the ill-fated Referendum.

---

372 My older son Laurence who had attended Harvard then Oxford went to the Sorbonne to polish his French before returning to Canada to complete his education at the University of Toronto Law School.

His final act as President was to press for a Referendum to change the social dialogue in France that failed to carry[373]. Perhaps he was influenced by Mao's cultural revolution as he wanted to change the social outlook in France and to emphasize citizen 'participation' in power sharing. When the Referendum failed, de Gaulle immediately gave up his office[374].

De Gaulle's solitary acts of leadership survived him and took him to the zenith of democratic leadership in the 20ᵗʰ century. In the end, he founded the Fifth Republic of France that survives and thrives as a leading democratic liberal power in Europe and he remains the most popular leader in French history.

Recall that de Gaulle was leader of France from 1944 to 1946. Suddenly in 1946 without conferring with his Cabinet, de Gaulle called them together and announced he was retiring from public life tired of domestic political divisiveness. He kept in touch travelling to Paris once a week to a small office to confer with political and cultural leaders. From the side lines, he led his political party Rally of the French People (RFP) almost to majority in the French Assembly. In midst of Algerian crisis, he deft paved his return to power in 1958 becoming President. As President in 1963, he led to the historic 'rapproachment' between France and Germany, enemies for over 100 years, with Konrad Adenauer that help stabilize Europe that led to the 'Élysée Treaty' which led to a new constitution which enhanced Presidential powers. Rebuffed in a Referendum, he suddenly left office in 1967, commenced his first memoirs, published one to wide acclaim before he died. The second remained unfinished[375]. He died shortly thereafter in 1970 where 63 heads of state attended his state funeral. As he said, like Moses, he 'crossed the desert'.

---

373 The substance of the Referendum included powers to enlarged regional governments, transforming the Senators into the New Regional Collectives who would share power with the new regional structures giving up the Senators 'direct' legal blocking powers. De Gaulle also preferred a two party system which was never accomplished. Many of the ideas in the Referendum came from Clemenceau's and Mandel's policies in the 1920's.

374 De Gaulle's last desire shortly before he died was to travel to China to visit with Mao.

375 Henry Louis Bergson books were constantly read and reread by de Gaulle as he penned his memoirs in retirement.

One aspect of de Gaulle's persona is often overlooked. He was and remained an officer and a gentleman. He was enchanted by women as they were intrigued by him, who dined with him or had lengthy encounters. Included in this list was Eleanor Roosevelt who admired de Gaulle unlike her husband; Pauline Vanier wife General Georges Vanier a World War II Canadian General and later Governor General of Canada; Princess Alice of Albany, wife of the Earle of Athlone, Governor General of Canada and the last surviving granddaughter of Queen Victoria; Clementine Churchill who carried on a long extensive correspondence with de Gaulle after she first met him and admonished de Gaulle to treat her husband less harshly[376] as she had earlier admonished her husband as well; Jacqueline Kennedy, wife of John F. Kennedy; Tina Rossi the opera diva; Edith Piaf the French chanteuse; Coco Chanel, the legendary designer; Lady Diana Cooper wife of Duff Cooper, U.K.'s liaison officer to Algeria during World War II and later Ambassador to France, who was a talented actress and writer. All these accomplished women spoke fluent French. Perhaps the most interesting, as de Gaulle loved the sight of beautiful women; he once spotted a youthful Catherine Deneuve racing past him in a fast car and commented, *"Why is she always in a hurry, she will soon be a star."* And she was.

De Gaulle accomplished extraordinary acts of statesmanship during his years of power. De Gaulle instilled a Gaullic catechism in his followers. No democratic leaders left such an entourage of acolytes of the left, centre and right to emulate and succeed him - Schuman, Bidault, Pleven, Faure, Pineau, Pinay, Mayer, Laniel, Mendes-France, Mollet, Pflimlin, Debre, Pompidou, Chaban-Delmas, Messmer, Giscard d'Estaing. Only Pompidou and d'Estaing became followers after de Gaulle had returned to France in 1944[377].

---

376 When de Gaulle finally resigned from public office he received a long moving letter from Clementine Churchill. He replied saying her letter was most moving *"...and it came to me, at the same time, in the name of the great and dear Winston Churchill. I thank you with all my heart."*

377 De Gaulle had a long relationship with Leon Blum, a socialist and first Jewish French Prime Minister in the '30s. Blum was receptive to de Gaulle's ideas increasing the

He restored France as a democratic power in world. While de Gaulle was a loner, self-absorbed, arrogant, stubborn, with an overwhelming sense of grandeur, he maintained an iron will to overcome patent failures and rejections. He was besotted with a sense of destiny and armed with a cool analytic, strategic tactical mind.

De Gaulle was intrigued by Churchill's raised forefingers in a V for Victory gesture. De Gaulle's iconic gesture occurred when he raised in both arms up right and with clenched fists in a gigantic V while roaring "*Vive Le France*" which remains an indelible memory.

He owns the tribute as the greatest democratic leader of the 20ᵗʰ century[378].

De Gaulle wrote the following:

- *La Discorde Chez l'Ennemi* (1924)
- *Histoire des Troupes du Levant* (1931) written by Major de Gaulle and Major Yvon, with Staff Colonel de Mierry collaborating in the preparation of the final text.

---

military budget at the time. They kept up a long correspondence. Blum stayed in France, was imprisoned first by Vichy and then by the Nazis. He was incarcerated with Georges Mandel in last part of the war in Buchenwald in Germany. The Allies bombed the entrances to Buchenwald that triggered Blum's departure. Earlier Mandel was taken away to die at hands of the Nazis and their Vichy collaborators while on a train. Blum survived his last hazardous trips to Germany taken from prison to prison (including Dachau near the centre of Munich) until he was miraculously liberated and survived. Immediately after his liberation de Gaulle met him on his return to France and offered him a post in de Gaulle's first provisional Cabinet. Blum, weakened by his ordeal, refused. De Gaulle was upset. They resumed a lengthy correspondence. Blum urged de Gaulle to commute Petain's death sentence.

378 In 1960 on de Gaulle's state visit to Washington, Walter Lippman, one of America's most respected journalists wrote the most glowing tribute he ever published for any public figure – "*The secret is that he is more than a great man... but truly a genius. De Gaulle has the capacity to see beneath the surface of events, to see through the obvious and conventional and stereotyped appearances of events to the significant realities, to the observed facts and forces that will prevail.*" It was the "*second sight of history*"... and with it "*the gift of prophesying what is going to happen because the seeing eye is already there*".

- *Le Fil de l'Épée* (1932)
- *Vers l'Armée de Métier* (1934)
- *La France et son Armée* (1938)
- *Trois Études* (1945) (Rôle Historique des Places Fortes; Mobilisation Economique à l'Étranger; Comment Faire une Armée de Métier) followed by the Memorandum of 26 January 1940.
- *Mémoires de Guerre*
- Volume I – L'Appel 1940–1942 (1954)
- Volume II – L'Unité, 1942–1944 (1956)
- Volume III – Le Salut, 1944–1946 (1959)
- *Mémoires d'Espoir*
- Volume I – Le Renouveau 1958–1962 (1970)
- Discours et Messages
- Volume I – Pendant la Guerre 1940–1946 (1970)
- Volume II – Dans l'attente 1946–1958 (1970)
- Volume III – Avec le Renouveau 1958–1962 (1970)
- Volume IV – Pour l'Effort 1962–1965 (1970)
- Volume V – Vers le Terme 1966–1969

English translations:

- *The Enemy's House Divided (La Discorde chez l'ennemi).* Tr. by Robert Eden. University of North Carolina Press, Chapel Hill, 2002.
- *The Edge of the Sword (Le Fil de l'Épée).* Tr. by Gerard Hopkins. Faber, London, 1960 Criterion Books, New York, 1960
- *The Army of the Future (Vers l'Armée de Métier).* Hutchinson, London-Melbourne, 1940. Lippincott, New York, 1940
- *France and Her Army (La France et son Armée).* Tr. by F.L. Dash. Hutchinson London, 1945. Ryerson Press, Toronto, 1945
- *War Memoirs: Call to Honour, 1940–1942* (L'Appel). Tr. by Jonathan Griffin. Collins, London, 1955 (2 volumes). Viking Press, New York, 1955.
- *War Memoirs: Unity, 1942–1944 (L'Unité).* Tr. by Richard Howard (narrative) and Joyce Murchie and Hamish Erskine (documents). Weidenfeld & Nicolson, London, 1959 (2 volumes). Simon & Schuster, New York, 1959 (2 volumes).
- War Memoirs: Salvation, 1944–1946 (Le Salut). Tr. by Richard Howard (narrative) and Joyce Murchie and Hamish Erskine

(documents). Weidenfeld & Nicolson, London, 1960 (2 volumes). Simon & Schuster, New York, 1960 (2 volumes).

- *Memoirs of Hope: Renewal, 1958–1962.* Endeavour, 1962– (Le Renouveau) (L'Effort). Tr. by Terence Kilmartin. Weidenfeld & Nicolson, London, 1971.

Below is a partial bibliography:

- *Charles de Gaulle. War Memoirs. Volume One. The Call to Honour 1940-1942*, translated by Jonathan Griffin, Simon and Schuster, New York, 1964
- *Political Leaders of the 20ᵗʰ Century: de Gaulle – A Political Biography* by Alexander Werth, Penguin Books, 1965
- *The General: A New and Revealing Portrait of the Man Who Is France* by Pierre Galante, Leslie Frewin, London, 1969
- *Georges Mandel and The Third Republic* by John M. Sherwood, Stanford University Press, 1970
- *The Duel: de Gaulle and Pompidou* by Philippe Alexandre, Houghton Mifflin, Boston, 1972
- *A Certain Eventuality... Britain and The Fall of France* by P.M.H. Bell, Saxon House, 1974
- *Charles de Gaulle: The Edge of The Sword* translated from the French by Gerard Hopkins, Greenwood Press, 1975
- *Malraux: A Biography* by Alex Madsen, William Morrow and Company Inc, New York, 1976
- *Leo Blum* by Jean Lacouture translated by George Holoch, Holmes& Meier Publishers Inc., 1982
- *White House Years* by Henry Kissinger, Little, Brown and Company, 1979
- *Charles de Gaulle: A Biography* by Don Cook, G.P. Putman's Sons, New York, 1983
- *De Gaulle* by Sam White, Harrap Ltd, 1984
- *Pierre Mendes France* by Jean Lacouture, translated by George Holoch, Holmes and Meier, 1984
- *Petain Hero or Traitor: The Untold Story* by Herbert R. Lottman, William Morrow and Company Inc., 1985
- *Duff Cooper: The Authorized Biography* by John Charmley Weidenfeld and Nicholson, 1986

- *De Gaulle The Ruler: 1945-1970* by Jean LaCouture, HarperCollins Publishers, 1991
- *The Locust Years: The Story of the Fourth French Republic, 1946-1958* by Frank Giles, Reed Consumer Books London, 1991
- *The General: Charles de Gaulle and the France He Saved* by Jonathan Fenby, Skyhorse Publishing, 2013
- *A Certain Idea of France: The Life of Charles de Gaulle* by Julian Jackson, Allen Lane, Penguin Random House, 2018
- *Left Bank: Art, Passion and the Rebirth of Paris, 1940-50* by Agnès Poirier, Henry Holt And Company, 2018

THE TWO GREATEST LEADERS IN THE 20TH CENTURY: R. MENACHEM MENDEL SCHNEERSON A.H.L. (1902-1994) AND POPE JOHN PAUL II (1920-2005)

The 20th century was populated by powerful leaders – both democratic and autocratic - who planted their oversized footprints on world history. Political leaders' with clear ideologies like Churchill, Roosevelt, Stalin and Mao reverberated till the end of the century. Other unique leaders with a religious bent like Gandhi, the Dalai Lama, Martin Luther King and Mother Teresa while impactful did not realize their goals of injecting tolerance and equality via civil disobedience and their good works or even convinced their leading followers to unite diverse publics behind their tolerant aims and principles.

No leaders in any field matched the indelible individual contributions of R. Menachem Mendel Schneerson and Karol Jozef Wojtyła, Pope John Paul II[379].

Most leaders possess a vein of narcissism inflated by the aphrodisiac of power. Most leaders thrive on their own conceits. These two men did what they did for the love of God and people.

Narcissism and power are inseparable. The human condition remains, as it has since time immemorial, flawed. Rare, when leaders' actions demonstrate that good can prevail over evil. The exceptions often prove the rule. Such is the case with Menachem Mendel Schneerson AHL known around the globe as the 'Rebbe' and Karol Jozef Wojtyła, Pope John Paul II, who became the two greatest leaders who set out to improve the human condition of the turbulent 20th century. No leaders' persona and actions made a deeper or more lasting positive impression around the globe on the 20th century and beyond.

Each man shared remarkably similar roots, traits and talents, though of different faiths. Both were born in Eastern Europe – the 'Rebbe' in a small town in south western Ukraine – Nikolaev, the Pope in a small town in south western Poland - Wadowice. Both, precocious as a youth, were recognized for their photographic memories. Both were considered prodigies by teachers and peers - the Rebbe was early considered a genius - an 'illui' - the equivalent in Hebrew. One of the Pope's earliest teachers likened to him as a 'genius'. Each had remarkable powers of concentration and retentive memories. Each were speed readers and devoured books. Each were superb linguists sharing the same languages – Russian, Polish, English, French, German, Hebrew and Yiddish amongst others. The Pope was brought up close to Jews in his small town neighbourhood. As a youth, the Pope lived next to a church as the Rebbe lived close to a synagogue. The Pope's closest lifelong friend was Jewish, a high school classmate in Wadowice, and a survivor who had moved to Rome after World War II and when Wojtyła became Pope revived and continue their fraternal relationship until the Pope's death. Jerzy Kluger, the Pope's oldest Jewish friend, was the first to experience a private audience in the Vatican when Wojtyła became Pope in Rome in 1978.

Both the Rebbe and the Pope were devout from early childhood. Both were indelibly influenced by their equally devout fathers. Both prayed and meditated regularly from youth. The Pope, as priest, Archbishop and then Pope, would privately prostrate himself especially when uncertainty and difficulties loomed. Both enjoyed deep, wide ranging, intellectual pursuits - the Pope - poetry, plays[380], languages and literature and the Rebbe – astronomy (who as a youth collected astronomy maps), chemistry, quantum physics, psychology, electrical engineering, math and even medicine[381],[382]. Wojtyła dabbled in science while Schneerson

---

379 Menachem Mendel from the Hebrew means to comfort or console. Jozef from the Bible Joseph means God will add, or God will increase.

380 The Pope as a young priest published poetry and a play that was staged.

381 The Rebbe was educated in math, physics and chemical engineering at Humboldt University, University of Berlin, Paris and later New York City. He audited classes in the humanities in Berlin, the Sorbonne in Paris and New York. While he was at university, he would take daily ritual baths and prayers to keep his mind pure and focused, and protected against secular influences.

382 The Rebbe fascinated by astronomy as a youth, studied quantum physics. Einstein's two theories – the theory of relativity was his overreaching examine of into the

enjoyed reading world literature. Both had wide circles of friends and admirers yet were considered loners. Both were profound biblical scholars. Both were voracious readers and maintained capacious libraries and delighted in collecting rare antique books on subjects of interest. Both enjoyed and were skilled at chess. Both attracted early attention and admirers for their undeniable talents and inviting, amiable, understated, modest personalities.

Each encountered and studied the evils of Communism and Nazism at first hand and were determined to bring a higher morality to the world. Both became a master, if unsung, organizer of the Soviet 'dissident' movement – the Rebbe across Russia and Ukraine, the Pope in Poland and European states under Soviet dominance.

Both reluctantly inherited the leadership of their religious institutions, and both, as reformers, modernized their faiths' finances, outreach and multiplied their global followership. Both went against the grain and the advice of even their closest advisors to adhere their own traditional belief structures. Both admired their fathers and sought to emulate them. Both were charismatic teachers and speakers in small or large audiences. The Pope adored his mother who passed due to illness while he was a youth[383]. The Rebbe was separated from his mother for decades[384]. Both were talented authors[385,386] and inveterate letter writers

---

nature of the universe while his quantum theory imbedded in quantum mechanics probed the substantial world. The Rebbe also studied the Kabbalah (The Reception) based on an 11th century school of Jewish mysticism that alluded to the 'black hole' theory of creation called the 'spark of blackness'. Stephen Hawkins, the brilliant thinker who sought to explore the 'meaning of everything' wrote, "...the ultimate triumph of human reason—for then we would truly know the mind of God."

383 The Pope's adoration of Mary was significantly part of his belief structure.

384 When the Rebbe's mother finally arrived in Brooklyn, he visited her every day until her death for decades.

385 The Rebbe wrote a masterful work on Maimonides. The Pope as Archbishop wrote a complex book analysing love, both sexual and spiritual called Love and Responsibility in 1960 assisted by a female psychologist.

386 As an Archbishop participated in Pope John XXVIII first Conclave, Wojtyła subtly disagreed with Pope John XXVIII who believed in co-existence with Communism. Wojtyła vigorously disagreed with him.

and letter readers[387]. Both shared the incessant goal of improving the human condition and imbuing a deep concern for each individual they encountered. Both leaders believed in the family as the core of civilized society. Both encourage large family units. Both fought secularism as they both believed that it was a harbinger of the weakening of the family and belief in faith. Both sought to rationalize their religious beliefs with science. Both believed in Biblical creation and carefully studied and applied notions of mathematics theory and scientific measurement to justify their belief.

Both opposed Marxist ideology that taught religion was the 'opium of the masses'. Both were experts in Marxist thought. The Rebbe insisted on rigorous religious education and maturity for young people before seeking a higher secular education. The Pope first attracted to 'Liberation Theology' then fought against its ideology because he felt it led to a drift towards Marxism and faithlessness[388]. Each became a confidante of world leaders and offered sage practical advice on the fissures and flaws of the world. Children flocked and adored them, which each easily reciprocated. Both were tolerant – the Pope in his homilies and brilliant Encyclicals and the Rebbe in promoting the 'Noahide Laws' and his prolific homilies on the weekly teachings in the Torah and the Talmuds. Both constantly sought to rationalize science with faith[389]. Both men and women were deeply motivated and attracted to them. Both recognized

---

387 The 'Rebbe' would weekly visit the grave of his father-in-law, the Sixth Lubavitch Rebbe in Crown Heights and pour over his voluminous mail each seeking advice and blessings and would then respond to each letter.

388 The Pope promulgated 14 Encyclicals all of which he carefully edited. Each was a clarity of precision.

389 The Rebbe was influenced by the medieval Jewish thinker Maimonides who wrote 'A Guide to the Perplexed' and often wrote and spoke homilies about him. Maimonides, a medieval Jewish doctor sought to rationalize his orthodox faith with science. Maimonides is buried in a small cemetery in Tiberius. My ancestor the Sheloh is buried next to him. The Pope's Encyclical in 1998 was titled 'Fides and Ratio – Faith and Reason'. He wrote "Science can purify religion from error and superstition. Religion can purify science from idolatry and false absolutes." In Genesis in the accounting of creation in seven days, the length of each day is not defined.

the equality of women in society and expanded the role of women within the spheres of each of their faiths.

Both, at first, craved worldly careers. Both devoured daily newspapers in several languages. Both worked eighteen hour days and more. The Rebbe longed to pursue an academic scientific career in electrical engineering[390], chemistry, math or physics. The Pope as a youth became a talented actor and wished, at first, to pursue a life in languages, poetry, literature and the stage. Both enjoyed music and had fine musical voices. Both were strong and athletic, the Pope a skilled skier and avid swimmer, and the Rebbe a youthful strong swimmer[391]. Both were reluctant to take on leadership unlike others like Churchill, Roosevelt, Stalin and Mao who harboured early ambitions of leadership and power[392]. Both the Rebbe and the Pope eschewed the attractions and pleasures of power. Both encountered the everyday travail and circumstances of totalitarianism – Nazism and Communism - that compelled their consciences to contest what they and their co-religionists confronted. Both believed in upholding ethical legal aspects of even autocratic regimes. Both believed in the sanctity of the individual[393]. Both gained superb instincts and when motivated to act swiftly to events, would carefully calibrate even his

---

390 The Rebbe living in New York City during World War II worked in the Brooklyn Shipyards and designed electrical systems for Liberty Cargo ships. The Pope worked at numerous jobs as a labourer, including stone quarries, hoping to be an actor, before choosing to become a priest.

391 As a youthful swimmer, the Rebbe dove into the frigid sea to save another youth from drowning. He recalled later that that swim effected his chest and he suffered discomfort for the rest of his life as a result. The Pope had a swimming pool built at his summer residence so he could swim for exercise.

392 The Rebbe waited two years after the Previous Rebbe's death hoping another would take on the mantle of Lubavitch leadership. When none appeared with a broad consensus, the Rebbe was reluctantly persuaded to take on the leadership of the Lubavitch movement. The Pope when he attended the 1978 Conclave to appoint the successor of John Paul I, refused to believe he would be elected. Reluctant to the end, he was surprised and overwhelmed when on the fifth ballot, he was finally chosen.

393 Pope John II called this the condition of an individual being a subject rather than an object.

minutest response. How each in his own way battled evil and autocratic regimes remains two of the most remarkable stories of the 20th century.

I was privileged to have two lengthy encounters with the Pope – first in Toronto and then in The Vatican in Rome in private audiences and two encounters briefly in Ottawa and Toronto[394] and two lengthy meetings

---

394 My first encounter with Pope John Paul II took place in the '70s at the home of Stanley Haidasz near High Park in Toronto. Stanley was a Polish born practicing doctor, a Polish nationalist and devout Catholic who knew of my father's record as a decorated Polish war veteran in World War I and who then went back to join the Pilsudski Brigade and to serve in the Polish War of Independence (1918-1921). Stanley was a friend, a Liberal member of Parliament, the first Minister of Multi-culturism under Pierre Trudeau. Stanley invited me to meet and have tea with his distinguished visitor, the Archbishop of Krakow, Karol Wojtyła. It turned out that his father and mine, both born in southern Poland less than 100 kilometers apart, had both served in the Pilsudski Brigades and in the momentous battle of Warsaw in 1920 where the Red Army led by Trotsky was defeated, for the first time despite larger number of Red troops. Wojtyła a tall, well-built man in an athletic frame who to my amazement spoke English, Yiddish and Hebrew. We both thoroughly enjoyed sharing stories of our late fathers. That slender but splendid thread led to two private audiences in Rome and brief encounters in Ottawa and Toronto when as Pope he attended a massive Catholic Youth Conference, a key organizer of which was my long-time friend and Catholic and Liberal activist Dennis Mills. In 1985, Dennis invited me to a small dinner where he seated me the only non-Catholic between Cardinal Carter and Cardinal Ratzinger, later to become Pope Benedict XVI, where we exchanged views at length and discussed his relationship with Pope John Paul II. The dinner was arranged by Father James Jim' McConica one of Canada's and the world's outstanding scholars who taught and studied at All Soul's College in Oxford where he befriended my son Laurence. Later Father McConica became head of St. Michaels College in Toronto.

Each time Pope John Paul II and I met, he would open the conversation with "Let's talk about our fathers" and our common Polish roots. Pope John Paul II trans-formed the church, its teachings and rooted out its discrimination towards Jews and Judaism and softened the church's previous history of antagonism towards Israel. He first visited Israel as an Archbishop. All progress by a winding staircase. Throughout his Papacy, he spoke out repeatedly and forcibly against the rising scourge of anti-semitism. He was the first Pope to visit a synagogue in Rome, to visit Auschwitz, to visit Jerusalem, to pray at the Wailing Wall, to pay his respects at Yad Vashem and to recognize the State of Israel.

with the Rebbe in his headquarters at 770 Eastern Parkway in Crown Heights, Brooklyn, first with my family and later alone. Up close each again demonstrated similar traits. Both had blue penetrating eyes who made one feel like they were reading your mind. They were both quiet avid listeners, digesting each word you uttered and then quietly responding concisely with startling insight into your thinking. Both were most careful with their words. Both, we are told, refused to make fun or bully others or tolerate these traits in others. Both made you feel you were the only person in the world at that moment of contact. Both men filled the room with their physical presence. Both were powerfully built handsome men with penetrating eyes. Both were quiet in private dialogue making you believe what you said was of the utmost importance and relevance.

In his 1994 book entitled '*Crossing the Threshold of Hope*', given to me by my great friend and mentor, the late Emmett Cardinal Carter, which I cherish, John Paul II wrote these words:

Through the plurality of religion... we come to that religion closest to our own... that of the people of God of the Old Testament...

... The declaration Nostra Aetate represents a turning point... since the spiritual patronage (of Jews) is so great, the... Council reminds and promotes a mutual understanding and respect...

Remembering in his hometown where his school backed upon a synagogue, the Pope wrote:

... both religious groups were united... by the awareness that they prayed to the same God.

The Pope continued:

... a personal experience. Auschwitz... the Holocaust of the Jewish people shows to what length a system constructed on... racial hatred and greed for power can go...

There he wrote:

To this day, Auschwitz does not cease to admonish... reminding us that anti-Semitism is a great sin against humanity...

Allow me to repeat the Pope's words, "*anti-Semitism is a great sin against humanity.*" The Pope went on:

... a truly exceptional experience was my visit to the Synagogue in Rome... the history of the Jews of Rome... is linked... to the Acts of the Apostles.

Each fell ill and faced their infirmities without complaint with internal fortitude. Each encounter was a memorable indelible experience. I will never encounter again the chemistry and magic of being in each of their presence. Millions have felt the same sense of exaltation by watching and listening to them from afar or via the media. Their major accomplishments were legendary and much unknown.

A short history of my encounters with the 'Rebbe' and a concise history of his Lubavitch predecessors.

When Rabbi Zalman Grossbaum in Toronto, Lubavitch's chief organizer in Toronto, first approached me to be the honouree for the 18th Annual Chabad Dinner in 1996, I declined. My wife agreed. We had never accepted such an invitation in the past. We both felt that there were others, many others, in this community, who were not only much more worthy of this honour, and would provide a greater magnet of attraction.

But Rabbi Grossbaum persisted. Rabbi Grossbaum possesses great powers of persuasion. After several months and calls from many friends, I reluctantly agreed. What finally convinced me was when Rabbi Grossbaum called to say he was about to visit the Lubavitch Rebbe's grave ('matzevah') in Crown Heights on the Rebbe's Yahrzeit and needed to know what he should put in his 'kwittel', his written message to the Rebbe. So I agreed still feeling unworthy of this singular honour.

Humility seizes and paralyses one just to have one's name associated with the grand and mysterious history of Lubavitch and their extraordinary leaders. In the Torah and Talmud, seven is a mystical number. We are told... 'all those who are seventh are cherished and all those who are seventh are most beloved'. Just as there was seven prophets from Abraham to Moses, so there have been seven great rebbes who transformed the Chassidic movement and created a living force within that movement called 'Chabad Lubavitch'. The 'Rebbe' was the seventh, left no offspring and so was the last of his line.

The founder of "Chabad", Schneur Zalman, was born in 1745 in 'White' Russia. Of first Rebbe, the Previous Rebbe (the Sixth Rebbe) once wrote, each man is like the burning bush seen by Moses. Each man burns with desire to do good deeds and have good thoughts, but Schneur Zalman, the first Lubavitch Rebbe - the 'ershte' Rebbe did much more as the most conspicuous, third generation successor to the 'Baal Shem Tov', - the acknowledged founder of the Chassidic movement in Eastern Europe who died in 1760. Reb Schneur Zalman created, through his personal leadership, by his humane ability to attract followers, and by his high standards of intellectual excellence, a precise and detailed and coherent formula for living a good life. 'Chabad', he wrote in his major Canon - *the Tanya* - Chabad is an acronym for three words, wisdom, understanding and knowledge.

Three words, yet each word, expressed within the mystical context of the Kabbala, a mystical rendition of creation and more, is replete with complexity and pierces the inner heart and awakens the soul of man. Awake, awake, he taught, as has each Lubavitch Rebbe after him, awake to the possibilities of a fuller, better life by good thoughts and daily good deeds.

1996 was the 200th anniversary of the first publication of the 'Tanya' - ('It is taught') the great platform and masterpiece of Lubavitch Chassidic thought written by the First Lubavitch Rebbe.

The last Rebbe, the 7th Rebbe, our Rebbe, may he rest in peace, said that each chassid, each faithful man, has it within him to be a leader. To lead, one must lead his own mind. One must lead his own soul. Only by actions and deeds, only by one's own conduct can we hope to have others follow. You cannot change yesterday, you can only improve today and tomorrow, he taught.

The Rebbe said 'to lead' means leadership in issues large and small. To lead oneself is a daily, hourly, even a minute by minute struggle. So leadership he taught starts and ends with oneself. The world can be changed by 'one man'. To 'repair the world', one must not neglect to repair oneself. This ideology lies at the core of Lubavitch Chassidism.

My own family roots had deeply rooted in 'Chassidism' or 'Hasidism'. My late father, Simcha Shlomo, as his father before him, was a Chassid, a Shomer Shabbos (a strict adherent to the rules of the Shabbath) and a lifelong student of the two Talmuds and the Torah. He was a 'Talmid Chacham', a scholar of the two Talmuds. He and his ancestors were followers of the 'Ger' Hasidism. Mother's father, my grandfather, of blessed memory, Israel Isaac Bleeman was a Chassid, a student of the "Sfas Emes" (the Mouth of Truth), the first Gerer Rebbe in Poland.

My maternal grandfather studied in Poland with the Gerer Rebbe's son and successor, the 'Imre Emes' (the Lip of Truth) before he emigrated to Canada planning to ultimately settle in Argentina based on his Rebbe's advice.

My maternal grandmother was a direct descendent of the legendary 17th century Rebbe and scholar Isaiah Horowitz called the 'Sheloh' – an acronym for his 'magnus opus' in thirty volumes – *The Two Tablets of the Covenant*.

The 'Sheloh' was born near Prague in 1570. His meteoric chassidic career, across Europe, led from Chief Rabbi of Dubnow, to Ostraha, to Prague and then to Frankfurt and finally, after the death of his wife, he left Europe to settle in the Holy Land in 1621 with the intent to settle in Safed (Sfat) to study the Kabbalah with the masters living there. Instead when he arrived in Jerusalem, he started a yeshiva there and was elected the first Ashkenazi Chief Rabbi of Jerusalem, where he completed his masterpiece - *'The Two Tablets of the Covenant'*. The 'Sheloh' was imprisoned by the Ottomans. Ransom was raised from co-religionists across the Middle East and when released, the 'Sheloh' made his way to north Safed (Sfat). On his way to Sfat, he died in 1727 near Tiberius. The 'Sheloh' was buried next to the 'Rambam' - the great Maimonides, in a small cemetery in Tiberias where a small number of famour deceased Rabbis are also buried starting in early post Biblical times. Why is this relevant to Chabad Lubavitch? The namesake. The namesake of the Seventh Rebbe was Menachem Mendel of Vitebsk, a Chassid leader who left his home in Vitebsk, Russia and settled in ancient Safed (Sfat) with 300 of his followers in 1777. He was a prolific book and letter writer whose fame spread throughout the Jewish world. When encountering difficulties with the Ottoman authorities, Menachem Mendel of Vitebsk (sometimes called 'of Horodok') and 300 of his followers settled in ancient city Tiberius in northern Palestine where he built a synagogue in 1786 that is still existing. When he passed in 1788, he was buried near this small cemetery in Tiberius that still exists near the Sea of Galilee where my ancestor, the 'Sheloh' is also buried along with Maimonides[395] and a few rabbinic leaders of antiquity. This small cemetery is considered one of the holiest sites in Israel.

The Seventh Rebbe was also named after his ancestor, the third Lubavitch Rebbe, who in turn had been named for Menachem Mendel of Vitebsk. Names are important. Schneur Zalman the first Lubavitch Rebbe was a friend and learned colleague of Menachem Mendel of Vitebsk.

Amongst the first discourses, the Seventh 'Rebbe' gave when succeeding the 'Previous' Rebbe in 1951 as the head of Lubavitch movement, he described the founder of Chabad, the first Rebbe, Schneur Zalman of Liadi, as a 'Sheloh Yid', a Sheloh Jew!, a follower of the Sheloh.

The Rebbe explained Schneur Zalman's reliance on the Sheloh's written masterpiece, the 'Two Tablets the Covenant', 'Shnei Luchos Habris' and he used the Sheloh's called the 'Shar Hashomayim' - the Gates of Heaven. These two principle texts, were used by both the First Rebbe and his son and successor, 'Dovber' as instruments of devotion and teaching. That's the good news.

The bad news is when the second Rebbe, Dovber (called the Mittler Rebbe) was in the process of consolidating his position as the head of the Lubavitch movement as a son and successor of Schneur Zalman in 1814, he was challenged by his closest friend and co-student, Reb Aharon Halevi. A fierce struggle for leadership broke out between their respective supporters based on differing principles of prayer and practise.

Reb Aharon Halevi almost succeeded in splitting Lubavitch in two camps. Rebbe Dovber met this challenge and succeeded in capturing the leadership of the Lubavitch movement and the vast majority of its followers with his superior cerebral erudition, devotion and ideas. The conflict was resolved when Reb Aharon left Lubavitch and set up a much smaller splinter group in Starosselye.

---

395 Maimonides together with one of the world's greatest lawgivers, Moses, each has a plaque of a marble profile, along with 21 other ancient lawgivers which are displayed, over the entrance to the United States House of Representatives in Washington. From *"Moses to Moses"* as the Rebbes and others have proclaimed - from one great lawgiver to the other – *"There is no lawqiver like Moses!"* Maimonides remains buried in Egypt were reburied in the small cemetery in Tiberius next to my ancestor – the 'Sheloh'.

That same Rebbe Aharon Halevi, of Starosselye, was also a direct descendant of my ancestor, the 'Sheloh.' So my family roots predate and yet are deeply entwined in the history of Chabad and stretches from the 16ᵗʰ century to the present day.

Privileged to meet with the Rebbe on two occasions, each time, I came away with the overwhelming belief that I was in the presence of an extraordinary man destined to be recorded as one of the great leaders in the 20ᵗʰ century and not just within the context of Judaism[396].

I started to study the lives of each of the seven leaders of the Chabad and their voluminous works when available in English. One could only scratch the surface. Each Rebbe lived a blindingly splendid life of devotion and prodigious intellectualism. Each Rebbe, through his writings and by his actions are considered 'Tzaddikim' – righteous men, the holiest of men. Yet all were not perfect. All made mistakes like the prophets of old.

Several were imprisoned for their beliefs. Many were detained and interrogated by authorities for their practises including the 'Previous' Rebbe who was imprisoned seven times. All, all risked their lives for their faithful. In the Tanya, the first Rebbe divided the Jewish community into two parts. The holiest men – 'Tzaddikim' - he wrote could achieve

---

396 On April 18, 1978, the Rebbe the secular date of his birthday (11th Nissan in the Hebrew calendar) started an international campaign to support education across the globe. For this effort, Education Day was established in 1978 by Jimmy Carter. In April 1993, this day was proclaimed again this time by a unanimous vote of Congress based on a Resolution proclaimed by President Bill Clinton. The Rebbe was the first religious leader to be awarded the Congressional Gold Medal on 5 January 1994 the highest Congressional award to citizens awarded to less than 100 others. A short personal experience. Rabbi Grossbaum asked me to arrange a meeting of Chabad Rabbis across Canada with Prime Minister Pierre Trudeau to commemorate Education Day hoping to influence the Canadian government to follow the American lead. This couldn't be arranged at the time. Later a meeting did take place in Toronto during a by-election in Eglinton. They presented him with a Bible in Hebrew and English as a gift from the Rebbe – a copy of the same Bible that had been presented to Presidents Carter and Clinton. Pierre Trudeau became fascinated with this group of bearded men. After a meeting that stretched to longer than an hour, Trudeau asked me if I could arrange for a meeting with Rebbe in Crown Heights. To my regret, that did not happen.

perfection in word and deed. While others in the wider community could only strive for perfection. Every man had his place in repairing himself and the world. Even a cursory glance at the works written by the first Rebbe or the mystical and majestic works of Rebbe Dovber, the second Rebbe who wrote magnificent discourses on ecstasy and on meditation, we find all the Rebbes' never lost sight of the importance of the ordinary Jew.

In fact, Dovber's books burst with brilliant ideas on pain and pleasure - precise definitions of emotions and mind, on human psychology, that preceded Freud and Jung by over 100 years. Only by a broken spirit, - only by 'tzubrochenheit' - he wrote, could one hope to rebuild oneself from within with greater truth or stronger vision or reach a higher state of self-awareness. Freud and Jung argued from the same premise. But the Rebbes taught that preoccupation with one's thoughts, one's own concerns, are not enough. Thoughts must be matched by good deeds to others to achieve a better life.

The 3rd (Rebbe Tzemach Tzedek), 4th (Rebbe Maharash) and 5th (Rebbe Rashab), each wrote equally impressive and voluminous works. Words are precious. They taught. Each word is essential. Words can teach or maim or kill. Care, great care, therefore, must be taken with daily speech, with each spoken word.

Nothing is unimportant. The Seventh Rebbe taught that each letter, each word, each combination of words or letters, even the pronunciation of each word is crucial. Even the humblest letter 'Yud', the smallest letter was used in the word that created the world. So all letters, all words, any words spoken or written, whether in private or public, whether in gossip or politics, must be used with great care. All Rebbes stressed repeatedly the importance and care to be given to each written and spoken word!

Reading the autobiography of the 'Previous' Rebbe, ('Rayatz') Rebbe Yosef Yitzchak, one is awestruck by the simplicity yet depth of his thought and the humility of his deeds. So scholarship is a tradition in the Chabad. In Toronto especially, the Schoichet family who are outstanding scholars on Rabbinics & 'Kabbala', in the Lubavitch tradition. Rabbi Immanuel Schoichet's books allow one to begin to lift the veil and penetrate the pathways of the Talmud, the Kabbala and Chassidism itself.

To even have a cursory knowledge or sure grasp, requires not only an understanding in English but in the ancient languages of Hebrew and Aramaic. So much is beyond my reach without greater scholarship.

Yet the work of the last two Rebbes and the still hidden impact that they made to capture the hearts, souls, minds of the millions of Jews trapped in Russia before 'Perestroika' is still not widely known or probed by historians of this era. They perform the greatest of 'mitzvot' - good deeds - they saved lives. They did more. They helped ignite the first sparks in the second Russian Revolution, the counter Russian Revolution, that led to the collapse of Soviet Empire seven decades later.

I came upon the hidden work of Lubavitch in Russia after the Russian Revolution in 1917 in a strange, almost accidental way. Carole and I, together with some friends, joined George Cohon and travelled to the U.S.S.R for the opening of MacDonalds in Moscow in 1990. We were so busy, crowded with public events, dinners and meetings that we didn't have time to visit Jewish synagogues in Moscow. When we arrived in Leningrad (now St. Petersburg), we decided to make it our business to visit the large Leningrad Synagogue that had fallen into disrepair and only partial use before we left. It was Friday afternoon. I insisted that our Russian guide take us there before sunset – the start of the Jewish Sabbath.

After much persuasion, our guide – a KGB officer, who first insisted it was impossible to visit since the synagogue was closed made the necessary arrangements. Quickly he relented when we advised we would complain to our Russian hosts. We arrived by bus at 3 o'clock with more than twenty friends from Toronto – Jews and Gentiles. A door in the synagogue wooden wall surrounding the closed synagogue was unlocked by a 'shamus' – the custodian. He spoke in Yiddish. I asked if we could hold a 'Minucha' (afternoon) service before 'shabbos' (Sabbath).

The Russian guide retorted again - it was impossible. The synagogue could not be used for services. I insisted. The 'shamus' asked who would lead the service. I said I would. So I counted a minyan of 10 Jews who were present and we recited 'minucha' service – the afternoon service in Hebrew in the large dilapidated dusty once majestic synagogue. As we finished, the shamus beckoned me to follow him through a different exit.

Attached to the synagogue was a small 'shtebel' – a long narrow 'study room'.

There, several boys were studying Torah with a youthful bearded teacher. On the wall, as I left, I noticed a large coloured poster of the Rebbe. Surprised, I asked the 'shamus', "*When did Lubavitch get here?*" He said, "*Lubavitch was always here. They never left.*" This statement aroused my curiosity. It turned out to be almost a mystery story.

All are familiar with the recent history in Soviet Russia. We all witnessed the rise of 'dissident' movement, both Jew and Gentile. The plight of Sakharov and Sharansky are well documented. What is less documented and less known is the deadly struggle within Russia for religious freedom that started after the Russian Revolution in 1917 and continued until the collapse of the U.S.S.R in 1989. Faith can move mountains!!

When the Bolsheviks took control in Russia in 1917, one of their immediate aims was to, in practical terms, to wipe out religious freedom and dismantle religious institutions. The 'New Soviet man' was to be freed of the shackles of religion. According to Marx, 'religion was the opium of the masses'. While the written Soviet constitution allowed for freedom of religion, in practice, religious services and Bibles were forbidden. Religious schools disbanded. Prayer books were effectively outlawed. Particular attention was paid to the small, powerful Jewish community. Russia had millions of Russian Jews, most of whom were religious in orientation. The object of the Revolution was to change all that and to transform each person into a 'new' Soviet man or a 'new' Soviet woman, free of religious training, free of religious cant!

This was a strange and turbulent time. Some Jewish families were deeply divided. The Rebbe's own brother, became, for a time, a Marxist, then a Trotskyite. A short time later, he became an early Soviet dissident. Jews, at that period, were haunted by pogroms. Communists believed that 'Utopia' could be achieved by "*the rejection... of all notions of religiously and ethnicity*". The Seventh Rebbe, in 1919, as a 17 year old youth, even joined the local Jewish defense force to physically defend Jews who were under threat and attack. Departments of the Soviet government were established, staffed by Jews, including former

Chassidic Jews, who chose to become Communist in their politics and secular, atheistic, in their beliefs[397]. Special sections of the government staffed with these Jews, aimed to dismantle Jewish institutions, specifically Jewish religious institutions. This branch of government was called 'Yevseksia'. A primary target was the Lubavitch movement which had spread to virtually from its origins in western 'White' Russia to practically all parts of Russia.

The 'Previous' Rebbe was living in Leningrad at the time. He was under surveillance yet he recognized that to keep Chassidism alive in Russia, an underground movement must be immediately established. As each synagogue was closed and each yeshiva was dismantled, an underground version was immediately established.

In 1924, the 'Previous' Rebbe secretly called together nine heads of the Lubavitch 'Yeshivas' and they each swore to continue to build Judaism, even at the risk of their lives by each creating an underground 'Yeshiva'. This was highly dangerous work. The Previous Rebbe was imprisoned seven times, the last in 1927. Then and only through the efforts of followers and representations by political leaders in the west was he released from prison. This date is still celebrated in the Lubavitch movement.

The Seventh Rebbe married the Previous Rebbe's second daughter in Warsaw in 1928 though his father also a Schneerson by descent and a Rabbinic leader in his own right was exiled to Kazakhstan where he is buried in Almaty, the old capital of Kazakhstan[398]. Meanwhile Schneerson and his wife studied first in Berlin and then Paris, he in physics, math and engineering and she in mathematics and architecture. Both were classical music lovers. He also attended classes in philosophy, Gestalt psychology and child psychology. Meanwhile he continued to take on tasks assigned him by his father-in-law.

---

397 The 'new' Soviet men in their Marxist utopia substituted traditional religious beliefs for Marxism.

398 While on a visit to Astana, the modernistic capital of Kazakhstan, at the suggestion of the Lubavitch Chief Rabbi of Kazakhstan, I urged the government to allow a heritage plaque to be posted at the gate of Jewish cemetery in Almaty where the Rebbe's father, exiled by the Soviets, was buried. Alas, still not done.

The 'Previous' Rebbe moved from place to place across Europe until, in 1940, he secretly left Warsaw and travelled to Riga, Latvia[399] and from there was brought to Crown Heights in Brooklyn, where the impoverished and decimated Lubavitch movement was recreated. The Lubavitch headquarters at 770 Eastern Parkway became firmly established in America.

Schneerson and his wife followed and joined his father-in-law, the 'Previous' Rebbe, months later in 1941. When he arrived in New York, he continued his studies in electrical engineering at a New York university. Throughout all that period to the end, the Previous Rebbe and Schneerson kept in close contact with dissident leaders in each community in Russia - with the underground. Indeed if one were to trace the dissident movement, a direct link can be made to the sparks that were lit by these efforts starting in 1917. These efforts were not sporadic. They were comprehensive. They were detailed. They were community oriented, house by house, street by street, synagogue by synagogue, yeshiva by yeshiva - one Jew at a time. The Previous Rebbe convinced his son-in-law and ultimate successor to take charge of this secret complex and dangerous activity starting in the mid '30s which he did with enthusiasm and skill.

Regularly Chabad messengers (shelichim) male and even male and female couples were secretly sent to live covert lives behind the 'Iron Curtain', to teach at underground schools and keep the flame of faith alive. The Jewish flame, the flame of religious freedom, was kept glowing at great personal cost and many times at the risk of death or imprisonment.

It is my hope that in the fullness of time, this remarkable, still hidden, still unknown history of the 20th century can be told by mainstream historians of this era. Historians will conclude as I did, that first cracks in the Soviet Empire were started by Lubavitch and widened by their silent, covert, yet relentless organized efforts. There are few stories which are known because they were published.

Many stories have been slowly published, but the story of Herman Branover, one of the world's leading scientists who was educated in Soviet

---

399   The fascinating story of the assistance the Previous Rebbe received to travel secretly
    across Nazi occupied Europe is in itself a miracle.

Russia, I found most instructive. Branover came from an assimilated Jewish family in Russia. His father was an atheist and was killed in World War II. His grandfather would take him occasionally to synagogue but he was educated in the Soviet system and was an atheist. He began his search for a better life after he has roughed up on the streets. This was during the anti-Semitic policies of Stalin in the late '40s and early '50s. While he swiftly moved up the academic ladder and was involved in the highest levels of strategic scientific research in the USSR, he became increasingly curious about Judaism. In the '60s, he decided to attend a small basement, an underground 'shtebel' in Moscow for Saturday services, to avoid detection. There he met his first Chabad Chassid. He was invited to the Chabadnik's home and they began discussions about physics and space.

They discussed the kabbalistic ideas of creation, questions of time, space and even Einstein's theory of relativity. He was persuaded to put on 'tefillin' (two black boxes, one for the forehead the other on the left arm containing scripts from the Bible) for the first time. Soon he learned about the Rebbe himself. He began to receive handwritten 'sichot' (teachings, speeches) of the Rebbe's in the mail because they could not be transmitted otherwise.

At the end of the '80s, he decided to emigrate from Russia to Israel. He applied for a visa and was immediately kicked out of his high position in the Soviet Academy of Sciences and imprisoned. After being released from jail, he decided to telephone the Rebbe directly. He got through, but one of the Rebbe's assistants intervened. Finally he heard a second voice on the line saying, *"Tell him he already has all the blessings, he must be sure that he will immediately go out."* After persistent protests, he was advised three weeks after the Rebbe's blessings that he had received his papers to emigrate.

Branover emigrated to Israel and soon after travelled to the United States to meet the Rebbe for the first time. Initially he could not figure out what the Rebbe was saying as he spoke to him in Yiddish. The Rebbe then in Russian asked him minute questions about dozens, indeed hundreds of families, everywhere in Russia including Siberia. The Rebbe wanted details, details, and Branover did not have the information.

He merely recognized some of the names. The Rebbe wound up telling him what each husband was doing, the wife, the ages of the children, the interests of the children, the family problems, their addresses, even their telephone numbers. Branover could not understand how so much precise information with such specific detail could come from one man. Branover was also surprised by the depth of the Rebbe's understanding of Branover's scientific training and work.

And now let me quote from Branover, directly, *"then I started paying attention to how the Rebbe was speaking. When he speaks about a certain Jew, a certain woman, a certain child, a certain man, the whole world doesn't exist. The only thing that exists is the Jew about whom the Rebbe is concerned at the moment."* He goes on to say that *"if the Rebbe is speaking about a Jew somewhere in Siberia, the whole world is non-existent."*

In 1985, one week before Gorbachev took office in Moscow as Secretary-General of the Communist Party and Soviet leader, Branover got a call from the Rebbe. He told him to call all of Branover's contacts in Moscow, Leningrad and other cities and tell them they should be assured that from now on the situation in Russia will improve. *"Not immediately"*, he said, *"it will take time. The whole thing will fall apart and Communism will come to an end and that whoever wishes to leave will be allowed. Everyone who wishes to stay will be able to practice Judaism."* This was unbelievable. No one, no one in 1985, predicted the U.S.S.R. collapse was at hand, but the Rebbe's prediction came true. Genius, like god, lives in the detail. The Rebbe kept the light of faith alive by herculean detailed efforts, by patient attention to the details of the life of each Jew, one at a time! Much of this story is still hidden from the public. This is what the Rebbe desired. The work was more important than the credit. The recognition, the attention might detract from the work at hand, the work of saving lives. Lubavitch had a different approach from others. At all times, both Rebbes insisted the Soviet Constitution be upheld. Unlike most, the Seventh Rebbe opposed public protests as he believed protests would curtail the massive immigration underway and might deny even one Jew his freedom from oppression.

The Soviet Constitution provided for freedom of religious practice and instruction. Yet the Soviet government failed to uphold its own 'rule of law' - its own constitution. Still, the Rebbes insisted. They always believed in the 'rule of law'.

So the Lubavitch's work, this particular work, the origins of the 'Refusnik' Movement, transcended the saving Jewish souls and became a universal message of hope for mankind. As an answer to a question I am always asked by non-Jewish friends. What do Jews believe about 'gentiles'? Do Jews consider themselves as 'Chosen People?' Why? Well, the Rebbe echoed the answer about gentiles, repeated by the 'Rambam' - the great Moses Maimonides on tolerance to other faiths.

In the 11th century, Maimonides wrote if non-Jews obey the seven simple laws of Noah - called the 'Noahide laws' - prohibitions against idol worship, blasphemy, murder, adultery and robbery, eating flesh from living animals and establishing courts of justice – establishing the 'rule of law', they are assured an equal place in the world to come. Thirty-six times in the Torah, Jews are repeatedly admonished to treat strangers better than themselves. The Jews chose and were chosen to place greater, heavier burdens of law and moral practice on themselves, to gain and sustain their place in the world (613 commandments in all).

It can best be summed up in the eloquent words of Rabbi Hillel over twenty centuries ago - do not do unto others what you would not have done unto yourself!

So the message of Judaism, the message of Lubavitch is universal. Belief ends where it started - with oneself!

The Rebbe was a master 'grass roots' community organizer, tactical strategist and building of institutions world-wide. How? From an impoverished small group of Lubavitch Chassidism headquartered in Crown Heights in a small cluster of three stone and brick buildings around 770 Eastern Parkway in Crown Heights, Brooklyn in the '50s, the Rebbe with a small circle of advisers modernized, innovated and expanded each aspect of his plans to reach every Jew across the globe. He carefully selected well over 400 couples to set up Chabad centres around the world wherever there was even a small cluster of Jews. He organized the production of newsletters, (both print and radio), comic books, magazines and had each of his speeches and homilies taped – all of which were meticulously dated and made accessible via first the phone and then the net.

He built primary, secondary schools and institutions of higher learning for male and female and vocational schools. He was the ultimate idea man reaching to the entire community with his education policies and 'mitzvas', daily good deeds for Jew and Gentile alike. He promoted the 'Mitzvah' Tank to take to the streets to entice Jews to discover or rediscover their roots. He reached out to the larger community by erecting giant Hanukah candles on public places to attract believers and non-believers to his message of hope, and possibility of miracles.

Don't waste a moment. Do a good deed now, he admonished followers and others alike. You can't change yesterday. You can improve the world today and tomorrow. Genius is infinite patience with detail. With his formidable education and formidable memory, relentless studies in all fields from science to environment to military strategy to diplomacy, he became a careful confidant and advisor of leaders in politics, faith, military strategy and literature and art. The Rebbe became both the message and the messenger. His 18 hour 7 days work week set an example for his followers[400]. A resolution declaring Education Sharing Day was passed unanimously by the American Congress to honour the Rebbe's 71st birthday. Then he rallied his followers to set up 71 new Chabad centres to celebrate his birthday around the globe which they did within a year. Starting in the '50s in Milan, London, Paris and Toronto, the Lubavitch movement under his watchful eye, one at a time, built Chabad centres which grew in number to reach 10% of the world Jewish population, in all states of the United States and each province of Canada and over 100 countries around the globe. His books, speeches and letters were meticulously collected and indexed in over 600 volumes. From the '20s, he began to write learned books and commentaries on 'Rashi' and Maimonides – two of the greatest Jewish thinkers. Then he gave lengthy homilies of each these masters after he became the Rabbe.

Organizations in every sector were established for young professionals and adults, male and female. He established vocational schools in Israel. He inspired writers like Elie Wiesel and Chaim Potok, poets,

---

400 Even on the Sabbath the Rebbe was active, reading and rendering accessible sexplication of the weekly Torah passage to his followers.

artists and teachers. By the end of the century, Lubavitch had spread to almost 15,000 families and established Chabad centres in over 100 countries and 950 cities around the globe. In the '70s, he advocated energy sufficiency to reduce the power of the oil states. In 1981, he became an active advocate of solar energy. To reach every Jew he encouraged young Chassids to go into the streets of cities and encourage each Jew daily to wear phylacteries (tefillin) (black boxes and black narrow straps to place on the left arm then wound around three fingers as 's' to remind one of G-d and a box on the forehead with straps to be ever remindful of one G-d. One box was turned to the heart to remind one of the hearts needs. For women, it was the simple act lighting Friday pre Sabbat evening candles to brighten their world and special schools for youth in need of better suited education. With a prodigious memory for detail, and endless rigour for long work days, he read, prayed and offered advice and blessings to each who wrote to see him, handing out new dollar bills to each supplicant to remind them to give charity. As a University student in Berlin and Paris, he arrange for a daily bath in a local 'Mikvah', a ritual bath attached to an orthodox synagogue to keep his mind and thoughts centred on the principles of his religious faith

The Rebbe was and remains a man for all seasons and for all reasons.

"Hasidism stands at the crossroads of the turbulent winds of history"

– **Isaac Babel**

Some select bibliographies include:

- *'Larger Than Life: The Life And Times Of The Lubavitcher Rebbe Rabbi Menachem Mendel Schneerson (Volume 1)'* by Shaul Shimon Deutsch (Chassidic Historical Productions, New York, 1995)
- *'Larger Than Life: The Lubavitcher Rebbe's Years in Riga & Berlin: 2'* by Shaul Shimon Deutsch (Chassidic Historical Productions, New York, 1997)
- *'Souls on Fire: Portraits and Legends of Hasidic Masters'* by Elie Wiesel (Jason Aronson Inc., 1993)
- *'Conversations With the Rebbe: Menachem Mendel Schneerson: Interviews with 14 Leading Figures about the Rebbe'* by Chaim X. Dalfin (JEC Publishing Company Inc., 1996)

- *'Rebbe: The Life and Teachings of Menachem M. Schneerson, the Most Influential Rabbi in Modern History'* by Joseph Telushkin (Harper-Collins Publishers, 2014)
- *'Maimonides: The Life and World of One of Civilization's Greatest Minds'* by Joel L. Kraemer (Doubleday, 2008)

Pope John Paul II was born Karol Jozef Wojtyła in Wadowice in 1920 - the same year that the Battle of Warsaw was fought on the outskirts of the and where the Bolsheviks were defeated when Poland achieved independence[401].

His father and mine, also born in southern Poland, less than 100 kilometres apart, both served in the Pilsudski Brigades in that momentous battle for Polish independence in Warsaw. This slender but splendid thread was noted again during my last audience in Rome with this charismatic personality.

More than common Polish roots, the Pope's transformation of the Church, its teachings and practices towards Jews and Judaism and its policy towards Israel shattered the Church's previous history and practices of anti-semitism which drew me and those of my faith towards him. While an Archbishop of Krakow[402], he allowed publication of a critique of Pope Pius XII and his questionable actions during the Holocaust.

All progress is by a winding staircase. The Pope spoke out repeatedly and forcefully against the rising scourge of anti-Semitism. He was the first Pope to visit a synagogue in Rome, to visit Auschwitz, to visit Jerusalem, to pray at the Wailing Wall, to pay his respects at Yad Vashem and to recognize the State of Israel.

---

401 The Red Army led by Leon Trotsky was defeated at the edge of Warsaw though Trotsky led a superior number of forces and had greater military resources, the only time that he was defeated with superior forces. Charles DeGaulle, always wearing white gloves and dressed in immaculate military dress, was a military advisor to the Polish forces at the time

402 Krakow was one of ancient cities of Poland and amongst the first to establish a diocese and an Archbishop in medieval Poland and home to one of Europe's oldest universities, where the Pope attended as a student and then taught as priest and Archbishop.

The life of Karol Wojtyła is instructive. Both his mother and older brother died prematurely. His mother was particularly devout. Wojtyła was born in 1920 in Wadowice, a small town in south west Poland. Brought up by his father, a sometimes officer in the Polish army who struggled to make a living at times as a tailor to sustain first his family, then his surviving son. His father was devout and prayed daily setting an example for his young son.

Wojtyła, a brilliant student, was devout from an early age, praying and then later meditating alone regularly each day. Popular, he was different from his circle of young friends. He loved sports and was a skilled athlete and he became a superb skier, skiing on all mountain regions across Poland and a strong swimmer and adept at soccer. A standout student in high school, he led his graduating class and gave a thoughtful grauating address in the presence of the leading church leader of Poland Cardinal Sapieha who remarked that Wojtyła was destined for great things. Wojtyła attracted two powerful mentors - Cardinal Sapieha and then Cardinal Wyszyński, who first disagreed with Wojtyła on his approach to the Communists especially when writing under a pseudonym for a socialist newspaper. Later however Wyszyński recommended Wojtyła for his Red Hat and then after refusing to believe Wojtyła had a chance to gain majority support amongst Cardinals, played a significant role to organize the campaign for his Papacy despite Wojtyła's continued reluctance and objections.

After high school, Wojtyła gained easy entry to University at Krakow[403] where he began to teach a range of subjects and later at University of Lublin where he deepened his studies of the history and practices of Catholicism after he was ordained a priest in his mid-20s. Meanwhile he published poetry and a play under an assumed name, and began scholarly works on the meaning of Catholicism. Catholicism, the indi-

---

403 As teacher at the Jagiellonian University in Krakow, one of the oldest universities in Europe, and later at Lublin University where he taught a wide range of subjects including introduction to the Old Testament, church art, Hebrew language, logic, metaphysics, cosmology, history of philosophy, logic and Greek and began his study of Spanish.

vidual and the family was the centre of his work as well as detailed work on relations between male and female. When ordained, he spent time in extra on confessions. He took young people on study and camping trips and would spend long walks with each participant as they strolled through the forests together and confessed their inner thoughts to him. As the Communist leadership began to isolate and imprison priests, he deftly avoided the authorities and taught underground classes first as priest, Archbishop[404] and then Cardinal. Keeping the flame of religious freedom alive was his most important mission.

Through his mentors' influence he travelled to join the Vatican in Rome, after he was named Archbishop of Krakow, where his circle of admirers widened and the depth of his piety and intelligence was admired. The rigour of his persona, his modesty and scholarship continued to draw attention to him.

He was a fervent follower of Pope John Paul I and Pope Paul VI who in 1967 elevated him to Cardinal and became the second Cardinal in Poland after Cardinal Wyszyński, his mentor. He participated in John XXIII's first Conclave[405] that resulted in the Encyclical that started to erase the roots of anti-semitism from the Catholic Catchism and reset Catholic Jewish relationships on a tolerant path. He continued writing and publishing under pseudonyms. As Archbishop of Krakow he met regularly and advised leaders of the dissident movement and later after he became Pope, leaders of Solidarity including Lech Wałęsa[406] and other underground leaders. He organized underground schools taught by priests.

---

404 As Archbishop he invited young immigrant men from Czechoslovakia to study with him and then secretly ordained then as priests and sent them back to Czechoslovakia to spread the faith underground.

405 As an Archbishop and attendee, he brought two leading female lay Catholic scholars to attend the Conclave to participate and advise him.

406 I met Lech Wałęsa in Ottawa and he gave me a signed Solidarity poster. Pope John II brilliant as a strategist, was demonstrative but careful with his involvement with the Solidarity Movement and its leaders. Even the name Solidarity was attributed to his public lectures broadcast to Poland. As Pope, he overrode Cardinal Glemp by radio broadcasts who advised Wałęsa and other Solidarity leaders to withdraw their demands for a labour union movement independent of the Communist regime.

He established 'safe' houses in churches, nunneries and monasteries. He was masterful in his relations with Communist leaders some of whom secretly maintained their youthful devotion to the church and advised leaders in the Solidarity movement and others who later became leaders in post-Communist Polish governments.

Wojtyła was surprised to be elected Pope. Yet he immediately set to work to modernize and expand the outreach of the Church, reorganize its finances and became stricter in his renditions of Catholicism.

He and the Rebbe both believed that the family was at the core of good practices and religion. Both felt secular education should be not instilled until the student's own character has matured or crystallized as the Rebbe taught. John Paul II while initially attracted to 'liberation theology' came to understand that its ideas might lead to Marxism and a loss of faith[407].

Pope John Paul II inaugurated his world tours, driven while standing up in what became known as the 'Popemobile' to travel amongst his throngs of audiences, attracting millions of Catholics and others in person or via the media to his banner of leadership across America north and south, Central and South America, Africa, Europe and the Middle East. The power of his persona and his electric teachings attracted millions. The Church turned outwards as he spread his message of tolerance and piety. His power attracted powerful enemies. A Turk attempted to assassinate him. Those behind this vicious attack were never discovered. The Pope survived but it would physically weaken him while he forgave his assassin[408]. As he began to visibly fail, he continued his work. Despite his infirmities, he refused to stop his global outreach travels[409]. He travelled to 129 countries during his Papacy. He became a visible lesson in how to overcome disabilities after he suffered a series of strokes.

---

407 The Pope once wrote: *"Freedom consists not on what we like but having the right to do what we ought."*

408 Who was behind the assassin was never definitely discovered and rumours of Soviet instigation were discounted.

409 My last audience with Pope John Paul II was in a small chapel in the Vatican. He passed away several weeks later.

Pope John Paul II continued the auspicious work of Pope John XXIII[410] and went on more aggressively to eradicate the roots of vestigial anti-semitism within the Catholic Church. John Paul II changed the course of history. The Pope made his first visit to Poland in 1979, in all eight eventful tours thereafter. His first visit was the one that offered Poles an alternative to Communist control.

In December 1981, efforts to dismantle the impregnable Soviet supported Communist regime in Poland coagulated in a somewhat disorganized yet intense way. A loose collection of students, priests, writers, journalist, farmers, teachers, workers, miners, leaders were all supported by the Pope. Together they began to push for intellectual, teachers, artists, workers and farmers uniting independent of the Communist government to protest for higher pay and better working conditions and independence. Lech Wałęsa, a shipyard worker, picked up the slender reins of leadership and became the public face of a nationwide strike. A network radiated by underground presses, joined by Radio Free Europe broadcasts, safe houses, mostly in churches, became depots for food, clothing, medicines, printing presses, radio transmitters, typewriters, ink, newsprint[411] and cash, smuggled into Poland by truck to assist the thousands of strikers in strike sympathy to support them and their impoverished families. Overruling Cardinal Glemp, Pope John II who coined the word 'solidarity', continue to urge by public broadcast, the strike.

When martial law was declared, thousands of strikers and fellow travellers were imprisoned. The Pope led in organizing trucks to smuggle aid into Poland for relief. Via his public broadcasts that reached Poland, he repeatedly use the word 'solidarity' to signal his support for the strikers and gain wider support amongst the Polish public. An underground university (The Flying University) and its teachers he organized

---

410 John Paul II disagreed with John XXIII's view to work on the theory of 'peaceful co-existence' with the Soviets, through this was in vogue in Church and the west at the time.

411 Canadian unions raised money to send newsprint paper to help the cause as did powerful American unions rendered aid. The American or Canadian governments did not aid 'Solidarity' and its network during these times nor did the C.I.A.

were key players. Many were released from prison due to his efforts and later became elected members of the Sejm – the Polish Parliament and the government, when Communist dominance crumbled less than a decade later. The Pope carefully found common ground to support the strike's aims and to crush the hegemonic hold of the Communists over Poland. The Pope's secret tactical and strategic moves were deft, keeping in touch by phone and secret correspondence with the Communist over-lords, especially Marshall Jaruzelski, the Polish soldier and leader of the Communist government who withstood the pressure of the Soviets and other Communist leaders in Eastern Europe especially Germany, restraining him and his government from harsher measures. A brilliant and surefooted campaign of protests were stealthfully encouraged.

One interesting footnote - Carl Bernstein the journalist of Water-gate fame, cowrote a book called 'His Holiness: John Paul II and the Hidden History Our Time' (Transworld Publishers Ltd, 1997) advancing the myth that Reagan and the CIA supported Solidarity and their strikes via an alliance with the Pope and the Church which was said by insiders to be false and dismissed by all sides. I could not find where Bernstein ever corrected his narrative.

The Pope's hyperactive outreach by carefully organized trips abroad continued through the '80s. Yet the issue closest to his heart was the liberation of Poland and sustaining Solidarity and its activists on the ground. The Pope travelled to Africa, Eastern Europe, Central, South and North America carefully treading a line between left and right govern-ments while purging the Church priesthood of its 'Liberation theology'. This was rife with difficulties as Pope's aim was a reduction of blatant poverty, hence an overlapping theme with 'Liberation theology'. The Pope believed in promoting democracy while concerned with unbri-dled capitalism forces displayed by autocratic governments. He sought a middle economic ground, a 'middle way', between capitalism and state enterprises. Concerned with the growing secularism, he forbade priests to adapt civilian attire and from holding public office. Priests and nuns seeking public office were forced to decide – the Church or public life.

Despite opposition, he elevated Opus Dei a secretive controver-sial Catholic society of clerics, laymen and laywomen, to expand in his outreach in their occupations and lives[412]. His outreach focused on other Christian denominations, Lutherans, Anglicans, Russian Orthodox and Greek Orthodox Christians and other faiths including Muslims and Jews. A special focus was on youth. Monster rallies of youth were organized in Europe, America and Canada[413] to attract a youthful new enthusiastic generation of the faithful. Rallies focused on the family were carefully organized and attended in the tens of thousands.

The Pope, the master communicator, publicized and broadcast all his trips especially to Eastern Europe like Prague in Czechoslovakia to fan the flames of the Soviet dissident movement there. After 1989 when the Berlin Wall came down, the Pope continued his drumbeats of outreach to expand the faithful and other admirers.

The Pope paid special attention to the Jesuits and elevated their order to a higher status despite internal opposition. The liberal waves in America to beat open the door of the Church to married priests and nuns, he slammed shut.

One consistent and faithful helper was Cardinal Ratzinger who met with the Pope each Friday for lunch in Rome when the Pope was not travelling. Both opposed the growing liberalism in the American Church and elsewhere by public addresses, encyclicals and by selective appointments of numerous archbishops and cardinals who agreed with their shared outlook. Though he and Ratzinger disagreed on topics from time to time, they remained inseparable[414].

In 1993 the Vatican finally recognized the State of Israel. It took 15 years for the Pope to override opposition within the Church to accomplish this feat of internal diplomacy. The first Pope to visit Jerusalem in 1964 was Pope Paul VI, Pope John Paul II's mentor and inspiration. In 2000 Pope John Paul II followed in Pope Paul VI's footsteps, visited Jerusalem,

---

412 Opus Dei (*Work by God*) was founded in Spain in 1928 by a priest Josemaría Escrivá de Balaguer for clerics and lay persons to pursue holiness through their chosen professions. The Pope canonized Balaguer in 1992

413 My friend Dennis Mills was a key organizer for this massive event in Toronto, Canada and led to another private audience for me with the Pope in Toronto.

414 Cardinal Ratzinger became John Paul II's successor as Pope in 2005 and took the name Benedict XVI.

met with leaders of other denominations, prayed at the Wailing Wall and visited and prayed in Yad Vashem and the Christian holy sites. The Church was never the same again. He visited 'death' camps in Poland and navigated the tricky ground between disagreeing with Polish nationalists in their sluggish support of the Holocaust while being prodded by an alliance of Holocaust survivors and Israel.

Astutely, he deftly supported the loose Solidarity movement to weaken Soviet hegemony in Poland then across Eastern Europe and Russia. His magical televised tours around globe opened the Church to new followers and new ideas. The Church became a source for peaceful change and transformed the outreach of Church to more tolerant relations with other faiths. He opposed the growth of nuclear weapons and Reagan's 'Star Wars' project. His outreach techniques were slavishly followed by his successors.

Poland, first victim of Soviet and Nazi collaboration when both regimes overran Poland in 1939, became the first state in Eastern Europe to hold free elections for the 'Sejm' (Polish Parliament) before the Berlin Wall was ripped down in November 1989. The Communist Polish United Workers Party gave up the Communist hold on power in Poland in April 1989. The election that year heralded the start of European Soviet satellites quickly returning to democracy and bringing to an end the cycle of Soviet monopoly of power in the 20th century.

Pope John Paul II led the way in the 20th century[415]. His persona and his ideas of faith married to tolerance continue to reverberate around the world[416].

Some select bibliographies include:

---

415 Pope John II led on another global front – debt of impoverished nations. He vigorously supported James David Wolfensohn's initiatives at the World Bank to write off much of debt incurred by these nations. He cited Leviticus 25 of the Old Testament about the forgiveness of debt.

416 In 2020, a report was released from the Vatican that criticized John Paul II for believing the American Cardinal McCarrick's denial of sexual misconduct. No doubt John Paul II was influenced by the Communists repeatedly attempts to besmirch priests' reputations during the Soviet era and gave McCarrick, perhaps unwisely, the benefit of the doubt.

- 'Man of the Century: The Life and Times of Pope John Paul II' by Jonathan Kwitny (Henry Holt and Company, 1997)
- 'Keepers of the Keys: A History of the Popes from St. Peter to John Paul II' by Nicholas Cheetham (Charles Scribner's Sons, New York, 1983)
- 'The Jesuits: A History' by David Mitchell (Franklin Watts, 1981)
- 'The Hidden Pope: The Untold Story of a Lifelong Friendship That Is Changing the Relationship Between Catholics and Jews' by Darcy O'Brien (Rodale Books, 1998)

Does history have meaning? Can individuals make a difference for good? Two extraordinary men, the Rebbe and the Pope, reaching out, one person at a time, helped repair our fragmented world, as each worked slavishly to return the 20th century to a virtuous cycle.

Let each reader decide[417],[418].

---

417 Coincidentally Winston Churchill shared the Rebbe and Pope John Paul II fundamentalist views of creation as set out in the Old Testament. *"We believe the most successful view, the most up-to-date and rationalist conception will find its fullest satisfaction in taking the Bible story literally... We may be sure that all these things happens just as they are set out according to Holy Writ."* Quoted from 'The Literary Churchill: Author, Reader, Actor' by Jonathan Rose (Yale University Press, 2014).

418 Mea culpa. I have always been fascinated listening to preachers and rabbis. In 1954 a classmate at Western University, Norman Rosenblood and I, arranged to audit classes at two leading rabbinical seminaries in America. Both of us were trying to choose between the law and the rabbinate as a career or rather a profession. Off we took that spring in Norman's convertible, travelling first to Hebrew Union College in Cincinnati, Ohio, the leading Jewish Reform Seminary in America led by Nelson Glueck, an archeologist and rabbi. We audited classes and dined with Glueck and listened to several of his lectures, steeped with references to his 'digs' in the Holy Land and to the Bible. Then we travelled to New York City to the home of the Jewish Theological Seminary led by Louis Finkelsten – the college for Conservative rabbis. Lectures by Finkelsten were pompous, boring and unimpressive. I went to listen to Rav. Joseph Soloveitchik (author of 'The Lonely Man of Faith') at Yeshiva College across town who was concise, insightful and mesmerizing. In the end it seems Norman and I were more interested in girls than rabbinics. I did not have the calling. I returned, and the following year, gained admission to law school at University of Toronto.

My fascination for sermons by preachers, priests and rabbis continues to this day. The diversity of just a few I listened and learned from was wide and varied.

My first Jewish experience was my teacher and Rabbi, David Kirsherbraum in London, Ontario. A Jewish Polish immigrant whose thunderous addresses as the news of the Holocaust seeped out in World War II made me awestruck. In Yiddish or English he would start quietly, building to a 'fire and brimstone' comparison of Hitler and the Nazis to biblical autocrats of old, from Egypt to Babylon and how their rule was obliterated for their misdeeds. Next was Reuben Slonim, a conservative Rabbi who dined at our home in London for Sabbath dinners. Slonim had a tenor's voice sonorous with many octaves, modern in his analogies and warm in his connection to his listeners. His successor in London was Shlomo Carlebach, quiet, serious, gentle and accessible to an impressionable youth. In Toronto, when I visited my blind grandfather I would escort him to afternoon shabbat meals in the small 'shtebels' of Rebbi Price and Rebbi Ochs, leading Orthodox Rabbis, when they each pronounced on the weekly Torah reading, in Yiddish and Hebrew, most of which I didn't understand but yet impressed, no less after my grandfather explained what they said as I walked him back to his home to Kensington Avenue.

At University of Toronto, I went to Convocation Hall and listened to Billy Graham's soaring address. When I joined Beth Tzedec Congregation, a conservative congregation in Toronto, I listened to Rabbi Stuart Rosenberg's thunderous orations as he grew to become a leading Toronto Rabbi and respected community leader. His speech at the opening of the New City Hall in Toronto was uplifting and inspirational. Later I came to know and admire Rabbi Gunther Plaut of Holy Blossom, Canada's leading Reform Temple, a brilliant scholar who published an accessible modern version of the Old Testament, and whose addresses were both intellectual, interesting and insightful. Rabbi Ben Friedberg at Beth Tzedec who loved as I did tales of Hasidic Masters who related to needs of everyday life. His successor Rabbi Baruch Frydman-Kohl became a friend whose liberal approach, storytelling and gentle wit from the pulpit and especially his eulogies were moving and informative.

Sunday morning of course was reserved for TV preachers starting with Fulton J Sheen, the Catholic Bishop who strode about and preached with passion and enlightenment as his Bishop's cape swirled around him. Then Johnny Swaggart, an evangelist, was always a stunning delight as he raised the Bible over his head with one hand and slapped it for emphasis with the other. Oral Roberts was another homespun handsome favourite. Cardinal Emmet Carter of Toronto's speeches and messages were enlightening and laced with wit.

Both Houses of Congress and Parliament from time to time echo with biblical references as public speaking began to wane and practitioners of the oratorical arts were overtaken by 'gotcha' lines.

In politics, the voices of Churchill (from recordings), all three Kennedys, Reagan and Thatcher and in Canada John Diefenbaker, Pierre Trudeau and the English accented words of David Lewis still ring in my ear. Of course, any address of Allan MacEachen both in the Canadian Commons and Senate were each masterpieces of artful persuasion and still resonate. Stephen Lewis followed in his father's footstep[s and was the best political orator of my generation. Men of the cloth remain my preferences to all alternatives in the art of powerful, literary soaked, rhetoric – a dying art form.

THE HOLOCAUST: VIEWS ON STATEMENT ISSUED BY THE VATICAN AS TEACHING DOCUMENT – MARCH 31, 1998 – IN THE SENATE OF CANADA[419]

More than 50 Passover and Easter seasons have passed since the furnaces of the Holocaust[420] cooled and closed down. Two weeks ago, in Rome, the Vatican issued a document assaying the role of the Roman Catholic Church, the papacy, the Vatican and its followers, titled, "*We Remember: A Reflection on the Shoah*". In a way, one could read the document as a collective mea culpa. In a covering letter, His Holiness Pope John Paul II hoped that the document "*will help to heal the wounds of misunderstanding and injustices.*" Some leading Catholic observers and others have noted that the document now leaves room for the Pope to make an even stronger statement in the future. Other Catholic observers expect that the document will serve as a teaching document for the church in all its aspects.

Much was heard of the centrality of Roman Catholic education in the lives of most Canadians. We have studied, debated and passed two constitutional amendments respecting religious education and the school systems in Newfoundland and Quebec. Thus, in a way, Roman Catholic education has been a preoccupation of this Parliament and, hence, any educational documents sanctified by the Vatican and gleaned for a wider audience should be carefully examined and placed on the public agenda, if not the teaching agendas of schools and, in particular,

---

419 This was a statement given by the author in the Senate of Canada on March 31, 1998 that was not debated.

420 The Holocaust was unique in the annuals of the 20th century. Unlike other horrendous genocides as befell the Armenians in Turkey, the aim of Hitler and his Nazi accomplices was to eradicate Jews just because they were Jews, no other reason. Other 'genocide' were allowed to flee but the Nazi 'Final Solution' meant to eradicate Jews.

the Roman Catholic school systems. I hope those in the church hierarchy - from whom we heard in abundance in the Senate respecting the importance of Catholic religious education - will advise us in the Senate what concrete steps by the Canadian Conference of Bishops and other professors of the faith will be taken to use this important historic document as a teaching tool in the schools, churches and beyond into the public arena across Canada.

Other observers have noted that the document falls short in its historical analysis of the responsibility or role of the church with respect to the root causes and the implementation of the Holocaust.

Before I turn to that aspect of this inquiry, let me remind honourable senators that I had previously drawn the Senate's attention to the consequences of nationalism as a source of 20th century malaise. Indeed, as if to support my contention, the Vatican document makes two telling references to the invidious role that nationalism played in the larger history that led to the Holocaust. First, the document notes that:

> ... in the 19th century a false and extremist nationalism took hold.

Later the document notes:

> ... that an extremist form of nationalism was heightened in Germany...

In that clear sense, the church reminds us all of the dangers inherent in nationalism. Nationalist ideology was a political engine that propelled a horrific state agenda of preference, then discrimination, followed by exclusion, segregation and, ultimately, extinction. The 'Final Solution' was seen as a considered, logical extension of a nationalist agenda.

The concerns about extreme nationalism in the Vatican document echoed one of Pope John Paul II's most passionate speeches condemning worship of the nation when he declared to the diplomatic corps at the Holy See earlier in this decade:

> This is not a question of legitimate love for one's homeland or respect for its identify but rejecting the 'Other' in his diversity so as to impose himself upon him... For this kind of chauvinism, all means are fair: exalting race, overvaluing the state, imposing a uniform economic model, levelling specific cultural differences.

For me, the first lesson of the Holocaust is the intrinsic danger of temporal nationalism encouraged or accommodated by a non-secular acquiescence if not acceptance.

Pope John Paul II has espoused the primacy of individuality over collectivity. In his encyclical *Centesimus Annus*, he wrote:

Something is owed to human beings because they are human beings.

Honourable senators, the church militant has always been a source of intense historic interest to me, in particular the nature of leadership. I belong to the school which believes that trends in history can be altered by individual leadership. Let me take this opportunity to share some of my thoughts with you respecting the role of leadership and, in this case, the papacy through the ages. What should we remember?

Let us start with the example of Gregory VII, the sixth-century Pope who supported laws preventing Jews from holding public office or building synagogues or practising trades. Promulgated as a papal bull, a successor, Pope Stephen IV, continued to promote these restrictions.

With the advent and the birth of the first idea of Europe, Christian Europe, the first European Holy Roman Emperor, Charlemagne the Great, showed leadership by ignoring and strongly objecting to a litany of papal edicts and restrictions against Jews at that time. Later, Clement III even tried to prevent newly baptized Jews from joining the church. This conduct contrasted with Bernard de Clairvaux, a founder of a Cistercian monastery, who warned:

Whoever makes an attempt on a life of a Jew, sins as if he attacked Jesus himself.

Bernard de Clairvaux earned his sainthood in that Dark and Medieval age.

Of course, we have Pope Urban V, who praised the death of Pedro I of Spain because that Spanish monarch established a liberal regime of privileges and sanctuary for Jews in his time. On the other hand, we discover the words of St. Thomas Aquinas, author of *Summa Theologica*, who harshly criticized the murder of Jews, contending that:

Jews should be preserved as eternal witnesses to the truth of Christianity.

Gregory VII repeatedly sought to restrict Jews holding any office. It was Paul III who protected Jews from proposed expulsion from Avignon in

France, but he was followed by the severe harshness of Pope Paul IV who cancelled letters of protection granted by past popes and accelerated the race to the Inquisition half a century later. We then have the case of Sixtus IV, who authorized the Spanish Inquisition under pressure from Ferdinand and Isabella of Spain. Thereafter, however, Sixtus IV tried to moderate the harshness of this miserable period by allowing peaceful relations with Jews within his domains in Italy.

In the 16th century we can turn to Leo X, who re-established privileges accorded to Jews in French papal territory despite the vigorous protest of the cardinals there. It was Leo X who ended the requirement of Jews wearing a badge in his French domain and let this obligation lapse into disuse within his Italian domain. He went further and encouraged Jews to practise professions and participate in the arts.

Later in the 16th century, we discover the leadership of Clement VII, who allowed Jews to profess openly, established courts to settle disputes between Christians and Jews, and allowed Inquisition refugees to settle in Anacona on the Adriatic as a sanctuary. Clement VII also allowed Jews to practise their trades and their professions. Through the thickets of European history, we can perceive the papacy oscillating from protection to prosecution.

Honourable senators, the road to progress and humanity is by a steep and winding stairway until we approach the common era in the gates of the Holocaust itself.

It was Pius IX, in the middle of the 19th century, who ascended St. Peter's throne and who refused the right of Jews to live beyond ghetto walls, acquire land, engage in trade or enter into professions in Rome. In a throwback to centuries past, he even forbade Jewish doctors to attend Christian patients. All these prohibitions served as eerie yet precise fore-runners of the infamous 1930's Nazi laws of discrimination and deprivation less than a century later.

Next we come to the heroic Pius XI who in 1939 issued an anti-Nazi encyclical following Germany's racist legislation and publicly told Belgian pilgrims:

In spirit, we are all Semites.

Pius XI went even further and condemned Mussolini's laws *"as a disgraceful imitation of Hitler's Nordic mythology"*. Reportedly the same Pius XI was planning even stronger denunciations when he died suddenly on February 10, 1939. Then he was succeeded to the papacy by Pius XII[421].

The Vatican document makes reference to Pius XII and stated that he personally and through his representatives saved hundreds of thousands of Jewish lives. In one study done about this period respecting Rome and environs, a historian came up with precise figures that 477 Jews were sheltered within the Vatican walls and another 4,238 found refuge in Rome's monasteries and convents. Yes, it is clear that in 1944, when Hungarian Jews were threatened with extinction, Pius XII did speak out loudly and clearly against the expulsions that ultimately led those Jews to the death camps. Of course, by then, Rome was safely in Allied hands. Perhaps the Vatican document might have made historical reference to French Cardinal Eugene Tisserant, who, in 1940, when the Nazi intentions of genocide were becoming clearer, wrote to a fellow cardinal in Paris of his futile urgings that Pope Pius XII issue an encyclical on what he said was the:

> ... *individual duty to obey the imperatives of conscience.*

Cardinal Tisserant went on in despair:

> *I am afraid that history may be obliged in time to blame the Holy See for a policy accommodated to its advantage and little more. Other Catholics can bear even stronger witness respecting that papacy's silence.*

While Popes may be 'infallible', they are not perfect. Yet no one can doubt the leadership the present Pope, Pope John Paul II, has taken in reconciling the role of the church and the responsibility for the roots and exercise of anti-Semitism. He was the first Pope since the founding of the

---

421 Later Pope John XXIII apologized for Pope Puis XII disgraceful disregard and silence to safely ward Jews hounded and massacred by the Nazis and their collaborative inclusion in Italian Fascists.

papacy, except St. Peter himself, to visit a synagogue, a ten minute ride across Rome. He was the first Pope to visit a 'death' camp, Auschwitz, located just 35 miles from his Polish birthplace. He followed Pope John XXIII's footsteps, who in 1959 ordered the first changes to Catholic liturgy to start to cleanse it of anti-Semitism, and the Second Vatican Council in 1962 when anti-Semitism and culpability were first denounced in Nostra Aetate. In 1988, Pope John II stated:

I repeat again with you, the strongest condemnation of anti-Semitism and racism, which are opposed to the principles of Christianity.

Pope John Paul II was the first pope to establish relations between the Vatican and Israel and the first pope to condemn anti-Semitism both repeatedly and forcefully. In his recent book, entitled *Crossing the Threshold of Hope*, the Pope wrote with sensitivity and insight of the necessity for the reformation of relationships between Jews and the church. It is clear from a reading of a voluminous biography, entitled *Man of the Century*, that this Polish Pope was almost himself a direct witness to the Holocaust, living as a hidden Polish student priest in southern Poland during the war. Later, as a Polish Cardinal, before he ascended to St. Peter's throne, he even encouraged a priest to write an article criticizing Pius XII, provided that criticism was placed fairly in three contexts; historical, psychological and moral.

There were the strong statements of accountability by the bishops of France and Germany, the latter who declared in 1995 that Christians had not carried out *"the required resistance"* to the Holocaust and now held *"a special responsibility to oppose anti-Semitism"*. Can we await a statement by the Conference of Bishops in Canada as to what role the church in Canada had prior to, during and following World War II in the documented unhappy attitudes of some of their priests and some of their adherents? May the newly appointed prince of the church in Toronto, His Eminence Cardinal Aloysius Ambrozic, himself born in Eastern Europe and reportedly interested in Catholic education, lead the way.

I see this Vatican document as a useful first step in the right direction to correct historic wrongs and accept accountability. I hope the

Vatican will find room to go further in the future, as even its adherents recommend, correcting the egregious errors of the past, perhaps moving from a 'mea culpa' to a 'mea maxima culpa'. Whether the Vatican document's carefully delineated distinction between centuries of 'anti-Judaism' as a religious teaching and the Nazi brand of anti-Semitism leading to the extinction, which the Vatican document says has 'its roots outside of Christianity', is a distinction without a difference remains for theologians and historians to explore. What is the nature of the gulf separating these two friendless schools of ideas? Which school of ideas occupies which of St. Augustine's two cities remains yet to be seen. The least we can do, as Elie Wiesel reminded us, is to ask good questions.

The Vatican files will be opened in the future. Scholars can examine for themselves the historical truth of the Holocaust which, for most of us, remains beyond imagination? In the first words of Pope John Paul II's papacy, *"be not afraid"*. Yet to study this carefully crafted document is a step, another step in achieving what His Holiness Pope John Paul II has said and written and preached: *"Never again"*.

Have the lessons of Holocaust been learned? Not yet.[422]

"When men choose not to believe in God, they do not thereafter believe in nothing, they then become capable of believing in anything."
- G.K. Chesterton

---

422 Perhaps one of the the most overlooked most influential historian was Jules Isaac (1877-1963), a French education bureaucrat and historian who survived World War II while his family perished. His wife's last note to him was to save himself, his life and save his work. He survived the Holocaust in 1947 completed his magnus opus *'Jesus and Israel'* (Holt, Rinehart and Winston, 1971). His scholarship brought him to the attention of Pope Pius XII and later to Pope John XXIII in 1960 when they met in the Vatican. Isaac's work influenced John XXIII who in 1965 introduced *Nostra Aetate* (*In Our Time*) which denounced anti-semitism in clear and unequivocal terms. One person can make a difference.

EXTREMISM AND TOLERANCE IN THE 20TH CENTURY – 'THE PROPER STUDY OF MANKIND', SIR ISAIAH BERLIN (1909-1997)

No one captured the origins and lure of extremism and the necessity for tolerance in politics better than Isaiah Berlin.

As education and literacy increased in the 20th century, so did the relentless search for 'utopia' on earth. The volume and cycles of extreme action and reaction moved with greater speed throughout the century accelerated by the rise of mass media. Vibrations were felt around the globe.

Isaiah Berlin became first a witness, then a recorder and idea person who throughout his life and works illuminated the excesses and antidotes to the recurring viruses of Communism and Fascism, and in their extreme forms of Stalinism and Nazism. *'The Proper Study of Mankind'* (Farrah, Straus and Giroux, 1998), is a collection of Berlin's essays that should serve as a primer for the study of political ideas in the 20th century. His essay *'The Hedgehog and the Fox: An Essay on Tolstoy's View of History'* became essential for the study of leadership after it was published in 1953.

Berlin was born in Riga, Latvia in 1909 of a wealthy Jewish family of lumber merchants who could trace their paternal roots to the founder of Chabad - Shneur Zalman - the Lubavitch movement[423]. His father would annually visit the fifth and sixth Lubavitch Rebbes to consult and seek advice and blessings on his business affairs. Berlin was brought up in comfortable surroundings. Though with orthodox Jewish ancestors, his father and mother were both well educated in secular schools, comfortable in their bourgeoisie culture in the early part of the 20th century.

---

423 Berlin was thus a cousin of the R. Menachem Mendel Schneerson - the Seventh Lubavitch Rebbe.

Precocious, with a gift for languages, steeped in the arts, Isaiah was named after great grandfather who married a woman who was a daughter of the 'Zemach Zedek' – then leader of Lubavitch.

In 1915, Berlin's family moved from Riga to a small lumber town, Andreapol, as his father sought to resolve business issues in Petrograd after the 1917 Russian Revolution.

Berlin's primary education included formal religious Hebrew instructions and an early orthodox teacher who taught *"...that in every one of the letters of the Hebrew alphabet there was Jewish blood and tears"*. In 1916 he and his family moved to Petrograd where his father worked to supply timber to the railway system. There Berlin was home educated in the Bible and the Talmud and, with a large family library, began to digest classics like *'Twenty Thousand Leagues Under The Sea'* by Jules Verne and Alexandre Dumas's *'The Three Musketeers'* in Russia. Berlin's early gift for languages that began with Yiddish, Russian and Hebrew, continued with German, French and English. At the dinner table he learned from his father and family members and friends of political events swirling around Russia and across Europe from Italy and else-where. In 1917 Berlin experienced the onslaught of Russian Revolution at first hand.

His neighbours included professors, musicians, artists and teachers who were being displaced from their vocations. Euphoria struck when he and his family received word in 1917 of the Balfour Declaration prom-ising Jews a national home in Palestine that lifted their hopes and spirits. When the Bolsheviks took over, his father joined the Revolution and gained a livelihood as a state contractor to the railways providing an ample lifestyle and a dacha.

Berlin continued to devour his father's ample library of Tolstoy, Turgenev, Goethe and especially a multi volume Jewish Encyclopedia. In 1919 overwhelmed by growing deprivation during Lenin's first year, his father decided to leave Russia to return to Riga. Then in 1921 with his remaining family dwindling, his father left for England to prepare the way for the family to sail for London where they quickly settled in comfortable middle class quarters. There Berlin started the climb up the ladder to a brilliant English academic career. Berlin began to experience

English tolerance that instigated his study of the notion of 'pluralism' which became his life's work.

His family moved from their orthodox Jewish roots and their kosher habits to a more secular home experience.

Having gained admission to Westminster, a top London private school, Isaiah decided, after the headmaster advised Berlin that changing his first name would make life easier decided instead to go to St. Paul's, another top private school in London, gaining a place but failing to receive a scholarship. A clumsy athlete he concentrated on his studies and became the top scholar and excellent debater.

In 1928 he gained admission to Oxford and attended Corpus Christi College. There he began his studies of philosophy, politics and economics and literature. Corpus Christi was an exclusively male College whose student body included Cyril Connoly, Harold Acton, Evelyn Waugh and Stephen Spender and other elite and accomplished students. There he won a scholarship to 'read' Classic and Modern history, and the 'Greats', both modern and ancient, at Oxford. Selected to edit the 'Oxford Outlook' gave him access to the 'brightest' and the 'best' of his generation. He befriended Fred Ayers, Ludwig Wittgenstein and Maurice Bowra, each outstanding scholars and soon, storied authors. No field of literature or philosophic ideas was not explored, and, each with passion and care. He relished Russian novels and poetry. Oxford, at that time, was the test bed for political ideas on Marxism and Fascism. Communist adherents split between Bolsheviks and Trotskyites dividing teachers and undergraduates alike. Summers he would travel to Europe especially to the Salzburg Festival in Austria where he deepened his love of music. He met and admired a classical music conductor, Toscanini, who was a fierce anti-fascist. In 1938, Hitler took over Austria in the 'Anschluss' and Europe became overrun with Nazi ideology.

Meanwhile Berlin had begun to dominate fields of study and two he made his own, the philosophy of history[424] and the theories of liberty. Berlin knit together the ideas of the ancients Greeks to St. Simeon, from

---

424 Berlin transformed this subject to focus on the interconnected and overlapping ideas of history.

the Germans Kant to Hegel to Marx, from the French from Constant to de Tocqueville to Rousseau, from the English – Locke to Mills to Bentham, from the Russians from Doesteyesky to Tolstoy, from the Americans from Paine to Jefferson, all in his relentless search to define the nature and limits of freedom, liberty and the narrow path to pluralism, from government to the individual. His lecture in 1958 'Two Concepts of Liberty' remains a classic.

Back in 1932 to his amazement, Berlin was elected to All Souls College, the most elite college at Oxford and the first Jew admitted and the third Jew to be elected a 'Fellow' of Oxford. Finally he found a totally congenial academic environment.

His time at All Souls - 1934-1980 - has been carefully documented in his authorized autobiography 'Isaiah Berlin: A Life' by Michael Ignatieff (Metropolitan Books, 1998)[425]. His book on Marx[426] brought him to wider attention. In 1939 he met Chaim Weizmann as a young Oxford Don and later became heavily invested in the Zionist cause during a stint in New York City. A failed trip to Moscow in 1940 left him languishing in New York where he was hired by the British Press Service, then part of the Ministry of Information. His job was to get the Americans into the war. He spent time in Washington (1942-45) widened his network of American academics, political insiders and journalists whilst he kept deeply involved with Zionist leaders in the U.S.A. and Europe.

In the U.S.A., he met Churchill who confused him with the American song writer Irving Berlin. Later Churchill became a friend and admirer. He became an intimate of Lord Maynard Keynes and other leading English and American political and academic notables. In 1945 he finally got to Moscow where he immediately made contact with Russian writers and dissidents learning at first hand their experience under the oppressive

---

425 I became well acquainted with Michael Ignatieff before and after he was elected leader of the Liberal Party of Canada. This slender volume of Isaiah Berlin is a concise clear comprehensive review of Berlin's ideas, made easy to understand especially Berlin's carefully polished nuances on freedom, liberty and pluralism.

426 'Karl Marx: His Life and Environment' by Isaiah Berlin went through more than four editions and remains in print. Marx was of Jewish descent. Berlin for some reason did not explain the basis for Marx's anti-semitic rants.

Stalinist regime. He returned to Leningrad (the old St. Petersburg) and the dense literary circles there, especially Anna Akhmatova, the great Russian writer and poet who, when they met, talked for hours which was later vividly recounted by both. He also engaged Boris Pasternak, the famed poet and writer and later Nobel Prize winner, in long cultural, literary and political discussions.

In 1946 he left public service and returned to Oxford and began a deep dive into political ideas of 'freedom', 'liberty' and 'pluralism' where he and became advisor to Churchill on his voluminous war memoirs. Through the Cold War (1949-53), he began lecturing at American universities especially Harvard as his reputation as an original essayist and teacher spread.

Suddenly in 1949 after having fallen in love and out several times, finally met and settled on a married woman, Aline Halban, an aristocrat French born of Jewish Russian extraction with three sons and married in 1953. Together they worked and translated works of Tolstoy.

In their comfortable home in London, Berlin hung a magnified painting by Leonid Pasternak, the famed painter and father of Boris Pasternak of a group portrait of Russia's leading writers, poets and artists that he relished.

In 1955 he lectured at University of Chicago and encountered Leo Strauss, a conservative political philosopher who was skeptical of Berlin's 'liberal' ideas. Between 1957 to 1963, Berlin began to publish his ground breaking essays and lectures rising in recognition for his original ideas. He met and influenced great leaders from President J.F. Kennedy to Chaim Weizmann. Berlin was enchanted by both Roosevelt and Churchill, and believed like Carlyle, in the 'Great Man' theory of history that animated his thinking. Unlimited liberty was inherently a flawed notion, he taught. Liberty requires limits. No historian probed the ideas of ancient renaissance and pre-modern thinkers, more deeply or comprehensively than Berlin[427], bringing to wider attention thinkers overlooked by others.

---

427 Perhaps Leo Strauss, the conservative historian matched Berlin's excavation of these ancient ideas. Leo Strauss brought Maimonides as an original thinker to a wider intellectual audience.

Berlin was attacked for his 'centrist' liberal ideas by both the left and the right and their 'relativity' to the politics of the era.

Berlin brought to wide attention the work of Alexander Herzen and the founder of modern political science, Giambattista Vico. His essay on Vico and Herder[428] clawed at the roots of modern political science. Berlin felt that the romantic writers had left a legacy of 'identity politics' that undermined and distorted rationality in politics. This romantic obsession led, he argued, directly to extremism and intolerance. Berlin believed in reason and truth was at the core of a 'positivist' liberal ideology. The 'utopian' visions of Hitler and Stalin (influenced by Lenin and Marx) that he experienced at close hand, he argued, were the curses of the 20th century. Romantic notions to transform the human condition led inevitably to extremism. His analysis on *'Two Concepts of Liberty'* changed the way historians analyse history.

To the surprise of his friends, he took on the Presidency of a new college at Oxford, Wolfson College, raised the funds and enticed top scholars to its precincts. After the buildings and campus were designed of a top architect selected by Berlin, he led the construction from scratch, organized and working until he found a worthy successor and left in 1975 to continue his writings and lectures.

Together with John Stuart Mill's classic work *'On Liberty'* and Berlin's essays in liberalism became the touchstones of the philosophy of liberalism in the 20th century.

From 1975 to 1997, Berlin continued to be the paramount source of liberal ideology in the west. In 1994, he lectured at the University of Toronto. I heard him speak of what he called his legacy, his 'Credo'. No one interested in liberal politics should fail to read this, his final address, to future historians and politicians.

Unlike most other historians[429], Berlin found a positive aspect even in extremists like the German philosopher and Nazi sympathizer Martin

---

428 Johann Gottfried Herder (born in Poland in 1744 and died in Germany in 1903) taught that an individual's 'roots' and 'belonging' different from romantic notions of 'identity' centres the person without alienating or denying others.

429 Leo Strauss, the conservative historian followed the same cause in his work.

Heidegger, as Berlin began to slowly and painfully connect the dots to outline a 'relativist' and persuasive tolerant school of politics and for politicians.

For anyone interested in 'liberalism' his legacy deepened, adding both followers and critics every day thereafter especially the latter part of the 20th century.

For a short cut in the study of the meaning and applied to liberalism, Mill's and Berlin's essays on liberalism will suffice. Berlin remains the most quoted modern political philosopher of the 20th century[430,431] – a must read for any 'wannabee' liberal.

> *"Few new truths have ever won their way against the resistance of established ideas save by being overstated."*
> – Berlin's quote from '*Communications and History: Theories of Media, Knowledge, and Civilization*' by Paul Heyer (1988), pp 125

---

430 Books by Isaiah Berlin include: *Karl Marx* (Thornton Butterworth, 1939), *The Age of Enlightenment* (New American Library, 1956), *Four Essays on Liberty* (Oxford University Press, 1969) and *Vico and Herder* (Chatto and Windus, 1976).

431 Berlin became noted for his luminous prose and polishing succinct quotes. Just a few of my favourite examples will suffice:

- *"Philosophers are adults who persist in asking childish questions."* – quoted in the Listener, 1978
- *"Injustice, poverty, slavery, ignorance - these may be cured by reform or revolution. But men do not live only by fighting evils. They live by positive goals, individual and collective, a vast variety of them, seldom predictable, at times incompatible."* – Political Ideas in the 20th Century (1950), *The Crooked Timber of Humanity: Chapters in the History of Ideas* by Isaiah Berlin & Henry Hardy (2013)

ABUSES OF HISTORY

Is history more than stories of the past?

History remains a mélange of facts, fictions and assumptions. Lessons of history live in opaque, murky pools of memory. Historians by design and inclination sift the sands of history through the sieve of the historian's belief structures. Facts, events and personalities are deftly arranged to meet the historians own subjective characteristics. Are their histories married to the historians' Marxist, socialist, conservative or liberal inclinations? We observe historians who embellish and polish the nuances and meaning of history through the lens of their biases. Rare is the historian who writes beyond his biases to illuminate fact based pages of history free of bias or personal ideology. Perhaps this is an impossibility but historians must try. Perhaps, in the end, history is only for other historians.

Four essays by Friedrich Nietzsche (1873-1878) entitled '*On the Use and Abuse of History for Life*' (1874) were not the first nor the last to explain how history is falsified for the purposes of a leader or wannabe leader or politician in need of support for a weak narrative abuses history, as history decays from abuse. Truth awkwardly gets in the way of political necessity. Even Plutarch and Voltaire were not immune from this malaise. Orwell in his book '*Why I Write*' (Penguin Books, 2004) unpacks the necessity of truth if we choose a path forward towards a better fuller life.

Historians always wrote and write history from the vantage point of their preconceptions. Herodotus, considered the first historian, is the first and prime example. Sometimes factual evidence is uncovered to change historians ruminations, though rarely. Having invested their reputation on a certain set of outcomes they rarely can recast their histories. Often historians look for someone to blame or seek to defend. Too often this results in a one sided story line that fudges history.

Examples abound. Most historians like Churchill are hero worshippers and especially of himself and enjoyed writing histories and biographies[432]. Churchill's collected works on the history of World War II edited at first by his son Randolph and then by Sir Martin Gilbert and his volumes on the history of the English Speaking People are both magnificent in scope, erudition and literary style[433]. Arthur Schlesinger adored Franklin Roosevelt and then John F. Kennedy, and wrote his versions of his hero-based history books accordingly. Schlesinger, in the need to justify errors in judgement by Roosevelt, developed a false counter narrative to blame the 'Cold War;' on Stalin's 'paranoia' or 'insanity'. Stalin was neither, except perhaps paranoid in his last years. Churchill called Stalin the 'greatest leader' he ever encountered after his visit with him in Moscow during World War II. British historian Eric Hobsbawm a devout Marxist till his death at age 102 in 2012, passed away, with no regrets as he wrote popular history through the distorted lens of his unwavering Marxist beliefs.

Barbara Tuchman (1912-1982), a popular American writer wrote a range of books on history imbedded with vivacious biographical sketches. Her first book in 1956 *'Bible and Sword: England and Palestine from the Bronze Age to Balfour'* (New York University Press, 1956) was an interesting introduction to the unfocused political frame of Palestine and Israel. She held no degree in history and believed this lack of historical training liberated her from being imprisoned by historians' norms and nostums. Turning points in history were her playing field. *'The March of Folly: From Troy to Vietnam'* (Knopf/Random House, 1984), *'The Guns of August'* (Macmillan, 1962) and then her excellent summary *'Practicing History: Selected Essays'* (Alfred A. Knopf, 1981). Her pithy quotes are

---

432 Churchill wrote lyrical biographies about his ancestor John Churchill, the first Duke of Marlborough who built Blenheim Castle where Churchill was born and buried and about his father and his idol Randolph Churchill who died prematurely and treated Churchill with distain.

433 As a life-long student of Churchill starting in 1950's, I wrote two essays on *'Churchill as a Zionist'* and *'Churchill as a Liberal'* published in my book *'Parade: Tributes to Remarkable Contemporaries'* (Mosaic Press, 2017). I sent my essay on *'Churchill as a Zionist'* to Sir Martin Gilbert when he was teaching at the University of Western

salient. *"War is the unfolding of miscalculations." "Dead battles, like dead generals, hold the military mind in their dead grip."* Though of a liberal bent, she painted magnificent portraits of leaders whose mistakes caused untold deaths in World War I. English scholar, Paul Johnson wrote history with greater balance and insight[434]. Jon Meacham, a prolific American historian who started with a conservative outlook, began to nuance his histories with a pronounced 'leftist' stance. Robert Caro's magisterial volumes on Lyndon Baines Johnson, still continuing, is balanced history at its apex, still sifted through an admitted liberal lens.

Margaret MacMillan, a Canadian historian also selected turning points in history for her popular histories. As Warden at St. Antony's at Oxford, she studied and pinpointed chilling failures of leadership. In her book, *'Dangerous Games: The Uses and Abuses of History'* (Modern Library, 2010), she pointed to the dilemma when leaders, baked in ideology, foster links between grievances and revenge. Her other books offer scintillating insights as she produced a series of volumes on turning points in history in the 20ᵗʰ century – *'Paris 1919: Six Months That Changed the World'* (Random House Publishing Group, 2007), *'Nixon in China: The Week That Changed the World'* (Viking Canada, 2006), *'The Uses and Abuses of History'* (Penguin Canada, 2008) and more recently *'War: How Conflict Shaped Us'* (Penguin Random House, 2020). MacMillan leads us through a scintillating romp through history and how nationalism, religion, the thirst for power, new technology and culture continuously provoke war that humanity moves ever slowly to limit.

In retrospect, my favourite historians are British. G.M. Trevelyan (1876-1962) whose elegant pen made 19ᵗʰ and 20ᵗʰ century history came alive with his 1928 *'History of England'* or his 1938 *'The English Revolution, 1688-1689'* just to name two. His student and historian J.H. Plumb

---

Ontario in my hometown of London, Ontario and he was kind to write me that he had learnt some facts on this subject about Churchill he did not know. Churchill's life is a treasure trove that keeps giving.

434 I had the pleasure to meet Paul Johnson in London when he served on the government board regulating radio, cable and television in the '80s. Afterwards, I became an instant fan of his popular histories.

published his own collected essays entitled '*The Making of an Historian: The Collected Essays of J.H. Plumb*', a wonderful jaunt through the lives and works of many of these historians.

No doubt the most difficult to decipher, yet worth the effort was the matchless works of Sir Lewis Namier, a strange difficult Polish Jewish immigrant to England who taught at Manchester University never making it to Oxford or Cambridge. Namier poured over the records and lives of the Members of Parliament in two periods – 17th and 18th century – to produce '*The Structure of Politics at the Accession of George III, England in the Age of the American Revolution*' and finally his majestic '*History of Parliament*' series. Namier came to the conclusion that politics and peripherally history was based on politicians' emotions and relation-ships rather than reason or principle. As he delved into the origins of party politics in the 1760's in England, he described the quest for power, cabals, factions, the origins of political parties and the relentless motion towards personal advancement that motivates all politicians[435].

Another favourite of mine for obvious reasons, is the works of Lord Alan Bullock from whom on the suggestion of the editor of my first book 'Beyond Imagination', he agreed to add his essay as a final chapter that laid out the undeniable facts of Holocaust that is still shamefully debated in dubious quarters.

My son also led me to Thomas Carlyle (1785-1881), an English histo-rian who was known for developing the 'Great Man Theory'. He argued some were born to lead and made a difference in the arc of history.

The lessons learned are that framing and informing oneself of history for veracity and accuracy is never ending.

---

435 The late John Stewart, a former Member of Parliament and later Senate with whom I shared offices in the Senate was one of the world's leading experts on David Hume. John led me to study the works of Sir Lewis Namier. My son Lawrence led to study the books and essays of the iconic historian A.J.P. Taylor who wrote of other British historians (including Namier), F.H. Carr, Hugh Trevor-Roper. What they had in common 'literary markers, great scholarship and clear convictions'. It was John Stewart – a graduate of the University of Chicago – who also introduced me to the 'Chicago School; scholarship on history led by Leo Strauss and Martin Friedman on economics, both worthy of careful study.

Of course there are leaders like Churchill whose words continue to be used and abused by politicians as flimsy validation to advance a shallow or unrelated usually ill-considered argument.

Leo Strauss, the conservative historian and philosopher argued that to dismiss ideas from ancient scholars because of their prejudices current in their times is to dismiss history. Historians should attempt to suspend their biases to extricate good ideas from bad. One idea is not superior to another simply on religious or political grounds except in the eye of the biased historian. Tolerance, both conservative Strauss and liberal Berlin argued, is the essence of liberals and conservatives endless search for truth.

Theories of history exploded in the 20th century. "War is the locomotive of history" wrote Trotsky who wrestled to become head of the new born Red Army and so saw history through his experiences as did other Communist leaders like Mao, or Ho Chi Minh or Stalin who were Marxist Leninists and saw history through perpetual social class war. Communists believed that changes in society could only happen by perpetual revolutions.

Before World War I, Churchill proclaimed early in his career that progress could only occur via European peace and stability. Later Churchill changed his views as Europe became mired in appeasement in the face of Hitler's aggression.

Every book of history has a view point. Every book of history is, in the end, an argument and history ever changes as more detail and facts are uncovered like relics that are excavated and dusted off from the mounds of the ancient past.

To uncover historic facts separated from opinion requires reading history from varied perspectives of 'true believers'. Only then can history's lessons be gleaned with some semblance of truth. While history remains a collection of stories written by historians with their biases, it remains equally difficult to divine messages that define lessons from history. Yet much can be learned from historians insights, if one can separate their slant of history from truth. Only by reading about the same events and the actions of political leaders described by a number of historians with different slants can a semblance of historic truth emerge.

Any student of history has a problem especially after the advent of the internet when history expanded and in process history accelerated. Still a careful culling can give an interested student a clearer picture of history, a daunting and consuming task[436].

---

436 If history is a collage of stories and clever staged plays, the backdrops or the stages of history are beginning to change. Looking back to the future through the rear view mirror will need wider different lenses. With the advent of the internet and big data collection, 'micro' historians will be augmented by 'macro' historians skilled in the collection and selection of megadata – on wars, civil discord, wealth accumulation and loss by elites and nations, educational trends (e.g. the growing gap between educated elite college graduates and a shrinking availability of appropriate job opportunities). Culture, climatic and nature's changing trends will also be coagulated and measured by sophisticated algorithms. Called 'cliodynamics' after Clio the Greek muse of history, this new approach to history seeks to treat history as a science with mathematical laws. It also seeks to integrate climatic, cultural, economics, macro sociology et al via mathematical constructs based on of historic databases and models.

'Cliodynamics' was coined by Peter Turchin, a Russian scholar who migrated to America to research to teach microbiology and then shifted to history. This method of mathematical models will provide new 'macro' backdrops to 'micro' historians and will continue to quickly evolve in the future, giving us a clearer picture of the past.

EPILOGUE

To ruminate, and make sense of the absurd jagged shards of the 20th century is a challenge. How best to distill the valorim of 'progress' embedded in the history of the fragmented 20th century. A narrative on outcroppings of historic events entwined with family history is not unique.

When I meet others, especially fellow Jews, I probe their roots, where were each of their parents born, their names, what route did they travel to get here – all marks on the scratches of historic events. Within each Jew lies elements of the richness and diversity of the Jewish diaspora. One woman I came to know in Toronto was born in Harbin, China where her family found refuge in World War II fleeing from Russia. Her husband was a son of poor Polish Jewish immigrants who built a successful engineering business across Canada. Another came from near Transnistria on the disputed borderlands of Rumania. Another came from Oslo whose family somehow escaped Germany. Still others from Bagdad, Tehran, Morocco and Egypt. South African Jewish immigrants in Canada mostly can trace their lineage to Latvia or Lithuania. Most in Canada came from Belarus, Ukraine, Russia or Poland. Israelis source their family roots from all the above and more.

This then is the palimpsest of history, the authenticity and the richness of diversity that lies in each hidden story of progress, one person's story, one at a time, and then each individual's voyage to tolerance as each story adds one more colourful strand in the tapestry of the vibrant history of our times.

The more you learn of another's roots the more history becomes less opaque and more informative. History changes constantly the more one reads and the more one listens to others stories.

AFTERWORD: LOOKING AHEAD

"The realization that life is absurd and cannot be an end, but only a beginning. This is a truth nearly all great minds have taken as their starting point. It is not this discovery that is interesting, but the consequences and rules of action drawn from it."

– Albert Camus

FROM PUBLIC CLARITY TO MEDIA SCRAMBLE IN THE 21ST CENTURY - THE ERA OF 'NEWISH' AND 'AGITPROP' PROPAGANDA[437]

On reflection and hindsight, the world's perspective on democracy and politics and the 'rule of law' in the 21st century is being deconstructed and not for the better. The 'centre' isn't holding. Almost like a slow motion car crash, the ball bearings of a smoothly purring engine have spilled out slowly rolling around in abound directions at the same time. Markets and institutions are imploding due to the impact of the 'attention economy and the net'[438]. More wealth and more 'unaccountable power' beyond the reach of governments obliterated the reach of governments around the globe and its accelerating.

More 'news' is consumed by more people on more platforms of delivery from print to TV, cable, radio and cyberspace, than ever before in world history. There are no longer core news sources.

The 'digital divide' has witnessed the swift transfer of manufacturing jobs from the working classes to the new digital millennials that continues to accelerate. Respect for all, all established institutions has crumbled. Religious observance is fragmented, and worse, demonized. There is an unreal, almost obsessional preoccupation with the 'middle class', while poverty continues at high unacceptable levels in Canada, especially amongst aboriginals and blacks, neglected by Liberals, Conservatives, NDP and Green, Quebec parties and pundits alike. The politics of envy is unleased and class warfare rife. 'Cancel culture' is now an accepted norm, obviously led by the 'woke' organisms proliferating United States of America.

---

437 *"Propaganda is the art of persuading others to do what you do not necessarily believe yourself."* - Abba Eban.

438 First coined by M.H. Goldhaber in a lecture in Cambridge in 1997.

Confronted with the easy inexpensive rise of the new 'propaganda' in varied unedited platforms: blatant lies, distractions, clever fabrications and hypocrisy lie hidden in the shadows of 'political correctness' as a prolix scramble of public policy is observed to our chagrin[439]. 'Narcissism of small things' wrapped in 'political correctness', distract public attention from underlying missing policy gaps. 'Identity' politics and 'victim' preoccupation has turned politics on its head. Clarity is baked into overcooked or underdone ideological party lines in mind-bending waves of distraction from the way forward to economic growth and prosperity. Sluggish growth – 'the inconvenient truth' - is left alone and unattended. Problems like clean drinking water not just for indigenous reservations but for places like outports in Newfoundland and the outlandish numbers of incarcerated indigenous youth are left unresolved. Boiled water advisories abound. Spiraling public debt is largely ignored and this was before Covid. While salaries stagnate and taxes increase and jobs for youth shrink, there is a growing restless malaise not detected in the media or political classes. Is the job market changing? What will be the impact of AI and robotics on the job market? No one knows or few care. Are good paying jobs a thing of the past? No. But we are distracted by smaller, less consequential issues – 'the narcissism of small things'. Small businesses, the best creator of jobs, have been neglected as more small businesses are lost than created.

My lifelong study of 'free trade' and 'free trade zones' as engines of economic growth continues[440]. Globalism has come under increasing

---

439   In Lenin's iconic book, 'What's To Be Done?' written in 1902 and studied by Stalin, he wrote that propaganda or half truths are all essential elements in Communist policy. When the Central Committee of Communist Party took over power in 1917, it set up a Department of Agitation and Propaganda ('Agitprop') and controlled the popular radio and print, films and cultural devoted to manipulate public opinion about towards Marxist-Leninism ideology. Trains with Soviets running active presses turned out and distributed 'heroic' posters and flyers all selling the Communist message. 'Agitprops' are alive and well in the west today, and, not only by Chinese Communists and their fellow travellers in the west, but others.

440   President George W Bush's 'tax free' zones in Egypt and Jordan to provide incentives for Israeli and Muslim businesses to work together to produce and export to the U.S.A., tax free, was established during his Presidency. Most recently, Trump's

attack. The cost benefit analyses are neglected. Overlooked in the slow torturous history of democracy is the relationship between 'free trade' to the creation and practice of democratic institutions. The best historical example is the origins and spread of Hanseatic League along the waterways in Northern Europe as 'free trade' became the precursor to open 'free' cities. Nascent tolerant business practices and diversity of business relationships became the harbinger of tolerant democratic political principles and practices. Business law and commercial practices set the framework and foundation for civil law, the foundation of a practicing democracy.

The heart of Parliamentary democratic principles lies in the Blackstone thesis of 'checks and balances' to restrain the impulses of the human condition. United States has ingrained constitutional 'checks and balances' and separation of powers[441] - Canada, less so.

The misuse and abuse of government power remains central to the human condition. Meanwhile in Canada, to denigrate the Canadian Senate is to neuter an invaluable constitutional 'check' on government and the Commons. The nature of its appointments while important pales in significance to its vital role as a 'check' on power. "*Put not your trust in princes...*", so goes the biblical injunction. There are less checks on power today as government grows in complexity and persuasiveness. Too often, courts in Canada avoid the plain reading of the Constitution and judge made laws are on the rise with often disastrous results as judges choose to legislate rather than adjudicate.

Accountability for the Canadian federal budget or indeed provincial or municipal budgets is not existent. A proliferation of tax payers dollars are spent on law suits, damage claims, or frittered away on absurd

---

'economic zones' to rebuild the core of those American cities fallen into decay and economic malaise with tax incentives are examples of positive growth policies and poverty reductions.

441 For a more thorough exposition of the Canadian Parliamentary system and its checks and balances, read '*A Leader Must Be A Leader: Encounters with Eleven Prime Ministers*' by Jerry Grafstein (Mosaic Press, 2019). The Canadian Prime Minister has more power than any other democratic head of state as he commands both the government, the executive, the public service and Parliament.

policies without oversight. Budgets are swiftly approved without M.P.'s, MLA's or Councillors even reading them.

Omnibus bills are the most egregious assault on Parliamentary oversight. Billions are approved in a few days of general debate. Same too at the provincial and municipal levels. Committee oversight, dominantly controlled by the government party, is weak and ineffective. Democracy is growing weaker yearly. The core of democracy blurred in the weak remains oversight of public expenditures. Since the Pierre Trudeau government, committees of Parliament no longer take the needed time to scrutinize the budget. Instead Parliamentary budget relies on parliamentary auditors. Six hundred years of struggles for Parliament oversight if not lost is diminishing. There is a blurring of accountability for the expenditure of the tax dollars between the federal, provincial and municipal governments. Responsible government grows weaker. The tax payer is confused, or worse, disinterested. The media's oversight is at best fragmented. Standing bipartisan oversight committees with skilled expert staffing may be one small answer.

Orwell, who valued truth, unvarnished truth, above all else, would not be surprised but certainly enraged, by the decoupling of truth from politics substituting 'opinion' and belief structures garnished with 'selected' facts to meet group machined belief structures. Propaganda replete with purposeful techniques are now adopted freely, without restraint, by democracies during elections and in public discourses. Giant tech companies gear public attitudes to their benefit. Artificial 'echo' chambers are deployed to manipulate public opinion to match political talking points that reverberate through the biosphere. Purposeful political surrogates as leaders act as ventriloquists to repeat their political lies. Emotive words like ethics or character no longer trigger public passion. The public has become jaded by information overload and, universities practice group think and 'cancel' history eroding the 'idea of a university' as place for meaningful debate.

'Identity' politics divides and drowns the public space at the expense of a deeper debate about economic and cultural choices. Descartes originated the modern preoccupation with individualism: "*Cognito, Ergo Sum*" "*I think, therefore I am*". The millenniums have brought forth the era of 'me first'. Obsession with 'identity' politics from gender to race to religion on close examination creates backlashes and increases the deeper divides in society's tolerances though 'progress' can barely be discussed. Does 'identity' or 'victim' politics enhance 'progress'? The reach for economic progress is sidetracked. Economic growth and economics both suffer from lack of attention, especially small businesses, that continue to create most new jobs. Equity where needed the most is scarce. Rigid belief structures in politics and the media easily paint over realistic facts with amoral actions. The interested public still believes what it chooses to believe. The 'new order' of the new 'news' is an odd scrambled mixture of entertainment and trash, and 'feel good' news vignettes. 'Character' and yes, 'honesty' and morality, in politics has been marginalized if not forgotten, submerged and no longer seems to register on the 'leadership' index. Patent lies by leadership elites are on the rise.

Politics and culture is so besotted with 'celebrity - figures who become instant 'gurus' on every aspect of life. The 'frenzy of renown' is not new[442].

Perhaps the word most misused by current politicos and the media is 'values'. 'Values' can be stretched to cover any definition or as means of disguising rationale for actions. Its 'values' this or 'values' that or 'core values' till the word has lost all semblance of meaning. I have learned to prefer the use of the word 'principle' or 'principles'. Citizens can agree more precisely with daily articulated 'principles' rather than obtuse 'values'.

John Locke's essays in 'Human Understanding' and 'Tolerance' have been neglected, and worse, forgotten. Jeremy Bentham whose theses to quantitatively serve needs of the greatest number, has now devolved with Parliament, provinces and cities preoccupied with entitlements, once granted, never easily returned. This dependence and muffled 'tolerance' fails to lift the growing number of Canadians adults and especially children living in poverty, pushing aside the scale of poverty as a measurement of democracy. David Hume, Scottish philosopher,

---

442 'The Frenzy of Renown: Fame and Its History' by Leo Braudy (Oxford University Press, 1986). The irrationality of 'celebrity' is not new, but magnified by the new world of cyberspace and media lusting to cover every minute aspect of a celebrity's life.

economist, historian and essayist, influenced by Locke, Montesquieu and Machiavelli once wrote *'Reason is and ought to be the slave of the passing and can never pretend to any other office then to serve and obey them.'*[443]

'Character', once a linchpin in politics, is fallen into disuse. Now character as a virtue is rarely used as a political polemic. Rather it is abused and ineffective as a political attack. Public attention is diverted. Abortive attempts to distract prevails over focus on principles and substance.

The 'Fourth Estate' is no longer the impartial watch dog of civil society. Journalist standards appear to dissolve before our eyes. The economic weakness of the print media is no doubt one part of the source of this derangement where the print media once served as the vigilant guard of 'virtuous' conduct. Instead the print media has been taken public hostage by its own economic distress and losing readership as competition for viewers races to compete with the simplicity of 'tweets' and ill-considered blurps on social media and wrestles to stem the flow of dwindling newspaper readership. Mindless soundbites of 'gotcha' newsflashes in both print media and TV and radio reign supreme. The blog sphere is worse. We need a balance of TV, print and cyberspace that at least declares its bias in each segment. Alas, 'gotcha' politics is preferred. 'News' is no longer 'news' but a toxic anemic mixture of garbled opinion and entertainment scrambled with 'cold case' murders and irrelevant so-called 'human interest' puppy-like stories. Two ideas collide. Fact based analyses and partisan ideological driven perception, with the latter usually winning the day. Context, historic context, has taken a vacation.

Yet I still retain high hopes that this cycle will pass and a virtuous cycle will return and hopefully a better tomorrow awaits. While an inveterate contrarian, I remain an incurable Liberal and liberal optimist. Perhaps the attention span of adults might increase to hold at least two opposing ideas together at the same time. Children can more easily multi-task.

---

443 John Stewart, born in Cape Breton and educated at the University of Chicago and Columbus University in New York City was appointed a Senator. We shared for a time an office in the Senate and became close colleagues. John was amongst the brightest and best in the Senate. He was a recognized worldwide expert on Hume.

What if media – both print and electronic - increased its resources in original investigative journalism, once the mainstay of major competing newspapers? A front page attention grabber each day! Would that attract wider, younger readership be attracted? Aspiring journalists would compete to join these news enterprises.

There was a time in the print media led by the New York Times in America and the Times of London in England exercised a rigourous fair and balanced approach to news reporting and opinion. The New York Times news, editorial and 'op-ed' embodied a 'Holy Trinity'.

News reporting in the New York Times was factual and sources were carefully scrutinized by skilled editors for accuracy and balance. The editorial page reflected the news editors' and owners' opinions. The 'op-ed' page quixotically had one journalist column on the left side of the page who held conservative views (e.g. William Safire) and another respected journalist's column on the right side of the page who held liberal views (e.g. William Reston). In between was a balance of other noted experts' opinion pieces. The editorial page had letters to the editor reflecting a balance of views. This practice is now history.

The electronic media was governed by the 'fair and balanced' regulatory rule for TV stations to retain use of the public airways. This changed dramatically when cable news not governed by the 'fair and balance' rules and regulations. Unverified opinion was allowed and unmarked. Both have had their way.

There should be a return to these norms. One way is have each opinion written and easily identify their bias. Public Broadcasting cable 'news' anchor or reporter in the U.S.A. on certain programs does this. This should apply to all electronic media in both Canada and the United States.

We can only maintain high expectations. Universities have retreated as a space for the 'free' exchange of opinions and fact. Is 'free debate' and diversity of opinion encouraged at universities? That's regretfully an open question. Who are the new 'fascists'? Both the 'right' and the 'left'.

There remains 'tender indifferences', as Camus wrote, to the reality woes of everyday life of massacres at home and overseas and the plight of the poor and the hard working lower middle class at home.

The Rebbe Kotzker, born in 19th century in Poland, a Hasidic master and a favourite of mine taught that the hardest task in life is to tell the truth - the 'emes' - especially the truth about oneself! Truth is no longer a mainstay in politics. Liars never change. Once a lair, always a liar. Fabricated opinion rules the print media while entertainment info infects hard news on T.V. It's hard to separate 'fact' from fabrication. Certainly nightly newscasts artificially tabled to one side do not help.

Was the 1990's, after the fall of the Berlin Wall in 1989, the last decade of limitless hope? For a sweet while, the ideological divisions that separated the world suddenly seemed to dissipate. It was incredible. All deep systemic political problems seemed solvable[444]. 'Progress' was on the march. Anything was possible. Or, at least, that's how many of us felt. The rise of the internet, the cell phone, 'tweets', and 24/7 news cycle did not waken us to the new reality of a more dangerous world that was coagulating beneath the surface as 'news' fragmented and 'fake' news proliferated. The world became 'woke'.

We have suffered from the loss of 'idea of the university' as promulgated by Cardinal Newman[445] and practiced by Robert Hutchins at the University of Chicago who preached the necessity of studying 'great books' of the past to so inform our free societies of the worth of virtuous cycles in history as lessons for the present and the future. Tolerance of opposing views is rarely practiced. Campuses have of late been taken hostage by extremists who have been allowed to flourish and stifle the free exchange of ideas. This absence of tolerance has seeped into our political parties. The study of morality and the humanities has dwindled. Academics fail in their primary task – to educate students to listen and tolerate discordant views as Cardinal Newman taught and wrote at Oxford over 150 years ago. Has the media tired overwhelmed administrators refuse to take

---

444 As Abba Eban, the articulate Foreign Minister of Israel, born in South Africa and educated at Cambridge, once observed, "*It is not forbidden for politicians to repeat errors, but it is not mandatory.*"

445 In 1858, John Cardinal Newman published his lectures titled 'The Idea of University' which envisaged a community of students with differing view-points debating ideas in an atmosphere of tolerance and curiosity. Alas, this idea is sinking in a sea of 'group think'. Can autonomy and Fascism from the left or right be far away?

courageous principled stands to ensure freedom of expression without vilification or fear, choosing to brand impressionable Canadian minds instead with the illusion of 'appropriate' extremist conduct. Group think has overwhelmed individual thought.

Timid university authorities, like the 'treason of the clerks', appease extremist ideology, weakening universities as beacons of 'free' thought and 'free' exchange of ideas. I lament the turbulent atmosphere at York University, one of Canada's greatest educational institutions where freedom of speech and freedom from fear is not practiced in parity and abetted by academic authorities. Student 'fascism' prevails. The 'idea' of a university is curtailed by egregious conduct where bigotry of verbal and physical abuse intimidate students for their views. Can universities return to leadership of tolerance and freedom? Of course, armed with or even the unfettered opportunity to articulate differing viewpoints in the university space which today requires courage and principle. Principle and practice march best when they march together.

We now live in the age of hyper-propaganda fabricated by politicians and media alike[446]. Fact, fiction, reality and perception are co-mingled beyond recognition. Truth, conventional truth, is neglected by all sides of the party system. Party has been supplanted ideas ripped from rigid belief structures. So one selects 'facts' to conform to one's 'belief' structure. Fact checkers in the news select the facts to coincide with their preconceived views as do pollsters. 'Character', 'truth' and 'morality' are no longer the beacons of politics or its leaders. Rather how they cut-and-paste and manipulate the social media is applauded. 'Values' smudge the clarity of politics even more. It was Sir Wilfrid Laurier who declared, *"...For my part, I ask only one thing that we be judged according to our principles."* Politicians call for adherence to a 'nucleus of values' which many in their party neither accept nor agree. A quote attributed to

---

446 George Orwell put it best in a slender volume *'Why I Write'* first published 1946 then in Penguin Books in 2004. *"Political language is designed to make lies sound truthful and murder respectable, and to give one appearance of solidify of pure wind."* For a through expose, read *'Propaganda: The Formation of Men's Attitudes'* by Jacques Ellul (Vintage Books, 1973)

Thomas Jefferson put it well: *"In matters of style, swim with the current; in matters of principle, stand like a rock"*. Educators continue to teach bias and exert censorship in exams by marking down those who refuse to follow their political line based in their 'ersatz' world view. Rather they should encourage students to debate different ideas, replete with cant and bias contraptions. The media spews its own line of bias. The last great newspaper editor of New York Times was A.M. Rosenthal, who I admired and whose gravestone in 1990 carves out his legacy, *"He kept the newspaper straight."*[447] Has the New York Times forgotten its own self-defining masthead: *'All the news fit to print'*? Fact based 'news' is supplanted by disguised opinion coloured 'news'. Alas. Experts tell us our biases influence our cognitive processes. More so, to be on guard.

Most disturbing is the hidden exploitation of meta data based behaviourable science, utilized to forage voter preferences in support of democratic leadership. 'Trigger' words are found to uncover voter emotions, anger, anxiety, hates and hopes. Mining this information spotlights wedge issues and breeds cross divisiveness. Personal data collection remains a deep dark tool to be plumbed and manipulated in the so-called 'public interest'. Has the 'Big Brother' era arrived, or gangs of 'little brothers', no less allowed or encouraged?

There has been a quantum dive into individual privacy. New rules should be explored to curb excessive misalliances in the interest of a free and open and democratic society. Facial recognition devices, without limits, obliterates personal privacy further. Beware – 'big brother' is here.

Hacking confidential political emails and leaking them to the public has become common practice illustrating the amorality of most political wannabees. Law making and political maneuvers are more obvious, too obvious. Perhaps Bismarck was correct – *"Laws are like sausages, it is better not to see how they are made"*.

In Canada should a constitutional amendment should be considered to protect the right of privacy or at least stricter legislative rules so that

---

447 Seymour Topping, a distinguished foreign correspondent became assistant to Rosenthal and ensured that Rosenthal's emotional outbursts did not veer from that policy.

personal data and facial images cannot be mined without individual consent[448]. Should not police at least require judicial assent to deploy these tools?

The fragmentation of media between old line print to the texting and tweeting universes continue to unbalance untutored analysts. The public is led to hear, see, read and learn and be persuaded by the profound bias in the mainstream media led by the so-called 'objective' experts who use their bias to manipulate what people come to believe as 'truisms'. Their biases are rarely noted. Why should not reporters, editorialists and journalists declare their biases as a first step? Trust in institutions like media, now reaching the low zone of popularity join politicians and lawyers, and most recently academia, continues frittering away. Trust in the media is at its lowest ebb in modern times. So too established religions. Scientists and the scientific establishment harbour their own biases. The universities are losing the modicum of trust they still hold as well. Their independence and merit leaves the public fast-tracked to mistrust as the public sense they are not being told the truth nor are their kids. Politicians are praised when they take obvious truth and deconstruct the meaning of words so that what matters according to their belief structure is more important than public morality. Words continue to lose their inherent meaning.

The most overused word in the political lexicon is 'transparency' which has come to mean a crutch and a cover for political activism and making bad choices under that cover. Apologies create the new traffic in politics so they too are meaningless. So we inhabit a different amorphous opaque space. Caveat elector!

The 'echo chambers' inhabiting the Fourth Estate now need fact checkers. Perhaps it's time for a new improved Fifth Estate, dedicated to truth and impartiality rather than opinion unless clearly marked. At least

---

448 Academia has not helped the cause of privacy in the cyber age. The argument against strict privacy laws have been based on 'freedom of speech''. But the major underlying economic argument against limiting government action on privacy concerns as to not inhibit economic innovation or even the lust for new taxes, cow and lull governments into inaction.

balance even in opinion journalism outlets should be essayed. The 'good' news is that 'fact' checking, even if unbalanced, seems to be on the rise against politicians, but less against the media itself.

The endless search for facts, objective facts, is a precondition to sound policy... so urged Pierre Trudeau. Facts before policy! Truth will ultimately emerge.

Instead, McLuhan observed, 'The medium is the message[449]'. Or the message became the medium. Which is it, we can ask!

Albert Camus, the French author, playwright and essayist, another favorite writer, maintains his currency and relevance. His novel 'The Stranger' and his prose in 'The Myth of Sisyphus' ring true today. Both were labelled works of the 'absurd'. Our world is both 'absurd' and surreal. Watching TV or cable news feels to me as if one were an 'alien' from another planet. The scramble of fact and fiction and perception and the scramble of the services into an indigestible omlettes of entertainment and news and its nonsensical coverage assaults the adult mind. All connection to objectivity reality seems abandoned. Words are no longer used with care or in context. Quick comparisons to previous events are usually distorted and bear little resemblance to history. Facts in the news remained tarnished and tainted by bias and rigid belief structures. Perhaps it is behavioural science's task to liberate 'fact' from belief dogma and rescue truth from hyperbole. Nightly TV news lacks context and factual balance larded with 'good news' snippets.

Caveat. When a leader uses the word 'plan' – beware. Rarely has a leader a well considered detailed plan and the people named and designated to execute it with consequences of removal for failure.[450]

---

449 Roger Ailes, the conservative TV guru who turned Fox News into the leading cable news network wrote 'You Are the Message: Getting What You Want by Being Who You Are' (Crown Business, 1989) to explain how TV news presenters could sharpen and stamp their non-elitist audiences and gain loyalty to a boisterous opinionated TV brand.

450 One anecdote. When Stalin surrounded by his key advisors reviewed a new 'fire plan', the meeting started at midnight in the Kremlin. Stalin was silent till dawn. Then he stood up, threw all the papers on the floor and asked – "Where are the men!"

Does history repeat itself when the leading media is in the bag of one political side? Perhaps the media should study the history of the thirties when appeasement was rampant and the leading press in Europe and America supported Chamberlain's mistaken appeasement policies. The media failed dismally to probe more deeply into the flaws of this one-sided cheering section for weak political leadership. They failed to speak 'truth' to power. Appeasement brought on war. Perhaps social media has some pluses after all as it empowers citizens an unparalleled opportunity to persuade confused public opinion swamped in a plethora of misinformation.

For whatever reason, the old model of traditional independent journalism with rare exceptions has come to an end. List them if you can! Perhaps because of technology or changing tastes, certainly because of education. The Fourth Estate as an institution and its purveyors, with rare exceptions, its anchors and editors are faulty and flakey and lack depth and historic lenses. Conviction based on perceptions are routinely supplied rather than objectivity. Whilst rapid change may destroy institutions and trust and extremism takes root, we remain optimistic. One suggestion to increase trust and reduce hidden bias is for media of whatever stripe to use journalists and commentators who expose and declare their political affiliations as does the public cable news service in U.S.A. in their news and information programs when seeking public interaction. CBC should try. News people should take a course in 'anger management' as well as deep rooted pessimism. Oft hard news is avoided especially if it comes from the politicians they dislike. Established media – print, cable, TV, radio – has become a relentless source of division. Based on the old saw of the three 'R's' – 'Robberies, Recks and Rapes' to attract followership and audiences – the mainstream media now systematically employs 'gotcha' stories and diversions rather than projects of unity[451].

---

451   For over 15 years, I was a Board Member of City TV with Allan Waters, the successful founder of CHUM Radio and later with CITY TV which I co-founded, who regularly bemoaned the fact that his mega-media outlets, radio and TV, never emphasized 'good' news enough!

What is missing most in the media is context. Journalists with little or no history training fail to excavate and place stories in past or current history so stories float without context to aggravate a 'faux' sense of domestic or foreign action. The past is usually the prologue.

Who can fail to lament the loss of the 'public intellectual' debate due to the invasion of the cybersphere? We need to support new platforms for essential intellectual engagement.

Easy for me to opine as I have left the public area. We can only pray that this vicious cycle too shall pass just as the 'sun also rises' and we will see the return of a 'virtuous' cycle in public life.

Margaret Atwood giving her take on the process of writing wrote this in her insightful book 'Negotiating with the Dead: A Writer on Writing':

> "Obstruction, obscurity, emptiness, disorientation, twilight, blackout, often combined with a struggle or path or journey – an inability to see one's way forward, but a feeling that there was a way forward, and that the act of going forward would eventually bring about the conditions for vision – these were the common elements in many descriptions of the process of writing. I was reminded of something a medical student said to me about the interior of the human body, forty years ago: "It's dark in there".
>
> Possibly, then, writing has to do with darkness, and a desire or perhaps a compulsion to enter it, and, with luck, to illuminate it, and to bring something back out to the light."

While Margaret wrote this about writing, for me, she also described, perhaps unwittingly, that 'desire to bring something back out into the light', that darkness that at times envelopes politics as the political process struggles to change course for the better. 'All progress is by a winding stair-case', as one astute observer once noted.

Adam Gopnik, a writer for The New Yorker, wrote 'A Thousand Small Sanities: The Moral Adventure of Liberalism' (Basic Books, 2019) and sought to steer a course between extremes in liberalism. For example, he argued that Edmund Burke's reaction to the killing of the French Royalty during the French Revolution ignited his fierce criticism of liberalism. Burke claimed chaos could follow with the belief that society could be remade all at once on the basis of a big idea whilst traditions and customs were annihilated.

Gopnik went on to list tenets that lead to bad results for a liberal society.

"*There is liberal secularism, indifference to faith that calls itself 'tolerant'.*" "*There is liberal cosmopolitism*", indifference to national loyalty. "*There is liberal permissiveness*", the disdain for simple moral ideas... as that all children should have a father... and... there is liberal relativism. Secularism, cosmopolitism, permissiveness, relativism... these ideas that liberals view as positive can have a catastrophic effect on reordering ordinary people lives is... "*This is the heart of the crime called populism... and the success of Brexit where cultural so-called elites look down at others.*"

These arguments for tolerance are only faintly heard by self-described liberals today.

In the confusion and intellectual chaos of recent events in the west, we need to re-read Thomas Paine's '*Common Sense*'. Paine influenced the American founding fathers and democratic movements around the world. He preached the separation of Church and State, freedom of speech, freedom of religion, help for the poor and pensions. No one could imagine that believers in democracy would morph into secular ramparts abetted by the free media, demolish cultural norms or symbols like the flag or Christmas celebrations or traditional crosses in the name of secular supremacy. Countries bereft of civic tolerance will drift in chaotic waves as their 'centres' fight to retain a semblance of balance, of restrained discourse.

For a brief moment in 2007, my expectations as a Liberal soared when the Liberal Government in Ontario passed the 'Poverty Reduction Act', voted unanimously by all parties, in the Provincial Assembly calling for a reduction of child poverty in Ontario of 20% within five years. Finally I had high expectations the Liberals would act as liberals.

Instead child poverty levels in Toronto have increased in the past decade from one in nine to one in four children who live under the poverty line, making Toronto the new child poverty capital of Canada, and now the poverty leader ahead of Montreal and Vancouver[452]. An increasing

---

452 In 2018, one federal riding held by a leading Liberal Cabinet Minister was found to have a youth poverty level of 40%, shocking!

percentage of our seniors continue to slip below the poverty line. It is a shocking tale of benign neglect by all of our political classes. Food banks cannot keep up with the demand especially from aging seniors - the new invisible well-dressed poor.

I remain bonded to the belief that the state of the poor in a liberal society is the best gauge of a successful civic society. If poverty goes up, liberals fail. When poverty levels go down, liberals succeed. Literacy remains a co-equal benchmark of a 'progressive' society.

Perhaps the most undernourished independent policy research in Canada relates to the cash-starved state of our cities. Canada is now a nation of state-like cities. As Dickens wrote in his classic *'Tale of Two Cities'*, our cities are divided between the glittery high rises and the invisible rampants of poverty hidden away below the public radar. The spiralling price of housing has denied new young families access to affordable housing. Policies to remedy these crises are too slow and too ineffective. Statistics are startling. Urban poverty is on the rise from the dearth of social housing, jobs for impoverish youth, to food banks that now run out of food. The elites of all parties focus on the 'middle class' while neglecting the rising urban blight of poverty. Shameful!

One place to start is to follow the lead of New York City that turned to the Manhattan Institute, an independent market driven think tank that provides thoughtful and cost effective non-partisan solutions about issues like policing, housing, traffic, city planning, and city budgeting to offer independent apolitical reasonable cost/benefit solutions.

There is an obvious absurdity in the current deployment of federal and provincial tax revenues. The cities are hobbled by its real estate tax base which is never enough to cover major and minor needs, like public transit or infrastructure renewal. Therefore there needs to be more appropriate visible sharing of tax revenues where the provincial or federal governors don't cherry pick or micro-manage each city's needs. Responsible government means direct accounting for the expenditure of taxes. Of course, there must be checks and balances. The City Councillors in Toronto, for example, have approved billions of dollars for city projects and expect the funding to come from elsewhere. There needs to be federal and provincial oversight to ensure City Councillors don't waste tax money they didn't raise. As more than one successful mayor said, *"You have to respect the taxpayers' dollar"*. Easy to say, hard to do. But this reform is vital to the new generations of urban Canadians[453].

We should look to successful oversight of major public capital expenditures. One accountable person should be named for each project. This was done successfully in the 1967 Expo in Montreal and in Pan Am Games in Toronto in 2015. Recall the public works in New York City by 'Czar' Robert Moses in the '20s and '30s who cut through public works 'red tape' and brought focus and cost containment to new housing and new expressways. Subways are good example. New York City built almost 15 miles of subway in less than five years and on budget opening in 1914.

Toronto, the city I love and where I began a law practice and raised a family in the '60s, as I was a Liberal volunteer politician party activist and organizing in every part of it, I came to realize Toronto is a collection of different neighbourhoods with different economic circumstances. My fear that the 'Toronto the Great' is slouching towards its future. One glaring example of neglect is while high rises are sprouting up, while downtown is almost barren of small grassy parkettes where people can sit, sun and enjoy nature. Why? And the number of families awaiting affordable housing continues to grow with no solution in sight. This alone is a harbinger of civic unrest.

Robert Moses in New York in the first part of this century was a bold civic leader who increased tax payer effectiveness when he oversaw new urban infrastructure, tunnels, parks and transit, the gaping holes in city affairs, keeping them on budget and on time.

In 2018, we note the 500th anniversary of the start of the Reformation in Europe. In 1518, an obscure Catholic churchman, Martin

---

453 I first heard this theme when I was involved in the Toronto mayoralty assisting Phil Givens, an energetic distant cousin and Liberal, who ran against William Dennison, an NDP stalwart and socialist. Dennison's daughter, Lorna Milne became a Liberal activist and later Senator. Phil made wonderful soaring speeches about Toronto as a global leader while Dennison had a tatty banner bearing his campaign theme at all his rallies and at the end of every speech, Dennison would point to the banner and repeat, *"You have to have respect for the tax payers' dollar."* Dennison won that election hands down. Lesson learned about municipal politics and realty taxes.

Luther, hammered 95 theses on a door of the local church condemning indulgences - payments made to the church in hope of remission from sins in the afterlife. Perhaps we need a new set of 'indulgences' that revolt against the drift of politics as usual. Are the cities captives of unbridled, unbalanced growth?

Clean drinking water on aboriginal reserves where over a third still live in third world conditions continues unabated. So too in many Newfoundland outports[454]. There is a simple example of the 'Absurd' in the 21st century as Canadians ship mobile clean drinking units to the undeveloped world yet cannot do the same for aboriginal communities across Canada. This remains a Liberal's lament in the second decade of the 21st century. Clean drinking water should be a 'human right'. And clean drinking water stubbornly refuses to be accessible to all Canadians - why?

As a student of 'magical realism' that invites one to look at situations with fresh eyes and glean symmetry out of the ordinary and extraordinary in everyday life, perhaps we need a radical relook in how to assure the aboriginal community govern themselves to enjoy the conveniences of the 21st century life as we do across Canada.

This experience, close and personal, is worth repeating. For over a decade, I was a member of the Bar of Northwest Territories and observed Judge John Parker from Alberta who officiated at criminal hearings of aboriginal youth across the western circuit of the far north. Judge Parker demonstrated how he quickly he could direct errant youth back into their aboriginal communities rather than languishing in prison. He showed how to rehabilitate these youth with strict rules of conduct and oversight without serving criminalizing inducing prison time. The justice system seems to have forgotten justice when it comes to aboriginals.

Another quick digression. I maintain a careful and disappointing overview of the Assembly of the United Nations, its well-formed

---

454 Imagine at the end of the 20th century mothers still carrying clean gallons of water to their homes for cooking, washing and bathing daily. Welcome to Canada. See my private Senate member's bills on clean drinking water that failed to pass Parliament. Easy to resurrect!

organs and compare it to Organization for Security-Economic Co-operation in Europe, the largest human rights organization in the world, that continues to illuminate my ideas about ways to expand the practice of democracy in states with unfulfilled or rudimentary democratic aspirations.

The UN Assembly is made of appointed diplomats to represent their member state governments rather than their publics. The UN remains composed of democratic and mostly autocratic nations, the latter unfettered by democratic practices or principles imbedded in the UN charter.

A brief historic review may be enlightening. The 'Cold War' started to thaw when the Final Act of the Helsinki Accords in 1975 between the West and the Soviet Union came to a stunning agreement. The UN was not involved. It was a grand starting point for the movement towards wider democratic practices and human rights in the later part of the 20th century across the face of Europe – West and East. The grand bargain was simple. Under those Accords, the Soviet Union would allow 'human rights' to be considered in return for the maintenance of the borders surrounding the Soviet Union and its Soviet satellites. The Russians bellowed they kept the bargain. The West did not, the Russians claim. The West widened its reach to expand NATO's membership to former Soviet dominated states like Poland and the Baltics and beyond when Russia was in turmoil. Hence Russia's distress over the expansion of NATO in former Soviet dominated states, stretching as far as seeking to welcome Ukraine always dominated by and adjacent to the Russian border into the NATO fold including major Russian ethnic enclaves especially in western Ukraine. Canada solved this problem of rights by bilingualism and multiculturalism. This contentious tale of history is still being re-written and lies in the roots of Crimea crisis. There are Canadian federalist solutions to this festering problem.

The two new OSCE international institutions that flowed out of the Helsinki Accords in 1974 were established in 1990 and 1992. Divided into government appointed representatives called the OSCE headquartered in Vienna, while its sister organization, the OSCE Parliamentary Assembly (OSCE PA) in Copenhagen. The OSCE PA is made up of all party delegations from each member state's assemblies who then annually or biannually vote for the 18 senior executives, made up of the President, Vice-Presidents and Treasurer. Each representative gets a vote to elect the Chair, Vice Chair and Rapporteur of each Standing Committee if serving on that Committee. When the annual report of each Committee is considered voted and approved in Committee, it is then voted upon by the Parliamentary Assembly as a whole. The OSCE is based on adherence to democratic principles and practices, including free and open elections, human rights and economic cooperation. Each delegate can decide to caucus with the Conservative Socialist or Liberal Party groups. I was elected and re-elected annually to chair the Liberal Group at the OSCE PA in Europe for over 12 years. The OSCE PA wanted more Canada. In each Committee Annual Report, each member had an active voice and a vote as well for the annual election of the Chair, Vice-Chair and Rapporteur who prepares a draft report for deliberation of each full Committee. Each Committee approved report by active members was then tabled in the full Assembly. The Committee's Rapporteur added wider comprehension and guidance and agreed to amendments and approval by the full Assembly. The OSCE is now made up of 93 states. I actively participated in all OSCE PA Committees during my tenure as Treasurer, then Vice-President. It was a remarkable lesson on how vital it was to teach democratic practices and procedures for democracy to bloom as it needs constant care and minute attention and reform like a garden.

The full-time OSCE Parliamentary Secretariat located in Copenhagen, was led by the Secretary General (Spencer Oliver, an American) who is chosen by the elected executives for five year terms. All parties are represented in most of state delegations. There was a healthy contest between both the government wings – OSCE in Vienna, and the parliamentary wing of OSCE in Copenhagen on a wide range of issues. Annual and biannual meetings of both institutions are held in cities across Europe as this contest of views played out in full public view - government representative against parliamentary delegates. Many times government views differed with their Parliamentarians and were fiercely debated.

Meanwhile, the UN Assembly and its committees are made of only government appointed officials. Their views reflect only the official line of their governments. The UN veers in its resolutions to be shaped mostly by majority of autocratic members, hence loses its credibility and legitimacy as a democratically mandated institution. Democratic principles are often overridden by autocratic members' resolutions. One glaring example. The only democratic state in the Middle East, Israel, is barred from chairing Committees or having membership in committees especially on 'Human Rights' Committees now dominated by the extreme autocratic state representatives who deny the principles they are there to maintain while the UN Assembly continues so-called endless rounds of debates failing to deal with this egregious members conduct[455].

Democracy practices was hard at work in each aspect of OSCE PA's chosen tasks from Election Monitoring to Economic Cooperation. Elections and monitored oversight are held in member states and meetings to show the ways and means of economic cooperation. When violence breaks out within the OSCE space that reaches from 'Vancouver to Vladivostok', active urgent emergency debates immediately are called and efforts made to send Assembly members to sources the tangled facts and mediate these volatile outbursts. Rarely is this painstaking work covered by the media. The work of OSCE is the best kept secret in the media and in the workhouses of foreign policy.

The practice of democracy is never-ending. It starts with democratic institutions with clear rules, to democratic practices in elections, to rules for popular assemblies, to democratic oversight of bureaucracies, to weeding out corruption. The OSCE PA issues a fulsome report after each national election it monitors, noting the successes and flaws in each election according to OSCE established democratic norms from advertizing to nominations to finances of candidate elections to oversight of election practices during elections. Democratic practices remain

---

455 The majority of UN Resolutions since the establishment of the UN Human Rights Council (UNHRC) in 2006 to replace the UN Commission on Human Rights against breaches of human rights since its inception have been directly to one lonely Israel, more than the rest of the world combined. Targeting Israel remains an alibi in denial of systemic 'anti-Semitism' of the overwhelming majority of UN States. The only 'ism' to be condemned as racism is Zionism, surely an example of the theatre of the absurd played out with regularity at the UN! Of course, this conduct contrary to the UN Charter remains for the most part unchallenged. Democratic realists live in hope!

a never-ending task carefully scrutinizing and reporting by careful monitoring of elections both in the West and East. It remains a fitting legacy of the 20th century.

The UN might better turn its attention to democracy building institutions in developing democracies training police, judiciaries, unions, free press, teaching how to organize parties, and democratic practices to point out weaknesses in potential election practices and oversight, and especially training capable bureaucracies with capabilities to handle the myriad tasks in elections. In this, Canada can lead in teaching these practices as it has done in policing and parliamentary bureaucracies. Toronto and other cities began to 'twin' with sister cities abroad that built ties and relationships from the ground up – a useful democracy building tactic as well. These should be encouraged city by city.

Of late, Canadians have been inundated by 'identity' politics and 'rights' advocates. 'We want our rights' - is the new mantra of the noisy interest groups, 'we are the victims'. The more they get, the more they protest. More with less accountability. These groups mindlessly shout, "*Rights, Rights, Rights!*" They demand their 'rights'. "*Only rights!*" Pierre Trudeau often reminded us of his belief that there could be no 'rights' without 'responsibilities', no freedoms without accountable responsible government. Meanwhile legislators should do the job they are paid to do and to be 'respectful of the taxpayer's dollar'. Extremism in 'identity' politics has deepened division and intolerance. Roguish politicians rant against the 'rich' as if 'class warfare' is the answer. New legislation is spewed out without cost/benefit analyses and without oversight so laws clog our clarity of focus on issues of 'progress' and impede justice. Deficits mount with no end in sight. Woe to future generations when governors regularly outspend what they take in.

The poor are forgotten in the melee for 'more' for the middle class. Little new social housing has been constructed amid skyrocketing condo and house prices further impoverishing the poor. If the cost of housing exceeds a family budget by 55%, that family is poor.

In Toronto, over 33 billion dollars of infrastructure projects have been approved by the City Council without any source of funding or independent assessment. Absurd. Irresponsible. The Toronto City deficit balloons as reserves are gutted. The City, all cities, need an independently elected City Treasurer to be directly accountable to the public. The city's financial tipping point is on the horizon. Beware. The ballooning Ontario annual debt shows no signs of restraint has created interest payments larger than previous budgets crowding out investment in infrastructure and other social needs. Canada's educational system, despite massive expenditures ranks 17th in the world at last count. Tax payers don't even wonder why? All this before Covid struck.

The biggest economic time bomb is the escalating costs of healthcare. In all provincial budgets, it is the largest fastest growing item. Other needs like infrastructure are being neglected. Time for governments to face economic facts and seek lower cost solutions more rigorously. E-health may be one answer, out-patient care another.

All this was written before the largest deficits at all levels in Canadian history due to the Covid epidemic.

It bears repeating the plight of aboriginals who continue to make up a majority of persons behind bars in Canada who cry for rehabilitation and liberty under the administrations who fail to provide teachers of vocational training to prepare them for freedom. Across the far North in the '70s and '80s, Judge John Parker of Calgary a Supreme Court Judge in Alberta, on his regular Arctic circuit tours, judged aboriginal youth caught in a criminal rut who dealt with their cases quickly and effectively allowing these wayward youngsters back into their small aboriginal communities on strict terms and conditions of good conduct[456]. Justice towards Aboriginals, especially of youth, is in a sorry state today in Canada, far worse now than then. Aboriginal justice remains an unattended priority of reform as our prisons remain crowded with forgotten incarcerated aboriginal youth, the highest in the world.

---

456 On a visit to Yellowknife in the early '80s to act as counsel for a small airline Northwest Territories Airlines before a Canadian Transportation Commission hearing, I was called to the Northwest Territories Bar by Judge Parker and learned at first hand Judge Parker's amazing work across the Canadian North, its far flung aboriginal settlements and towns.

Canada became a leader in international institution building through the good offices of Louis St. Laurent and Mike Pearson at the founding of both the United Nations and NATO[457]. The United Nations is in obvious distress[458]. While considered the arbiter of international law, it rarely reflects democratic norms. Urgently needed is UN reform to restore it to its democratic principles and ideals. The community of nations is lawless against democratic principles. Read the founding documents of the UN and see how it fails in its legal mandate. Canada could once again lead 'middle' powers to reform the UN returning to its founding principles. The United States has been crying for reform. Recall that NATO was conceived when Mr. Pearson and the Allies realized that the UN was deadlock by Security Council vetoes and manipulated by autocrats. Mr. Pearson believed that NATO membership, limited to democracies, would be the best safeguard for peace. NATO is also in desperate need of reform. Envisioned as it was by Pearson to be a 'league of democracies' to foster democracy and act as an effective actor protecting democratic and state borders. Now it is equally, if not more, important to protect

---

457 As a diplomat, Mr. Pearson was a key architect of the U.N. Then disappointed with UN gridlock, he turned his attention and reliance to the construction of NATO – an alliance of democracies. He added section 5 of the NATO Chapter to insert economic cooperation. He believed that a coalition of democracies like NATO was more effective for world peace than the UN, which he never gave up trying to improve. He was a key architect of the Colombo Plan to organize aid to the underdeveloped nations. Both initiatives were undertaken despite reluctance by King and St. Laurent. This initiative laid the foundation of Canada's outreach to the 'Third World' and was part of Pearson's belief in spreading a secular social 'gospel' as a moral imperative for Canada's foreign policy.

458 In 1961, the 16th anniversary of the founding of the UN, Abba Eban, the first Israeli ambassador to the UN wrote, "*The founders of the UN assumed that the whole human future was their responsibility, that their work would become a blue print for a positive order of society. The truth is the UN has outlived all the basic assumptions which attended its birth.*" Indeed, the history of the UN is largely a story of unintended collapse. Key functions of the UN have been captured by autocrat regimes working in concord to neutralize the UN Charter. Pearson was not surprised, but never gave up hope of UN reform. It is never too late to renovate the UN. Abba Eban once noted, "*Diplomats touch nothing they do not adjourn.*" How true!

innocent people from violent attack within states. NATO is not working as it should[459]. States are not paying their agreed share. Most States have become freeloaders demanding security without sharing the burden of their own defense. All must step up to make NATO more effective. NATO reform remains another pressing unfinished work in the 21st century as the world gets even more dangerous in narrower slices.

NATO has outgrown its Charter. After WWII, its original mandate was the mutual protection of borders of democratic states[460]. NATO's Charter is crying out for change to meet the 21st century threats of asymmetrical war. NATO's actions have continued to outrun its mandate. New reforms are necessary to keep up with NATO's activities and the ever present international need for policing errant nations that are not democratic in their practices. A fresh zero sum look is imperative. Who will lead on this?

Under our laws, ignorance of the criminal laws of land is no excuse or defence. Of course, no one is capable of knowing all our laws or regulations, either criminal or civil. Laws flow endlessly from law-making bodies. Parliament, Provincial Assemblies and County Governments and City Councils never stop. And the regulators are worse. They never cut or delete outmoded regulations. Recall Lord Hewart's book, '*The New Despotism*' when bureaucrats, the faceless unaccountable masters of government and regulations were shown to become so intolerable and invisible that the sinews of democracy were weakened. Eliminate those unnecessary, outmoded laws and bring the law closer to popular compliance may help to regain public trust in our lawmakers. Perhaps a solution

---

459 Canada should lead by both advocating and funding studies and policies oriented to solving asymmetrical wars by investing in 'Think Tanks' in universities and elsewhere to study this 21st century phenomenon. Canada has displayed little intellectual interest in this subject though billions of dollars have been deployed in these aberrant wars and foreign aid. Asymmetrical wars don't receive the benefit of the Geneva Accords and those rules of war of state against state. Perhaps a comprehensive study by the Canadian Senate or a Royal Commission might be a good start.

460 Mr. Pearson, an avid architect of the UN, deeply disappointed in the repeated deadlocks of the UN Security Council and the irresponsible actions of the UN assemblies became an avid advocate for the NATO Charter having drafted some of its articles but early believed that NATO should evolve with changing conditions.

would be an accountable public watch dog who's primary precondition to any new legislative initiative would be to include a 'sunset clause' inserted at the end of each law and regulation requiring the legislators to re-examine legislation to decide if these laws conform to their original objectives after a 'five year period'. Meanwhile Parliamentarians first and the House and Senate Committee could start an annual review of all existing legislation, regulations and in decade wipe from the law books all outmoded superfluous laws and regulations while examining all existent legislating power since confederation. This is hard work for politicians but necessary for democracy to be renewed, effective and regain trust by our citizens.

What is often overlooked by Canadians and observers is the almost absolute power a leader in Canada gains once he reaches the pinnacle of politics, the Prime Ministership – less so in either Parliamentary democracies in Britain, Australia or New Zealand. The Prime Minister is absolute master of his Party, the elected members of his Party, the government bureaucracy, all government agencies. Most of his appointments serve at his 'pleasure' and can be removed. He appoints or 'green lights' Party officials, both elected and paid. He appoints all senior bureaucrats and all ambassadors, boards and heads of all government agencies and Crown Corporations, the heads of RCMP, all intelligence agencies, the heads of the armed services and senior assistants. He 'green lights' the Speaker of the Commons to run for Speaker, appoints the Speaker of the Senate, the Government Leader of the Senate, Parliament officers, all Senators, all federal judges especially the Supreme Court of Canada and Chief Justice of the Courts of each province, Chairs of each Committee of House, and at times, the Senate. He 'green lights' all political staff of his own and all ministers and, in some cases, M.P's. He chooses his election campaign committee and pollsters. He chooses the party media team. He chooses his House leadership and his whip and their assistants to corral his members to vote. He approves the national caucus chair, each chair of the committees of the caucus and the chairs of each committee of both Houses. Most serve at his pleasure!

Awesome in scope and reach and rarely understood, the Prime Minister also determines the policy, the agenda and legislation and regulations put before Parliament while in office. No one democratic leader in the world has this wide range of powers. He chooses his spokesperson to the media. He decides where and when to travel and who should represent him abroad when he chooses not to travel. He sets foreign policy by his own travels. All ministers' policy speeches require his approval. The budget and additions require his prior consent. Until recently, he remained only accountable to the 'confidence' of his elected caucus. The Canadian Prime Minister cannot be fired as leader by the caucus alone. It now requires the Party in convention to do so. The Canadian Prime Minister is more powerful than the British, Australian or New Zealand Prime Minister. The future of democracy in Canada lies in the hands of the caucus, the opposition, the Senate, the press and the electronic media, TV, cable and social – and of course, polls, distorted as they are, that now act as 'checks and balances' on political power that is in obvious need of constant reinforcement and balance[461].

Perhaps a salutary democratic reform to curb democratic spending excesses is the need for a cost/benefit analysis as a precondition to the enactment of each new regulation or law. No 'rights' without 'responsibilities' as Pierre Trudeau would reiterate – the essence of 'responsible government'[462].

Final thoughts about liberalism in the 21st century. Liberals by definition should be suspicious of power - whether from the left or the right. *"Put not your trust in princes"* as the Scriptures demand. Abuse of political power doesn't differentiate between party lines. 'Transparency' of power is a synthetic 'trigger' word proven to be a 'snag', a 'self-delusion' and a trap especially for the advocate. Beware voters. Government is taking over an ever increasing slice of our economic and social life. Rights and Freedoms are being slowly eroded[463].

---

461   For a fuller exegeses of Prime Ministerial powers, read *'A Leader Must Be a Leader: Encounters with Eleven Prime Ministers'* by Jerry Grafstein (Mosaic Press, 2019)

462   When the City of Toronto Council vote for expenditures for projects in the billions without any viable way to obtain funding from the taxpayers, that's a screaming example of irresponsible government.

463   In *'Churchill and Orwell: The Fight for Freedom'* (Freedom Press, 1917), a marvelous work by Thomas Ricks reminds how in Orwell's masterpiece *'Animal Farm'*, "... the

If this has been on recurring trope of the 20th century in almost every sudden turn of history has included violent action. Wars large or small continue, the immediate consequences are waves of want and human displacement, large and small, with major collateral effect resulting in innocent deaths. Lessons of war never do seemed to be learned ('*Small Wars, Faraway Places*' by Michael Burleigh (Viking Press, 2013).

Canada is a 'trading' nation. Canada's growth is predominantly based on international trade. Almost 70% of Canada's GDP originates from trade. More than one out of two jobs in Canada depend on 'free trade'. 'Free trade', is the major key to Canada's economic growth. Canadians should never cease negotiating and refining 'free trade' agreements around the globe. The linchpin to trade remains 'free trade' with the U.S.A. This linchpin needs constant care and attention[464]. There should

---

pigs steadily revise the rules of the farm to their own advantage, and along with it their accounts of the history of the farm. To Orwell, such behaviour, controlling the past as well as the present and future, was an essential aspect of total state control. He later would conclude, "Totalitarianism demands, in fact, the continuous alteration of the past, and in the long run probably demands a disbelief in the very existence of objective truth." That thought would become one of the core themes of his final book. It is not just the future that belongs to the all-powerful, but also the past."

464 As a senator, I was elected annually by all parties in Parliament as Senate Co-Chair of the Canada-U.S. Interparliamentary Group for over 15 years. Through regular meetings with U.S. Senators, Congressmen and Governors, an all party delegates, we travelled to Washington and to every region of America. Our task was to mediate irritating trade issues from salmon on both coasts to softwood lumber, to steel, to milk products, to coal, to potatoes, to 'clean water', to 'hot' pollution spots along the Great Lakes, to border issues, to movie subsidies, to cattle, to meat and food labelling, to human rights to foreign policy and so on. Policy and changes to American legislation was a constant preoccupation. We discovered that all issues effecting Canada are 'local' in origin in the U.S.A., so work must be done at the state level before the issues harden and reach Washington. During that period, we became familiar with lawmakers and American law making. Sometimes we made a difference. But we never gave up. It was an education in the American political system. When I retired from the Senate, I received two gifts that I cherished for this unsung work. One was the Red Maple Leaf, the so-called 'Two Week Flag' that flies over Parliament Hill in Ottawa, then, the 'One Day Flag' (the Stars and Strips that flies over the Capitol in Washington). A signed declaration of 20 Congressmen, 10 on

be a Senate and Commons Committee dedicated only to free trade. The traffic lanes and the clearance procedures of borders need to be more efficient to enhance just in time trade. Innovation in the modern world is a key to future growth. Canada's if off to a good start but funding continues as a pressing priority for start-ups.

So for me, the 1990's remain the last great decade in the modern history of the world. The 'Holy Trinity' of a true believer – a liberal democratic realist – in the chaotic changes of the 21st century - is simple:

- Help those that cannot help themselves.
- Follow 'due process' and the 'Rule of law'.
- Obstinately search out the 'vital centre', as acute observers have coined, to seek compromise and consensus between the extremes of the 'left' and 'right'.[465]

In Canada all change was possible. Reform was a constant. Liberal reform was continuous. 'Progress' was inevitable. We believed we were privileged to live in that virtuous cycle and I yearn for that era still.

Or, in retrospect, was I deluding myself? Is 'progress' a continuum or merely intermittent? And how do you define yourself as a 'progressive'

---

each side of the aisle, is required to obtain this American flag 'Stars and Stripes', for which I am ever grateful was sent to me after I retired from the Senate of Canada to my surprise and delight.

465 *"To bring those of different faiths together, navigate towards the 'Noahide Laws'"*, so admonished the Seventh Lubavitch Rebbi (AHL). This was the clear path forward, for all faiths, the 'Rebbe' taught.

1) Do not deny God

2) Do no blaspheme God

3) Do not murder

4) Do not engage in illicit sexual relations

5) Do not steal

6) Do not eat from a living animal

7) Establish courts of legal system to ensure obedience to these laws.

According to the Talmud, there is agreement that the seven laws were handed down by Noah to his seven sons. Six of the seven laws are derived from Genesis given to Adam and Eve. The seventh establishing courts of justice came later.

if poverty especially in developed countries continues to expand.? Do we suffer from a pseudo sense of optimism or dystopia? Was the 20th century just a series of preludes or aftermaths between war and peace? Is war continuous? Is war inseparable from the human condition? Is war arrested only by short interludes of 'progress' in the twisted chronicles of the bloody history of the 20th century?

Is progress a myth or at least obtuse?[466] Writers live via the electronic media, the leaps of progress and the lurches in barbaric regression. Is progress inevitably leading to greater happiness or despair because of outbreaks of barbarity and depravity and the visible and invisible poverty? Have we reached even the outward boundaries of Hegel's promise of the 'perfect government'? Some writers like Steven Pinker is his book *Enlightenment Now: The Case for Reason, Science, Humanism, and Progress'* (Viking Press, 2018) argue that by every measure, especially in the last two centuries propelled progress is on an upward curve. Others argue we have entered a new era of barbarity. Still others think that AI (Artificial Intelligence) means machines, will soon predominate over human kind diminishing human control over our lives and our futures leading to a new global autocracy controlled by a few monopolistic hegemonies. Machines cannot replace man's greatest gift – creativity. The debate between religion and secularism continues unabated. The extremes in political debates seem wider, more divisive, than ever.

The circle of history repeats itself as autocracies always leave behind extremism of the left or the right. Examples abound – South America, Middle East, Asia and Africa. Democracies, too, never seem to learn to behave according to their agreed principles. Faux liberalism mired in celebrity politics has moved from its liberal progressive base to a strange space without due process or reason or free speech – to a new form of

---

466 No more intriguing account of the deep roots of 'progressive' policies in the 20th century as formulated and practised in Russia, the United States and Israel is the dense but masterful work by Yuri Slezkine, a Professor of History at the University of California entitled *'The Jewish Century'* (Princeton Cambridge Press, 2004). All of Isaiah Berlin's books should be primers for politicians of all stripes. Berlin relentlessly seeks to illuminate how political ideology is rooted in the human need to organize a better, fairer, freer society.

excommunication or cancel culture's where free speech is excluded a new slavery is formed. Hopefully this is a cycle that will swing back to its virtuous groove. The onslaught of rapid scientific advances will change the world as we know it. Technology can be endlessly improved by individual innate drive for creativity.

Pestilence outbreaks and public health responses remain in continuous need of reformation. Public health officers with public advocacy skills are in scarce supply.

The impact of the perception of climate change continues to roil public policy. Advances in clean energy like fusion and tidal wave turbines could change the current public preoccupation.

The most baffling issue confronting Canada and the world is climate change as the visible melting of the Arctic ice cap continues. Visionary leadership is missing, as the world lurches from fossil fuels to less dependable 'cleaner' energy sources.

Meanwhile the untapped treasures including precious and rare metals especially in the 'Ring of Fire' in Ontario's north and Quebec 'Nord' are barely touched. Fusion energy and 'clean nuke' energy is not encouraged in the growing clamour of the divisive climate change debate. Meanwhile other solutions like hydrogen await. The United States Energy department has two experimental stations testing new energy technology in New Mexico[467] and California. Canada does not yet.

Hudson's Bay has the second highest daily tidal waves in the world. Mobile water turbines are now cost-effective available and visible only lacking infrastructure to carry this 'clean' renewable energy to southern markets. Nor is Canada prepared for the looming advent of the ice-free Northwest Passage to Europe and Eurasia. Russia and other circumpolar nations are heavily invested in ice-breakers and their northern ports. So has China.

Neither the Russians or Americans, now at odds, can be convinced to cost effectively build a tunnel under the shallow Bering Straits between Russia and Alaska closer than the European 'Chunnel'. A tunnel wide

---

467 At the invitation of Governor Richardson, I visited the Experimental Station in New Mexico. Canada should copy it.

enough for rail and electric cars could connect and then via the Yukon by road and rail to the rail and road networks in northern British Columbia to Canada and America. Imagine connecting London across Europe and Russia via rail and then to this tunnel to rail and roads to Alaska, Yukon and British Columbia down to American's west coast, heartland and east coast. Fast trains, now available, could be deployed. Japan leads this way on fast rail. Collaborative infrastructure would reduce pollution and enhance greater climate co-operation. Meanwhile Canada's north could become the global food basket as vast tracts of northern lands became arable. Immigration could be encouraged with the promise of 'free land' to Canadians and new immigrants to be cultivated. All that is missing is vision and political will.

Carlo Rovelli[468], a marvelous Italian theoretical physicist who teaches at Aix-Marseille University in France, understood that before Einstein's papers from 1905 to 1917 time was an illusion and rigid in structure. He wrote, *"Time is not a line with two equal directions: It is an arrow with different extremities. And it is this, rather than the speed of its passing, that matters most to us about time. This is the fundamental thing about time. The secret of time lies in this slippage that we feel on our pulse, viscerally, in the enigma of memory, in anxiety about the future. That is what it means to think about time. What exactly is this flowing? Where is it nestled in the grammar of the world?"*

So our world, constructed on a singular perception of time, remains a slowly uncovering mystery as does the future. History, after all, is comprised of true stories waiting to be recovered.

The private citizen in our civic society now has new and easy tools to become directly engaged in the issues of our time. National narratives take on newer and curious aspects, widen public knowledge, and, what seems to matter most, is which new wave attracts most public attention on the social media, as the next 'new' wave overtakes and floods the overcrowded public space.

---

468 *'The Order Of Time'* by Carlo Rovelli (Penguin Publishing Group, 2018). Read also *'Einstein's Shadow: A Black Hole, a Band of Astronomers, and the Quest to See the Unseeable'* by Seth Fletcher (Harper Collins, 2018).

In this chaotic rapidly changing 21st century, at times shocked by new absurd surreal news events, we are admonished by our Hasidic masters, to clarify our thinking, seeking to ask good questions. I leave each patient reader to decide for themselves! The questions become more difficult, the answers even more elusive. Perhaps, as in the saga of Zionism, we have yet to reach the peaceful 'Promised Land'. When you cannot answer the question, you live the question![469],[470].

"Common sense is not so common"
– Voltaire

"In a free society, where terrible wrongs exist,
some are guilty, but all are responsible."
- Abraham Joshua Heschel

"Look on every exit as being an entrance somewhere else."
– 'Rosencrantz and Guildenstern Are Dead', Tom Stoppard

"Eventually, all things merge into one, and a river runs through it. The river
was cut by the world's great flood and runs over rocks from the basement of
time. On some of the rocks are timeless raindrops. Under the rocks are the
words, and some of the words are theirs. I am haunted by waters."
– Norman Maclean

"Once you stop believing in religion, you can believe in anything"
– Charles Krauthammer

"Imagination is more important than knowledge. Knowledge is limited.
Imagination encircles the world."
– Albert Einstein

---

469 Mikhail Svetlov, a popular late Soviet era writer and critic was quoted, *"What is a question mark?"* *"It's an exclamation point that has grown old."*

470 In 1941, Stefan Zweig (1881-1942), an Austrian-born prolific writer of an endless stream of polemics, newspaper articles and books including a stunning novel *'Confusion'* (Insel-Verlag, 1927), and his masterful concise work *'Decisive Moments in History'* (Ariadne Press, 1999) from ancient times to Lenin's 1917 fateful train ride from Switzerland through Germany to St. Petersburg, Russia that changed the course of the 20th century.

*"Make your own Bible. Select and collect all those words and sentences
that in all your reading have been to you like the blast of a trumpet out of
Shakespeare, Seneca, Moses, John, and Paul."*
– Ralph Waldo Emerson

*"Most live only for the here and now.
Others seek to observe each elusive turning
point in history as they make their bow.
Still others ruminate about life in all its different invisible dimensions.
And attempt to uncover the hidden keys to each declension.
Still others ponder the mysteries of the universe gazing at the limitless sky,
And wonder what, when and why."*
– JSG

*"In times of deceit, telling the truth is a revolutionary act...
If liberty means anything at all, it means the right to tell
people what they don't want to hear."*
– George Orwell

*"No steel can pierce the human heart so
chilling as a period at the right moment."*
– Isaac Babel

The most compelling concise lessons of the 20ᵗʰ century are encapsulated in 'Witness: Lessons from Elie Wiesel's Classroom' by Ariel Burger (Houghton Mifflin Harcourt, 2018). Wiesel, a Holocaust survivor and witness, concluded the world has still not learned the lessons of history from the 20ᵗʰ century.